About the Hearth

About the Hearth

Perspectives on the Home, Hearth and Household in the Circumpolar North

Edited by
David G. Anderson, Robert P. Wishart
and Virginie Vaté

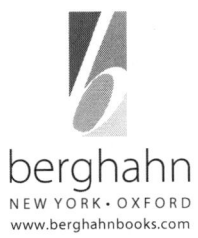

berghahn
NEW YORK · OXFORD
www.berghahnbooks.com

First published in 2013 by
Berghahn Books
www.berghahnbooks.com

Library of Congress Cataloging-in-Publication Data

About the hearth: perspectives on the home, hearth and household in the
circumpolar north / edited by David G. Anderson, Robert P. Wishart and
Virginie Vaté.
    p. cm.
Includes bibliographical references and index.
ISBN 978-0-85745-980-0 (hardback: alk. paper) --ISBN 978-1-78238-
787-9 (paperback: alk. paper) -- ISBN 978-0-85745-981-7 (ebook: alk.
paper) 1. Dwellings--Arctic regions. 2. Vernacular architecture--Arctic
regions. 3. Households--Arctic regions. 4. Social archaeology--Arctic
regions. 5. Arctic regions--Antiquities. 6. Arctic regions--Social life and
customs.
I. Anderson, David G. II. Wishart, Robert P. III. Vaté, Virginie.
GT170.A46 2013
392.3'6091632--dc23

2012037873

British Library Cataloguing in Publication Data
A catalogue record for this book is available from the British Library
Printed in the United States on acid-free paper

ISBN 978-0-85745-980-0 hardback
ISBN 978-1-78238-787-9 paperback
ISBN 978-0-85745-981-7 ebook

Contents

List of Illustrations

Figures

Tables

Acknowledgements

The intellectual work that went into this volume was the result of a unique international funding initiative coordinated by the European Science Foundation's EUROCORES programme. The research topic, 'Histories from the North – environments, movements, narratives' (BOREAS), was designed to direct attention to the unique voices of northern peoples within humanities research. The ESF provided a forum wherein funding agencies from a large number of European countries, and Canada and the United States, pledged research funding which supported the field research and analysis in this book.

Most of the contributors in the volume worked under the auspices of the collaborative research project entitled 'Home Hearth and Household in the Circumpolar North' (HHH), which was based at the University of Tromsø in Norway and supported by research funding from the Research Council of Norway (NFR 179316), the National Science Foundation of the United States (NSF OPP 0631970), the Social Sciences and Humanities Research Council of Canada (SSHRCC 861-2001-0003), the Academy of Finland (08431003) and the Royal Swedish Academy of Letters, History and Antiquities (KVHAA CRP014/004) in Sweden.

The research of Dr Virginie Vaté was supported by the NEWREL collaborative research project and the Max Planck Institute for Social Anthropology. Prof. Ingold was one of the designers of the theme 'Histories from the North' and served on the strategic governance committee for the network. The ESF also provided three networking grants which allowed many of the authors to meet and discuss their chapters in Irkutsk (May 2006), in Tromsø (Oct. 2008) and in Calgary (Nov. 2010). Some of the support for the editing of this volume came from the Advanced Research Grant 'Arctic Domus' from the European Research Council (295458). On behalf of all the authors in this volume, we thank all of these sponsors for their support. We would also like to thank two anonymous reviewers for their helpful reflections on an earlier version of this manuscript.

Although work within this international network had its peculiar challenges, one of the joys was the genuine exchange of ideas between members of different national teams and between different collaborative research grants. Although this type of 'synergy' is a formal requirement of large framework grants, it is quite rare to see it unfold out of natural curiosity. We feel that this volume represents many aspects of that sharing, both through the contributions of authors from different projects, and through the coauthoring of chapters by scholars funded by different national funding agencies. Finally, the editors would like to thank Alex Oehler for his work on the index.

CHAPTER 1

Building a Home for Circumpolar Architecture

An Introduction

Robert P. Wishart

The hearth is at the centre. It is a simple statement with profound implications. As Stephen Pyne (1995: 3) reminds us, humans are 'uniquely fire creatures on a uniquely fire planet'. And yet the hearth, the place where we ignite and tend to so many of our fires, is not simply a container for, or a site of, this particularity. Take, for example, the hearth as philosophized and mythologized by the ancient Greeks. Hestia, the goddess of the hearth, was also the goddess of the home, architecture and the symbolic and ritual centre of the inhabitants, the 'oikos' or household (Vernant 1969: 132).

To the ancient Greeks, the hearth, the home and the household were inseparable, and as Carsten (1995b) illustrates, this understanding is not unique to the classical world. The relatedness of the hearth, the home and the household correspond to the complex and creative relatedness inherent in kinship.[1] But would it be reductive to understand the house as container for and site of the household, and would it ignore the coextension of the hearth, house and household with the environment and the cosmos? Furthermore, would these reductions also serve to eclipse real lives with representations that might serve other interests? For the collective effort of the authors gathered here, these questions became fundamental to the inquiry about the ways in which the hearth in the circumpolar North is at the centre of something much larger.

There are few other places that one could imagine the crucial interdependencies and relationships between the hearth, home and household would be as apparent as that in the circumpolar North. Indeed, they are essential for human inhabitation in this region. This collection makes a unique contribution, not only in recognizing the necessity of this climatic adaptation within the circumpolar North, but goes much further in demonstrating how the North is in itself uniquely situated to illuminate how finding solutions for meeting these necessities is part of engaging in finding solutions to equally important aspects of being human and of living complex political lives.

This connection is not without its challengers. In the colonial imagination, the latter set of solutions did not follow from the former – indeed, it was quite the opposite. Northern people's lives were imagined to be simple, fragmentary and ephemeral, and so were their homes. So rectifying this image is a further contribution made by the authors collected here.

Building a home, making a fire in the hearth, being part of a household – in the circumpolar North these are all enmeshed with other activities and events of life. Indeed, the entanglements are of such a high degree that the activities and events often obscure what is at the centre, and we forget the profound role that these have in the unfolding of people's lives in the North.

It is not that they were each ignored – as the chapters in this book attest, the form of homes, the physical and symbolic affordances of the hearth and of fire, and the social structure of households have each had their moments of being in multiple academic foci and in the gaze of the circumpolar states. A common frustration expressed by almost all the authors is how these various attentions can also often present themselves in 'unhealthy' ways. Whether it is in a portrayal of the primitive north, an obsession with reform and domestication, or a state-sponsored snapshot of its northern peoples, of where and with whom they live, there has been an ossification of the home as form, of transforming the hearth into its base utilitarian necessity, and fixing the household in time as a human resource or a social problem.

Each of the papers in this collection deals in some way with the problem of eclipse, and each is also trying to bring to light the problems of ossification so that we might understand the relationships between homes, the hearth and the household as sites of 'becoming' (Carsten 1995b: 223) that have very deep foundations.

As part of this collection's purpose is to document the intellectual history of circumpolar hearths and how it is embedded in state projects, it behooves us to recognize our own position and how the particularities of this collection unfolded. This unique collection of papers represents the multidisciplinary thoughts of an international body of authors who have been working together to tie the significance of dwellings in the circumpolar North to relational metaphors arising out of our various investigations into history, cosmology, demography, colonialism, economy and architecture.

Bringing the authors in this collection into conversation has been the work of David G. Anderson, who recognized the common problems and lacunae in anthropology, archaeology, museum studies and historical demography in the study of homes, hearths and households in the circumpolar North, and sought to bring together scholars who were interested in these subjects. These conversations began in the early 2000s, but did not find a real centre until 2005 when the European Science Foundation put out a call for humanities research networks focusing on the circumpolar North. Aptly named BOREAS, the central theme and organizing title for the research agenda was 'Histories from the North – environments, movements, narratives'. An insistence on histories from the North, rather than histories of the North, has the effect of shifting the focus and allows for a return to the centre of social practice: the home, the hearth and the household.

In recognizing this potential for reinvigorating the study of circumpolar architecture, religious practice, social organization and indigenous political expression, the fire was lit and the result was a project on the dwellings of the circumpolar North. One of the stipulations of the proposal process was that each project should have a recognizable anagram, and HHH (Home, Hearth and Household) best reflected the fact that we are working with three general metaphors that serve as relational anchors in northern people's lives.

While BOREAS provided us places to gather and with funds to network, the building blocks of research were made possible by various grants that were awarded in the researcher's home country (please see the acknowledgements for details on funding). This book is just one of the outcomes of the research and the ongoing conversations of the people who were directly involved in the HHH theme, but like any conversation others – Nakhshina, Loovers, and Vaté – entered the discourse and became crucial to its diversity at other points along the way. Also included in this book, but not an official member of the HHH team, is Ingold, but he has been part of the conversation from the very beginning as one of the designers and builders of BOREAS. What makes this book different from the other publications that have developed out of these individual projects is that this is the only place where the research trajectories come together. It is, in effect, a home and an intellectual household.

As a key symbol of northern indigenous lifeways, the conical lodge served to structure the first level of inquiry. Here is an architectural form that is known throughout the circumpolar North, but what can we really say about all the relationships that go into its design, the sourcing of its materials and its construction? From this seemingly straightforward question came the complex of problems reported in this book, and none would argue that this is exhaustive.

What can the conical lodge tell us about the way people live? What about the centrality of the fire – is this not what really transcends geography and time? After all, it is the remains of the hearth that forms so much of the important archaeological evidence of northern lives. What about other vernacular architectural forms practised today and throughout history? What do we know about the make-up of the household, and how do we know these things? As the site of reference for this conversation, the conical lodge became a meeting place for the entangled trails of inquiry that sometimes seem to be leading off into the distance but always, somehow, come back again.

Vernacular architecture is made without a strict preformed plan but it is not chaotic. A classic argument about whether there is something fundamentally different between an architect and a 'folk builder' rests on the relationship between ideas and spatial form, and whether or not the individual working without a blueprint is creative or is merely reproducing a form (Hubka 1979). As others have argued more recently, this debate positions the relationship as that between two distinct, separate entities – the mind and the physical world – and leaves out the essential element of materiality (e.g. Godelier 1986, Tilley 2004), or materials and their 'affordances' (Ingold 2007b: 3).

Until quite recently this is how most building was accomplished. It was the combination of building with designs and materials that flowed and mingled during the creation of any particular structure. If it is the case that vernacular architecture exists in this flow between designing and building, and is always going through a process of alteration as it is reflected in the imagination of the builder in relation to place and variable materials then why, at a superficial glance, is there such consistency in final form?

It is not possible for this book to answer fully this question of consistency, although it does go to some length to explain it. What it does do to great effect is demonstrate that the quick glance really does miss a great deal. Certainly, much can be said about the conical lodge as a solution to the complicated problem of meeting the demands for a lightweight, mobile form of architecture that will not only provide shelter but will be reasonably thermally efficient. More can be said of the materials that make up its construction and how they need to be replaceable. Learning how to do all of this 'properly', and passing this knowledge on, is equally complicated, as is the experiential significance of the final form. Finally, more can be said when the demands change and new solutions are found.

If this book is a home for this academic household, and if the conical lodge with its corresponding hearth is to some degree at its heart, then how should it be built? Like many homes in the vernacular style, it went through many changes and partial rebuilds before a good compromise could be reached between the parts and the final form.

At first it seemed best to use the preexisting framework of the HHH project. The book could be organized into three sections on home, hearth and household. While this provided a good triangular frame, the chapters did not wrap neatly around it. Many of the chapters covered all three themes but some jutted out and left gaps where they should join together with their neighbours. The next solution was to organize the chapters around the disciplines at their centres. This solution made for a better cover, but there was something missing in the structure to hold it all up. What was needed was an organization that combined these two approaches, so in this book the chapters flow around the circumpolar North geographically, like following the wall of a canonical lodge, but with a vertical structure provided by organizing papers within each geographical section into a narrative that acknowledges discipline and theme.

In the building of a dwelling a key question must be asked: where is the entrance? In many traditions, and there are good examples to be found within the chapters of this book, the entrance is regimented. Sometimes the entrance is located for practical reasons – in the circumpolar North, it makes sense to use climatic knowledge to locate the entrance away from the potentially harsh forces of weather. Equally important is the orientation of an entrance to coincide with cosmological and spiritual understandings, and these can be as regimented as the climatic considerations. Then there are the forces of social organization and larger infrastructural considerations: entrances to homes are often placed in accordance to the relationship between the household and the larger community.

Two chapters in this book ask fundamental philosophical questions about northern forms of architecture and could serve as a passageway into the geographical discussions, those of Anderson and Ingold. As an entrance is also an exit, these two chapters serve to bring us in and out of the conversation.

Returning to the theme of the conical lodge, it is apt that this book begins with the thoughts of Ingold on the place of the lodge in larger circumpolar themes of relationality. Ingold argues that the lodge, as a home for circumpolar people, is also a nexus in a multidimensional world of relations. Building from an understanding of the home as the centre in the rhizome-like interactions and experiences of animals, people, plants and the land that have become so important in our understanding of northern life, Ingold asks us to consider what happens when we situate ourselves beside the fire at the centre of the lodge and follow the smoke. By looking up through the interlocking poles of a conical lodge and out through the smoke hole we get a new sense of the relationships between those who inhabit it and the cosmos. He argues that the place of the lodge is one that is located in a world made up of relations between the land and the people, but that we need to also stop neglecting other possibilities such as that of relationships within an 'earth–sky' world.

The book then moves on to discuss the building of a conical lodge in a new context. Ingold starts his philosophical treatise on the conical lodge with an example of his experience with a lodge that was set up on the grounds of the Tromsø Museum. This particular lodge was provided by a combined effort of the Prince of Wales Northern Heritage Centre and the Tłįchǫ Nation, Northwest Territories, Canada.

As curator of the lodge, Andrews describes how this particular dwelling was constructed and the context which led to its creation. As a part of a repatriation and revitalization project, the construction of two Tłįchǫ lodges (one of which was brought for a short time to Tromsø) brought together museum staff and the Tłįchǫ Nation, and the chapter describes how differing agendas between the parties were overcome and coalesced into new understandings of how museums can learn to dwell and, in so doing, relate in more egalitarian ways to the communities who are the source of the materials in their exhibitions.

The revitalization of the conical lodge with the Tłįchǫ brought together a community, and the teaching of skills in working with skin and building with wood became important outcomes of the construction of the dwelling. The skill in building another form of home is taken up by Wishart and Loovers, whose chapter shifts the geographical focus north, to the homes of the Teetł'it Gwich'in. In this chapter, log cabins are examined as important elements in Gwich'in human–land relationships, and in their articulations about tradition and political jurisdiction. In the wider scope of this book, this chapter introduces the fact that while the conical lodge might be undergoing something of a revitalization, there are other architectural forms that arose in more recent history that have become as central to practice and life on the land. This theme is explored in other ways as the book moves eastward to examine the homes of the Sámi.

In common with Wishart and Loovers, Bjørklund asks why certain architectural forms come to be paradigmatically linked to indigenous identity. In Norway the conical lodge, referred to in Northern Sámi as *lávvu*, has come to be a key symbol in Sámi ethno-politics and it is duplicated in published materials, website banners, and incorporated into the planned architecture of government buildings and private businesses. Bjørklund argues that the emphasis on this one form eclipses the diversity of historical Sámi architecture, and he provides evidence that it had its fluorescence during a period of reindeer-herding intensification for the Sámi, and then only as a form that was used during the movement of reindeer. However, as a symbol which instantly links the Sámi to international indigenous rights discourses, the conical lodge is of greater value now than when solely considered as a home.

Picking up this conversation on Sámi vernacular architecture and the revitalization of form is the chapter by Beach. Like Bjørklund, Beach writes about the historical use of different architectural forms, but he focuses on one particular site and documents his own observations over the last 35 years. This detailed account of one site allows for a discussion of the revitalization and devitalization of forms, and includes insight into how the adoption of certain technologies, such as a metal stove, can change other practicalities of house life.

In the oscillation between revitalization and devitalization, Beach anticipates that should there be a revitalization in certain Sámi architectural forms – such as a prefabricated conical lodge – it is entirely possible that there would be a corresponding devitalization of Sámi practices that have developed in relation to the changing Sámi architectural world. Above all, Beach argues that practicality is of central concern for Sámis with whom he works, and that the alterations in the last 35 years in structural design and building technique are most often in response to practical concerns rather than an outward projection of tradition.

The discussion on housing forms arising out of the chapters thus far asks under what conditions northern people will seriously alter their architectural preferences. Beach and Bjørklund remind us that these changes can be attributed to a range of factors, but what is clear is that northern people have many options available to them, and that the result can be contrary to what one would anticipate. Part of the problem in figuring out what is going on with the forms of homes is, as Beach reminds us, that we tend to neglect the changes that have occurred in the household. To remedy this problem, we now redirect the conversation back onto the people who are living in these homes and how their social structure has also gone through interesting changes. Staying in Scandinavia, the next two chapters present a view of changing household structure that can be built from an application of historical demography.

Brännlund and Axelsson present an interesting problem in Swedish Sámi demography. According to the historical data accumulated by Swedish authorities there is very little difference in the composition of Sámi and non-Sámi Swedish households. As Brännlund and Axelsson argue, this finding presents an anthropological problem. It is known from the Sámi literature that household structure was not similar to that of the wider Swedish community, and there are a few possibilities for explaining this disconnect between bodies of evidence. The authors conclude that the data were accumulated using categories that make it appear as if the Sámi are the same as the wider Swedish community. They present an alternative way of organizing the data that works with indigenous categories for the household, and then demonstrate how this changes the view completely.

Brännlund and Axelsson argue that one of the key factors in how the household has been misrepresented is in how heads of households are determined in the statistical account. Sommerseth is also interested in accounting for heads of households, but in the case of the Norwegian Sámi. The literature on household change in the North tends to argue that there has been a tendency towards the creation of nuclear families at the expense of traditional family structures. Sommerseth argues that this may be true, but not in the way that is predicted, and that in fact multiple strategies were used by the Sámi to maintain the elderly as the household heads while allowing the younger men to pursue dangerous, but lucrative, economic activities. What then appears as a move towards one household type is actually a change that increased variability and flexibility, corresponding to Beach's argument about the implications of revitalization and practicality.

The image of the Sámi house and household provided by the previous four chapters is one that flows in relation to internal and external forces. These chapters discuss Sámi history over the last few centuries, but how does this relate to the archaeological evidence of the more distantly related residents of these lands? The chapter by Halinen, Hedman and Olsen reports on the archaeology of Sámi hearth row sites from the late iron and early medieval periods in northern Norway and Finland.

The archaeology of hearth rows returns us to the centre, to a discussion of the heart of the dwelling. A stereotype of the past in the North is that of primitive simplicity, and caught up in this baggage is the idea that the hearths of the past were always round, as right angles are a thing of advanced cultures and more modern times. As Halinen et al. describe, the discovery of rectangular hearths that are arranged in a linear fashion, also dating from the Iron Age, seriously challenges this stereotype of static primitive simplicity. What is revealed in the work by these authors is that the picture of the more distant Sámi past is as complex and shifting as that of more recent times. However, what is also revealed in this chapter is a remarkable degree of consistency with the ethnographic literature on Sámis in regards to the positioning of artefacts in relation to the hearth. It is this contradiction between the conservation of some elements and flux in others that presents an analytical challenge.

Vaté continues the discussion on the hearth and brings us to the final geographical set of chapters on Russia and Siberia, with her analysis of a Chukchi reindeer herding ritual. Vaté's chapter gives us a clear ethnographic illustration of how the hearth serves as a central focal point in both the ritual and practical lives of people in the North. Her insistence that the hearth connects people's relationships to the cosmos and the material world simultaneously brings into question how the hearth works to bridge people's histories (as expressed in ritual practice) and their present-day activities.

Following from Vaté, Nakhshina approaches the elements of time and the symbolic capacity of the built environment in the small Russian village of Kuzomen'. Like many other places where the indexical qualities of the past are engaged with differently between the permanent residents and seasonal inhabitants, the houses and ruins of Kuzomen' provide Nakhshina with a collage of materials and symbolic representations to document how incomers are often far more interested in the past, while the permanent residents are mindful of the past but are far more interested in the present and future affordances of their homes and the village. This chapter allows us to engage with a similar situation as described by others in this book, that while it can be difficult to live an idealized past, materials and homes can tell stories and memorialize while the inhabitants go on with the business of everyday life.

Nakhshina introduces the idea that homes can become like museums and that sometimes people living in them treat them this way. This idea begins to bring the book back around to the question of how a particular home may find commonalities with others. Oetelaar, Anderson and Dawson take this conversation forward and present a chapter that compares how the Inuit and Evenki, two groups of people separated by huge distances, geological barriers, language and culture, nevertheless build homes that are similar in various important ways. The key to these similarities is how both build their homes and organize the internal space in relation to a set of cosmological beliefs that architecturally serve as a mnemonic, or perhaps a holographic relationship between the parts of the home and the whole – the landscape.

Oetelaar et al. conclude their chapter by arguing that material and economic similarities are certainly relevant in the discussion of why house forms are similar, but it might also be true that both Evenkis and Inuit are in conversation with the land and hear 'whispers' of how things should be. Ziker continues the conversation on the symbolic relationship between the home and the environment with his discussion of how virtuous practices are communicated and serve to reinforce beliefs in the cosmological and physical worlds of the indigenous people of northern Siberia. The structure of the household, the building and organization of the house, and the insistence on referring to the hearth in kin terms, are all reasonable social norms in the interconnected web of relations that is dwelling in Siberia.

Ziker's chapter brings the book back to the beginning, not only in a geographical sense but also in the way that it asks questions about the norms of practice and how these are related to experience and cosmological belief. The book began with Ingold asking how the dwelling is situated in an earth–sky world, but as a way of exiting this collection it is only fitting that the architect of the HHH project should have the final word. Anderson thus provides the final chapter, where he brings it all together with his ability to situate the house that has been built of these chapters into the wider academic world of international scholarship.

One of the key ideas that emerged in many of our discussions about homes, hearths and households is the way that in the North homes never seem to be complete. The Gwich'in elders I worked with were continually adding to their cabins and sometimes they would take parts of them apart to use the bits elsewhere. So, in this tradition we have built a home in this book but the parts are available to the reader to make all sorts of new things as well.

Notes

1. This idea is further elaborated upon in the edited collection *About the House: Lévi-Strauss and Beyond* (Carsten and Hugh-Jones 1995a) from which this collection's title takes its inspiration.

CHAPTER 2

The Conical Lodge at the Centre of the Earth–Sky World

Tim Ingold

I

In the grounds of Tromsø Museum, a conical tent or lodge had been erected of a kind traditionally used among indigenous, forest-dwelling peoples right around the circumpolar North (Figure 2.1). The frame was made of long, stout wooden poles that converged at the apex, but splayed out at ground level around the perimeter of a circle. This was covered with laboriously prepared caribou skins, carefully sewn together. Although extending all the way to the base of the frame, they reached not quite to the apex but to a level just short of it, leaving the apex itself uncovered. Entering through the door-flap, I found myself in a remarkably capacious, interior space, at the centre of which was a place for the fire. I knelt on the ground. It was still daytime and the light was streaming in through the apex, which remained open to the sky. Looking up, it made me blink (Figure 2.2). At the same time, through my knees, I felt the clammy depth of the earth which gave me support.

In a moment of revelation, I understood what it meant to inhabit a world of earth and sky. It was to be at once bathed in light and rapt in feeling. But it also dawned on me how closely the idea of landscape to which I was accustomed from my own upbringing is linked to a particular architecture: to the habitation of rooms with hard floors below, ceilings above, and windows set in vertical walls. Imagine yourself as the resident of a modern suburban apartment, with large picture windows that afford a commanding, panoramic view of the surrounding countryside. When you look out from the windows you see the land stretching out into the distance, where it seems to meet the sky along the line of the far horizon. Inside the lodge, however, there were no horizons to be seen. Earth and sky, far from being divided at the

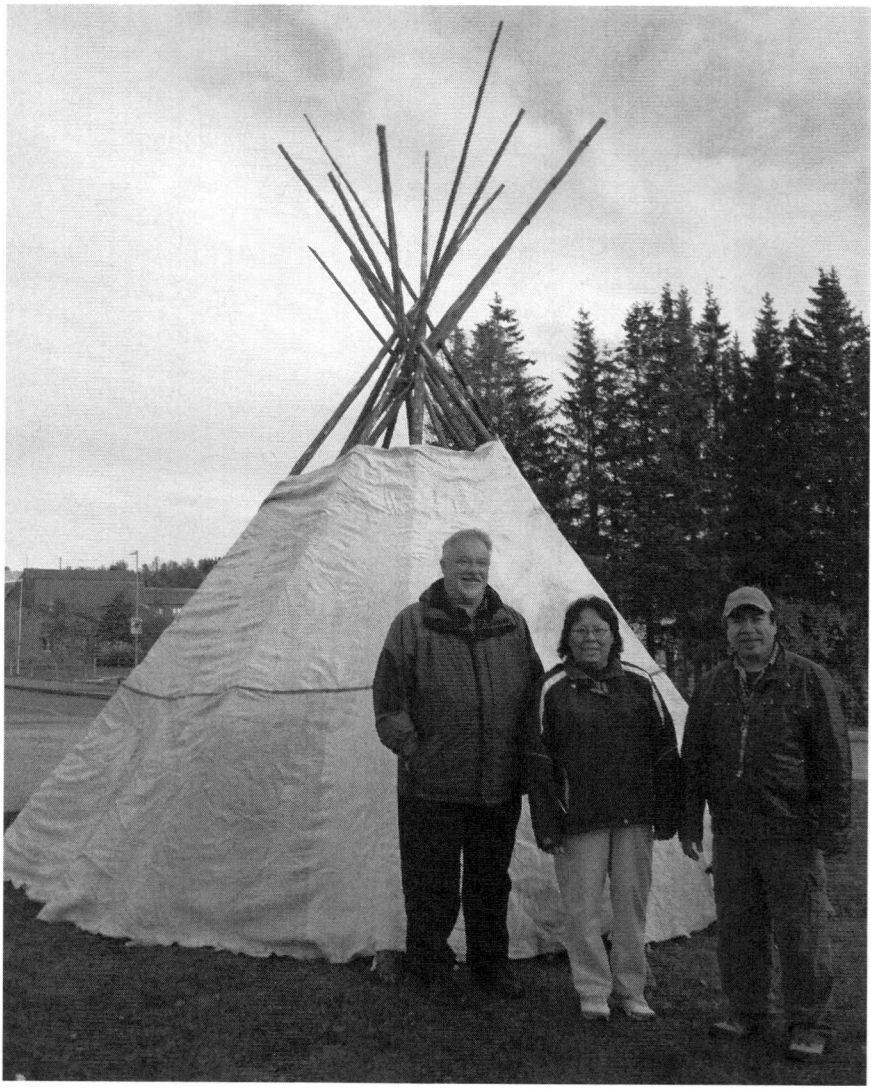

Figure 2.1 *The Tłįchǫ conical lodge, viewed from the outside, in the grounds of the Tromsø Museum. This lodge, made from 30 caribou skins, was one of two made in 2000 by Tłįchǫ seamstresses from Behchokǫ and Whatì. L-R: Tom Andrews, Alizette Drybones and Sam Drybones. Photo by Hilde Sommerseth.*

horizon, seemed rather to be unified at the very centre of my emplaced being. Enwrapped within the lodge I nevertheless felt open to a world. But this world was not a landscape – it was what I shall henceforth call the *earth–sky*.

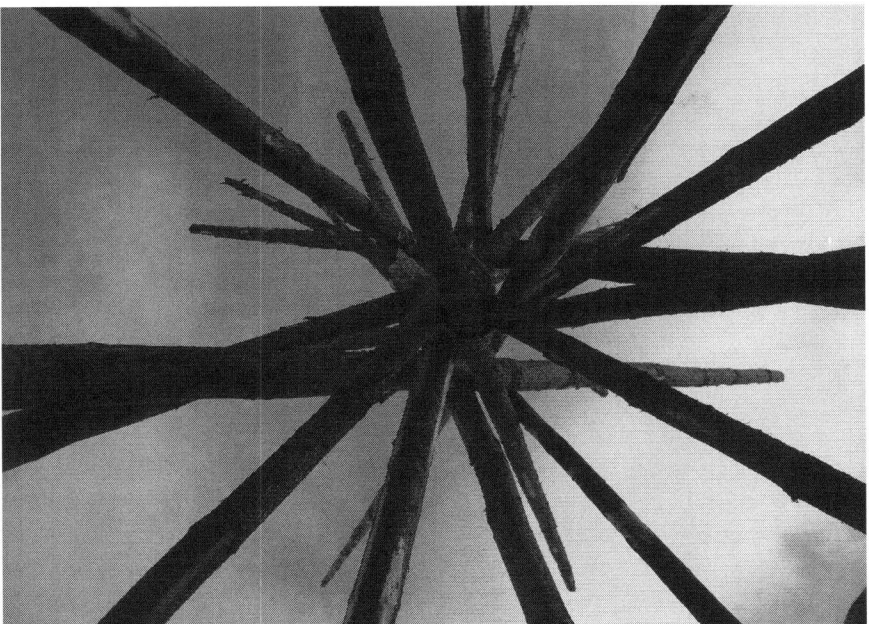

Figure 2.2 *Looking up through the apex of the tent, the linear poles interweave to comprise a complex knot, from which each nevertheless continues, reaching up into the open sky. Photo by Hilde Sommerseth.*

Further reflection led me to think that what is at issue here is not just a particular architecture but the very idea of architecture itself. For more than five centuries, it has been both the claim and the conceit of the architectural profession that every building is a monument to the genius of its creator, standing as the enduring realization of an original design concept. In the mid-fifteenth century, in his treatise *On the Art of Building in Ten Books,* Leon Battista Alberti had painted an unashamedly self-aggrandizing portrait of the architect as a man of 'learned intellect and imagination', who is able 'to project whole forms in mind without any recourse to the material' (Alberti 1988: 7). As one of the founding figures of the European Renaissance, Alberti can be seen in retrospect to stand at a pivotal juncture in the process that ultimately led to the professionalization of architecture as a discipline exclusively devoted to design as opposed to construction. His treatise both looks back to the time of his predecessors, the master builders and journeymen of the medieval era, and forward to a time when the architect would prescribe only the formal outlines of the building, leaving its actual construction to masons, carpenters and other practitioners of the building trades.

Yet in this idea of making or building as the projection of precon-ceived form onto inert matter, Alberti drew his inspiration from the more distant past of classical antiquity – from the philosophical writ-ings of Aristotle. In the making of any artefact, Aristotle had reasoned, ideal form *(morphe)* is unified with material substance *(hyle)*, such that the artefact is finished when the once shapeless material has taken on the form intended for it. Likewise for Alberti, any building 'consists of lineaments and matter, the one the product of thought, the other of Nature; the one requiring the power of reason, the other dependent on preparation and selection' (1988: 5). What Alberti calls 'lineaments' *(lineamenta)* are the abstract lines of Euclidean geometry, comprising the elements of formal design as conceived by the intellect. But neither linea-ments nor matter, Alberti was quick to add, would on their own suffice to make a building. To fashion the material according to lineaments, in the work of construction *(structura)*, called for the skilled and capable hands of workmen.

Not only was the idea of architecture entirely recast through its har-nessing to the Aristotelian, so-called *hylomorphic* model of making. So too was the idea of landscape. There is indeed an intrinsic connection between the two ideas. Though art historians are inclined to associate the landscape ideal with a certain style of pictorial representation, originally perfected by Dutch painters in the seventeenth century (Alpers 1983), the word itself is of early medieval origin, and refers literally to the shaping of the land, from Old English *sceppan* or *skyppan*, meaning 'to shape' (Olwig 2008a). Medieval land shapers, however, were not artists or architects but farmers and woodsmen, whose purpose was not to lend ideal form to the material world, or to render it in appearance rather than substance, but to wrest a living from the earth. Like their counterparts in the building trades – the masons and carpenters of medieval times – their work was done close-up, in an immediate, muscular and visceral engagement with wood, stone and soil, the very opposite of the distanced, contemplative and panoramic optic that the word 'landscape' conjures up in many minds today.

For it is not in agrarian or building practice that the roots of the modern landscape aesthetic are to be found, but in architecture. Serving as both stage and scenery, the landscape is commonly taken to furnish not only the solid foundations on which the architectural monument is erected, but also the scenic backdrop against which it is displayed or 'set off' to best advantage. Together, the monument and its landscape are understood to comprise a totality that is complete and fully formed. Here, land is to scape as material substance is to abstract form, and the land is shaped by their unification. As historian Simon Schama writes, introduc-ing his magnum opus on *Landscape and Memory*, the scenery 'is built up as much from strata of memory as from layers of rock … it is our shaping perception that makes the difference between raw matter and landscape' (Schama 1995: 7, 10). If the bedrock of the physical world provides the matter, then the human mind contributes the form. Land–scape, in short, equals matter–form.

With these reflections on the meanings of architecture and landscape in mind, let me return to the conical lodge. In what follows I argue that we misunderstand the lodge by imagining it as an instance of architecture: that is, as a structure built to the prior specifications of a formal design, and set upon the stage and amidst the scenery of a landscape. Those who hold such a view – and they include a substantial majority in the fields of ethnology, cultural anthropology and material culture studies – do recognize, of course, that as an example of what is called 'vernacular' architecture, the lodge manifests a design that is attributable to the genius of cultural tradition rather than individual creation. The builders of such traditional structures, according to architectural theorist Christopher Alexander, do not knowingly implement designs of their own making but rather submit to the reproduction of forms sanctified by weight of tradition. Their building is, in this sense, 'unselfconscious' (Alexander 1964: 36). Nevertheless, the fundamental assumptions of the hylomorphic model remain: that while the raw materials of the lodge are supplied by nature, the form is added by culture, carried unknowingly in the minds of the people and passed from generation to generation through force of custom and habit. It is supposed that in building the lodge, this ideal form is projected upon the substrate of the material world.

The alternative view, which I shall now attempt to establish, is to comprehend the process of building not as a projection of form onto matter but as a binding together of materials in movement. Thus the lodge, far from being built upon rigid and impervious foundations, is stitched into the very fabric of the earth. Instead of thinking of the lodge, then, as a material artefact set in a landscape, it would be better understood as a nexus of materials in a world of earth and sky.

To establish this view, I will proceed in four steps. In the first, I examine the difference between two ways of thinking about building: as the assembly of elementary solids and as the weaving and splicing of fibrous material (Ingold 2000b: 64–5; 2011: 211). In the second, I consider the essential mutuality of earth and sky, and what it means to say of the lodge that it is both of the earth and of the sky. In the third step, I link the idea of the earth–sky, in contrast to landscape, to that of smooth space, and show how this linkage is manifested in the materials of the lodge. Finally, I explain the conical form of the lodge as an upended spiral – the envelope of a process of growth and regeneration.

II

We are continually being told, these days, that the world we inhabit is built from blocks: not just the world that we ourselves have made – of artefacts or the built environment – but the worlds of nature, the mind, the universe and everything. Biologists speak of the building blocks of life, psychologists of the building blocks of thought, physicists of the building blocks of the universe itself.

So pervasive has this metaphor become that we are inclined to forget how recent it is. I had not even realized this myself until a year ago, when I chanced to read a little book entitled *The Most Beautiful House in the World,* by the architectural historian Witold Rybczynski. It was not until the middle of the nineteenth century, Rybczynski tells us, that the metaphor of 'building blocks' came into common use, along with a domestic architecture – of prosperous homes equipped with dedicated nurseries – in which building with blocks could literally become child's play (Rybczynski 1989: 29–36). Before that time, most play was out of doors, and even when it took place indoors, floors were too uneven, and too busy and cluttered, for any construction to stand up. From the 1850s onwards, however, the architectural profession actively promoted the development and marketing of sets of building blocks for children. Inculcated from our earliest years, the assumption that the world is built from blocks has since become part of the stock in trade of modern thought. For the most part, it is invoked uncritically, and without a moment's hesitation or reflection.

It is precisely this assumption that I want to question. I shall do so by considering what would happen if we were to think of the building not as a construction put together from solid blocks, but as a thing woven from pliant materials. In more technical terms this is to draw a distinction between *stereotomics* and *tectonics*. Stereotomics – derived from the classical Greek *stereo* (solid) and *tomia* (to cut) – is the art of cutting solids into elements that fit snugly together when assembled into a structure such as a wall or a vault. These elements are, of course, the building blocks to which we are so accustomed. Tectonics, by contrast, is the art of assembling a frame from linear components, held together by joints or bindings rather than simply by the gravitational force of heavyweight elements bearing down on those beneath and ultimately on foundations. One might think, for example, of the frame of a boat that has still to be covered with planks or skins, or the beams of a roof that has still to be thatched, slated or tiled. The term tectonic comes from the Greek *tekton*, originally referring to the work of the carpenter but subsequently extended to building or making in a more general sense. It goes back to the Sanskrit *taksan*, which signified the craft of carpentry and specifically the use of the axe *(tasha)*. Our question, then, is about the balance – or the relative priority – of stereo-tomics and tectonics in the building of things.

This was a question that much preoccupied the historian of art and architecture, Gottfried Semper. Writing in the middle of the nineteenth century, just as the stereotomic idea of building blocks was on the rise, Semper argued in just the opposite direction, namely that the threading, twisting and knotting of linear fibres were among the most ancient of human arts, from which all else was derived, including both building and textiles. *'The beginning of building'*, Semper declared, *'coincides with the beginning of textiles'* (1989: 254, original emphasis). Thus the first walls were plaited from sticks and branches: they were fences and pens. From there it was a small step to the plaiting of basts, and thence to the technique of weaving. This, in turn, gave rise to pattern, and the weaving of patterns led to the emergence of the carpet. We tend to think of walls as made of such solid materials as brick or stone, and of wall-builders as masons or bricklayers. But following his chain of derivations, Semper concluded, quite to the contrary, that the first 'wall-fitters' *(Wandbereiter)* were weavers of mats and carpets, noting in his support that the German word for wall, *Wand*, shares the same root as the word for dress or clothing, *Gewand* (1989: 103–4). He also found etymological support for his idea of the evolutionary priority of the textilic arts in the affinity of the words for the joint *(Naht)* and the knot *(Knoten)*, both words being connected, in modern German, to the concept *Verbindung* (binding). Thus the carpenter, joining beams, and the weaver, basket-maker or carpet-maker, binding and knotting threads or fibres, are engaged in the activities of the same general kind (Frampton 1995: 86).

The primordial dwelling, according to Semper, comprised four fundamental elements. These are the earthwork, the hearth, the framework and the enclosing membrane. To each of these he assigned a particular craft: masonry for the earthwork; ceramics for the hearth; carpentry for the framework; and textiles for the membrane. The key issue for him, however, was the relation between the stereotomic base of the building, the earthwork, and its tectonic frame – and thus between masonry and carpentry. Admittedly, the earthwork could rise up into the fabric of the building itself, to form solid walls or fortifications of rock and stone. But Semper was careful to distinguish between the massiveness of the solid wall, indicated by the word *Mauer*, and the light, screen-like enclosure signified by *Wand*. In relation to the latter's primary function of spatial enclosure, Semper thought, the former played a purely auxiliary role, to provide protection or support. The essence of building, then, lay in the joining or knotting of linear elements of the frame, and the weaving of the material that covered it. Even with the addition of stone walls and fortifications, building never lost its character as a textile art.

Semper's essay on *The Four Elements of Architecture* was published in 1860. It was not well received. Leading figures in the histories of art and architecture lined up to ridicule it. Indeed, the idea that building could be a practice of weaving akin to basketry seemed as strange to Semper's contemporaries as it does to most of us today. It takes a bold intellect to question it. One such was the eccentric philosopher of design, Vilém Flusser (1999). Writing in the final decades of the twentieth century, Flusser reminds us that for any structure that would afford some measure of protection from the elements, such as a tent, the first condition is not that it should withstand the force of gravity but that it should not be swept away by the wind. This leads him to compare the wall of the tent with the sail of a ship, or even the wing of a glider, the purpose of which is not so much to resist or break the wind as capture it into its folds, or to deflect or channel it, in a way that serves the interests of human dwelling (Flusser 1999: 56).

What if we were to follow Flusser and commence our understanding of walls by thinking about, and with, the wind: by flying kites rather than building with blocks? Rather like Semper before him, Flusser distinguishes two kinds of wall (corresponding to *Wand* and *Mauer),* the screen wall, generally of woven fabric, and the solid wall, hewn from rock or built up from heavy components. Without going into the question of relative antecedence, this for Flusser is the difference between the tent and the house (1999: 56–7). The house is a geostatic assemblage of which the elements are held firm by the sheer weight of blocks stacked atop one another. The force of gravity allows the house to stand, but equally can bring it tumbling down. Within the cave-like enclosure formed by the four solid walls of the house, Flusser argues (1999: 57), things are possessed – 'property is defined by walls'. The tent, by contrast, is an aerodynamic structure that would likely lift off, were it not pegged, fastened or anchored to the ground. Its fabric screens are wind walls. As a calming of the wind, a locus of rest in a turbulent medium, the tent is like a nest in a tree: a place where people, and the experiences they bring with them, come together, interweave and disperse in a way that precisely parallels the treatment of fibres in fabricating the material from which the tent's screen walls are made. Indeed, the very word 'screen' suggests, to Flusser, 'a piece of cloth that is open to experiences (open to the wind, open to the spirit) and that stores this experience' (1999: 57).

As house is to tent, then, and as the containment of life's possessions *over and against* the world is to the weaving together of life-paths *in* the world, so is the closure of the solid rock wall to the openness of the windblown screen wall. 'The screen wall blowing in the wind', Flusser writes, 'assembles experience, processes it and disseminates it, and it is to be thanked for the fact that the tent is a creative nest' (Flusser 1999: 57). Of course, like all sweeping generalizations, this is far too crude, and any attempt to classify built forms in these terms would immediately collapse under the weight of exceptions. There are tents that incorporate rock walls, and houses whose walls are screens. One has only to think, for example, of the screen walls of the Japanese house. Paper-thin and semi-translucent, these walls defy any opposition between inside and outside, and cast the life of inhabitants as a complex interplay of light and shadow. The traditional Japanese house, as the architectural historian Kenneth Frampton has observed, belonged to a world that was woven through-out, from the knotted grasses and rice straw ropes of domestic shrines to *tatami* floor-mats and bamboo walls (Frampton 1995: 14–16). Indeed, in its commitment to the tectonic, Japanese building culture stands in stark contrast to that of the Western monumental tradition with its emphasis on stereotomic mass.

The general contrast between the geostatics of the rock wall and the aerodynamics of the wind wall remains, however. Independently of Flusser, but drawing directly on the earlier work of Semper, Frampton takes us back to the foundational distinction between stereotomics and tectonics, and to the question of the balance between them. Traditions of vernacular building around the world reveal wide variations in this balance, depending on climate, custom and available material: from buildings – such as the Japanese house – in which the earthwork is reduced to point foundations while walls as well as roofs are woven, to traditional urban dwellings in North Africa where stone or mud brick walls arch over to become roof vaults of the same material, and in which brushwork or basketwork serves only as reinforcement (Frampton 1995: 6–7). In the former case the stereotomic component, and in the latter case the tectonic component, is reduced to a minimum. In some instances, materials are transposed from the one mode of construction to the other, such as where stone is cut to resemble the form of a timber frame (as in the classical Greek temple), or where bricks are not so much heaped upon one another as bonded into coursework that has all the appearance of a weave. Frampton's interest, however, lies in the 'cosmic associations evoked by these dialogically opposed modes of construction; that is to say the affinity of the frame for the immateriality of sky and the propensity of mass form not only to gravitate toward the earth but also to dissolve in its substance' (ibid: 7). In these associations, the building is revealed as a marriage not of form and matter but of earth and sky, and as the consummation of their union. To think of the building as such is to situate it in an earth–sky world.

III

It is in these terms, then, that I propose to consider the conical lodge – not as an artefact in the landscape but as a particular synthesis of earth and sky that allows human life to take root and grow, drawing sustenance from the earth even as it breathes the air.

In order to understand the nature of this synthesis, let us start from the ground. I have already noted how the idea of 'building blocks' presupposes a ground that is level and rigid: a foundation upon which the objects of our interest, or that afford everyday life, are mounted. In his manifesto for an ecological psychology, James Gibson compares the surface of the earth to the floor of a room. Like the floor, he argues, the ground is 'the underlying surface of support' on which all else rests (Gibson 1979: 10, 33). Yet a bare ground, devoid of features, would be no more habitable than an unfurnished room. To be rendered habitable, a room must be furnished with the miscellany of objects that make possible the everyday activities carried on in it. Similarly, the ground can harbour life only because it, too, is furnished with objects of one kind or another. 'The *furniture* of the earth', Gibson insists, 'like the furnishings of a room, is what makes it livable' (1979: 78). Just like the room, the earth is cluttered with all manner of objects which afford the diverse activities of its innumerable inhabitants. Among them would be such objects as trees, stones – and buildings.

Gibson was among the first to challenge the once dominant view that people see the world in pictures, projected onto the back of the retina as if on a screen. As I shall show below, there is a direct link between this notion of projection and the idea of landscape in its modern sense. Arguing against this, Gibson placed perceivers at the centre of a world that is all around them rather than arrayed in front of their eyes. He imagined this world as comprising two hemispheres – of the sky above and the earth below. At the interface between the upper and lower hemispheres, and stretching out to the great circle of the horizon, lies the ground on which perceivers stand. Both littered on the ground, and suspended in the sky, are the objects of our perception. Thus the inhabited environment includes not only earth and sky, nor only the universe of objects, but both together. In Gibson's words, it consists of 'the earth and the sky with objects *on* the earth and *in* the sky, of mountains and clouds, fires and sunsets, pebbles and stars' (1979: 66, emphasis in original). To return to the conical lodge, then, we could pose the following question: is the lodge an object on the earth? Is it part of the furniture? Or is it rather, recalling our earlier discussion of the aerodynamic properties of the tent, an object in the sky? Is it perhaps both, or neither?

The answer I wish to propose is that the lodge is not an object at all but a thing. The object exists as an entity in a world of materials that have already precipitated out and solidified in fixed and final forms. It stands before us as a fait accompli, presenting only its congealed, outer surfaces to our inspection. The thing, by contrast, is ever-emergent as a certain gathering or interweaving of materials in movement, in a world continually coming into being, always on the threshold of the actual. Whereas the object, as Flusser notes, 'gets in the way' and blocks our passage (Flusser 1999: 58), the thing draws us in along the very paths of its formation. Each, if you will, is a 'going on' – or better, a place where several goings on become entwined. As the philosopher Martin Heidegger put it, albeit rather enigmatically, the thing presents itself 'in its thinging from out of the worlding world' (Heidegger 1971: 181). The example that Heidegger used to illustrate his argument was a simple jug. The jug's thinginess, he argued, lies neither in its physical substance nor in its formal appearance but in its capacity to gather, to hold and to give forth (1971: 166–74).

There is of course a precedent for this view of the thing as a gathering in the ancient meaning of the word, as a place where people would gather to resolve their affairs. As the historical geographer Kenneth Olwig (2008b) observes, in a brilliant account of the political geography of early medieval Jutland, the thing–place gathers the lives of people who dwell in the land, holds their collective memories and gives forth in the rulings and resolutions of unwritten law. Jutland is dotted with such places. To attend a thing, then, is not to be locked out but to be invited into the gathering. If we think of every participant as following a particular way of life, threading a line through the world, then perhaps we could define the thing, as I have suggested elsewhere, as a *'parliament of lines'* (Ingold 2007a: 5). Thus conceived, the thing has the character not of an externally bounded entity, set over and against the world, but of a knot whose constituent life-lines, far from being contained within it, continually trail beyond, only to mingle with other lines in other knots. The conical lodge, I suggest, is such a thing (Figure 2.2).

As such, to return to our earlier question, the lodge is neither on the earth nor in the sky. For far from being confined to their respective domains by the hard surface of the ground, in the constitution and dissolution of things earth and sky continually infiltrate one another. Indeed, wherever life is going on the interfacial separation of earth and sky gives way to mutual permeability and binding. The painter Paul Klee beautifully evoked this binding in the image of a seed that has fallen to the ground. 'The relation to earth and atmosphere', he writes, 'begets the capacity to grow … The seed strikes root, initially the line is directed earthwards, though not to dwell there, only to draw energy thence for reaching up into the air' (Klee 1973: 29). The growing plant is not mounted upon the ground surface but rooted in it. For that very reason it is simultaneously earthly and celestial. It is so, as Klee pointed out, since the commingling of sky and earth is itself a condition for life and growth. It is because the plant is of (and not on) the earth that it is also of the sky.

The same applies to the conical lodge. It, too, is at once of earth and sky: a place where earth and sky are brought together in the growth and experience of its inhabitants. Evidently, then, the ground of the lodge is no mere platform. It is rather an enveloping matrix that both anchors and nourishes the lives of its inhabitants, just as the ground beyond its circumference nurtures the vegetation that grows there and the animal life that feeds on it. Thus, the ground outside the lodge does not resemble the ground inside because it is similarly furnished with objects. Rather, it is the ground inside the lodge that resembles the ground outside, since it provides shelter and nourishment like the surrounding earth. It is *in* this ground and not on it, as Heidegger put it – in this earth, this zone of growth and transformation – that 'man bases his dwelling' (Heidegger 1971: 42). In an admittedly florid passage, Heidegger describes the earth as 'the serving bearer, blossoming and fruiting, spreading out in rock and water, rising up into plant and animal' (ibid: 149). Yet this earth, Heidegger insisted, is unthinkable without also thinking of the sky, and vice versa. Earth and sky are not, then, separate hemispheres which, put together, add up to a unity. Rather, each binds the other into its own becoming. The earth binds the sky in the tissues of the plants and animals it sustains and nourishes; the sky sweeps the earth in its currents of wind and weather; and at the centre of this world of earth and sky lies the conical lodge.

IV

Even if this argument is accepted, however, we have still to account for the specific way in which earth and sky are brought together in the conical lodge. How, for example, does the lodge compare in this regard with the traditional dwellings of people who lived by farming and forestry rather than by pastoral herding?

One way to think about this difference might be in terms of a distinction, introduced by philosopher Gilles Deleuze and psychoanalyst Félix Guattari, between smooth and striated space. This distinction takes us back to what Flusser called the screen wall of the tent, and more particularly, to the material of which it is made. Recall that for Flusser, the tent wall is a woven fabric that gathers, holds and disseminates the lives of those who dwell within. As such, it epitomizes the very 'thinginess' of the lodge, in Heidegger's terms. It is 'open to experiences', Flusser says (1999: 57), and draws people in. But does it really? Semper, after all, had assumed to the contrary that the function of the woven wall was, first and foremost, to enclose (Semper 1989: 254–5). As the wall of the fence or pen, woven from sticks and branches, enclosed crops or herds, so that of the traditional house, whose woven walls might have been plastered with wattle and daub, enclosed its people.

Writing more than a century later, in 1980, Deleuze and Guattari appear at first glance to concur. Fabric, they say, encloses, but the wall of the nomadic tent is nevertheless open to experience in a way that the house wall is not, precisely because the exemplary material of the tent, in their view, is not fabric at all, but felt. Whereas the weaving of fabric entails the intertwining of separate threads, with felt there is 'no separation of threads, no intertwining, only an entanglement of fibres'. In this regard, they contend, felt is the very opposite of fabric. It is an 'anti-fabric' (Deleuze and Guattari 2004: 525). They proceed to use this opposition to exemplify their distinction between the striated and the smooth. The former is the ruled and regulated space of an agrarian regime, straked with rigs and furrows, as is cloth with intersecting parallel threads of warp and weft. It was in this sense that the land was shaped by farmers and woodsmen, in times gone by, thereby fashioning the landscape in the original, medieval meaning of the term. The latter, by contrast, is the open space of nomadic herdsmen: a heterogeneous mélange of continuous variation, extending without limit and in all directions. As felt is made up of entangled fibres, so the ground of smooth space is comprised of the entangled trajectories of people and animals as they wend their ways, following no predetermined direction but responding at every moment to locally prevailing conditions and the possibilities they afford to carry on.

However, there is a catch in the argument which even Deleuze and Guattari themselves are forced to acknowledge. While felt is the predominant tent material of herding communities throughout Inner Asia, it is by no means common to pastoral peoples everywhere. In many parts of the world, tents are covered with prepared animal hides, as indeed was the case in the lodge from which I began, clothed as it was with a patchwork of caribou skins. Deleuze and Guattari are quick to assimilate the patchwork – 'an amorphous collection of juxtaposed pieces that can be joined together in an infinite number of ways' – to their idea of smooth space (2004: 526). It is like felt in having no consistent direction, or lines of striation. The use of fabric as a tent covering, however, presents more of a problem. The nomadic pastoralists of North Africa, for example, know nothing of felting, nor do they cover their tents with animal hides. Rather, they use wool to weave their tent-cloth. How can we take woven fabric to be a hallmark of agrarian life, when it is found equally among pastoral nomads?

To get around the problem, Deleuze and Guattari displace their initial distinction between felt or patchwork and fabric onto one between two kinds (or conceptions) of fabric, corresponding respectively to the striated and the smooth. On the one hand, they argue, among sedentary farmers – inhabitants of the striated – fabric enfolds the body and the outside world within the confines of the immobile house. Here, its function is to enclose. The fabric of nomads, on the other hand, 'indexes clothing and the house itself to the space of the outside, to the open, smooth space in which the body moves' (2004: 525). Just how one might distinguish a fabric of the first kind from one of the second is hard to say, and with no means of doing so, the argument does suffer from a certain circularity. Nevertheless, with this qualification, the respective claims of Flusser and of Deleuze and Guattari, apparently in contradiction, can be readily reconciled. We have merely to acknowledge that Flusser's 'screen wall' – open to experience, spirit and wind – is a woven fabric of the second kind. And the implication is that as the setting of fabric shifts from tent to house, so the open screen becomes a closed solid wall or, more probably, a wall-covering or tapestry that hangs from it.

Exactly the same happens with the carpet, another invention of tent-dwellers, as Flusser goes on to show. The carpet, he writes, is 'to the culture of the tent what architecture is to the culture of the house' (Flusser 1999: 95). Initially, when carpets entered the house they went up on the walls. Recall that even Semper referred to carpets as wall-hangings and to carpet weavers as among the first wall-fitters (Semper 1989: 103–4). Nowadays, however, it is not on the walls that you would expect to find a carpet. For modern urban dwellers, the proper place for a carpet is the floor. As we have already seen, the popular idea of building blocks calls for a floor that is perfectly level and rigid. For the occupant of a house or apartment in a modern metropolitan city, this is all a floor should be. It is but a base, upon which can be mounted all the appurtenances of everyday life. Strip all these things away and the floor is left barren and lifeless. It cries out to be covered. We are even inclined to extend this idea metaphorically to the ground outside, which we say is 'carpeted' with vegetation.

With this idea of the ground as a solid floor, covered with a carpet and cluttered with objects as the interior room of the house is cluttered with furniture, the agrarian landscape of medieval times gives way to the stage and scenery of the landscape in its modern incarnation: as a space not of gathering but of projection. Deleuze and Guattari (2004: 543–4) distinguish between the *haptic* space of close-up, hands-on engagement – for example of the weaver with threads, the ploughman with the soil, or the carpenter or mason with wood or stone – and the optical space of distance and detachment, wherein the forms of the architectural imagination, conceived off-site, are projected onto material substance. They are right to point out that this distinction cross-cuts that between eye and hand: thus one can see close up (as in weaving) and touch at a distance (such as on a keyboard). They are wrong, however, to equate the opposition between the haptic and the optical with that between the smooth and the striated. It would be closer to the mark to recognize that the optical and the haptic correspond to two ways of striating space. This, indeed, is what distinguishes the modern sense of the landscape from its medieval precursor (Ingold 2011: 134).

The landscapes of modernity are striated, but not by the warp of the loom, the furrows of the plough, or the marks and cuts of masons and carpenters, whether etched in stone or following the grain of timber. Rather, they are striated by the abstract *lineamenta,* and by the ratios and proportions, of projective geometry. These striations, then, are of an entirely different order. To amplify the difference, we can return to Flusser's idea of the screen wall. With this idea, Flusser is primarily thinking of the woven fabric of the tent covering. For many contemporary readers, however, the word 'screen' is more likely to bring to mind the opaque screens of projection – such as in the cinema or conference room – upon which are cast images of one kind and another. Curiously, Flusser (1999: 57) believes that they, too, assemble and store experience, in just the same way as the fabric walls of the tent. This, however, is precisely what they do not do. In the cinema, the movements of life are projected onto the screen, not drawn into its fabric. The screen itself remains blankly impervious to the images that play upon its surface. Light, sound and feeling, the fundamental currents of sensory experience for the tent-dweller, are reduced in the world of cinematic representation to vectors of projection in the conversion of objects to images.

Indeed, the difference between the screen as a woven fabric and as a surface of projection precisely parallels the contrast in ways of thinking about building, between the gathering together of materials in movement and the projection of ideal form onto material substance, that I have sought to establish. 'The unavoidably earthbound nature of building', writes Frampton (1995: 2), 'is as tectonic and tactile in character as it is scenographic and visual'. Only in the former sense could it be said, with Flusser, that the screen wall is 'open to experience'. This leaves us with one problem, however, that has still to be resolved. How, exactly, does the perception of nomadic pastoralists, the archetypal denizens of smooth space, differ from that of sedentary farmers in their hands-on activities of shaping the land? How do the gatherings and weavings, and the sensory engagements, of smooth space differ from those of the striated? Only when we have answered this question can we finally put our finger on the specificity of the way in which earth and sky come together in the conical lodge.

V

All life is lived under the sun, and in this the farmer is no exception. People who wrest a living from the land have also to contend with the vagaries of wind and weather, whatever their mode of subsistence. 'It is evident that the peasant', write Deleuze and Guattari, 'participates fully in the space of the wind, the space of tactile and sonorous qualities' (2004: 530–1). This is not an optical space – a space of projection – wherein the world is revealed to the beholder in a manner akin to images on a screen. Nor is it a haptic space of close-up engagement with the materials of life. It is rather atmospheric – a space of light, sound and feeling that infuses the body, saturates awareness and both constitutes and underwrites the capacities of inhabitants to see, to hear and to touch. To inhabit the atmosphere is to see with the light of the sun, to hear with the sounds of the elements and to touch with the breath of the wind (Ingold 2011: 134).

But while nomad and peasant may live under the same sky, and imbibe the same atmosphere, their respective relations to the earth are fundamentally different. For in the peasant's labour of shaping the land, the earth presents itself as a field, not of forces to be harnessed, but of resistances to be overcome. Here, earth and sky meet not in unison but in discord – a discord played out in the construction of the dwelling, as we have already seen, in the opposed principles of stereotomics and tectonics. Whereas in the tent of the nomad, earth and sky meet at the hearth, in the house of the peasant they are divided between the stereotomic mass of the walls and foundations, which gravitate towards the earth, and the tectonic frame and covering of the roof, which mingles with the sky. In the division between roof and walls, the peasant dwelling is divided against itself. The world of the peasant, we might say, is not so much an earth–sky as an earth/sky.

To highlight the contrast, let me introduce another comparison, between the farmer's life on land and the mariner's at sea. The ocean is surely smooth space par excellence. The mariner ensconced in his vessel, feeling the waves as they lap the hull and catching the wind in his sails, all the while scanning the sky for the movements of birds by day and of the stars and other celestial bodies by night, is a point of rest in a world in which all around is in movement (Gladwin 1964: 171–2). In striving to rein in the forces of the elements he is the precise opposite of the farmer who bends muscle and sinew to counteract the friction of an immobile and often unyielding earth, dragging himself and his equipment over the hard ground and inscribing tracks and pathways in the process. To describe the mariner's surroundings from the farmer's perspective, as a seascape (Cooney 2003), would be to confer on waves and troughs, or on becalmed or turbulent waters, a permanence and solidity that they lack in reality. Setting sail, the mariner does not simply relinquish one set of surfaces, of the land, for another, of the sea. Rather, he enters a world in which surfaces take second place to the circulations of the media in which they are formed. Here the grounded fixities of landscape give way to the aerial fluxes of wind and weather above, and the aquatic fluxes of tide and current below. These fluxes, and not the surface of the sea, absorb the mariner's effort and attention. The world he inhabits is not, then, a seascape but an ocean–sky.

Could the same not be said of the nomadic pastoralist? Much as mariners ride the waves, nomads ride the pastures, carried along on the windswept expanses of sand, steppe and snow, and responding in their movements, at every moment, to real and imaginary forces, both celestial and subterranean (Ingold 2011: 133). At home in the lodge, the nomad feels the earth with his body as his gaze mingles with the sky. As a centre of stillness and a calming of the winds, the conical lodge is indeed comparable to a vessel at sea, and not just in the fact that the covering of both boat and lodge is stretched over a tectonic frame. We have reports of Micronesian mariners lying on the bottoms of their canoes when travelling far out of sight of land, sensing the swell with their bodies while gazing directly heavenwards (Mack 2007: 13–14). If for the mariner in his boat, the world is a blend of sky and ocean, then for the nomadic pastoralist in the lodge, it is likewise a blend of sky and earth. This is to think of the land as smooth rather than of the sea as striated. There are surfaces in the earth–sky world, of course. But they are surfaces of a different kind. The landscape, carved and striated, has turned against the sky. It is, as Deleuze and Guattari say (2004: 530), closed off and apportioned. But in the smooth space of the earth–sky, the surfaces of the land – like those of the sea – open up to the sky and embrace it. In their ever-changing colours, and patterns of illumination and shade, they reflect its light; they resonate in their sounds to the passing winds; and in their feel underfoot or under-hoof they respond to the dryness or humidity of the air, depending on heat or rainfall. In smooth space, to continue with Deleuze and Guattari, 'there is no line separating earth and sky' (2004: 421). One could not exist without the other.

In his *Tristes Tropiques*, Claude Lévi-Strauss linked the birth of architecture to the invention of writing, and both to the creation of cities and empires with their attendant structures of power and exploitation (Lévi-Strauss 1955: 299). Both writing and architecture strive for hierarchy, monumentality and permanence. Their forms are stereotomic, assembled from blocks and made to last. In the tectonic world of the earth–sky, however, nothing lasts: there are no indelible records, enduring monuments or rigid hierarchies. From an architectural point of view, the built forms of the earth–sky world appear ephemeral – as ephemeral, even, as spoken words. It would seem, indeed, that the monument is to the lodge, and the landscape to the earth–sky, precisely as writing is to speech. Just as the words of oral narrative dissolve in the very act of their production, so the binding of materials in smooth space is always accompanied by their unbinding.

And yet the lodge, as we have seen, is a thing, and the thing – to recall Heidegger's words – carries on 'in its thinging, from out of the worlding world' (1971: 181). To inhabit the lodge is to join with its thinging, in the material flows and circulations of vital force of which its form is the ever-emergent outcome. Whereas the monument was built, once and for all, the lodge is always building and rebuilding. Thus for the inhabitant of the worlding world, it is the architectural monument that seems ephemeral, buried in the sands of time while life goes on. As writing eventually fades, so also – in time – the monument, though designed to last in perpetuity, cracks and crumbles. The lodge, however, persists in a constant process of renewal, just as do the narratives that inhabitants tell in it.

I have sought to understand the conical lodge as a locus of growth and regeneration in an earth–sky world, where materials welling up from under the ground mix and mingle with air and moisture from the atmosphere in the ongoing production of life. As a gathering place of forces and materials, the lodge is not closed over. It does not turn its back on us. It is open: a confluence of persons and materials, drawn together in the movements of its formation. At the generative heart of the lodge is the fireplace, the hearth. And where life binds, in the growth of living things, fire unbinds, in their combustion (Ingold 2011: 122). In the smoke of the fire, materials nourished by the earth, and bound together in life, are released once more to the sky, whence they will fuel further growth.

To conclude, I want to suggest that it is in relation to this perpetual cycle of binding and unbinding that we should understand the conical form of the lodge. Instead of thinking of this form in terms of pure geometry, as a Platonic solid set upon a plane, we should perhaps regard it as the envelope of an upward spiral – that is, as an upended vortex with the hearth as its eye. The spiral is a movement that goes around and up, rather than a surface that divides inside from outside. It thus signifies growth and regeneration rather than enclosure. In short, as a vortex in the currents of earth and air, where the smoke from the hearth rises to meet the sky, the conical lodge brings to a focus the generative fluxes of the worlding world.

CHAPTER 3

Mobile Architecture, Improvization and Museum Practice

Revitalizing the Tłı̨chǫ Caribou Skin Lodge

Thomas D. Andrews

In recent years, museums have become more attuned to community desires to interact with objects in their own ways (Fienup-Riordan 2005: xvii), providing opportunities for both indigenous people and museum staff to learn valuable lessons about their own practices. This chapter is focused on one such project, the revitalization of a Tłı̨chǫ caribou skin lodge. The lessons learned from this project were crucial to the way that the skin lodge has now become embedded in Dene practice and has been given a new life. By facilitating community access to objects in ways that stretch the boundaries of museums – by taking objects out of their cases and back to the communities of origin – museums are redefining both their purpose and purpose of their collections.

When it has been allowed, an important aspect of this new trend in museum practice has been the way that objects can become revitalized through pedagogical exercises. Elders, wearing white cotton gloves, will now hold objects to demonstrate particular uses or techniques of manufacture to school children. Allowing children, elders and museum professionals to engage these objects with all of their senses allowed for the objects themselves to be mnemonic devices, triggering memories for the elders that they were willing to share with all. For the Tłı̨chǫ elders I have worked with, such sessions allow them to repurpose museum collections to fit better with their own educational priorities. In my experience of working with numerous elders over my career, they have all shared a single objective when participating in a collaborative project: that youth be provided with educational opportunities through direct participation whenever possible.

While museums tend to focus on collecting and managing objects, measuring their heritage value often in terms of rarity, aesthetic quality, a sense of representativeness and other factors, for the elders these held less importance than the skills, knowledge and experience that the objects embodied. What can we learn from Dene values that might help us understand this contrasting appreciation of objects? What implications might this hold for museums operating in the twenty-first century, especially those with a mandate to serve a primarily aboriginal audience?

A series of related projects focused on Tłįchǫ caribou skin lodges provides an opportunity to explore these questions. Designed to be light and mobile, the conical lodge was considered one of the most important of the few possessions a family owned. Recent collaborative cultural revitalization projects focused on conical lodges in museum collections, provided opportunities for the Tłįchǫ to teach youth about the history, design, manufacture and social context of these durable, portable structures, while participating in a creative practice guided by tradition. In the process, important lessons about museum practice were learned as well.

The purpose of this chapter, therefore, is twofold: first, to briefly examine the ethnographic context of two collaborative repatriation projects involving Tłįchǫ caribou skin lodges; and second, to explore lessons learned from these projects in light of Dene value frameworks, the process of creativity and improvization in relation to ideas of tradition, and how this might inform the collecting practices of museums today.

Part I: hearth, home and revitalizing Tłįchǫ lodges

Since 1981 the Prince of Wales Northern Heritage Centre has collaborated with several northern aboriginal groups on more than ten major cultural revitalization projects (Andrews 2007). Whether the projects focus on recreating traditional watercraft or hide clothing, or arranging for the temporary display of parts of nineteenth-century museum collections in the communities of origin, the projects always engage skilled practitioners and museum experts in a collaborative setting. Sometimes called 'knowledge repatriation' projects, these efforts employ objects from museum collections to revitalize or enhance cultural knowledge or practice in a way that does not seek to reclaim or repatriate the objects 'but to re-own the knowledge and experiences that the objects embodied' (Fienup-Riordan 2005: xxvii). Two of these projects – both involving Tłįchǫ caribou skin lodges – will be briefly explored for what they have contributed to the ethnography of Dene mobile architecture in the Northwest Territories (NWT).

A tale of two lodges

Historically there were several different types of Tłįchǫ shelter, ranging in complexity from simple wind-breaks to skin lodges. Winter houses, called *tsimǫkǫ* ('spruce house') used a conical structure of spruce poles banked with branches and snow. Elders often refer to them as 'pitiful', implying that they were constructed only when absolutely needed and that people preferred to live in caribou skin lodges.[1] An A-frame house, called a 'split stick house' was also sometimes constructed in winter, and elders note that it was particularly good for two families. It wasn't until the late 1800s that the Tłįchǫ began experimenting with log buildings, copying styles seen at trading posts.[2]

However, the conical lodge with a caribou skin covering was the primary habitation. Data from the 1891 Canadian census estimates that 711 Tłįchǫ were trading into Fort Rae, NWT – a Hudson's Bay Company post established in 1852 (Helm 1980). Assuming a conservative extended family size of seven to ten people, and that each family might possess a single skin lodge, we can estimate that 70 to 100 Tłįchǫ lodges may have existed in 1891. Although lodges were repaired frequently, with damaged skins or entire panels replaced as required, the effective life of a lodge, elders tell us, was about ten years (see Figure 3.1). Thus, the number of lodges that might have been made from first contact with Europeans to the time when the use of canvas tents replaced skin lodges – a period of approximately twelve decades from 1796 to about 1920 – was relatively large, with an upper range of about 1,200. Tłįchǫ oral tradition notes that due to their proximity to vast numbers of migratory barren ground caribou, Tłįchǫ seamstresses made lodges to trade with Slavey and Chipewyan living south of Great Slave Lake.[3] Consequently, the actual number of Tłįchǫ lodges produced during the first twelve decades of the contact period might have been significantly more than 1,200. Despite this, and to the best of our knowledge, only two lodge coverings have survived in museum collections.

The older of the two was purchased at Fort Rae on July 18, 1893 by Frank Russell (1894: 14), a graduate student from the University of Iowa, who was travelling through the Northwest Territories on a natural history collecting trip. Russell purchased the lodge from a prominent Tłįchǫ trading chief known as Bear Lake Chief.[4] Russell's journal (Russell 1894; 1898) records that he paid $25 for the lodge and he used it as his primary habitation throughout his travels, eventually bringing it back to Iowa at the end of his trip, where it was given to the Natural History Museum at the University of Iowa, along with his other ethnographic and natural history collections.[5] In 1997, with the assistance of the late anthropologist, June Helm,[6] the University of Iowa gifted the lodge to the Tłįchǫ and the people of the Northwest Territories and it now rests in the care of the Prince of Wales Northern Heritage Centre (PWNHC) in Yellowknife (Helm and Andrews 1999).

The second lodge covering, a generation younger, was collected by an unknown collector in 1923 from 'Chief Martin' in Rae,[7] and purchased

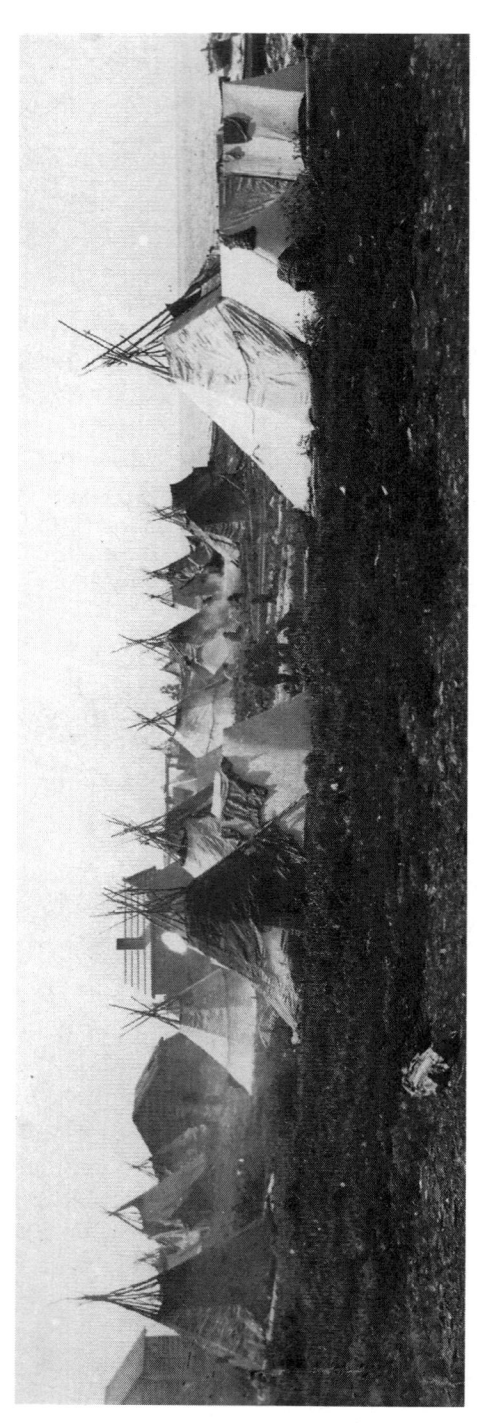

Figure 3.1 *Tłı̨chǫ caribou skin lodges, many decorated with a red ochre band, at Fort Resolution, 1924 (NWT Archives/Porritt/N-1987-016:0066).*

Table 3.1 *Comparison of the lodge coverings*

	Prince of Wales Northern Heritage Centre, Yellowknife	National Museum of the American Indian, Washington
Current museum collection		
Originating museum collection	University of Iowa Natural History Museum, Iowa City	Heye Foundation, New York, NY
Accession #	997.6.1	23891.000
Collector	Frank Russell	Unknown
Year collected	July 18, 1893	1923
Original owner	Bear Lake Chief	"Chief Martin"
Maker	Likely Emma Kowea, wife of Bear Lake Chief	Unknown
Height	3.4 m (11 feet)	3.2 m (10.5 feet)
Weight	15.8 kg (35 lbs)	Unknown
Length of bottom edge	17.4 m (57 feet)	15.4 m (50.5 feet)
Total number of hides	30	29
No. hides in bottom panel	15	15 + 2 infill sections
No. hides in middle panel	11	9
No. hides in top panel	4	4
Decoration	3 hide tassels coloured with bands of red ochre; red ochre band painted over seam between bottom and middle panels	3 tassels made from red and blue wool stroud and hide fringes; faint traces of red ochre at several locations, but no pattern apparent
Condition	Excellent; much evidence of smoke staining on interior side; small holes (from warble flies) have mostly been sewn closed	Excellent; little evidence of use on interior suggesting that the lodge was made for trade or on commission?

by an agent of the Heye Foundation in 1951. Originally part of the Heye collection, the lodge is now in the care of the National Museum of the American Indian (NMAI) in Washington, DC. No record of the purchase price has survived. Virtually identical in design and engineering to the 1893 lodge, we are confident that the NMAI lodge is Tłįchǫ in origin and there is no reason to doubt the purchase location. See Table 3.1 for a comparative summary of both lodges.

In 1995, June Helm began to lobby the Board of Governors at the University of Iowa and the Director of the Natural History Museum to return the 1893 lodge to the North. Although carefully stored, it had never been displayed and was unlikely to be in the foreseeable future. The University Board of Governors agreed and representatives of the Tłįchǫ and the PWNHC travelled to Iowa City in 1997 to attend a gifting ceremony. When the 1893 lodge returned to Yellowknife in early 1998 the PWNHC hosted a large celebration and exhibit highlighting the Tłįchǫ lodge. Attended by over 1,500 people the opening still stands as the largest public event ever held at the museum, testament to the lodge's importance in the eyes of the numerous Tłįchǫ elders who attended (Andrews and Mackenzie 1998).

The lodge remained on exhibit for nearly eight months, and was eventually retired to the collection's storeroom to prevent the further impact of gravity pulling on the lodge's sinew-sewn seams. The day after the exhibit was dismantled, however, two Tłįchǫ elders arrived at the museum and were disappointed to find that it was not available for viewing. Though they were invited to examine the folded lodge in storage, the moment demonstrated that elders expected that the lodge would always be available for viewing. In response we approached the Tłįchǫ Treaty 11 Council[8] to invite them to participate in a revitalization project which would see the creation of two replicas[9] of the 1893 lodge. And so, in the fall of 1999 staff from the PWNHC joined the fall community caribou hunt at White Wolf Lake in the barrens in order to collect the 75 hides needed for the project. Over the fall, winter and next spring, the hides were brain tanned and sewn into two new lodges, modelled on the pattern of the 1893 lodge. The entire project was documented on video, and 29 and 42 minute versions of a documentary were produced (Woolf and Andrews 2000).

The hide tanning camp was established at a location near Rae that had road access, permitting regular visits by school buses. School children from Behchokǫ, Yellowknife and Fort Providence visited the site to learn about the process of tanning and sewing hides. In addition, a small group of youth from the local school in Rae were selected to be 'apprentices' and allowed to spend more time at the camp to learn firsthand the traditional practices of tanning and sewing. Finally, in August of 2000, the two replicas were complete and erected at the Tłįchǫ Government's annual assembly in Rae. Attended by hundreds of Tłįchǫ from four communities it offered an opportunity to celebrate the completion of the lodge and the skilled work of the seamstresses. It also provided yet another opportunity to talk about lives lived in lodges, their history and their use. This will be discussed below.

When we learned of the second lodge at the National Museum of the American Indian in 2001, we began a dialogue with the museum

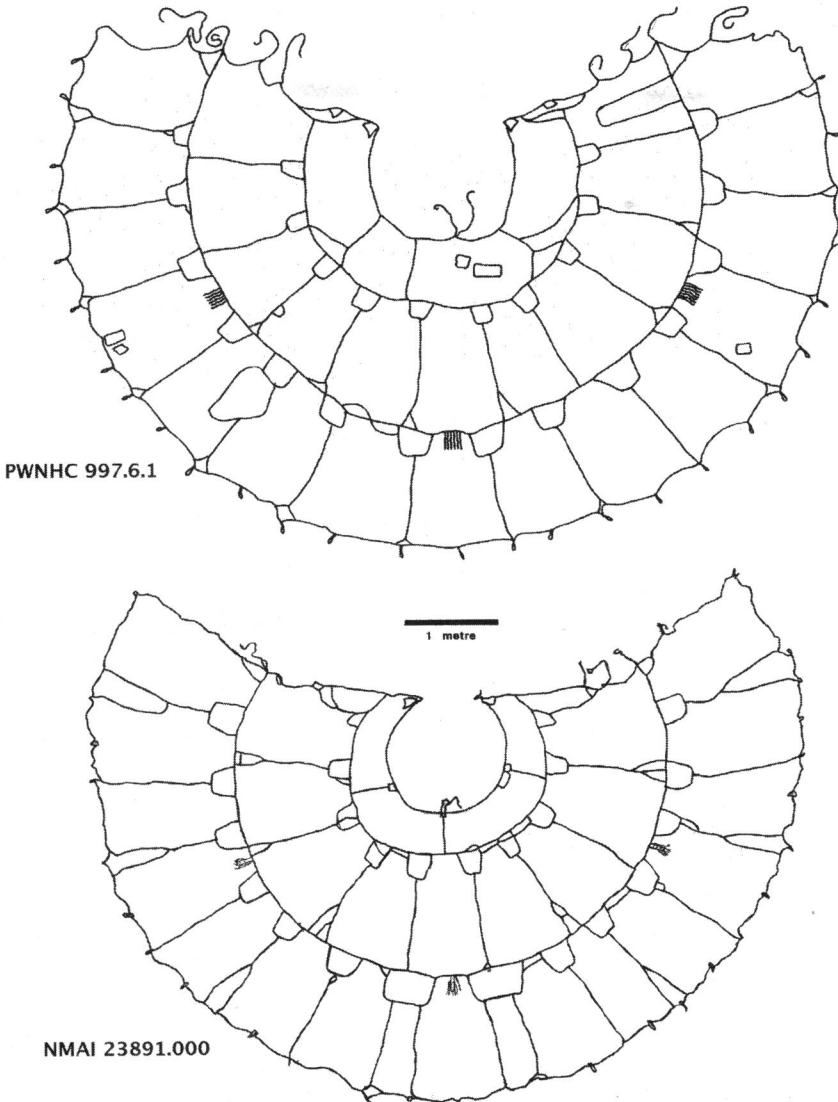

Figure 3.2 *Scaled patterns comparing the two Tłı̨chǫ caribou skin lodges in museum collections.*

and later, as a component of the Boreas Circumpolar Home, Hearth and Household project, a group of elders and staff from the PWNHC made two trips to Washington to study it. The 1923 lodge covering, as discussed above, is very similar to the 1893 lodge and differs only in a few details (see Figure 3.2 and Table 3.1). Importantly, the visits to the NMAI began an ongoing relationship between the Tłı̨chǫ and the museum that continues today.

As these projects evolved, there were numerous opportunities to focus discussions with elders on the culture of lodges. The information presented in the next three sections summarizes ethnographic data provided during these discussions, supplemented with data from historical accounts, archival photographs, and other ethnographic descriptions.[10]

Making lodge coverings

Made from tanned caribou hides, the lodges are light, durable, easily erected and waterproof, providing safe, warm habitation. Archaeological evidence suggests that conical lodges were used in this region for at least 5,000 years (Wright 1972; 1976), although they have probably been in use for much longer than that. Unlike the towering tipis of the North American Plains, Tłı̨chǫ lodges were lower in height, broader at the base in relation to height, with less steeply angled sides, and had a much larger smoke hole without the elaborate wind flaps found on Plains tipis (see Figure 3.3). In form they are more similar in shape to reindeer lodges used by Evenkiis and other central Siberian peoples (Anderson 2007), although they are significantly smaller in overall size and consist of a single panel as opposed to the separate overlapping panels used in Siberia.[11] Caribou skin lodges are known as *ewò kǫ̀ nı̨hmbàa* (literally 'skin hearth lodge').

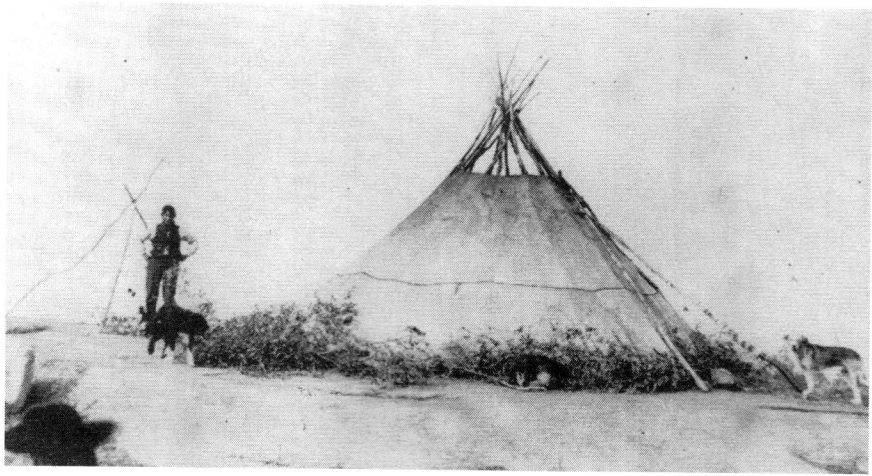

Figure 3.3 *A Tłı̨chǫ lodge ca. 1910. Note the brush piled around the edge and the ever-present dogs (from Wheeler 1914: 62).*

Having been tanned with the hair off, the hides are arranged with this hair side facing out and then sewn into three panels – a bottom panel called *nįhmbàachąą* (glosses as 'lodge bottom'), a middle panel known as *nįhmbàatani* ('lodge middle') and a top panel called *nįhmbàakwį* (or 'lodge head'). The three panels are then sewn together. Women often worked in groups to tan and sew lodges, processing numerous hides and several lodges at a time. Although tanning[12] was often done near a lake in a camp setting, the ideal location for sewing the covering was a large, flat area of exposed sloping bedrock. The open area allowed women both room to work on such a large object and perspective to ensure that the lodge panels were taking the appropriate semi-circular shape. The slight slope allowed the lodge covering to drape properly, making it easier to achieve the right shape – in essence, the land helps give both life and shape to the lodge.

Autumn hides were regarded as the best – from late August to early October – because they are thicker and the numerous holes created by warble fly larvae exiting from under the skin on the caribou's back in early summer were healed over. Caribou killed during October have strong tasting meat from the rut and women would make drymeat from it, saving it for dog food. Warble scars, sometimes opened during the tanning process, were sewn closed. In the bottom and middle panels, hides were sewn in anatomical position, with the neck pointing to the head of the lodge. This left two spaces on either side of the neck – called *wek'ohgà*, or 'neck beside' – that were filled in with small pieces of hide. The hides are sewn with sinew using an overcast stitch (known as *echìwa k'èè nàedli*). The strands of caribou sinew are taken from the thoracolumbar fascia of the animal's back. When the animals are field dressed, hunters take great care in preserving the thoracolumbar fascia, which is dried and later abraded to soften it. Individual strands – about 30–38 cm in length – are pulled free and three small bundles (about 10–15 strands each) are lightly braided and stored for later use. Forty-five or more braids of sinew might be needed to complete a single lodge.

To affect the necessary drape over a cone-shaped pole structure the number of hides in each consecutive panel is reduced to create a curved, semi-circular covering. Although both of the museum examples are slightly different sizes (see Table 3.1 for comparisons) they contain nearly the same number of hides: 29 for the NMAI lodge and 30 for the PWNHC lodge. Larger lodges were said to have existed, made for large or cohabiting families. Accounts of lodges using 40, 45 or 60 hides were common from elders.[13]

Both of the museum lodges are decorated with three tassels sewn into the seam between the bottom and middle panels, such that they are equidistant when the lodge is set. On the 1893 lodge these tassels are made

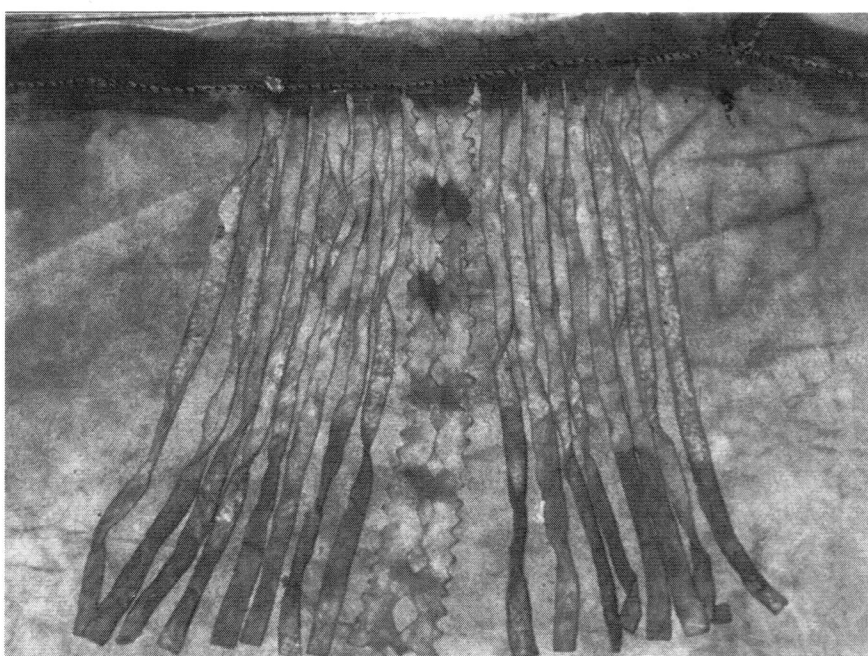

Figure 3.4 *A hide tassel decorated with red ochre from the 1893 lodge (T. Andrews/ GNWT 1998). Ochre shows as dark grey at the ends of the leather fronds and between the diamond-shaped cut-outs on the central decoration. The red ochre band painted over the seam joining the bottom and middle panels is visible at the top of the image.*

from tanned hide and consist of a central tab, cut with a serrated edge and with 11 small diamond-shaped holes cut in a row down the middle axis. Five red ochre bands have been added between the diamond-shaped holes. On either side are sewn eight thinner strips of tanned hide. The bottom half of the 16 strips have been rubbed with red ochre (see Figure 3.4). In addition, a red ochre line, about 4 cm in width, has been painted around the lodge over the seam between the bottom and middle panels.

The tassels on the 1923 lodge are much simpler in construction. The central tassel has a broader band of red wool stroud with four thin hide strips on either side. The other two are the same except that blue stroud is used in place of red. There is no red ochre line painted over the seam or on the tassels, although faint traces of ochre do appear at various places on the hide. In 2007, the NMAI used a variety of photographic techniques in an attempt to raise a pattern, although none could be discerned.

Red ochre, or *chii*, was used to decorate numerous objects such as snowshoes, toboggans, canoes and lodges. Closely associated with *ik'ǫǫ,* or medicine power, ochre was regarded as a powerful substance, in part because of its colour which brings to mind the powers associated with blood, and was used as a way of protecting the object's owner or user from harm. Knowledge of places where ochre might be collected was protected and elders are still aware of them today. To make the lodge replicas, ochre was collected from a location on the Marion River *(Gòlò Tì Deè)* by a group of men who were married to the seamstresses, and joined by two others who had specific knowledge of the location. The ochre was weeping from cracks in a rock face just a few feet from the river. Each man had a small can or plastic pail and attempted to collect fine powder and small chunks, but only after leaving a votive offering of a cigarette or a few coins, accompanied with a short statement of thanks in Tłįchǫ. After returning the ochre to camp, the women began to prepare it by removing larger pieces, breaking smaller ones into a fine powder, and then mixing the powder with water to make paint. Using their first two fingers, the women took turns painting red bands around the lodges.[14] Only the women participated in painting the lodges and rejected requests from men who offered to help (see Figure 3.5). Surrounding the lodge with ochre protected the occupants from harm. The tassels on one of the replicas were painted with ochre, mimicking the 1893 lodge. It was said that by blowing in the wind they would frighten malevolent entities wishing to gain entrance to the lodge.

Analysis of historical photographs suggests that few other design motifs existed. A close examination of photographs dating from the early 1900s to the late 1920s has revealed only two other design motifs: numerous examples of no decoration at all, and a single example where what appears to be a thin (perhaps 6 cm in width) white appliqué of caribou hide (or canvas?) is sewn around the middle of the top panel. In terms of the relative frequencies of the four design motifs, the lodges with no decoration and ones with tassels and an ochre band seem equally popular and significantly outnumber lodges with just tassels. As noted above, only a single example of the white appliqué was found. Elders were unable to recall whether there was any symbolic significance for the different decoration motifs, with one noting that they may have simply been expressions of choice made by the seamstresses.

Setting, moving, living

When a new lodge was made, it was 'christened' with a feast and a dance. As elder Elizabeth Mackenzie reported:

> The birchbark canoe, the willow bark net, the toboggan and the *ewò kǫ nįhmbàa* were the most valuable of possessions and were 'christened' with a feast and dance.

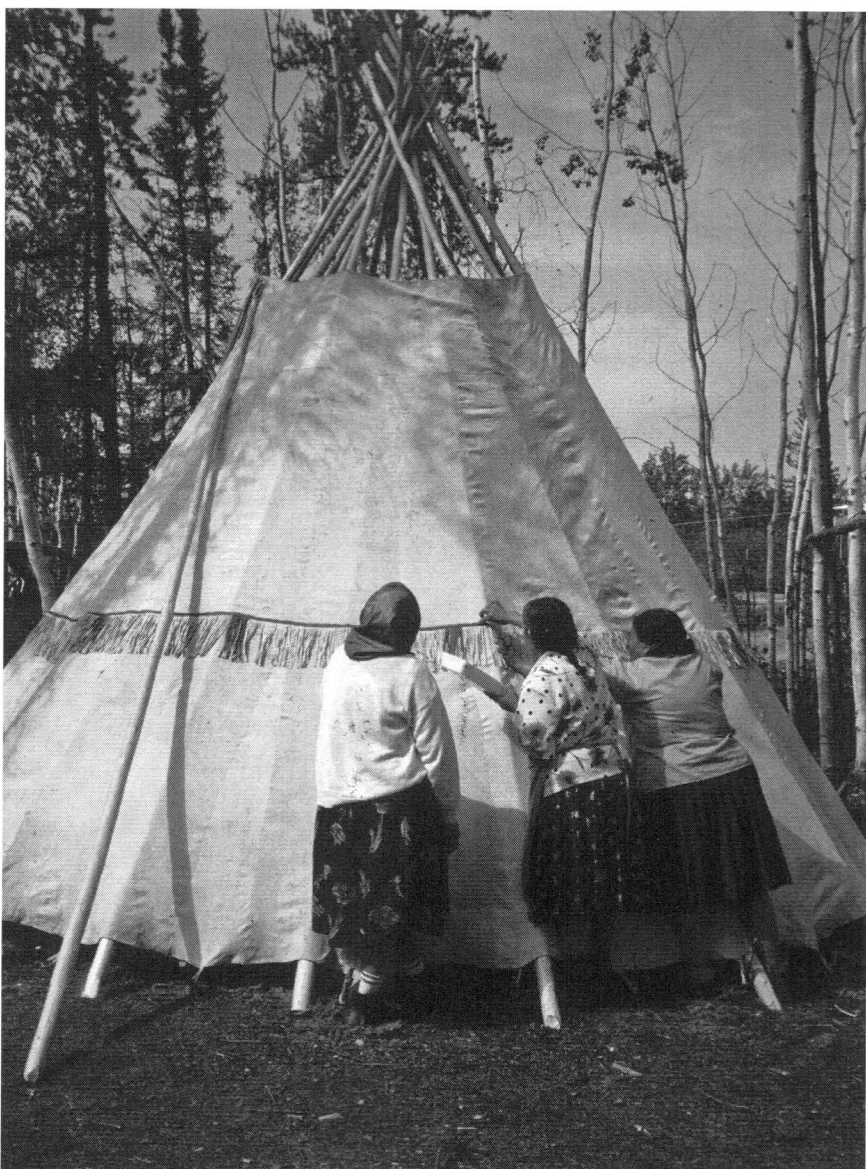

Figure 3.5 *Painting ochre on the lodge seam (T. Andrews/GNWT 2000).*

When a new lodge was finished the women would ask a man, 50 years old at least, to cut poles. It was an honour to be asked. In the old days, when we lived out on the land, the woman's husband would travel to Rae for supplies and then they would feast and dance.

Women not only made lodges but also set them up, maintained them and carried them between camps; often this meant that women would play a significant role in choosing the camping location. When breaking camp, the poles were either left standing or leaned against a high branch in a nearby tree to prevent them from rotting on the ground. Between 14 and 20 spruce poles, about 5.5 to 6 m in length, were needed to set a lodge. Three poles were tied together, lifted into place, and the remaining poles set against the upper arms of the tripod.[15] Poles were always trimmed of bark, unless the camp was for a brief, overnight duration. As old poles were frequently used when arriving at previously inhabited camp, removing the bark helped ensure they would not be weakened by sawyer beetles. As much of the Tłıchǫ landscape is formed by the Canadian Shield, large cobbles would be used to hold the skin covering to the ground on exposed bedrock. Lodges were also fitted out with peg loops, and wooden pegs were used when possible. When travelling in summer, islands were preferred locations for camps. Being more wind-swept, they kept flying insects at bay and made bear encounters less likely (cf. Wheeler 1914). Smoke holes on Tłıchǫ lodges were broader than on Plains tipis and therefore did not need the elaborate wind flaps common on the latter. They were constructed with small pockets on the outside surface in the corner of the free ends of the lodge head, called *nįhmbàadzi* (which glosses as 'lodge corner, extends into') into which special poles, called *wedzįįa* (glosses as 'into the pocket') were placed (see Figure 3.6). Used primarily to help set the lodge, they could also be adjusted to help direct the smoke out of the lodge when required.[16]

In winter, lodges were set in an area swept clear of snow by snowshoes, often in thick copses of trees, protected from wind. Toboggans, turned on their side, might be leaned against the outside of the lodge to act as a windbreak and to keep dogs from entering. Brush and snow might be added as well (Mason 1946: 20). In summer, brush was frequently piled along the outside edge of the lodge to keep dogs from entering or from urinating on it. When travelling alone in the barrens in winter, hunting caribou, musk ox, or for trapping, men would load sleds with firewood at the treeline, carrying their tent poles on top. If their journeys took longer than planned, lodge poles could be burned. In times of necessity, lodges could be set with just two poles, using lines and weighted toboggans as counter balance (Mason 1946: 16). In both winter and summer, the floor was always covered with spruce boughs, providing insulation from the cold ground, and a fresh fragrance to the lodge. A central hearth was used and will be described in the next section.

Skin lodges were the primary form of habitation until the early 1920s when canvas tents replaced them. Introduced as a trade item early in the 1900s, canvas tents at first proved impractical since there was no way to

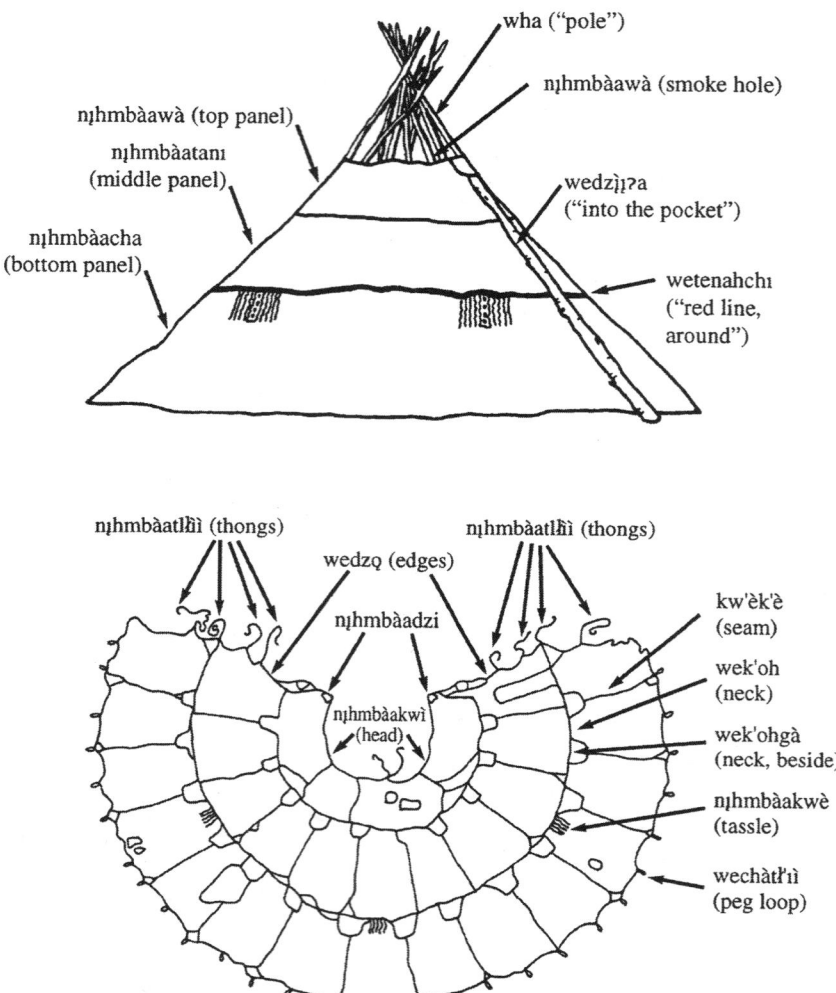

Figure 3.6 *Tłįchǫ names for the lodge's components.*

let smoke from the hearth escape. During this period of transition, photographs from the early 1900s often show hybrids of caribou skin lodges with canvas tents attached. During this period, photographs also show lodges with canvas patches and some made entirely from the material. With the introduction of portable steel stoves in the late 1920s, however, canvas tents became popular and quickly replaced skin lodges, giving women tremendous time and labour savings in the bargain, at the cost of having to carry a much heavier habitation. The 1893 lodge weighed

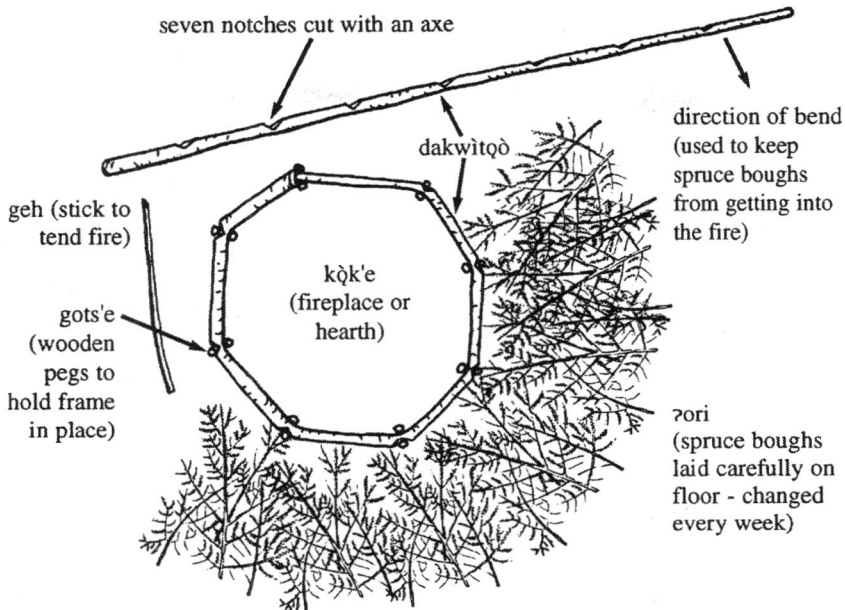

seven notches cut with an axe

direction of bend
(used to keep
spruce boughs
from getting into
the fire)

dakwìtǫò

geh (stick to
tend fire)

kǫk'e
(fireplace or
hearth)

gots'e
(wooden
pegs to
hold frame
in place)

ʔori
(spruce boughs
laid carefully on
floor - changed
every week)

Figure 3.7 *The layout of the interior hearth.*

just under 16 kg, whereas an 8 by 12 foot canvas tent will weigh more than twice that. During the exhibit opening in 1998, Tłįchǫ elder Joe Mackenzie told this humorous story about this time of change:

> In the old days when we went to trade at the [Hudson's] Bay, they gave us a canvas tent as a gift. We had never seen one before and they didn't tell us how to set it up. We took the tent back to camp and the women spread it on the ground. For three days we left it there. We walked around it trying to figure out how it worked. Finally the women cut it up and made a lodge out of it. It made a very good lodge.

Interior arrangement and social space

At the centre of every lodge was the fire, called *kǫ*, contained in the *kǫk'e*, meaning 'fireplace' or 'hearth'. Fire is so central to life that the word is also used to denote 'house', 'building' and 'town' or 'settlement'. Hearths were surrounded by a spruce pole cut with seven evenly spaced notches and bent to form a hexagon. Called a *dakwìtǫǫ*, it was held in place by wooden pegs. Filled in with dirt and ash it created a raised *det'ǫ*, or 'nest' for the fire, which provided for better draft (cf. Wheeler 1914) (see Figure 3.7). Sometimes, when lodges were set over bedrock, a small pavement of stones would be used to create the 'nest'. In settings where expedience was required, a ring of small rocks or larger pieces of firewood could be used to contain the fire.

Fires were not only critical for survival, but were used to communicate with a world where ancestral spirits dwelled. Through ceremonies called 'feeding the fire', inhabitants would provide food offerings to ancestors, asking for safe travel conditions, luck in hunting, good weather or other similar wishes in return. Since the coming of Christianity, these ceremonies were often held on Sundays near a grave of a prominent elder. Offerings of food were made into the lodge hearth or wood stove on Fridays, a practice continued by many elders today. Because the fire could be used to reach another world, the stick used to tend it, called a *geh,* was never used for other purposes and always treated with reverence.

Although lodges lacked purposeful doors, as any part of the edge could be lifted to enter, the main entrance was where women tended to work and sleep. Called *kaga,* or 'front', it was also where small amounts of wood for the fire were stored and where the main cooking preparation would be done. Opposite the entrance was the *kwèelǫ,* or 'back' of the lodge, an area usually reserved for men or guests (cf. Mason 1946: 20). As such, the lodge had informal male and female sides. Wishing to avoid proscriptions for women stepping over the blood of freshly killed animals, especially at menses, men would lift the edge of the covering near their sleeping place to bring fresh meat or hunting equipment into the lodge.

There were no set rules for the orientation of the lodge. In situations where numerous lodges were set together, the entrances might face each other. In situations where the lodges were set on a narrow clearing beside a lake or river they might all face the water. Personal gear was stored at the edge of the lodge and people generally slept with their feet towards the fire, although other arrangements were common. In winter, the canvas or moosehide 'wrapper', the long open bag attached to a toboggan, might be removed and brought inside the lodge to line the edge and be used to store tools and supplies. Bedding was rolled up each morning and kept at the edge, clearing the main part of the floor for work. Spruce boughs were replaced every two or three days by the women, often with the assistance of young children.

Above the fire, at head height, a rack made from spruce poles was used to suspend meat for drying, or to dry articles of clothing. A long cord with a wooden hook attached to the end was suspended from the centre of the rack, allowing metal pots, metal baskets or other cooking apparatus to dangle over the fire. Collecting firewood and tending the fire was a shared duty and both women and men were proficient with axes. Heavy cutting and retrieval of large logs was left to the men, and young people would often be encouraged to do much of the light collecting. Though gender roles were important and respected, both men and women were generally proficient with all tasks and could get by in any emergency.

Dogs were never allowed inside, although they often had houses built for them in nearby dog 'yards'. Frequently dogs were left loose in camp, which meant that brush needed to be piled around the outer edge to keep them at bay. Other functional spaces outside the lodge were linked with interior ones. For example, food was moved from outside to inside hearths, or vice versa. Waste created in the lodge was disposed of outside in designated waste areas and always in accordance with spiritual beliefs. For example, the remains of terrestrial animals such as caribou or moose could not be disposed of in the fire[17] or water and were usually piled neatly and discretely at the edge of camp. Waste from aquatic animals (fish, beavers, ducks etc.) was always returned to the water. Wood was cut outside the lodge and small amounts would be stored near the women's entrance and near the fire. Many tasks – making or repairing tools, cutting fish or drymeat – could be moved inside or out, depending on weather or season. When working outside, however, one always needed to be cognizant of the presence of dogs and that they might steal food or upset a project.

Part II: values, enskillment, creativity and implications for collecting in the twenty-first century

Turning now to Part II of the chapter, I would like to explore how these revitalization projects find meaning in the context of Dene life and reflect core societal values. Following an examination of basic values and value frameworks, I will discuss how creativity and the process of improvisation directs an enskilled practice. Finally, I would like to reflect on how this might inform modern museum practice.

Many Athapaskanist anthropologists have noted four basic values common to all Dene societies. These include individual industriousness and capability, generosity, personal autonomy, and emotional or personal restraint in social interaction (Rushforth and Chisholm 1991). Rushforth and Chisholm (1991) demonstrate that not only are these values held by all Northern Athapaskans, but also among Pacific Coast and Southern Athapaskan societies as well, which suggests they have great antiquity and predate the Pacific and Southern Athapaskan diaspora. Furthermore, they demonstrate that these values have remained historically stable, persisting through times of rapid change that have had dramatic impacts on other aspects of culture.

Although these four values are interrelated and indivisible for defining what constitutes a competent or capable person, two values – individual industriousness and personal autonomy – are particularly important to the discussion here. Being industrious and self-reliant by 'knowing how to do things' is highly valued in all Dene societies. June Helm has noted that individuals who exhibit a 'commitment to hard work and physical endurance' (for the Tłı̨chǫ; Helm 1972) or 'superior ability' (amongst the Slavey; Helm 1956), are recognized as being capable and self-reliant. These qualities, she argues, are related to prestige and are central to Dene leadership (Helm 1956). Autonomy, or 'being your own boss' as Rushforth's (1984) Sahtuot'ine consultants phrased it, is also important. Indeed, in current wage-labour settings, positions such as 'foreman' or 'manager' are translated into the Tłı̨chǫ vernacular as the insult *k'àowo dee,* or 'big boss' – someone who shows no skills of their own and only oversees capable persons.

In reviewing Sahtuot'ine values, Rushforth and Chisholm (1991) describe and analyse a fifth value, called *séodı̨t'e* (which loosely translates as 'care' or 'control'), that acts to integrate the other values in an operational framework. When Rushforth and Chisholm asked the Sahtuot'ine to describe *séodı̨t'e,* they noted that it is the most highly esteemed type of behaviour but that they preferred to recite a series of stories which demonstrated it in action, rather than try to define its basic characteristics. In these stories the protagonist, although proficient in some skills, often exhibits weakness and an inability to conform to cultural norms with respect to a variety of other activities, most notably those related to hunting, and is teased and chastised by members of his group as a result. In response, the protagonist rises to the occasion, often involving mitigating a critical food shortage, and exhibits proficiency in all of the areas he was criticized for earlier, bringing food or other resources to his family and other members of his group, all the while showing no hubris. Through this skilful display, always performed alone and without the assistance of others, and his subsequent restraint and generosity towards his former tormentors, he becomes a highly respected member of society. Individuals, either men or women, with *séodı̨t'e,* are thus recognized as 'capable' individuals, mastering the values of industriousness, autonomy, generosity and restraint.

The Tłı̨chǫ have similar ways of denoting a capable person that are rooted in core values. Anyone, including animal-persons, who carries out a particular task proficiently can be described as being *nàghòò,* or 'capable'. For example, a young boy skilfully using an axe to chop wood, or a fox pouncing on a mouse under the snow, might be said to be *nàghòò.* People who are capable of complex tasks, or who exhibit a wide-ranging capacity, would be known as *hats'ele ha dii-le,* or 'someone who can do [the task]'. For example, the seamstresses may assess their capacity for completing a lodge and conclude *weghàlats'eda ha dii-le,* or 'we can do it'. The phrase recognizes their skilful capacity to complete the task at hand. Finally, someone recognized widely as being an extremely capable person may be said to be *wexǫ̀zǫ*, or 'a very capable person'. These expressions operate in a fashion similar to *séodı̨t'e* in that they provide a way of denoting individuals who uphold the values important to all Dene societies and who are known for their skilful, creative practice.

As Tim Ingold (2000a: 5) has noted, skills are 'incorporated into the *modus operandi* of the developing human organism through training and experience in the performance of particular tasks'. He also notes that stories are an important means for guiding the attention of listeners into the world (Ingold 2000a: 190). Recently, Thorsten Gieser (2008: 299) has suggested that emotion plays a role as a learning mechanism in developing skills, by filtering the attention of the apprentice through empathy with a skilled practitioner. Could it be that stories act in the same way by allowing the apprentice to learn through an empathetic relationship with the story's protagonist?

Listening to stories, especially those that highlight the Sahtuot'ine qualities of *séodı̨t'e,* allows the apprentice to become immersed in the allegorical world of a capable and skilled practitioner, thereby contributing to his knowledge (cf. Cruikshank 2005: 9). Being inside a story world, young apprentices can imagine themselves using their own personal knowledge, experience and skills to perform the feats of the narrative protagonist, without the emotional cost of criticism that might ensue in an experiential setting. When combined with the hands-on experience gained from working closely with skilled practitioners, young apprentices have an opportunity to gauge their own proficiency, at least at an imaginary level. During the conduct of the various revitalization projects, storytelling formed a significant part of the experience, clearly intended as part of the apprentices' education. If we can accept that Dene stories serve a kind of archive (cf. Andrews, Zoe and Herter 1998) that skilled practitioners can call upon, perhaps when a need to improvise arises, then the emotional embodiment of the stories is a way to organize them for later recall. In the process, the stories also help youth learn important societal values, an important aspect of becoming Dene.

During our various revitalization projects evenings were almost always spent listening to elders tell stories. Stories about hand games were a popular subject. Tłįchǫ hand games (see Helm and Lurie 1966 for an extensive treatment) have tremendous societal significance, and stories about them often relate supernatural activities of important individuals from the past.[18] Traditionally played by men at times of ingathering to the trading post (treaty time, Christmas, Easter) and frequently associated with other festive activities (feasts, dances, etc.), hand games are fast-paced guessing games played by two opposing teams. While one team (of up to 12) secretly hides an object (called an *idzi*) in one hand or the other, the other team appoints a captain who tries to guess which hand it is hidden in. The captain uses a complex set of over 50 hand signals to indicate the particular hands he is guessing. With a loud clap, the captain gestures one of the signals, simultaneously guessing for each man of the opposite team. Sticks are used to keep tally, and the teams switch back and forth taking turns at guessing and hiding, and the team that wins two rounds wins the game. Behind each team sits a row of drummers, but only the drummers behind the side hiding the *idzi* drum, playing a loud, fast and powerful rhythmic drum song. The powerful drums resonate in the chests of the players and spectators alike, making for an exciting embodied experience shared by all. The *idzi* men move rhythmically with the beat and in combination with grand gestures with arms and bodies it makes for an emotional spectacle that, with the loud drumming, serves to disconcert the opposition. Often associated with betting, the game is still popular today, with significant prizes being awarded in large tournaments.[19]

In the evening, after a long day of practice-led teaching, elders will entertain youthful apprentices with stories, and hand games are always a popular subject. Hand game stories typically focus on the amazing feats of individuals who used their various capacities to win games in challenging or even dangerous, sometimes life-threatening, situations. Sometimes the stories lead to an impromptu game, recalling a time when they were a popular pastime for families encamped during fall caribou hunts (Helm and Lurie 1966: 82). Regardless, the impact on the youth is apparent for several days as young boys pair off to try newly learned hand signals or body gestures on their opponent, and can often be seen consulting with elders about the finer points of the game. The stories highlight the qualities of *séodı̨t'e,* and help the youth learn societal values and in the process what it means to be Dene.

Creativity, improvization and enskilled practice

During the course of the first lodge project, it became clear that the two 'replicas' were anything but exact copies of the 1893 'original'. Although one was a reasonable likeness – it would have fitted well within the range of lodges in any of the historical photographs surviving from the early twentieth century – the other was not, since the seamstresses added an elaborate fringe that ran entirely around the lodge. It was also apparent that the best of the caribou hides were incorporated into this lodge. When I asked why they had chosen to 'break with tradition', they explained that they wanted the best looking lodge to go to the museum and were taking steps to dress it up a little by adding the fringe (see Figure 3.5).

In an epilogue to a book presenting the Athapaskan collection of the Haffenreffer Museum (Hail and Duncan 1989) entitled 'Women's Work, Women's Art' June Helm (1989: 121–2) notes:

> A woman's aesthetic standards and pride in her handiwork do not start with the decorative elements with which, past and present, she has embellished items of hide apparel. The hide itself is subject to aesthetic appraisal. To gain approval, the dressed hide must be supple, smoothly and evenly scraped, and smoked an even, rich golden brown. An elegant pair of moccasins must display not only attractive designs and colors executed in fine floss-work or veil-stitched beading; the hide must also be handsome. ... For many of the finest creations of a 'bush' Indian wife, her husband served as a kind of travelling art gallery. When men went by dog team to the trading fort, particularly at Christmastime and Eastertime, to trade their furs, their wives usually stayed behind. But the embroidered or beaded yoke of her husband's parka and his decorated moccasins, newly-made for him to wear at the fort, advertised a woman's handiwork afar.

Not surprisingly I think, the creative practice of making things – where skilled practitioners use knowledge and experience to complete objects (even utilitarian things such as lodges and articles of clothing) – can serve as a way of demonstrating one's creativity. Reflecting on the process of creativity and cultural improvisation, Ingold and Hallam (2007: 7, emphasis original) note that following a tradition 'is a matter not of replicating a fixed pattern of behaviour, but of *carrying on*'. Copying something, they note (ibid: 5), is not a 'simple, mechanical process of replication' but rather a complex interaction between a skilful practitioner and a model (or tradition), a process that is more in line with the concept of improvisation.

The Tłįchǫ use the word *gonaèwo*, to describe 'our way of life'. For the seamstresses, while tradition or *gonaèwo* may have been the architect, they were the 'builders' and improvised on the 'original' design as the situation dictated. In so doing, they uphold Dene values of personal industriousness and capability. In short, their actions demonstrate that creativity and improvisation are essential components of enskilled knowing and enveloped within value frameworks such as *séodįt'e* or the Tłįchǫ concept of *wexòzǫ*. Their actions support the notion that tradition is not a set rule or dictum blindly followed, but rather a design guiding skilful practice, while allowing improvisation when appropriate. In other words, a skilled practitioner must also be a creative one, capable of improvising when required to do so. Young apprentices watch and listen to skilled practitioners as they carry out their tasks and, later, use their own hands to improvise on what they have been taught – in this way, as Ingold and Hallam note, culture carries on.

Implications for collecting in the twenty-first century

What does this mean for museums collecting today? Clearly there is an important role for anthropology in all aspects of museum practice – something that Nancy Lurie (1981) called for more than 25 years ago. For a museum like the one I work for, where a majority of our constituency is comprised of aboriginal communities, a focus solely on collecting objects would seem to be missing an important aspect of Dene culture. Collecting objects must also involve recording the practice of making them. In situations where the knowledge and skills have been lost, museum objects should be used whenever possible to help restore them.

For my own institution, despite years of collaborative work with aboriginal communities doing just these sorts of things, there exists no formal mechanism, either in the museum's mandate or its collections strategy, to endorse or facilitate this approach. Collaboration has been the practice of a few staff, not endemic to the operational procedures of the institution. Yet these projects have clearly demonstrated the profound benefits for aboriginal communities, as they provide meaningful opportunities for elders and youth to interact in a traditional setting where apprentices learn from skilled practitioners. They provide benefits for museums as well, by having knowledgeable elders and artisans examining their collections to provide sources of information pertinent to the objects' history, manufacture, use, cultural context and setting.

Consistently, whether making moose skin boats, birchbark canoes and kayaks, or caribou skin lodges, elders agreed to participate only if the project was designed to involve young apprentices, usually in a camp setting outside of the community. Indeed, as educational experiences, the further from the distractions of 'town' the more successful the projects were likely to be. For elders, it provided an opportunity to return to a traditional teaching setting, where the direct hands-on experience of making things can be interspersed with opportunities to interact with youth in other ways: sharing a tent, communal making and eating of food, checking fishnets or collecting firewood together. Telling stories was a particularly important part of these projects and elders were careful to make time for them at night, where they served to broaden the cultural context for the hands-on work that consumed much of the day. For elders, the context was more important than the object.[20]

It should come as no surprise that for highly mobile Athapaskans, individual skills, knowledge and experience are regarded as more valuable than the objects created through skilled practice, something that Robin Ridington (1982; 1983; 1994) has spoken about at length. He observes that northern Athapaskans value knowledge and skills over material possessions, noting the adaptive advantage that techniques held in the mind, in concert with tools that are easily fashioned from local materials, have over a complex material culture that is difficult to carry long distances. He suggests that these technologies emphasize artifice over artefact. Expressed another way, practice is more important than product.

Recognizing that 'improvisation is a cultural imperative' (Bruner 1993: 322, as cited in Ingold and Hallam 2007: 2) challenges the need for stringent, inflexible tests of authenticity so commonly applied in the field of heritage preservation and museum practice (cf. Andrews and Buggey 2008). Whether they are acknowledging the skilled practice required to make utilitarian objects such as willow bast nets, or improvising on tradition when decorating a skilfully constructed lodge, the primary focus of elders is to contribute to the experiential education of youth, allowing youth to learn core Dene values through the process of becoming skilled practitioners. For museums today, replicating this setting in the context of knowledge repatriation or cultural revitalization projects brings significant benefits to all participants, while helping to ensure that both artifice and artefact are carried on.

Acknowledgements

To undertake and successfully complete projects of the scale of the ones described here many skilled and dedicated partners need to work together, and I am grateful to numerous people who worked with me on these projects. Although too numerous to catalogue in full, I would like to acknowledge the many Tłı̨chǫ who participated, particularly Melanie Weyallon and the other seamstresses, Elizabeth Mackenzie, Rosa Mantla, George Mackenzie, and John B. Zoe. Pat Nietfeld and staff at the National Museum of the American Indian, provided extraordinary access to their collections, helping to redefine the role of museums in the twenty-first century in the process. The late June Helm, George Schrimper, and the staff of the Natural History Museum at the University of Iowa played a critical role by facilitating the return of the Russell lodge. These projects would not have been possible if not for the support of my colleagues at the Prince of Wales Northern Heritage Centre. Funding for the projects described here came from the Government of the Northwest Territories, the Museums Assistance Program (Department of Canadian Heritage) and the Tłı̨chǫ Government. A grant from the Social Sciences and Humanities Research Council (Gerry Oetelaar, Principal Investigator) supported a significant portion of the research. Finally, the chapter benefitted from critical commentary from Glen MacKay, Ingrid Kritsch, Rob Wishart, Shelley Crouch and Susan Irving, who read an earlier draft.

Notes

1. Mason (1946: 20) suggests that, among the Slavey, until the introduction of the gun, only the better hunters could secure skin lodges.
2. Today, modern 'stick-built' houses are often procured through government building programs. Conical lodges, now typically covered with polyethylene tarps or plywood, sit adjacent to the house and are used as a 'smoke house' or storage facility.
3. Tłı̨chǫ trade practice would sometimes take them to Fort Resolution on the southern shore of Great Slave Lake, where they would have encountered local Slavey and Chipewyan groups.
4. Bear Lake Chief was born in approximately 1852. His Christian name was Francis Yambi and his Tłı̨chǫ name was *K'aawidaa*, which glosses as 'highest trader'. However, he had other nicknames as well. Helm and Lurie (1966) have referred to him as 'Slim Ekawi' and Russell referred to him as 'Naohmby' (Russell 1898).
5. Russell (1894: 14) also purchased a birchbark canoe ($5) and a dog team ($15) from Bear Lake Chief. A sum of $45 dollars had tremendous purchasing power and measured in the currency of the fur trade was equal to about 90 MB ('made beaver' – a unit of currency during the fur trade) (Russell 1894: 294). By way of comparison, a large beaver pelt traded at the HBC post would be worth about 8 MB in 1893.
6. June Helm, an anthropologist based at the University of Iowa, had undertaken extensive research in the NWT beginning in 1951, mostly with the Tłı̨chǫ. June Helm passed away in 2004.
7. Fort Rae had moved from its original location to a new one about 24 km to the north. The new location had become popular when free traders, Hislop and Nagle, established their post at the site in 1898. The new location was known as 'Rae'. Today it is known as Behchokǫ and is the largest of four Tłı̨chǫ communities (including Gameti, Whati and Wekweeti).
8. Now the Tłı̨chǫ Goverment, following successful implementation of provisions of their self-government and land claim completed in 2003.
9. One lodge was for use in the Tłı̨chǫ school system, the other for permanent display at the PWNHC. Although the Tłı̨chǫ use their copy regularly in school programming, the PWNHC has yet to erect theirs in a permanent gallery installation.
10. One elder, the late Elizabeth Mackenzie, was very important and I would like to acknowledge the time that she spent with me talking about lodges. Much of what is presented here expands on the exhibit guide we produced for the 1998 exhibition (Andrews and Mackenzie 1998).
11. Samuel Hearne (1958: 207) noted that Chipewyan made lodges in separate panels of no more than five hides, tanned with the hair on.
12. The tanning process has been described elsewhere (see Andrews and Mackenzie 1998).
13. Mason (1946: 20) noted that lodges as large as 40 hides were used.
14. Mason (1946: 27) described an almost identical process in 1913.
15. Mason (1946: 20) describes a four-pole foundation used during his visit in 1913, although I have never seen this practised. The system he witnessed in 1913 used a forked pole into which three others are set, forming the four-pole foundation, to which the remaining poles were added. I have only seen people lay three poles on the ground, tie them together tightly with a stiff cord about 2 feet from the top, and lift the three-pole unit into a tripod. Perhaps the introduction of inexpensive cord sometime after Mason's 1913 visit inspired this innovation.
16. Although it was not discussed in the context of the museum projects, June Helm (personal communication 30 October 1998) was told by a Tłı̨chǫ elder that a separate small tarp (made from two hides sewn together), held in place at the top of the lodge by poles, was used to direct the wind from blowing down the hole. Ernest Thompson Seton (1911: 149) illustrated a similar set-up for the Dene Sųłiné (or Chipewyan).

17. This may appear contradictory to findings from numerous archaeological deposits where diminuted and calcined bones, presumably from terrestrial animals, are frequently found in hearth deposits in subarctic contexts. Harry Simpson, a Tłįchǫ elder, explained that the practice of making 'bone grease', where the bones are smashed into small fragments and boiled to render their tallow or 'grease', is not seen as being disrespectful to the animal, and that this transformation permits the waste bone fragments to be disposed of in the hearth.
18. See Helm and Lurie (1966: 86–7) for a story involving Bear Lake Chief using his medicine power to win a hand game.
19. Today hand games are also played at the international Arctic Winter Games and other regional sport gatherings where the traditional practice of only allowing men to play has been discarded.
20. See, for example, Andrews and Zoe (1997) for a list of the conditions required by elders in order to agree to participate in a cultural resource inventory project.

CHAPTER 4

Building Log Cabins in Teetł'it Gwich'in Country

Vernacular Architecture and Articulations of Presence

Robert P. Wishart and Jan Peter Laurens Loovers

The introduction of the log cabin as a type of housing in the Canadian sub-arctic has been positioned as an indication of the far-reaching implications of culture change during the Canadian fur trade. Indeed, cabins have been part of a larger narrative about the apparent radical departure of Canada's northern Aboriginal peoples from a land-based, foraging economy.

We would like to argue that this is far too simplistic an argument, at least for the Teetł'it Gwich'in with whom we have worked. The rise of log cabins as a dominant housing type can be located historically in the cultural exchanges that took place between the Gwich'in and those who came to their lands to participate in the fur trade and other extractive industries such as early forms of gold mining. This fact, however, tends to obscure an already existing use of logs for Gwich'in architecture at the time of contact, how cabins are actually built, and how the raw materials are gathered from the land. It omits how the fur trade was understood from a Gwich'in perspective, how cabins serve as a Gwich'in expression of that particular understanding, and how cabins continue to be constellations of Gwich'in social and political engagement with their lands and with neighbours and outsiders.

In this chapter we will provide a brief history of log cabins and working with wood for vernacular architectural purposes, followed by demonstrating how and why cabins serve as reminders of a time period that is considered to be one of cultural florescence for the Gwich'in rather than decline. We will then illustrate how cabins continue to be an aspect of living on the land, finally demonstrating how they have become important reminders of occupation and use of the land.

Log cabins: general history

Pre-contact architecture among the Gwich'in can be difficult to determine (Osgood 1970: 55). One possible reason might be due to environmental factors that have resulted in poor preservation. When vernacular architecture appears in the early anthropological record it has been used predominantly as an index of social evolution. For example, anthropologist Lewis Henry Morgan was fascinated by architectural form and what it indicated of the builders. In Morgan's monumental *Ancient Society* (1877) he makes mention of the evolution of architectural form, but in the case of the Gwich'in he left out the discussion of their architecture deeming it to be superfluous. However, he returned to the question of Gwich'in houses later in life and included fur trader Strachan Jones's drawing of a Gwich'in skin lodge in his book *Houses and House-Life of the American Aborigines* (1881). Citing Jones's discussion of Gwich'in dwellings, Morgan ends his short reference with the conclusion that '[t]he Kutchin must be classed as savages, although near the close of that condition as they still live in simple structures' (ibid: 113).

In an interesting counter claim to the European social evolutionary view of their own homes, some Gwich'in wondered if Europeans were related to beavers because of their penchant for building, and living in, permanent log lodges (Slobodin, in Loovers 2010: 93). Leaving the evolutionary disposition of the early anthropological record for the Gwich'in aside, and what this meant for the analysis of architecture, there are oral historical, archaeological and early written historical sources that describe Gwich'in pre-contact architecture.

Despite his reservations on the subject, Osgood (1970: 48–57) provides a fairly elaborate summary of traditional Gwich'in dwellings divided into three types: primary dwellings, secondary dwellings, and special shelters. The primary dwellings are the moss-house or *nyin-kun*, the semi-spherical skin-covered tent or *nivaze* (*nìivaa* or *nivyaa*), the thin-caribou lodge or *dityie*, and the gable-roofed log houses. This corresponds closely with Gwichya Gwich'in oral history. The Gwichya Gwich'in distinguish four types of dwelling: *nee kanh* (moss house or Osgood's *nyin-kun*), dome-shaped with a wooden frame and a moss and earth covering, the *nan kanh* (ground house or Osgood's gable-roofed log house) which was gable-roofed and more semi-subterranean than the moss house, the *dizhoo nìivaa* (Osgood's *nivaze*) which was a caribou skin tent with hair left on for winter use, and finally the *aadzii nìivaa* (Osgood's *dityie*), which was a smoked caribou skin tent without hair for summer use (personal communication; see also Andre and Kritsch 1992: 24–5; Heine et al. 2007: 133–5).

According to Osgood (1970), the preferred dwelling structure, when the Gwich'in were moving around their country, was a semi-spherical shelter (*nivaze*) that was partially subterranean. This is partially contested by oral history – Gwichya Gwich'in elders mention that they would just clear the snow and even out the ground (see Heine et al. 2007: 103–7). Bent poles were covered with various materials, caribou skins and spruce and/or birch bark being of primary importance. The Peel River (Teetł'it) Gwich'in would construct larger more permanent dwellings during the late autumn. The *nyin-kun* (Osgood 1970: 49) formed a permanent dwelling during the first winter months until mid-January. The tops of the four corner posts and the two taller centre posts were cut in a v-shape, somewhat like a dove-tail corner, and the ridge-pole fits in accordingly. Surrounded with smaller poles and rafters, a circular architecture was formed and moss was placed around the tent with dirt, or mud, to support it.

Andre and Kritsch (1992) refer to 75 to 80 moss-houses in the Gwichya Gwich'in region, and one can conclude that there were other traditional Gwich'in settlements of moss-houses. The floor of the moss-house was first dug to the permafrost and afterwards layered with willow mats. For the beds, the Gwich'in would use spruce boughs. Another form of this type of structure was the gable log design, where logs were used to construct the walls and roof of the structure. Osgood (1970: 51) referred to birchbark houses, tipis, and snow shelters as secondary dwellings. These dwellings were more temporary and built less frequently as the primary dwellings. The special shelters included ceremonial grounds, caches, spruce-bark smoke houses and sweat lodges. The building of these dwellings was an endeavour that brought together different timber-cutting techniques with the skills and knowledge of the land.

During the very early years of direct trade (mid-nineteenth century), Gwich'in dwellings remained relatively true to their pre-contact design. At this point in history, the fur traders were almost totally dependent upon the Gwich'in to sustain their material needs and not the other way around. Trade in this area of the Mackenzie District ran at a loss to the European companies who calculated it to be worthwhile because of the potential for future trade wealth that could come from holding this territory (Wishart 2004). Therefore the traders were more inclined to adopt and adapt to Gwich'in ways of doing things during this period, but they also started building permanent log cabins at centralized trading posts and forts.

Log cabins as a replacement for the timber and moss or gable-roofed permanent structures were constructed later when the Gwich'in began to a have more direct relationship with European traders (Vuntut Gwich'in First Nation and Smith 2010: liv) during what is locally referred to as 'the Old Days', a period lasting from the mid-nineteenth century to the early twentieth century. In this era things changed markedly, for example there was an increased capacity in transportation at the turn of the twentieth century to bring European trade goods into Gwich'in country and to take furs out (Asch with Wishart 2004). From the south, barges and steamers came down the Mackenzie River and would bring or haul materials that were now being transported to hubs in western Canada by the new railroads far more frequently and in larger quantities.

A further change was the Klondike Gold Rush, where Gwich'in traded meat with miners for cash or goods. From the money earned, the 'Dawson Boys' (Slobodin 1962; 1963), as the Gwich'in hunters became known locally, bought new luxury goods such as canvas tents and cast iron stoves. The Klondike Gold Rush, and to a lesser degree the whaling era in the Beaufort Sea, accelerated the changes and the incorporation of canvas tents and log cabins. Once available, canvas tents were adopted quite quickly by the Gwich'in and have remained an integral part of Gwich'in life on the land because they are relatively easy to set up, portable, and warm when coupled with small steel wood-burning stoves. The canvas tents replaced the skin tents that were used for times of travel and short stays. Although there was a rupture or break from incorporating skins in vernacular architecture, the canvas tents – like the skin tents before – continued to require the skill of using timber resources in their construction similar to that of their pre-contact counterparts.

Slobodin (1962: 26) argues that this period of increasing change is talked about by the Gwich'in as a period of stability, when the fur trade was sufficiently developed to allow for relationship building between the Gwich'in and the European traders, employees, gold miners and whalers. It is a period in history that Gwich'in still talk about as being relatively positive, a period when newcomers were adapting to Gwich'in practice and Gwich'in were also learning things of local value. Emerging out of this period was certainly a materially changed Gwich'in tradition, but one where core values were not in any sort of danger or collapse; indeed in our experience, and that of Slobodin (1962), it is a period often indexed as being the good old days when things 'worked well'. Throughout Dene country, greater disruption occurred later (beginning in the First World War and intensifying after the Second World War) when a Canadian government policy shift tied its fiduciary responsibility to resettlement in prefabricated towns where social management could be closely scrutinized (Asch with Wishart 2004; Berger 1977: 85). Amongst the politics was the establishment and enforcement of residential schools in which Aboriginal children were educated and manipulated to become like southern Canadians.

The effects of the 'move to town' have been many, but for the purposes of this chapter we would like to highlight the following: first, it meant that many Gwich'in were now moving to homes that for the first time in their history they did not design themselves. As one Gwich'in elder told

Wishart in 1998, 'the new houses came from people who thought they knew better about our land than us'. Second, it meant that certain places where Teetł'it Gwich'in used to live for large parts of the year, such as the former village at the Mouth of the Peel, were largely abandoned and the cabins that were built there became mostly disused. This correlated with the shift to using snowmobiles instead of dog teams as a means of transportation, which implied that Teetł'it Gwich'in fished less.[1] The death of Gwich'in elders further led to a decrease of traditional fishing villages such as Mouth of the Peel. Third, it meant that those wishing to continue pursuing land-based activities started to build more cabins in places closer to town so they could spend time hunting, fishing or trapping and then return to their houses in the town. In some cases, this meant continuing to build and maintain cabins at the old family camp sites or village sites as well. Fourth, it meant that those who wished to have an alternative to the prefabricated house in town started to build their own log houses within its boundaries. And, finally, Gwich'in realized, and have now actively resisted, part of the rationale for the government's desire to have them move to town: i.e., opening up the North to other sorts of development that, unlike the fur trade, did not include a Gwich'in presence on the land as a key component of the economic strategy.

Building cabins

Often when we talked to Gwich'in elders about activities such as gathering logs to build a house, they emphasized the idea that one has to know the trees, what they are good for, and how to use them properly. In our experience this is often spoken about as a search or a hunt for trees. Once we transform the idea of 'harvesting trees', in the language of management, to the idea of 'hunting for trees', it highlights the actual process of engagement and relatedness with the landscape which is a more accurate statement about how the Gwich'in gather the materials for their building projects.

Gwich'in (and other boreal forest Aboriginal people) steward and 'manage' their wood places. The 'management' and stewardship follows the knowledge of the place and the trees. Hunting for trees, then, becomes an activity in which one selectively chooses trees to be cut, while blazing others to make them dry or to clean around them, letting them grow so that more can be harvested in the future. The area further provides knowledge about the way that elders were working and cutting wood and how they 'watched' – taking care of or maintaining and acting within – their area. They are continuously 'growing' the area. Moreover, a shift to a watchful or hunting engagement allows anthropology to understand the fit between a sentient landscape (Anderson 2000) and the gathering of logs, in a way that is similar to how the extensive literature on northern hunter-gatherers hunting for animals has influenced the understanding of human–environment relations (e.g., Brightman 1993; Fienup-Riordan 1994; Tanner 1979).

The process of hunting for logs for cabins, and indeed for larger community efforts, follows a distinctive pattern. The process of selecting the trees is complex as it requires ending up with a set of straight logs all with relatively similar dimensions. The Mackenzie Delta is on the edge of the tree line and the trees are highly variable in quality, so unless the site that one is building upon is blessed with a stand of very good trees, those that produce these logs must come from many locations. Each project requires trees of different sizes and those that require the longest logs are also those that use the largest trees. Community projects on a grander scale use very large trees indeed, while the average cabin in the Delta uses trees that are considerably smaller. Many cabins only require logs that are between 4 and 5 metres long with a butt diameter of 30 to 35 centimetres. These logs are easier to obtain and are easier to handle. It is considered far more practical (both from the point of view of labour and the amount of wood one needs to heat it) to build a small cabin – with average wall dimensions of $4 \times 4.5 \times 1.6$ metres – and then, at a later date, extend the building by attaching another identical or smaller section to it which usually acts as the kitchen or storage room. More sections may be added at a later date as well. The end effect is often a long, narrow, segmented cabin, although there are many cabins that have been built using different strategies and there are those to which no additions have ever been made.

The process by which log cabins are constructed first requires that a suitable site for construction be found. A site needs to be determined prior to getting the raw materials because the logs are often floated downstream from their source to the building site – sometimes (in the case of Fort McPherson) more than 70 kilometres downstream. As the end user of the cabin is often the same person who hunts for the trees that will go into making it, unlike in places where there may be several intermediary layers of different labourers, there is far more attention paid to where the raw materials come from.

Once the location has been determined, the logs can be hunted. In the case of building a cabin along the waterway, the preferred method of obtaining these logs is to cut them in the spring just after break-up. In spring, the water is high and people can travel by boat up the creeks and the rivers with more ease. It is a great deal easier to cut and haul other types of wood when the ground is frozen and the materials can be packed out using snowmobiles on top of the ice and snow. The harvesting of

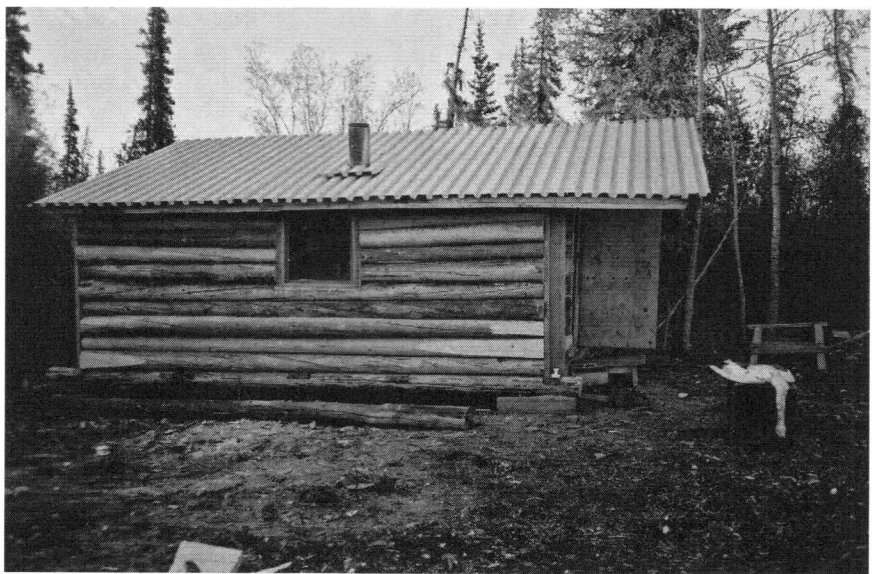

Figure 4.1 *Cabin built at Dry River by Thomas Koe. Photo by Robert P. Wishart.*

logs for cabins can follow this pattern, but because the trees need to be debarked it is far easier to do so when the sap is running in the spring. At this time of year it is easier to peel the bark off the trees.

A selected tree is first felled and then the limbs are taken off. The top of the tree is removed at the point where the desired length of the log ends, and is put aside. The topped log is then peeled with an axe. The log can be moved to the riverbank in a variety of ways, including people getting together to help move the log, harnessing it to skidoos, or using dogs as in the old days to drag the log out. Once the logs have been gathered from upstream locations they are lashed together into a makeshift raft and then floated downstream to the desired location. The logs are then stored until they are seasoned, or until enough have been gathered for the job. This process may take a few years. Sometimes, during spring run-off, people get 'really lucky' and good-quality logs come right to them. After break-up, people who are building cabins keep an eye out for such logs as they float down from way upriver. In the case of upland cabins, there needs to be considerably more attention given to the location of the cabin, ensuring that they are close to several stands of good trees so that the logs may be harvested and moved during the winter. Although this necessitates considerably more effort in cleaning the trees of the bark, moving them during the spring and summer over the distance from the stands to the building site is far more onerous.

The actual building of these cabins is done rather quickly if three or more men are working together. If the logs have been allowed to season they are considerably lighter than in their green state and can be manipulated without much trouble. Despite the rapid construction of these cabins, they are far from a prefabricated design. Cabins, like other constructions, implicate knowing through making and the weaving together of materials within an ongoing field of relations. Furthermore, as Hallam and Ingold point out (2007: 4), buildings are organic. Rather than considering cabins or tents as a predetermined plan, cabins and tents need to be understood as processes of makings in which improvisations (following Hallam and Ingold 2007) and creative designs stand central. With Heidegger (1971), buildings grow and unfold in ways that are not separate from dwelling but through and with dwelling. Vernacular architecture, then, expresses being in a particular way and emphasizes knowing-through-making and making-through-moving or thinking-in-movement.

In contrast, prefabricated houses in Fort McPherson eradicate aspects of these processes for many Gwich'in. Instead, others have controlled and dominated both the planning and the building of these prefabricated forms. The houses and the buildings follow architectural plans designed in an office away from the community, and the making processes are controlled and executed by outsiders. Improvisations and building-through-knowing are bounded by regulations. In comparison, each part of any particular cabin calls upon sets of skills and the ability to improvise. There are no written plans; no blueprints to work from. There is usually one person, the boss, who has the vision of how to proceed, but this too is altered and adjusted through advice, conversation and adaptation to the materials as the building proceeds.[2]

Log cabins and being Gwich'in

When we were young girls everybody decided to move to town (Fort McPherson). The pensions … you know, you had to be in town. So all the people who had houses built at Mouth of the Peel, upriver, Husky River came to town. There was lots of talk about it then, still is, same thing, that everyone should get a house, part of the agreement with the government. My Jijuu (grandmother) told me not to take one of those houses, that we should build a cabin ourselves like before. That way you still have to go get the stuff to build it, get wood for the stove, go get water to use. It was important to go out for her, same for me now; it's what I tell my grandchildren.

This is a part of a conversation Wishart had with Teetl'it Gwich'in Elder Bertha Francis in her former home, a log house in the town of Fort McPherson, NWT. This particular conversation evolved out of a discussion he was having with a few elders about some logs that had been stacked at the side of a road for a couple of years. The logs had been cut by the renowned late Chief Johnny Charlie in order to build a log house for his family. It was said that, like others in the community, Chief Johnny Charlie felt that a log house was superior to the Government prefabricated houses – not only in structural design and the practice of getting the materials, but also in indexing a continued presence of Gwich'in in their 'country'. Unfortunately he died before he had the chance to build with the logs.

In an application of ethnohistory to studies of development (Asch with Wishart 2004; Feit 1988), these cabins illustrate one pivotal way in which Gwich'in have continued a form of architecture that speaks at once about an idealized past – a period of florescence in many of the outward expressions of Gwich'in culture – and about the importance of continuity in land practices and about competing jurisdictional claims. In this way vernacular architecture can be thought of, and indeed mobilized, as a concrete expression of local meaningful practice, serving to remind and stimulate other forms of politics and action.

Much has been made of cases when oral history is combined with – or perhaps better conceived as anchored to (Hojer, in Basso 1996; Palmer 2005) – a feature of the landscape, thus unlocking considerable potential for remembrance, instruction and moral direction (i.e., Basso 1996; Cruikshank 2005). Certainly, built elements of the landscape – in this case vernacular and larger community-sponsored constructions – have similar potentials to anchor historical narratives and to speak of the varieties of Gwich'in skilled engagements with the land. Cabins are returned to in visits while people travel on the land. Many times, in both of our research experiences, Gwich'in would make a point of stopping to visit old abandoned cabins. Often tea would be made and stories would be told of building the cabin, events that transpired there, family histories, and why the cabin was eventually abandoned. The stories would continue as the site was examined – often humorous and sometimes tragic, the stories were remembered and the cabin was as much a reminder as it was a member of the audience.

Given the evocative power of cabins to act as anchors in the telling of Gwich'in history, one might be tempted to understand them as a part of a past existence rather than as an ongoing participant in Gwich'in lives today. The fact that cabins continue to be built out on the land to become homes for Gwich'in while they practise land-based activities contradicts this temporal frame. Moreover, the examples of the community-sponsored building of log constructions in Fort McPherson, and a log cabin at Bear Creek, neatly illustrate why this understanding of a lost past is too simplistic and misses the wider community engagement with cabin architecture.

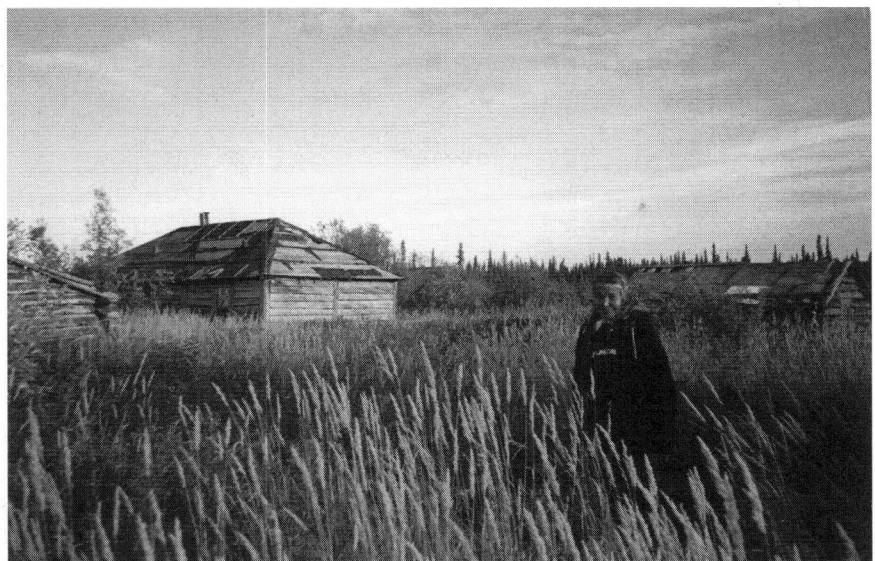

Figure 4.2 *Abandoned cabins at Mouth of the Peel being visited by Eileen Koe. Photo by Robert P. Wishart.*

In 1999, when the Co-op store in Fort McPherson decided that it was time to replace the restaurant and hotel that had previously burned down, there was a great deal of consultation with elders and community members who decided that the building should be made out of logs so that 'it would be really nice, just like Tl'oondih'. Tl'oondih used to be a place of healing on the land and was located about 30 kilometres upriver from Fort McPherson.[3] Its main building, a lodge, is an impressive log construction. In effect, a log cabin on a grand scale made out of Peel River logs. The construction of the healing camp of Tl'oondih is positioned as another example of doing things properly, and it resonated as a place of Gwich'in personal discovery and social reintegration that has considerable currency.

The logs for the Co-op were all harvested upstream along the Peel River and its tributaries. Individuals were allowed to bring ten logs each to the site and were paid per log. The specifications were that the logs had to be relatively straight with a diameter of 25 centimetres at the top and at least 6 metres long. Due to the number of people involved in getting these logs and the strict specifications of the planners, many people talked about the practice of harvesting spruce trees for building logs. While many of the logs were harvested from trees fairly close to the construction site at Eight Miles,[4] many others came from more than 20 miles up the Peel.

Ara Murray (2002: 76) explains the decision-making process:

On the day that we arrived in Fort McPherson in 1999 I [was] greeted with a hot meal of caribou meat. Later that day when an elder and I were waiting for the ferry in order to get into town, I noticed a large pile of big logs on the other side of the river … She explained to me that they were building a new co-op store in Fort McPherson, with a restaurant, hotel and conference rooms attached. Part of this was to be built out of logs.

The Co-op committee had decided that they did not want a logging company from outside the community to come in and cut down their trees. They were especially concerned about the effects of clear cutting. Clear cutting seems to be well known as an activity that happens frequently 'down south', and the effects of clear cutting are well known as they are shown on television and other media. It was then explained how the logs for the Co-op building were to be collected, and made plain that clear cutting was an irresponsible practice. It was therefore more appropriate to create a system based on the existing community model. By opening up the collecting of logs to the community, the Co-op committee was taking advantage of the way that the community uses the land in the local manner. This was seen as a good alternative to clear cutting, as the people who provided the logs took them from different areas, ensuring that no single area was overused.

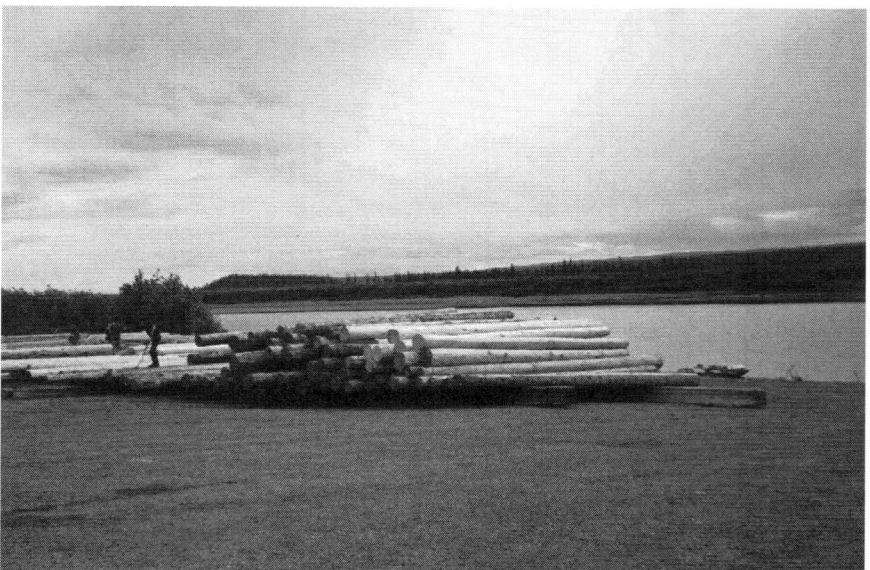

Figure 4.3 *Logs piled up at Eight Miles in preparation for the building of the new Co-op. Photo by Robert P. Wishart.*

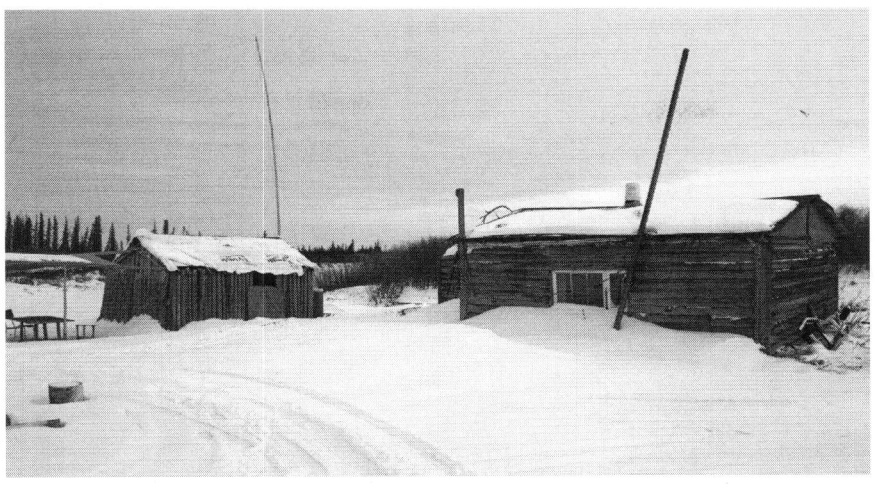

Figure 4.4 *Two different types of log constructions: the late Mary Wilson's smokehouse (left) and old cabin (right) at Rat River. Visited and photographed by Peter Loovers.*

Indeed, many elders have made it a point to discuss the community building projects as an extension of their ethos of living in their country, a combination of locally meaningful patterns of ecological and cultural sustainability. To the elder and to the others who made the decision, a building of the scale that they were proposing could not be ignored, and the fact that it would be made out of logs that were hunted 'on the land' makes the message clearer. As another elder said, 'I just think it's good. For the kids'. As a product of confirming the rights of indigenous people to govern themselves and their jurisdiction, construction projects on a grand scale incorporating First Nations design features, symbols, and cosmologies are being recognized for their power of affirmation. Just as building a log cabin or house for the Gwich'in can serve practical purposes while countering federal jurisdictional claims at a family level, the control of community building design and construction also follows this oscillation between jurisdictional claims and creating a practical, locally meaningful building.

In 2007 Loovers (2010: 248–67) participated in the building of a cabin at Bear Creek – about four hours away from Fort McPherson by snowmobile – to replace a pre-existing cabin. The building of the new Bear Creek cabin was sponsored by the Teetl'it Gwich'in Renewable Resource Council in cooperation with the Government of the Northwest Territories. Since the old cabin could potentially flood and had been built several decades ago, the decision was made to make a newer and bigger cabin which could function as an emergency shelter, a hunting camp and an educational camp. This effort, done on behalf of the community, followed the way that family cabins are built. The site was chosen, the logs were gathered from stands that had been managed, and the cabin built using experience, discussion and improvisation. These types of cabins that are situated at a distance from Gwich'in towns allow for a way of life that depends upon these cabins being there, and also provide emergency shelter for any other travellers in the area. The cabin enables Gwich'in people to continue their traditional way of life and illustrate Gwich'in presence to governments and commercial enterprises that have entered Gwich'in lands on the premise that the land is uninhabited. Thus, in several cases a log cabin is built to emphasize this – to show outsiders that the Gwich'in continue a certain occupation of the land distant from town.

Discussion

Cabins, like trees and logs, can be said to narrate events; like the squaring of logs, the turning of the foundation, or the discussion concerning the roof. They may begin with a set of past experiences, but they then 'become' with skilled improvisation. Thus, cabins become alive and are constituted by movements, narratives, skills and knowledge. Each cabin, or indeed each of the new community buildings, is made out of logs that have a social history that ties them to individual Gwich'in actions on the land and, furthermore, they are talked about as being the result of proper, positive ways of behaving while on the land. The choice of the log house design, rather than that of a skin tent or a semi-subterranean lodge, as an expression of Gwich'in tradition, illustrates how the Gwich'in have incorporated the relationships between Gwich'in and fur traders of the 'old days' as pivotal to their way of living.

The exploration of the social lives of things (Appadurai 1986; Strathern 1999) has tended to focus on the manner in which commodities acquire new significations as they flow through the world markets from producers to middle agencies and finally to the consumer. In the case of a log cabin in Gwich'in country, the same frame of analysis is not exactly apt. Instead, each cabin can be thought of as a constellation of activities which have occurred out on the land and as a final product of interactions with the trees that have been hunted by people who dwell. Indeed, the same thing can be said of all the forest products which Gwich'in seek out – while they may be ephemeral, in the sense that the evidence does not remain as long as say a cabin or a log hotel, Gwich'in are cognizant that it is all part of the same process.

As reminders of presence and continuity, log structures are desirable for the simple fact that they do 'stick around'. In recent years, some people within the community of Fort McPherson have made the decision to construct new homes out of logs that have been hunted by themselves while out on the land, undertaking activities they consider to be continuous with those of their ancestors and that are consistent with the local understanding of the proper way of being. Each log house, each cabin and each large public structure made in this way can also be thought of as a positive act of resisting imposed landscapes. This resistance may not be apparent without the words of elders and others declaring the cabins, or the relatively new Co-op building, as being somehow proper. Webb Keane argues that among the Anakalangese of Indonesia:

> At the practical and conceptual base of authoritative actions Anakalangese insist on a simple but critical requirement: words and things must be transacted together. The requirement is a local peculiarity, but the problems it seeks to master, of *weaving together* and containing power, value, authority, performative efficacy, material resources, and communication, are widespread concomitants of representational practice. (Keane 1997: 20, our emphasis)

Without the 'weaving together' of words and things, other people – Gwich'in included – would not be able to recognize that a cabin constructed ostensibly just to provide shelter is also a powerful indicator of presence and continuity. Not only does the cabin contradict what Gwich'in consider to be irrational 'clear cutting', it also backs up their own understandings and provides evidence that this understanding exists and thrives. They are also carefully critical of the government housing schemes,[5] sometimes talking about them as another attempt at assimilation. Thus, cabins become complex woven articulations with histories, personal narratives of experiences, bodies of knowledge and particular political implications that allow them to continue to play a pivotal role in Teetł'it Gwich'in lives.

Acknowledgements

The authors want to acknowledge the community of Fort McPherson and the Gwich'in Social and Cultural Institute. They want to thank in particular Alestine Andre, Johnny Charlie Junior, Bertha Francis, Thomas Koe, Eileen Koe, Ingrid Kritsch, Ara Murray, and the Snowshoe family. Funds for the research were provided in part by the Social Science and Humanities Research Council of Canada, the Carnegie Trust for the Universities of Scotland, the 6th Century Fellowship of the University of Aberdeen, and the RAI Urgent Anthropology Fund. The writing and some of the theoretical work on this chapter was partly supported by ERC Advanced Grant 'Arctic Domus' 295458. All shortcomings are those of the authors.

Notes

1. Alestine Andre explains that this differs for the Gwichya Gwich'in. Gwichya Gwich'in continue to fish extensively during the summer and fall fish-runs for consumption, for their own or local dogs, or for dog mushers in Inuvik. Several Teetł'it Gwich'in men also set nets on the Mackenzie River and Arctic Red River (personal communication).

2. See Loovers (2010) for a detailed description of his interactions with a group of Gwich'in men while building a log cabin.

3. Very recently, February–March 2012, several of the Tł'oondih buildings, including the main building, have been moved into town and there are plans to turn it into a cultural tourist centre. The relocation, and change of purpose, of the camp has been critiqued by a number of Gwich'in.

4. Eight Miles is the place where the Dempster Highway crosses the Peel River. Its name is an artefact of the Hudson Bay Company's practice of assigning toponyms according to distance from the trading post. Eight Miles is thus eight miles from the original location of Fort McPherson.

5. When talking about the choice to build one's own home out of logs, people often talk about how they want to do it themselves but do not make any sort of judgement about those who, for a variety of reasons, depend on government housing or government support.

CHAPTER 5

The Mobile Sámi Dwelling

From Pastoral Necessity to Ethno-political Master Paradigm

Ivar Bjørklund

One of the main goals of the Home, Hearth and Household project was to look into the organizing principles of mobile dwellings and their functional, cosmological and political contexts. Furthermore, focus was set on the silent knowledge displayed by these dwellings, and the project thus aimed at reviving some of this knowledge through the involvement of indigenous craftsmen. Following this strategy, a Sámi traditional winter tent was constructed by a couple of older Sámi reindeer herders and through this process further information was gained about both the historical and political dimension regarding the use of these tents.

The tent used by the herders today while on the move is called a *lávvu* (Figure 5.1). What can this tent tell us about former and present relations between the users and their social and ecological setting? The answers to these questions might inform us both about the development of reindeer husbandry and about some particularities within Norwegian ethno-politics. Today the *lávvu* has gained iconic status in Norwegian mainstream debates. This tent is considered the real Sámi dwelling – in other words, it is a well-established cultural stereotype. Let us therefore take a closer look at the story behind this stereotype. By tracing the development of the Sámi mobile dwelling, we should be able to achieve some insight into the changing forms of social and economic relations between Sámi and Norwegians in the northernmost part of Norway.

This particular kind of mobile dwelling is closely connected to the development of reindeer husbandry in Scandinavia. Dating the beginnings of reindeer domestication is an old debate among Scandinavian academics (Storli 1996). The prevailing explanation states that the emergence of Sámi pastoralism took place in the sixteenth century (e.g. Vorren 1978), although some regional variation is accepted. In analytical terms,

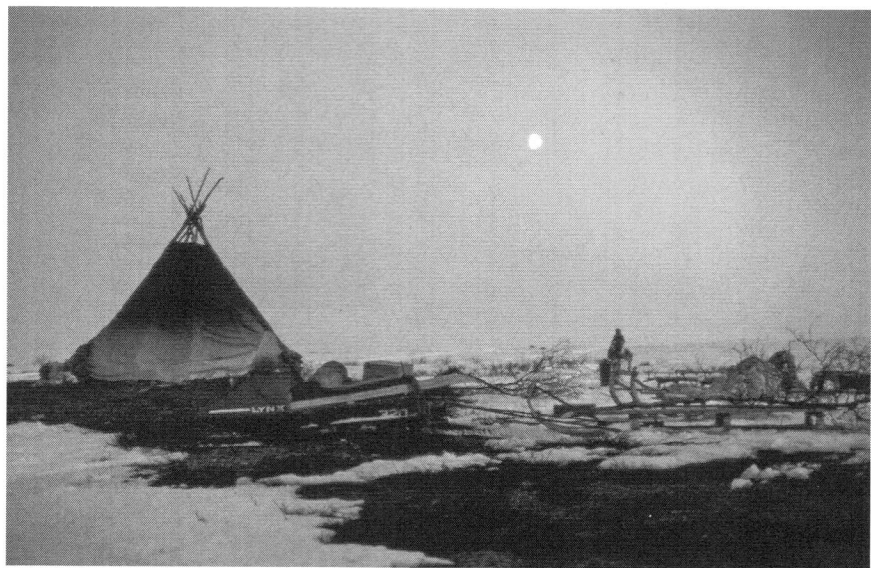

Figure 5.1 *Reindeer herder on the move between winter and summer pastures. Kautokeino 1985 (Arvid Petterson, Tromsø Museum).*

'pastoralism' is used to characterize an economic adaption solely depending upon a herd of domesticated animals. According to the stated theory, this development was due to new markets, expanding taxation and the introduction of firearms, which led to the depletion of the wild reindeer stocks. Historically, Sámis were quite dependent upon the exploitation of wild reindeer, hunting them collectively by the use of large numbers of pitfalls and corrals. A more recent – but contested – point of view argues that Sámi pastoralism is much older. Referring to archaeological findings and the Saga literature (the travels of Ottar), Sámi pastoralism is dated back to around 1000 A.D. (Storli 1994).

Whenever domestication occurred, this development probably brought about profound changes within the Sámi society. According to Hansen and Olsen (2004: 203–14) – referring to Ingold (1980) – one such change might have been a transformation from collective to private ownership of the main resource: the reindeer. If so, one has to be able to understand what this change could have meant to the Sámi way of life. It is therefore necessary to look into the characteristics of pastoralism. Basically, all pastoral adaptions depend upon the relations between labour, animals and pasture. The pastoral challenge, then, is to obtain the optimal relation between these three factors, given the economic and political context in which they are situated. A key dimension of this challenge is the ongoing quest for flexibility (Bjørklund 2004: 125–6). Pastoralists need to make sure that all their strategies and circumstances are as flexible as needed. This also applies to their dwellings, and consequently tents became a preferred construction because they are mobile.

As mentioned earlier (cf. Figure 5.1), the *lávvu* is one solution to this need. Highly flexible, it was the preferred kind of dwelling for herders while staying out with the herd or being on the move across the tundra. Construction wise, it is a rather crude conical arrangement consisting of just some poles (ideally 12–14) and two pieces of canvas. However, the preferred kind of tent for the household on a daily basis was the *bealljigoahti*. This was the main dwelling among the Sámi pastoralists (Figure 5.2). Archaeological and written sources state that this type has been in use for at least 500 years (Sommerseth 2009: 201).[1] The construction is not the conical type also known from Canada, the US or Siberia – this particular kind of tent is unique to the Sámi in northern Scandinavia. The construction consists of two pairs of *beallji* (double-arched poles), 12–14 straight poles, two pieces of cover and a door – all made of cloth (Vorren 1966). It is put up or taken down in a few minutes and provides room for between one and eight people. All can be transported on two sledges (*geris*) with one draft reindeer (*hergi*) in front of each one, or on the back of two reindeer in the summertime. In other words, this kind of dwelling is very well adapted to the need for flexibility embedded in the pastoral Sámi way of life. The *bealljigoahti* has always been considered a

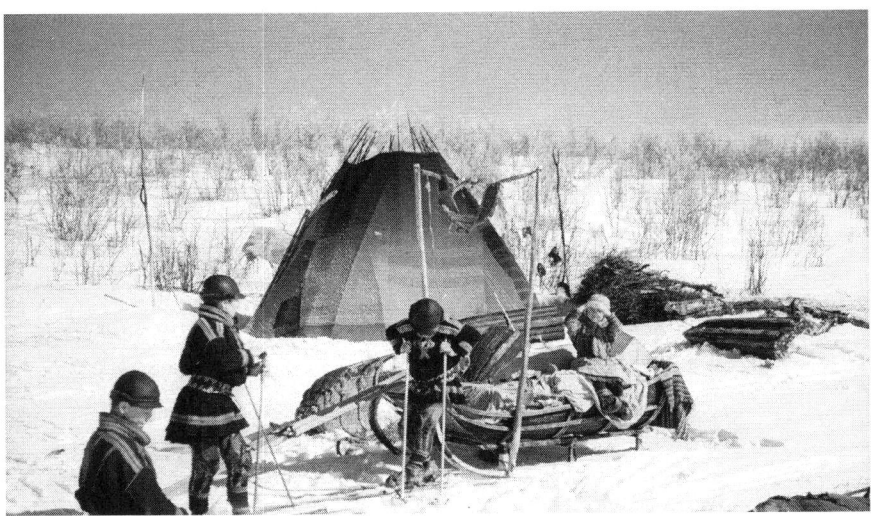

Figure 5.2 *The* bealljigoahti – *the traditional household dwelling. Karesuando 1947 (Rolf Arnstrom, Tromsø Museum).*

valuable object, the wooden double-arched poles *(beallji)* could be given as a wedding gift and the cover was valued as an expensive trade item.

Returning to the question of the emergence of Sámi husbandry, a closer look at the *bealljigoahti* might give us further information. We do know that the wooden construction of this tent is identical to the dwellings used by the Sámi living by the coast (Figure 5.3).[2] The existence of a coastal Sámi population of hunters and gatherers can be traced back at least 2,000 years, and that also goes for their dwellings (Olsen 1993). Such a depth of time actually makes the *beallji* construction one of the few material artefacts with continuous use among the Sámi almost to the present day. The coastal Sámi were involved in a transhumance practice; moving between summer and winter locations within a single fjord. They had permanent dwellings in both places – a wooden *beallji* construction covered with turf.

The emergence of reindeer husbandry meant a growing need for flexibility, specifically a more mobile form of dwelling. Being on the move with a herd all year round, one needed transportable solutions. This was solved through the combination of the traditional *beallji* construction with woven cloth for cover. Canvas made out of linen or hemp was available through the Hanseatic trade from the twelfth century, but for winter use a warmer cover was needed. The preferred solution was the *radno* – woollen blankets manufactured by the coastal Sámi and sold to the nomadic Sámi (Figure 5.4). Having no sheep for themselves, the need for such wool blankets established trade relations between the two Sámi groups. Consequently, the tent itself testifies to the fact that the reindeer owners were involved in external trade relations from the very beginning. There are no sources whatsoever referring to the use of reindeer hides as

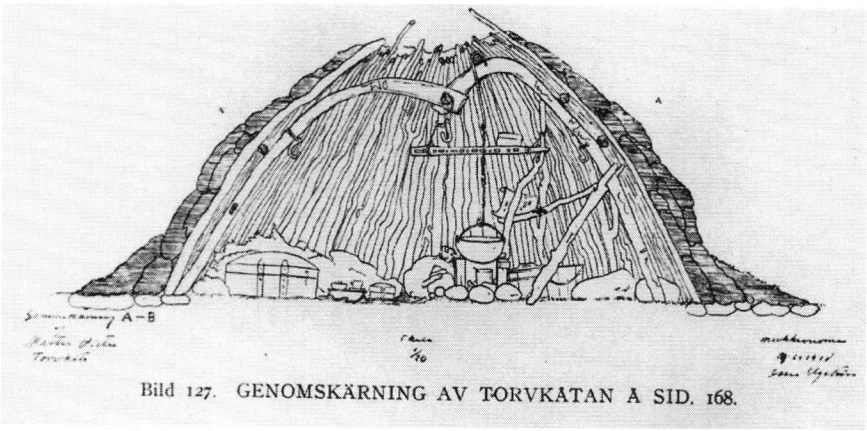

Bild 127. GENOMSKÄRNING AV TORVKÅTAN Å SID. 168.

Figure 5.3 Bealljigoahti *covered with turf (Ossian Elgstrøm, Tromsø Museum).*

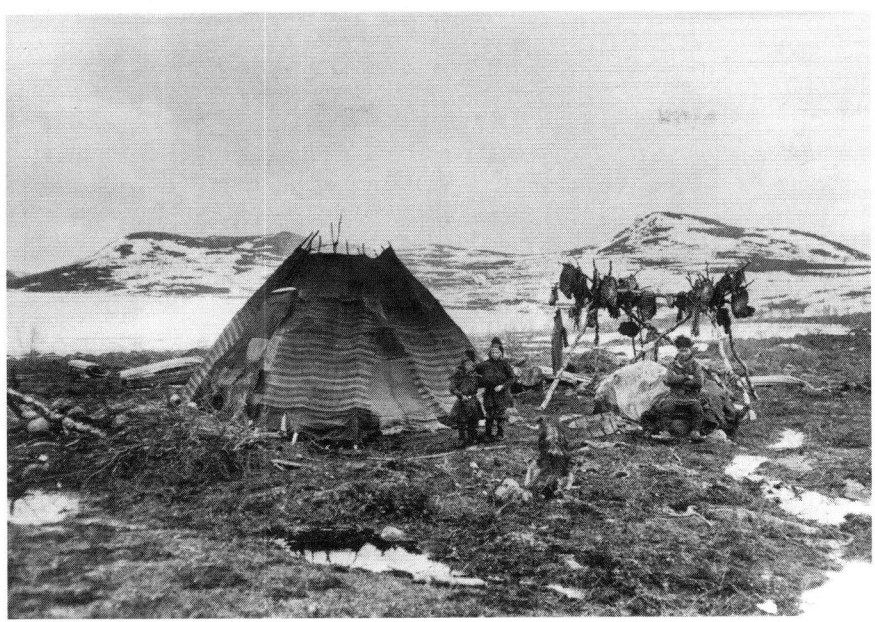

Figure 5.4 Bealljigoahti *with a cover made of woollen blankets. Indre Troms ca. 1910 (Tromsø Museum).*

tent covers. For winter use, a cover made with fur would be too heavy to transport and also demand a much stronger wooden construction. A summer cover made out of scraped hides *(sisti)* would also represent a rather expensive solution, demanding the use of 20–30 hides. Under such circumstances, a woven cover was preferred.

It is also quite likely that the use of tents was a precondition for the hunting of wild reindeer in some areas. The hunt took place in the fall – especially during the rut – and the *lávvu* was probably the preferred dwelling.[3] This activity also depended upon the use of domesticated reindeer for transport and decoy purposes, which facilitated the transition from hunting to a pastoral economy.[4]

In other words, dating the access to woollen blankets and canvas could indicate the potential age of reindeer husbandry. The first written sources we have regarding the use of these woollen blankets are Swedish tax records between 1555 and 1624. It seems that the *radno* at the time were well established as products for trade and tax payment – the coastal Sámi traded them for reindeer hides, sinew, butter and iron equipment from the reindeer-herding Sámi.[5] When, then, did the coastal Sámi start rearing sheep and when did they acquire weaving technology? Until quite recently, the accepted view was that domesticated animals such as sheep and cows were introduced among the coastal Sámi around 1500–1600 A.D. However, recent archaeological findings indicate the existence of sheep among the Sámi between 500 and 1000 A.D. (Andreassen 2001: 35; Schanche 2000: 150; Hedman and Olsen 2009: 8). Furthermore, the knowledge of milking, cheese making and weaving is confirmed in linguistic evidence dating back to ca. 700–800 A.D. or maybe even in earlier pre-historic times (Qvigstad 1893; Nesheim 1954; 1967: 135). As for technology, the warp-weighted loom *(oppstadvev)* was in extensive use among the Norwegians in the Viking age and such intermediate technology was in use among the Sámi too – at least in Western Finnmark and Troms (Hoffman 1974: 75–103). *Snaldu,* the Sámi word for the spindle whorl, is derived from an Old Norse word – *snelda* (spinning whorl) – which went out of use ca. 1300–1400 A.D.

Another indication that woven wool cloth was available along the coast of northern Norway has to do with the need for sails. The introduction of the sail along the Norwegian coast seems to have taken place around 500–600 A.D., and reflects the development of Norse chieftain societies which depended upon clinker-built seagoing vessels and thus a large-scale production of high-quality wool cloth for the sails (Lightfoot 2005; Andersen and Nørgård 2009). We do know that Sámi fishermen probably took part in seasonal fisheries along the coast of Finmark in the twelfth century (Bratrein 1998) – an economic activity which tells us that sailing must have been introduced in the local fishing fleet by then. The main fishing boat was the *tre-roring* – 20–22 feet in length, with oars and sail manned by three persons.

A conclusive remark then, is that a local production of woollen blankets might have taken place in some of the coastal Sámi areas between 800 and 1000 A.D. – a time when Ottar reports on the presence of domesticated reindeer. By then, sheep rearing might have been a part of the Sámi economic adaption along the coast – at least from Western Finnmark and southwards. Sheep were kept for wool and cheese production and brought along by the household between the different seasonal locations in the fjords (Figure 5.5). One should also bear in mind the important export from Iceland to Norway of woollen cloth *(vadmel)* all through the Viking age – a product which very well might have found its way to the north of Norway. Consequently, the use of the mobile *bealljigoahti* – which suggests the existence of reindeer husbandry activities – could have been a reality from that time. The emergence of reindeer pastoralism, then, has to be seen in the context of sheep husbandry as well as trade relations.[6]

When more written sources appear in the eighteenth century, the use of the mobile *goahti* is firmly established (Leem 1767). As stated, it is a form of dwelling well suited to the flexible adaption of the nomadic Sámi in the

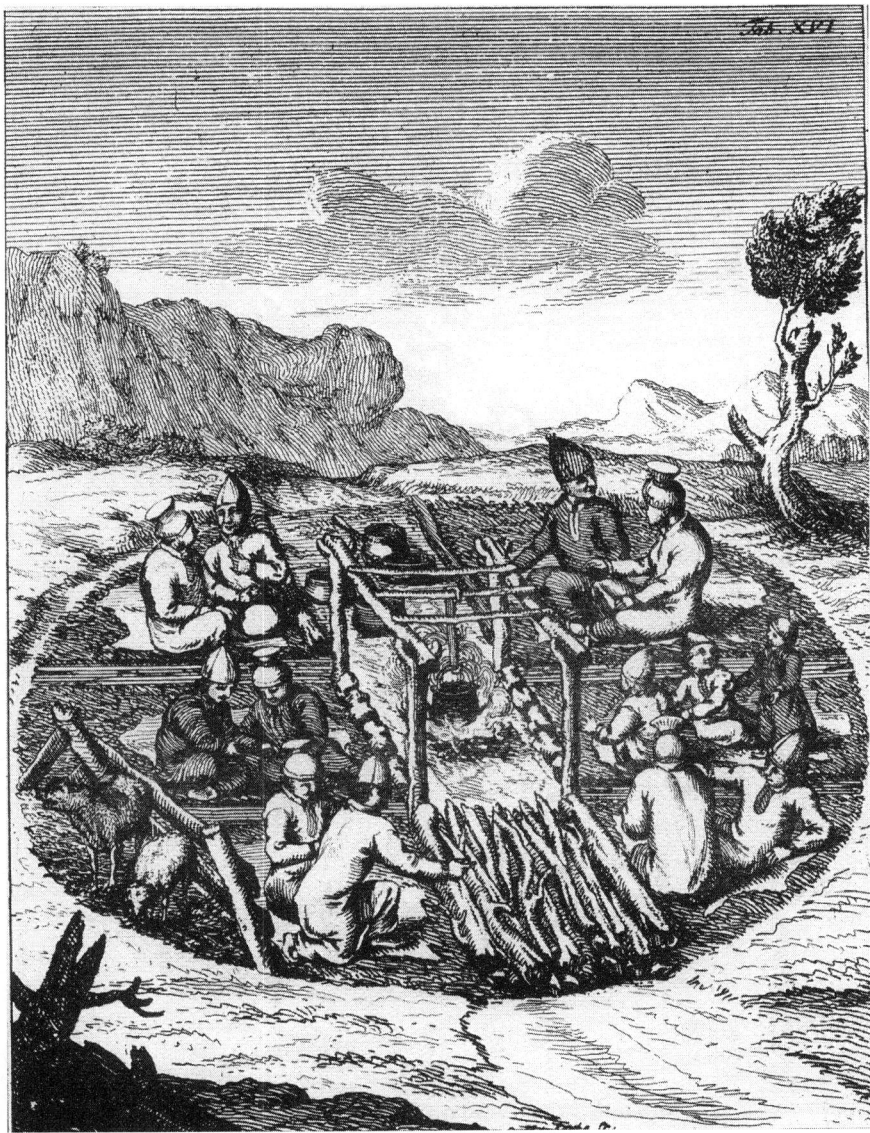

Figure 5.5 *A* bealljigoahti *presumably covered with turf inhabited by coastal Sámi with sheep (Leem 1767 [1975]: Tab XVI).*

inland area. It is flexible both with regards to their social organization and to their land use. On the organizational side, the pastoral management regime as known in the twentieth century was organized through bilateral kinship relations (Pehrson 1957). The work group (*siida*) changed composition throughout the year according to grazing and herding requirements. The need for seasonal regrouping, then, made flexible and mobile dwelling arrangements necessary.

In the period 1800–1900, reindeer husbandry turned into a general pastoral adaption in Fenno-Scandia and expanded in territorial terms. Slowly it took a more extensive character, although with some important regional variation. Areas outside Scandinavia, such as Alaska, Labrador and Greenland, became pastoral options for herders migrating from Inner Finnmark. But the core area remained the tundra plateau of northern Scandinavia. As the size of the herds grew larger, more extensive herding techniques developed, which again became more labour intensive. It was not until the 1960s that new technologies such as the snowmobile were introduced, which strongly reduced the need for labour and led to new forms of herding management. The snowmobile made it possible for the reindeer-herding Sámi to settle down in houses at a permanent location in the winter area, instead of moving around with a tent. By snowmobile one could now travel back and forth to the herd and do the herding on a rotational basis. Consequently, the *bealljigoahti* fell out of use and in a few years disappeared altogether. Only the *lávvu* – the herding tent – survived the test of time, as it was still needed when the herders moved between winter and summer pastures.[7]

In the last 30 years a strong revitalization of Sámi culture has taken place. This development reflects international ethno-politics and the emergence of indigenousness as a political and cultural concept. Today, the pastoral Sámi have achieved iconic status in the ethno-political world, and the *lávvu* has become the strongest ethno-political symbol available in Scandinavia. This in many ways presents a paradox, as less than 10 per cent of the Sámi population are involved in reindeer herding. The reindeer herder has become the Sámi stereotype and the *lávvu* has become the Sámi architectural master paradigm. The *bealljigoahti* however – historically the main Sámi dwelling as long as reindeer herding has existed – has ended up in oblivion and today hardly anybody knows of its former existence. This development is partly due to the lack of symbolic potential to be found among the remaining 90 per cent of the Sámi population – involved as they are in occupations shared with other Scandinavians. Fishing, farming, or any kind of tertiary work, do not involve any material differences in ethnic terms and are therefore not very potent when it comes to the production of ethno-political symbols.

The cultural revival in the last decades among the Sámi could be described as an ethno-political revolution. In Norway, a common acknowledgement of the political failures embedded in the so-called Norwegianization campaign – which lasted for 150 years – has led to the political acceptance of the Sámi as an indigenous people and the establishment of a Sámi

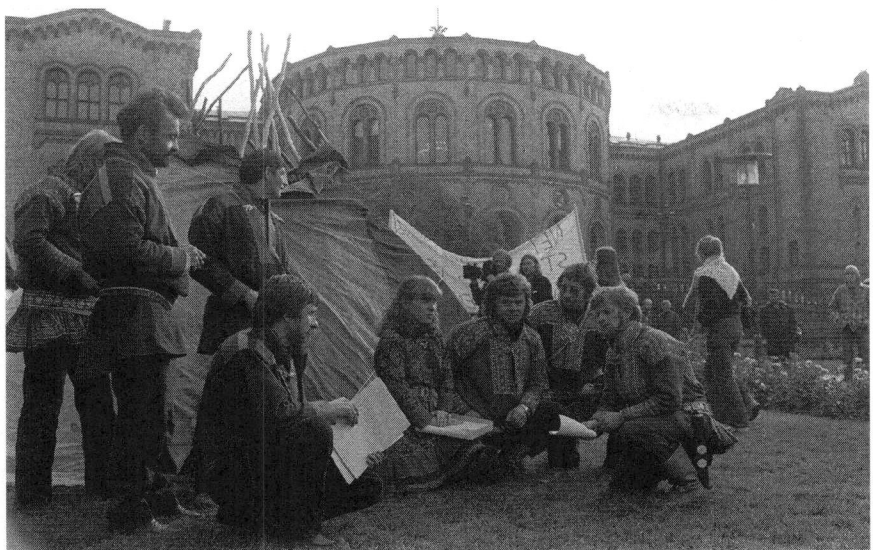

Figure 5.6 *Sámi demonstration outside the Norwegian Parliament, 1981 (Vidar Knai, Scanpix) (Tromsø Museum).*

Parliament. It is within this context that the conic form of the *lávvu* has achieved a paradigmatic status. This very shape has become the visual expression of the long existing asymmetric relationship between the Sámi and the national state. The starting point of this new paradigm was probably the Sámi demonstrations against the hydroelectric development of the Alta-Kautokeino river around 1980. The symbolic breakthrough of the *lávvu* came with the Sámi hunger strikers putting up a *lávvu* in front of the Norwegian Parliament (Figure 5.6). Since then, the figure of the *lávvu* has been adopted as a logo by all kinds of Sámi institutions and organizations.

Parallel to this development, the *lávvu* itself was turned into an industrial product. A growing number of companies started to manufacture a 'high-tech' kind of *lávvu* with folding metal poles, stove and waterproof cover.[8] This was marketed as the 'traditional Sámi dwelling' and sold to reindeer herders, the Norwegian public, and now the world.[9]

In a few years, the *lávvu* became the standard tent among herders on the move, but even more interesting was its gaining popularity among Norwegians in general. Being a nation where outdoor activities are highly regarded, the *lávvu* soon established itself as a very popular kind of tent. It was used not only for camping purposes, but also became part of the standard equipment used in schools, kindergartens and, in furthering its symbolic capital, tourist enterprises. It was perceived as a 'Sámi cultural contribution' to Norwegian outdoor life and has been displayed as a Sámi icon both in Europe and in the US.[10]

Maybe the most spectacular example of the paradigmatic status the *lávvu* holds today is the way Scandinavian architects have perceived and presented their ideas of Sámi dwelling forms. As the Nordic countries came to acknowledge the existence of the Sámi as an indigenous people, a governmentally financed infrastructure was established to facilitate Sámi cultural and political activities. Part of this was a growing number of public houses, and the way architects chose to design these buildings has been characterized by the Sámi architect Joar Nango (2009) as a 'Giant Lávvu' syndrome. What these structures have in common is the conical shape – but enlarged to quite a magnitude (Figures 5.7 and 5.8). They seem to encapsulate the architect's idea of the characteristics in Sámi dwelling design – and thus confirming the existing stereotype of the conical *lávvu* as the traditional Sámi dwelling. Consequently, the architectural potential of the round-shaped *bealljigoahti* is still a non-explored territory. The *lávvu*, in contrast, has more or less left the tundra. It exists today mostly outside the Sámi world, continuing to remind the rest of the world of the ethno-political success of the Sámi people.

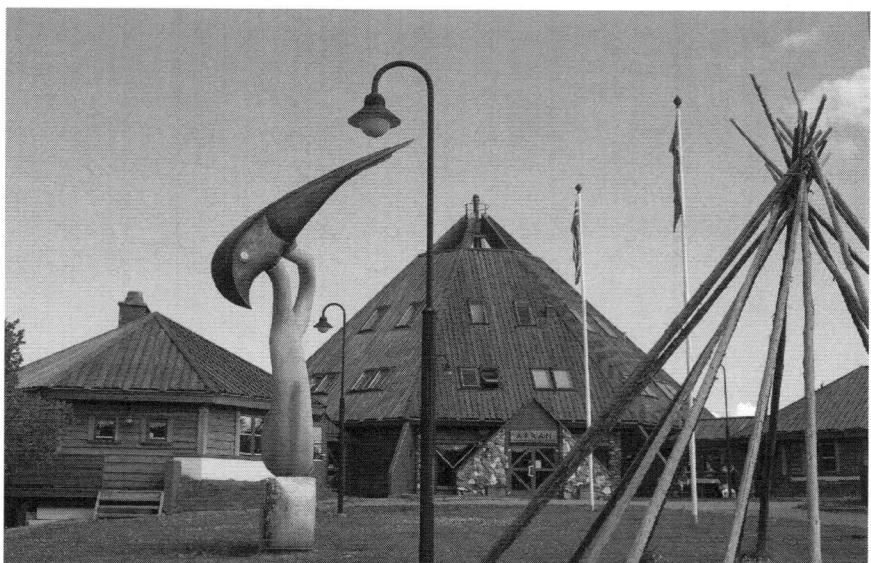

Figure 5.7 *Arran – the Sámi Cultural Center in Tysfjord, Norway (Lars Magne Andreasseen, Arran).*

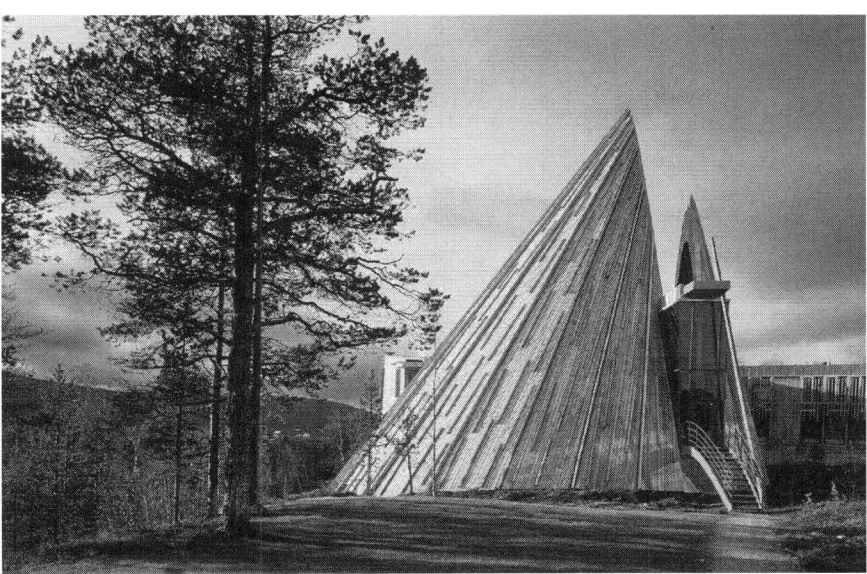

Figure 5.8 *The Sámi Parliament in Karasjok, Norway (Jaro Hollan).*

Notes

1. Based upon the existence of a particular kind of hearth – the *geadgebearpmet*.
2. Both the tent and the sedentary dwelling are called the same in the North Sámi language: *goahti*.
3. I am here referring to hunting by means of bow and arrow, and spears, not to the large pit fall and coral systems known in eastern Finnmark.
4. The hunting of wild reindeer continued alongside pastoralism for a long time (Bær 1926: 71), possibly until the twentieth century (Bjørklund 1985: 46).
5. The reindeer-herding Sámi and traders (*Birkarler/Qvener*) brought iron tools and butter to the coast from settlements in northern Sweden and Finland.
6. The same argument goes for market-related fishing. The woollen sail was a precondition for taking part in large-scale fishing (Lofoten, Finnmark), producing dried cod for export.
7. Beach, in his chapter, gives an interesting account of how pragmatism is an underlying dimension regarding the vitalization of Sámi dwellings in Sweden.
8. www.venor.no
9. A similar development took place in Sweden, cf. Hugh Beach's article in this collection.
10. http://lavvu.com/

CHAPTER 6

The Devitalization and Revitalization of Sámi Dwellings in Sweden

Hugh Beach

This chapter analyses the determinants of change to dwelling types, their placements and timing of use among Sámi reindeer herders in northern Sweden over the last 35 years. I document this period, 1973–2008, from my first-hand participant observations (although with shifting intensity), affording grounded detail to complement theoretical discourse. I also contextualize this period by looking back on the history of architectural types in the region up to the seventeenth century. Naturally, the price of such detail, accrued over such a stretch of time, demands that one concentrates on one place. Therefore the focus of this chapter is on Staloluokta[1] – one of the main camps of the Tuorpon Sámi today. The site is inhabited essentially during the calf-marking summer season. Hence this chapter follows the relatively recent and rapid disuse of the traditional Sámi permanent turf dwelling, the limited revitalization of the temporary Sámi mobile tent, and the shift to Swedish-styled frame cabins (which I argue can also be considered to be linked to the revitalization of kinship ties to the landscape).

When I arrived for the first time in Staloluokta, one of the main summer camps for the reindeer-herding families of Tuorpon *sameby*[2] in the Jokkmokk mountains of northern Sweden in the summer of 1973, the south-eastern shoreline of Lake Virihaure was dotted with permanent turf dwellings[3] made of double-arched birch frames, waterproofed by birchbark (or synthetic tarpaulin) and covered by a thick layer of turf for insulation (Figure 6.1). I lived for a number of years with the Tuorpon herders (Beach 1993), returning each summer to Staloluokta, and even after permanent employment as a professional anthropologist at Uppsala University far to the south, I frequently return to join my herding friends during the summer calf-marking season. Each time I am there, I climb the same slope, stand on the same rock and take a picture of the same village.

Yet in many ways it is not the same village. When comparing two of my pictures, separated by 35 years, I am struck by the number of relatively new permanent and winterized frame cottages interspersed among the older turf-covered dwellings (Figure 6.1). Many of these old dwellings remain, but the photos do not tell us in what way they remain in use, or when they are used. Obviously, the coming of the new dwellings impacts radically on the old, whether or not they are replaced. While pictures can tell us much, there is more that can never be conveyed by any picture – the differences, which can be viewed in pictures, do not tell us why.

In the following pages I wish to plumb the social and cultural changes that, while often reflected in the pictures, cannot readily be discerned by them alone. For this task, I must rely on my own memories and experiences, along with those of the herding families I continue to visit. It is an easily conceived project whose main insight and methodological tool derives from little more than the stubborn return to a cherished place over many years and having a kind of home there. Yet it is not so simple. I have learned that this work is far from merely battling against fading memories and dredging forth a chronology of past events. All of us find new motivations behind past actions depending on our current positions and the ever-changing larger patterns with which we come to interpret our past in light of our present.

Dwellings and the extensive revolution

The traditional Sámi turf dwelling is called, in local Sámi, a *goattieh* (pl. *goattii*), a *goahti* in North Sámi, or a '*torv* (turf) *kåta*' in Swedish to distinguish it further from other possible types of Sámi dwelling.[4] Ruong (1937: 45) has proposed a fascinating evolutionary sequence for Sámi architectural development, from the elemental tripod to the double-arched, conical, nomadic tent and the permanent turf *goattieh* (Figure 6.2A). However, as we shall see, social and economic factors allow structures to appear and disappear out of sequence.

In 1973, when I arrived in 'Stalo' as it was commonly called, the elementary double-arched conical tent in Ruong's scheme was already a thing of the past. The distinctive double-arched structural design was by then only to be found in the permanent turf *goattii*, which bordered the lake. There was, however, a mobile Sámi tent form remaining in use. It was the less refined conical *laavo* (or *lávvu* in North Sámi) made from straight wooden poles without the curved double-arched birch frame. This 'straight-pole' *laavo* was ever attainable as it was made from a frame that hardly warranted transport, since it could be obtained and replaced if need be from the nearest stand of trees. In comparison to the *laavo*, the

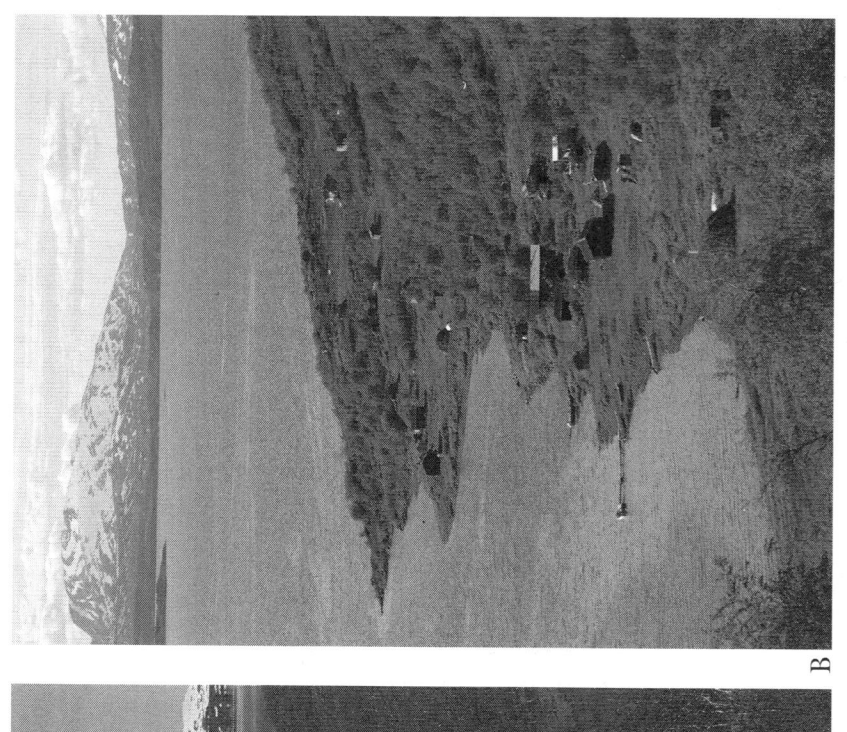

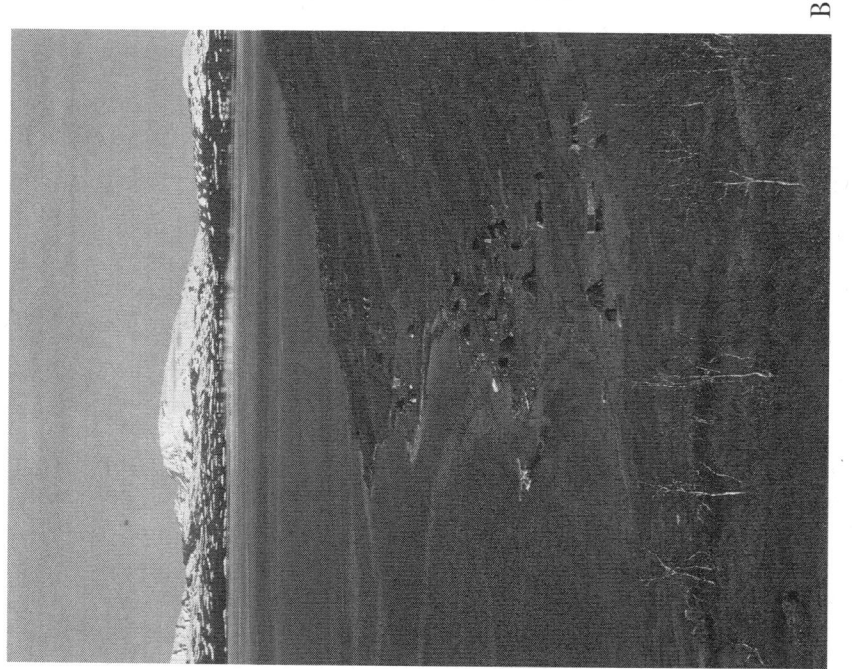

Figure 6.1 *This paired set of photos shows Staloluokta, Tuorpon sameby, summer camp. 1973 is represented in image A. The summer of 2008 is in image B.*

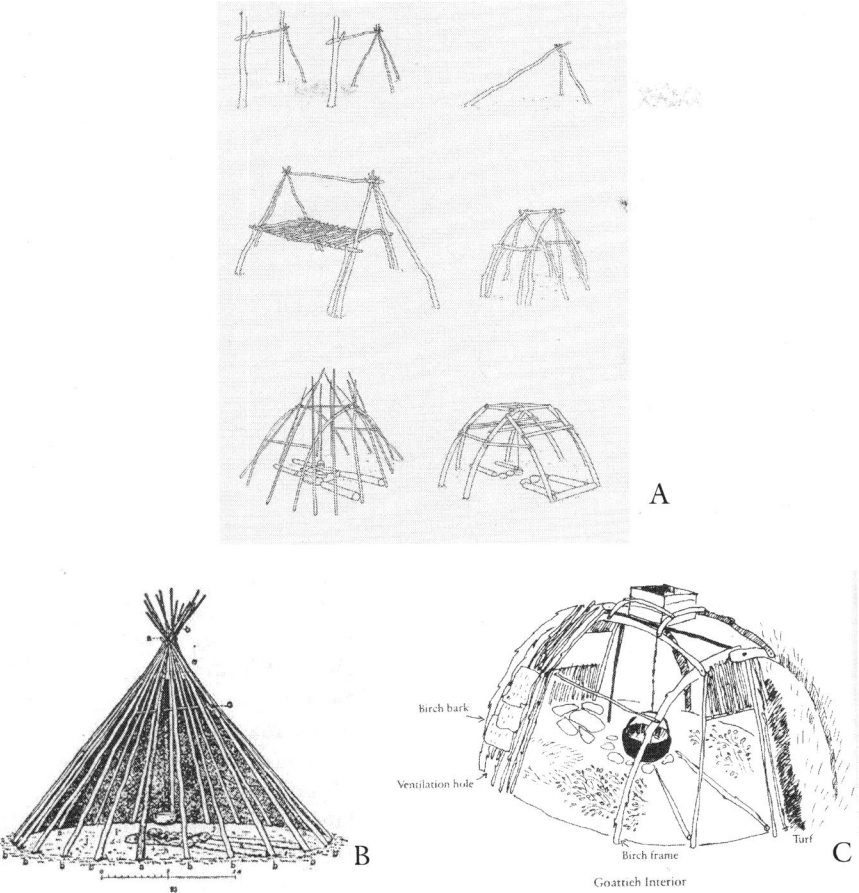

Figure 6.2 *A collage showing the developmental sequence for* goattieh *architecture. Image A shows Ruong's developmental sequence for the Sámi* laavo *(Ruong 1937: 45). The frame on the bottom left of the panel is the frame for a double-arched nomadic tent. The frame on the bottom right shows the basic frame for the permanent turf* goattieh. *Image B shows a cross-section of a Sámi* laavo *according to Ruong (1969: 106). Image C shows the double-arched northern Sámi* goattieh *type common in Stalo (Beach 2001: 48).*

'devitalized' double-arched tent gave more 'floor space' (with good head-room), which would have required far more straight poles, of the *laavo* tent type, to achieve.

In a sense, the older double-arched tent was ideal for reindeer caravan migrations. The fewer structural parts of the double-arched tent meant a much lighter load for the reindeer. When families were moving over bare ground, the tent structure – disassembled arch halves and poles – was distributed evenly on the sides of the last tame transport deer. One end of the long poles was tied behind the shoulder of the deer, the other dragged over the ground. When they were moving over snow cover, the entire structure was hauled along on the last sled of the reindeer caravan. This double-arch *goattieh* could be easily set up, anywhere on the tundra or high above the tree line where *laavo* poles could not be cut. I came to appreciate all of these features when visiting Norwegian Finnmark where the double-arched tent, the *bealljigoahti,* was still used in migrations with reindeer caravans (see Chapter 5). However, in the Jokkmokk mountains it was already rare for entire families to travel by reindeer sled. Snowmobiles and the demands of the Swedish school system for the children had already ended the era of full-family reindeer sled migrations with mobile double-arched tents. Instead, stationary turf dwellings dotting the migratory route at critical points were preferred: dwellings which took advantage of the dawning of what came to be called the extensive revolution in reindeer herding.

It is important to mention that the surviving *goattieh* turf dwellings themselves had already been modified by 1973. Not long before my arrival, these turf dwellings were located higher up on another slope of the mountain Unna Titir overlooking other mountain slopes and snow patches rather than the lake. When I came to Stalo, the older generation still remembered their old *goattieh* sites, when the village was around the other side of the mountain and quite a distance from the lakeshore. To some degree, this older alpine setting is associated with multiple meanings of 'tradition' and a different type of reindeer husbandry.

Still earlier records give evidence of a different adaptation. The native Jokkmokk herders who first used this site from the seventeenth and eighteenth centuries spoke the Lule Sámi dialect. They followed a so-called 'intensive-herding' lifestyle where the reindeer were milked and kept under year-round careful control. They used the excellent grazing pastures around Lake Virihaure and migrated with their small herds across what later became the Norwegian border, all the way to the North Sea coast (Linnaeus 1732; Hultblad 1968; Beach 1981: 132). However, while one might say that these original Lule Sámi herders occupied this site first, these small groups did not remain at Staloluokta very long, nor did these families always cohabit together. Before the arrival of relocated Karesuando herders from further north who mixed with the local Jokkmokk herders, the Viri group used mobile dwellings which could be pitched just about anywhere. To this day one can find the remains of their tent sites dotting the western end of Lake Virihaure (Beach 1981: 132). The earliest photographs show that these tents (as expected, being the primary, long-term dwelling) were of the double-arched type.

I think it is fair to say that while certain people at the dawn of time might have been the first to populate a tract of land, nowhere have they been first to populate a landscape, for they have generally filled it themselves with spirits, monsters, trolls, legendary peoples or dead ancestors well in advance of their own arrival. In this case, the troll, Stalo, who has given his name to the place, is said to have lived in a cave in a huge rock on the other side of the lake. He used to terrorize the Sámi living there until one day a brave Sámi walled up the cave opening while Stalo was asleep inside. In fact, the positioning of settlements, probably at any time in the past as well as today, depended and depends upon the physical characteristics of the land (in relation to their form of resource use) as well as for the (not-merely-human) social map of the landscape. Usually there is a very human social landscape to deal with, be it another group or groups of people of variable social distance ranging from total strangers of different ethnic groups, or strangers within recognizably the same ethnic group, to well-known members of the same community. Each of these types of social relation played a role in the clustering and internal positioning of the first permanent *goattii*, which in time became known as Staloluokta 'village'.

With the dissolution of the Norwegian/Swedish Union in 1905, the ensuing national restrictions on grazing access and the relocation (both freely but in the main forcibly by Swedish authorities) of many northern Sámi families with their reindeer to grazing lands further south, the grazing lands around Lake Virihaure hosted numerous waves of northern Sámi herders, some who moved on, but many who stayed. Not only did these newcomers, speaking a different dialect of Sámi, bring with them herding traditions originally adapted to other conditions, but their reindeer were also forced onto lands to which they were not accustomed. Naturally, the new group formed its herding partnerships based on kinship bonds (Paine 2009), which did not incorporate native Jokkmokk Sámi. Marriages across the Jokkmokk/Karesuando divide were practically unheard of and are still uncommon today. All of this resulted in the widespread disruption of local intensive herding practices and friction between northern relocated Sámi and local Jokkmokk Sámi groups. This is a story of huge complexity (not least legal), which is still unfolding with many regional variations (Elbo 1952; Åhren 1979; Walkeapää 2010). The social and cultural disruption among Sámi groups, both for the newcomers but also for those forced to make room for them, still lingers throughout the length of Swedish herding territory caused by the forcible relocation of northern Sámi (Beach 2008). For our purposes here, we must limit our discussion to note that Staloluokta, as the defined place along Lake Virihaure's shore, came to be a situated village of permanent *goattii* of northern Sámi type due to the coming of the northern Sámi. Previous to this, it signified a rather more diffuse zone in which the early intensive-herding Jokkmokk Sámi pitched their double-arch tents during the summer.

In previous works (Beach 1981; 2000; 2008) I have elaborated on the change from the era of so-called 'intensive' reindeer herding, which relied on the intimate relation to reindeer as a source of milk, to more 'extensive' herding characterized by the loose control of the deer used as a meat-producing animal. The explanation for the decline in the use of the traditional double-arched nomadic tent was brought on by these changes through a set of linked processes. As reindeer-milk pastoralism declined, reindeer calves, no longer deprived of their mother's milk, grew stronger and more independent. This meant that there was much less reason to monitor calves closely during the summer. Herds, which were more dispersed during the summer, were also spared epidemics of hoof and mouth disease, which occasionally decimated tightly controlled herds. As a result of increased extensivity, herds increased in size, and even individual reindeer became better 'meat-producing units'. With the reindeer running freely under loose, extensive control all summer, husbandry tasks during the bare-ground, pre-rut period came to be mainly confined to calf marking (Beach 2008). Freed from milking and monitoring the herd at all times, and with more time on their hands, herding families could take up permanent dwelling. They began to leave supplies at a storage site conveniently located near a sufficient source of birch wood and a good fishing lake, which could provide for their main summer diet.

The so-called 'extensive revolution' soon came to sweep far beyond anything practised by the northern Sámi newcomers and continues its forward march today, driven by inexorable market demands to maximize profits within the limits of sustainability. This is characterized by regulated herd sizes per *sameby* and ideals of selective breeding, calf slaughter, and optimal age/sex composition of herds – that which is known as 'rational herd management' (Beach and Stammler 2006) and which must today hearken to increasingly global dictates and conditions of possibility.

These were the conditions that led to the establishment of Stalo village with permanent *goattii* in the early 1900s, when it was situated rather high on the 'back' side of Unna Titir. This site provided people living in the *goattii* with a good view towards Kierkevare, a focal mountain with snow patches where deer habitually escaped insect pests. At this time, a modicum of intensive control was still desirable, to protect the herd (especially the young calves) from predation, to know when would be the opportune time for calf marking at various corrals and to assure oneself of the ability to assemble the necessary trained pack reindeer needed for further movement toward the lowlands as autumn arrived. Eyes were basically 'mountain oriented'.

The fishing that occurred here was quite limited and not essentially for sale. Private boats in the mountains at that time were small and light and had to be hauled into the highlands by reindeer sled while the land was still covered with snow. Boat motors, demanding a supply of gas, were still unheard of in Stalo, as were the nylon nets which greatly increased fishing productivity. The fish caught were for immediate consumption, and perhaps some for the salt barrel to be freighted out by reindeer.

All of this changed with the advent of the seaplane. Gradually, turf dwellings were relocated and swivelled to be 'lake oriented'. Proximity to the lake meant easy access to boats for fishing as well as to seaplanes for the freighting of caught fish to the lowlands and the distribution of mail and supplies brought by these same seaplanes. Should the time for marking reindeer calves approach, and the herders find themselves with the need to set out on foot to sweep the surrounding slopes and valleys for reindeer, the seaplane pilots could help the herders to position themselves strategically by setting them down at any small lake large enough for landing. During their many trips, the pilots also kept an eye out for wandering reindeer and thus became a major source of information for the herders on where the herds were congregating.

At this time herders began using conical tents again, both of the double-arch and *laavo* type, to extend the fishing reach of families in various shifting directions from the village hub, but tent use of this kind never replaced the permanent turf *goattieh*. The old double-arch tent structure used previously on migrations was too bulky and would cost too much to be put in a seaplane, but it could be transported by boat. The *laavo* could be erected wherever access to trees permitted, and it was also quite common to leave the poles behind at a site where recurring visits were to be expected. The making of a double-arch tent structure, requiring the search for four matching 'ear' arches, took considerable effort, and caused them to be valuable family possessions. They were not likely to be left behind at a campsite, and as their main purpose as a migratory home ebbed away, so were they soon to become a rarity in the mountains, even at short-term fishing camps.

Calf marking was still the number one concern of herders in the summer. More prolonged fishing expeditions would therefore often be left to the elderly who would not have to rush off to a corral at a moment's notice. Tent cloth and nets could be flown out with a fishing couple to any one of a multitude of small lakes, or a fishing camp could be established anywhere along the shore of the big Lake Virihaure. Supplies of all kinds from the lowlands would then be flown up while the catch of arctic char was brought out. It was soon unnecessary to keep goats, as practically any fresh food item available through the lowland road network could be in the mountains with little delay. Seaplanes could be used to transport large cans of gas for boat motors, and commercial summer fishing gained a dominant place in the herding cycle with considerable financial importance for herding families.

Given the new importance of fishing and the seaplanes, it is understandable that the families began to shift their dwellings to the Viri (short for Virihaure, i.e. the lake) side of the mountain when *goattii* needed rebuilding and young families started out on their own. Eyes shifted to the lake, and lake weather of consequence for seaplane traffic and fishing conditions became often more important than mountain weather. The *goattieh*'s (often single) window – the presence of any window at all made possible only through relatively modern means of transportation – turned towards the lake.

Kinship relations are still the best predictor of the relative placement of permanent *goattii* within the village (and are even noticeable when tents are erected near a corral). However, many factors might fine-tune final placement within an area made probable by kinship. As fishing became increasingly important, residents began to experiment with changing the ceiling heights in the *goattii* in order to make a dwelling that could also be used for smoking fish. The technical challenge was to maximize the draw of air without making the lower section too uncomfortable for inhabitants. A dwelling that is situated wrongly in relation to the surrounding slopes can cause prevailing winds to drive smoke back down the smoke hole. For a time, in the early 1970s, dwelling placement for a new construction could even be influenced by (though hardly decided by) the desire to maximize the signal strength of walkie-talkies in various directions.

Technological change further altered the number of different types of dwellings a family would maintain. The growing density of the road network, followed by the coming of the snowmobile, quite swiftly obviated the regular need for sled-deer family transport caravans.[5] Speed and ease of transport made it possible also for herders to work with the herd much farther from a single base. Reindeer could still access winter pastures far westward without it being necessary for the herding families to live there. Therefore, the maintenance of separate spring/autumn and winter settlement dwellings became for many quite redundant. The active herders (usually male) could base themselves at one spot and cover such a broad timespan of herding work from there that a single permanent dwelling for the snow-cover period was adequate. This also allowed the rest of the family to extend their stay in these winter quarters and accommodate more easily the regular Swedish school programme.

As seaplane freight-and-fish-delivery companies grew in number and capacity, they were soon entrusted to fly families and all their seasonal bare-ground-period packing into the mountains for the summer, and then eastward towards the lowlands again with the autumn. The reindeer might migrate in the company of some herders necessary for the job, but families could move up and down independently by seaplane. In effect, the movements of the reindeer, the herders and their families all became split and were no longer harmonized by the migration of caravans. This meant that the old spring/autumn camps, commonly set midway along the migration route between westernmost summer pastures (and camps) and easternmost winter pastures and scattered homes, gradually fell into disuse and were abandoned.

Larger regional economic development motivated change of the main permanent dwellings towards a completely new form where a family would live for about nine months each year. When the construction of new hydroelectric dams stopped, when agriculture also ebbed and machines replaced manpower in the timber industry, jobs became scarce in northern inland Sweden. Labourers began vacating their homes, releasing a large number of Swedish-style houses onto the market at cheap prices in the lowlands. Herding families began to take over regular homes built to Swedish standards central to their snow-cover grazing lands (for the Tuorpon *sameby* herders, in or around the town of Jokkmokk). In short, when I first reached Stalo in 1973, the time spent at the so-called winter home in the lowlands for the herders had lengthened (extending over all but the summer months in the mountains), and dwelling forms (for the main family) had become permanent and relegated to two main positions in the grazing cycle: the westernmost summer turf *goattieh*, and the easternmost winter (Swedish-style) home.

35 years later

Returning to my two photographs (Figure 6.1), one finds that the most immediately striking difference between the two pictures, which are separated by 35 years, is in the vastly increased number of four-sided cabins, insulated for all weather conditions (not to be confused with the much smaller four-sided outhouses and storage huts). Bedding and gear can now be left in summer homes all winter, and travelling up and down between mountains and lowlands can be done with minimal packing. With generators, TV, satellite phones and gas stoves, life in summer camps has become increasingly similar to life during other seasons in the lowlands – increasingly similar but for a decreasing amount of time.

The number of permanent turf *goattii* has decreased, although I can attest to the fact that at least a couple of them are indeed still there, only hidden behind a cabin or submerged in greenery. What is not immediately discernable in the pictures is how use of these dwellings has changed and why.

Today, most of the turf *goattii* are used minimally and some hardly at all. They might still be used for the baking of traditional flat bread, 'ember cakes' over an open fire, or for the smoking of fish still taken from the lake for household consumption or sale in small numbers to hikers passing by. However, large-scale fishing for sale to air-companies with swift daily flights to lowland restaurants has all but disappeared. The *goattii* can still serve as quarters for the many summer guests, extended family members and good friends who often prefer to experience the old life on a reindeer or moose hide around the central hearth (Sámi *arran)*, but this will often demand a good deal of preparatory work – for example, cutting a new floor of birch branches and keeping a large supply of firewood. Some owners have eased this work by laying a wooden floor in the *goattieh*, and maybe by installing an iron stove with a permanent smokestack and bringing in cots.

The old turf double 'ear-arched' *goattieh*, like the traditional reindeer-drawn double-arched mobile tent, as well as the straight-poled *laavo*, all shared the same basic floor plan, with the same rules of movement for people inside and the same social significance of seating positions (Beach 1993). But once the *arran* gets replaced by an iron wood stove (often positioned at the *goattieh*'s perimeter, since a smokestack does not require a central position), and floors are laid with permanent wooden planks instead of the annual renewal of fresh birch saplings, the way people use the space changes. For instance, a larger unified floor space unbroken by a hearth in the middle allows for the central positioning of a table with chairs. Since the smoke is funnelled out the smoke pipe and does not hover throughout the interior, pressing inhabitants towards the floor, people are far more prone to stand or sit in chairs. Such modernized accommodations can even be rented out to summer visitors, but it is not common to bring complete strangers into the village for extended periods, as this can bring an imposition to all villagers. Most of the old *goattii* are paired with a new cabin, both owned by the same family, with the shift of use as indicated above. However, there is no simple binary opposition between traditional and modern in permanent dwelling form, as illustrated by the turf *goattieh* or the frame cabin. There are a few herders who maintain a good deal of the old style of life who use (often modernized) *goattii* as their prime residences during the summer, and who have not (yet) built a cabin.

Maintenance of the old *goattii* is to some degree supported by grants provided expressly for their restoration by the Swedish National Heritage Board. Funds have been given to *goattieh* owners to cover both the cost of new materials and also the labour necessary to restore the *goattii*. Not all applications to the Heritage Board are granted, however, for the Board wants to promote the preservation of traditional dwellings and to ensure that they will remain in use (so that there is a real incentive to keep them in repair). Were it not for this restoration programme by the Heritage Board, a number of old *goattii* made redundant by cabins as primary dwellings would surely have lapsed into disrepair and then been torn down. Usage accepted by the Heritage Board encompasses use of the *goattii* for such things as baking and smoking fish, uses which give them a purpose and value to their owners. Heritage Board funds are not granted, however, for the modernization of *goattieh* architecture or of the interior layout.

Besides individual predilections, there are also other reasons governing the choices taken about what kind of dwelling to live in, how to construct it and how to furnish it. Among these, the most important is a law declaring that the construction of permanent dwellings on Crown land is allowed at certain sites for herders only.[6] Within the large national-park areas of northern Sweden (overlapping most of the summer grazing territory of many *samebyar* like Tuorpon), restrictions are all the more elaborate. Children of herders who would not themselves become herders would not be granted permission to build a home on Crown land, especially not in a park's mountain regions. However, they are always allowed to inherit any such property from their parents.

The so-called 'structural rationalization' of the herding industry, which began seriously in the 1970s, squeezed herders out of their livelihood through carrot and stick policies (cf. Beach 1981: 323ff.; 1983). The logic of these reforms was that those remaining in the industry might enjoy a greater slice of the total herd limit, increasing their profits and their living standards. This meant that the children of herders, more than ever, embarked upon non-herding livelihoods. While they were still active herders, herding parents who were unsure of their children's future as herders saved money[7] in order to build cabins to replace their traditional Sámi-style dwellings, both to have a more comfortable pensioned life, and also to have dwellings of value that could attract even their non-herding children and families into the mountain camps – prime 'nursing grounds' for Sámi identity and social cohesion.

The building of expensive permanent Swedish-style cabins in the mountains was naturally hampered by problems transporting building materials. Almost all of the material for the building of the traditional *goattii* could be obtained in situ, but the lumber, insulation, windows and other materials for the cabins had to be purchased in the lowlands and freighted to the mountainside. Heavily laden snowmobiles could take much more than the reindeer caravans, but even snowmobiles have their limits, and the job could be treacherous. The helicopter, able to lift and carry huge burdens suspended underneath for placement anywhere, revolutionized transport. However, the advent of new transportation possibilities was insufficient to bring about a building boom in Stalo. Instead, herders had to struggle against government regulations.

While herders have the right to build dwellings to serve them in pursuit of their reindeer-herding livelihood on Crown and Park lands, the building permits most often issued were minimalist to say the least. State authorities would commonly allow only very small buildings, without any standard comforts, insulation or plumbing. A permanent turf *goattieh* was, in effect, all that was allowed. The first tiny, makeshift cabin permitted for a herder in Stalo was granted in the 1970s because he had become severely asthmatic, and with a letter from his doctor could certify that he should not be overly exposed to the smoke from the open hearth of a *goattieh*. However, it was not until 1982, after a year of negotiations with park authorities, the Environmental Protection Agency and the County Administrative Board, that a larger cabin with higher standards was permitted. Informants in Stalo have explained that the thawing of tight building restrictions was largely due to the enlightened attitude of the current head of the Crown lands in the park area, Bengt Edholm, who had stated that the herders 'were after all not animals and should be allowed habitations befitting people as they wished'. Once this cabin was built, other herders rapidly followed suit to take advantage of a window of opportunity they feared might shut at any moment. This led to the blossoming of new four-sided buildings at the site in my second photograph (see Figure 6.1B).

Flying dogs, labour, and time spent in camp

When comparing contemporary summer life in the village with that of 35 years ago, I find that one of the most significant changes is not to do with location, building type, interior layout or mode of use, but rather with the timing and extent of use of the dwellings. This change cannot be seen in the photographs. Most of the herding families spent far less time in Stalo than previously. They were also far more mobile than ever before. This change can be explained by the arrival of the helicopter. It is also linked to the revitalization of the mobile tent – as we shall see below – but again in a surprisingly new form.

Of course, seaplanes had been in operation for more than 20 years – bringing herders, families and their supplies into the mountains, and taking them out again in many places – before the job was taken over by the helicopter. Not only is the operational cost of a seaplane less than that of a helicopter, but herding families were also given considerable discounts for seaplane transport, since they could be counted as the main fishing employees of the seaplane businesses. Why then should there have been a transition to helicopter use at all?

Both seaplane and helicopter may be flying machines, but their airborne capabilities differ enormously. Significantly, the helicopter does not need water for landing and take-off, and it can easily lift heavy loads for transport almost anywhere. Hence the helicopter is far more useful than the seaplane for work within the National Parks, to lift mobile bridges and construction material, but also for difficult rescue operations. It can fly tourists in and out of the mountains no matter how rough the lakes are. It is also of far greater assistance during the moose hunt, when heavy moose carcasses must be transported with haste from anywhere in the vast mountain-taiga area. The mountain air companies must serve a number of different customers to make ends meet, and reindeer-herding interests and the profits derived from that sector are but a part of their larger business puzzle. Moreover, even if they are more expensive to use, helicopters afford far more flexibility in mode of use for reindeer herding.

When I first came to Stalo in the early 1970s, helicopters were rarely used to transport herding families to the mountains and only occasionally in herding work. Its most likely use then was during the pre-rut slaughter of the bull reindeer, whose rapid hormonal shifts would cause their meat to be inedible if they were not slaughtered before mid-September. The deer were still rather far westward in the mountains then, far from the winter lowland road network. Not only was it critical to bring the bull deer to the corral in the mountains in time, but once slaughtered there the carcasses had to be removed swiftly down to the slaughterhouse trucks waiting at the end of the road. The helicopter could serve both needs. It was used to round up the deer, to drive them into the corral, and later to freight the bodies, five at a time, from the mountain corral to the trucks farther east (Beach 1993: 135ff.). Use of the helicopter to freight bull carcasses from the mountains to the road is not necessary in those *samebyar* where roads penetrate into the autumn lands, but the use of the helicopter to round up the bulls to ensure their time-critical delivery into the corral has become the rule. Of course, there was a period when the air companies maintained both seaplanes and helicopters, but once large-scale commercial fishing faded to a level that left no profit, and profit from helicopter use rose further, the seaplanes disappeared.

This fading of large-scale commercial fishing by herding families in the summer and the dependence on the helicopter in herding are intimately related, and both of these have influenced greatly the timing of summer occupancy in Stalo. As will be explained in more detail shortly, expanded use of the helicopter, now encompassing the actual driving of the herd into the calf-marking corral (not merely the positioning of herders – as with the seaplane – to perform the gathering on foot) has caused all the calf markings to be completed on a tight schedule, early in the summer. Once these are over and done, and without large-scale fishing to motivate prolonged stay in the mountains, many herding families have begun to return to their lowland main homes after only a few weeks.

Not only can the helicopter serve to scout for reindeer and to position herders anywhere on the ground. Anyone who has watched a helicopter at work when collecting and driving reindeer to the corral can understand the appreciative but somewhat ironic term for them: 'flying dogs' (since real dogs are so rarely used in herding nowadays). A helicopter can hang still in the air; it can turn on a dime, and it can move slowly, close to the ground. Flocks that try to run off from the sides of the herd can be brought back swiftly into the fold if need be, while the deer can be driven ahead at a calm tempo towards the corral with the helicopter zigzagging at the bottom of the herd. Should the entire herd stampede off in the wrong direction, the helicopter has the speed and commands the 'authority' to turn it back. With a skilled herder sitting beside a skilled helicopter pilot, the flying dog can do the job of many in a fraction of the time. When the helicopter gathering is joined by youths on motorbikes, the drive to the corral is all the swifter. Of course, the final push of the deer into the corral 'arms' and the rolling across of the wire fencing gate requires the presence of 'ground troops', perhaps others on foot waiting by the corral, but the helicopter rarely fails (weather permitting) to deliver the animals into their hands.[8]

Contemporaneous with the increasing use of the helicopter, a development which requires a sizeable expenditure from the *sameby's* collective purse, is the practice of paying herders' wages from the *sameby's* collective funds to accomplish special tasks. As we shall see, the payment of wages and the use of helicopters are intimately related, and together they have impacted on the dwellings herders choose to occupy. I have described the wage system as structured by the reindeer-herding law previously in considerable detail (Beach 1981; 2000), and will only summarize its essential features here to inform our understanding of its impact on dwelling patterns.

The Reindeer Act of 1971 restructured the *samebyar* into collectively responsible economic business units, according to the ideals of a rationalized reindeer industry. The new business units were designed to run on balanced budgets. If a *sameby's* initial annual budget figures showed a deficit, the final account had to be brought into balance by levying a per-head fee on each reindeer owner for the care of the reindeer. The handling fee could change year by year as long as it was set at a level at least high enough to balance the *sameby* budget. Of course, a *sameby* might require no herding fee – for example, by significantly avoiding collective labour expenses, or if the *sameby* in question had money on hand from environmental compensation payments from hydroelectric dams, or from predator damages to cover expenses.

The wage system was devised to go hand in hand with the herding fee and would protect herders with few deer from having their labour exploited by those with big herds. Big herders can rest assured that they will always have enough deer to satisfy their needs for sustenance at any winter corral, whereas the small herder must be far more actively engaged in bringing the animals into the slaughter corral and be sure that all of his new calves are properly marked in summer (see Beach 2008 for the dangers of not doing so). Under the fee/wage system, herders would pay a sum into the collective purse according to the number of deer they owned, but then they would also be compensated by the *sameby* for any labour that they provided (for the collective good) during annual activities.

In terms of a budgetary strategy a particular *sameby* could choose to proceed along the traditional route of minimizing or avoiding all cash expenses, and instead use moral pressure to ensure that each family supplied at least one person to take care of common tasks. Or a *sameby* could choose to take on contracts, even very costly ones, for the collective good, and pay for it by raising the necessary herding fee per reindeer. In effect, there is a great deal of choice to be exercised by a *sameby* when it comes to setting the annual herding fee and deciding how much work to put under the wage system (and at what rate of salary), and what other expenses are incurred.

The helicopter, although extremely costly, will do the work of many men, thereby offsetting the cost of herding fees. Ideally, if a helicopter's 'down time' is reduced, the *sameby* is faced with the salary of only one herder. To rationalize costs even further, adjoining *samebyar* make cooperative schedules for helicopter use. Among the *samebyar* in the Jokkmokk Mountains, a tacit agreement has been reached that one *sameby* must complete its calf markings before the next *sameby* starts. All *sameby* sub-groups and all *samebyar* in the area are thereby forced into the new time schedule. Nowadays the calf markings occur back-to-back, in a few weeks of frenetic activity. There is no time for fishing, and no helicopter is available to transport fish even if fishing were practised commercially.

This rationalization of time leads to the further rationalization of the use of space. When the calf markings are over, in the early summer, there are few if any opportunities for people to earn salaries from the *sameby*, nor any unspoken moral pressure to be on hand for communal work. Herders begin to leave the mountains early. Those who remain in the mountains a bit longer are often the pensioners and perhaps some young grandchildren for whom the post-calf-marking period becomes a kind of vacation and immersion in a Sámi social context. Pensioners can supplement their incomes by providing fish and ember bread to hikers, while older youths might be enticed to stay on in the mountains for the income they can gain through park maintenance and tourist-oriented jobs. On the whole, however, even these lingering summer residents move down much earlier than before, and my informants complain that the old relaxed summers when families circulated among the *goattii* for long coffee visits are no more. Residence patterns, therefore, have become intense, abbreviated and extremely mobile. This in turn has affected people's choices in architecture.

The mobile Sámi tent

The pressures of contemporary herding life, including such developments as abbreviated wage payments, combined with the costly but efficient transport of helicopters, and new building codes and inheritance legislation, have led on the one hand to an increased use of the *laavo*-type mobile tent in a modernized form, and on the other to a decrease in use of the traditional permanent turf *goattieh* in favour of the Swedish frame house. Calf-marking events are now so frequent and compressed in time that herders are often flying from one corral to another, day by day, forgoing even the luxury of flying home in between. This has led to a preference of a new type of light, highly mobile dwelling, the Moskosel *laavo,* which shares a common conical shape with the traditional Sámi *laavo* and is marketed on the basis of its indigenous heritage, but uses high-tech synthetic materials. The conical form is achieved thanks to a set number of aluminium poles fitted into a rigid 'crown' holding-rig at the top. The covering is made from synthetic cloth. This internal shape-holding architectural device is entirely new and without roots in Sámi tradition. A gathering of Moskosel tents full of children near a corral can appear in a few hours, only to disappear after the corralling with equal speed. The helicopter can replace the old reindeer caravan when it comes to hauling the home; in fact, the new tents (even of a size hosting five people) are made of such lightweight materials that they can be carried by a single person without difficulty (Figure 6.3B). The tents appear again at the next corral, but after two or three weeks of most intensive marking activity, they are more or less gone for good (for that summer). The tents allow families to bring children and grandchildren along to enjoy the seasonal events. They help herders to achieve tasks and to enjoy each other's company, but they are rooted in a radically new social environment.

In the early 1970s herders walked to the calf-marking corral and might have to wait there for a day or two if the reindeer proved difficult to drive. Walkie-talkie communication in the mountains was often haphazard, and it could be extremely difficult to follow the whereabouts of the gathering team. Small children could not embark on a long hike to a corral; nor

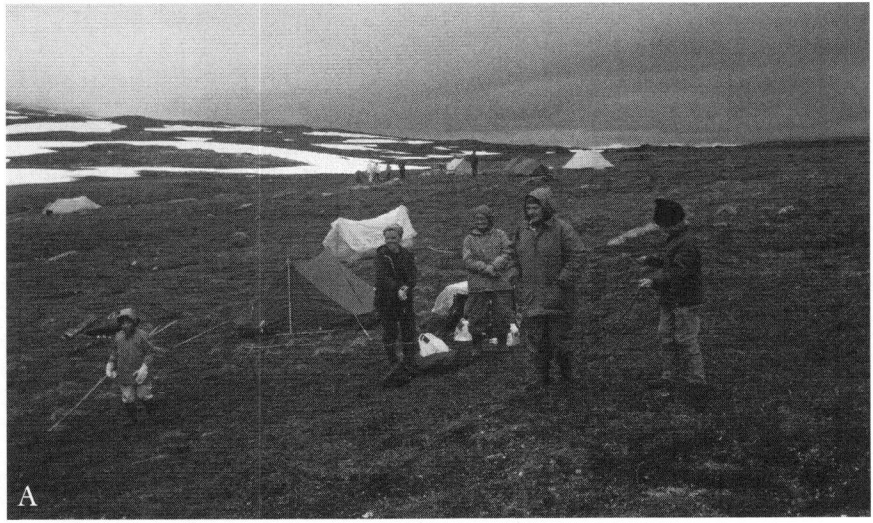

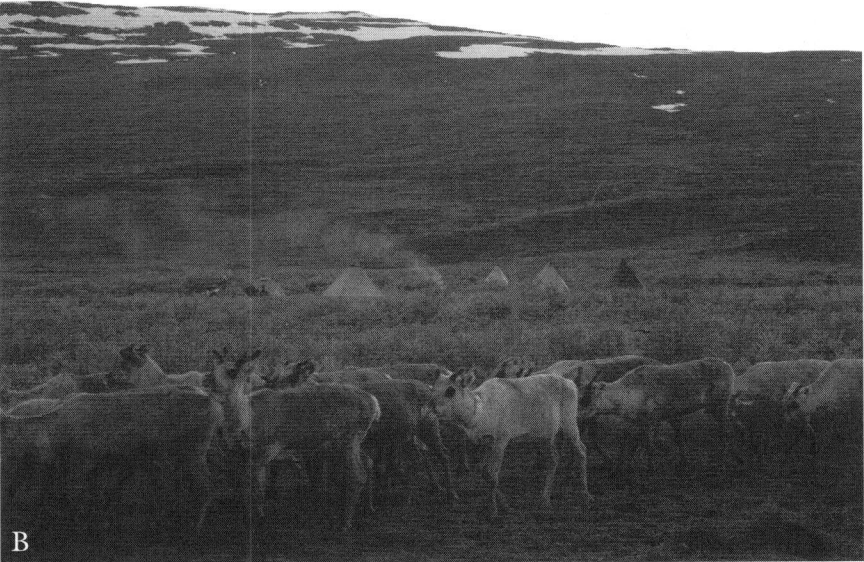

Figure 6.3 *This paired set of photos shows family tents at a calf-marking corral. Both are taken near the Arasluokta village in Jåkkåkaska sameby territory near a spot (and river) referred to as 'Melädno'. Image A on the top is from 1973 and Image B on the bottom is from 2008.*

were their young mothers likely to attend the corralling. There could be a long wait, the work could also last most of the night, and living conditions were not particularly comfortable, especially in poor weather. Nowadays, on those occasions when corrallings are not too far from the village, families, even those with small children, can congregate there for the marking with a modicum of comfort, with considerable assurance that the marking will occur, and without long periods of waiting. Mobile telephones provide sure communications. Before the calf marking, a few *sameby* members have probably been sent ahead of time by the *sameby* to prepare the corral and the camp for both the herders and their families. In the case of those calf markings which occur in another *sameby*, possibly quite far from the range of a herder's home *sameby* (and therefore less likely to have its reindeer at the corral), it is common today for the *sameby*'s collective purse to finance the attendance of a few herders, chosen carefully for their wide knowledge of ear marks, to perform marking tasks for all of their *sameby* mates, thereby sparing them the considerable (private) flight expense. Lightweight poles and roles of wire fencing can also be transported by helicopter to set up corrals in many new places. The advent of flying corrals, flying dwellings and flying herders with less time but longer 'reach' brings together herders from greater distances, from *samebyar* farther away. Their herding schedules grow increasingly entwined.

With a helicopter in constant use by many *samebyar* during the marking season, its schedule of bookings is tight. The pilot must give top priority to the transportation of herders rather than accompanying family. Nor can the helicopter be booked for days sweeping vast tracts to bring a large mass of deer to a single corral. Each corralling must be a one or at most two-day affair, if schedules (and budgets) are to hold. As the herders say, 'We have begun to bring the corrals to the deer rather than the deer to the corral' (cf. Beach 2008).

That old-time feeling (perhaps romanticized but present in memory nonetheless) when children ran between lasso practice and the hearths or outdoor, more collective fires where their parents congregated to chat leisurely around the coffee pot, depends precisely upon the waiting for the reindeer. Inclement weather and delay in bringing the deer into the corral creates the calm to socialize across family lines, at least for the old timers, the women and small children. Poor weather will find groups eating and talking outdoors with eyes scanning the mountainsides and ears assessing the nearness of the helicopter. Truly foul weather will push everyone inside the tents, but here too fires will gather people around them, although naturally people will tend to disperse into smaller tent-family groups. Usually, however, the weather, even if poor, will be sufficiently good for the helicopter to bring the herd to the corral. The smallest children can be fed or put to rest sporadically in the tents, but most of the time the tents stand vacant, their erstwhile inhabitants congregating with the reindeer in the corral and chatting with each other in abruptly ending bursts between breaks to catch a calf for marking. The talk grows longer as the majority of calves become marked, but once the job is all done and the herd released, the herders also quickly disappear, and the tents are hurriedly dismantled. Only a few smouldering fires and unused piles of willow brush remain as an indication of the whirlwind of work that occurred at the corral site not long ago.

Admittedly, these temporary clusters of tents can hardly emulate the tent camps of the old days of intensive reindeer herding. The tents may still be pitched with some regard for family connections, but such concerns must now accommodate more immediate concerns such as being placed close to the corral but out of the path of the herd. Inside the tents one will find usually only the barest of essentials for eating and sleeping. Of course, such things as baking stones, wrought-iron frying pans or thickly matted birch branches covered by moose or reindeer hide on the floor, common in village tents in the past, will not be found in these short-term dwellings. Nevertheless, the conical tents put a much more indigenous stamp on the landscape since they allow smoke to rise from Sámi tent clusters – in contrast to nylon backpacker tents where lone herders would be forced to make their fires outside.

Yet for the herders there are tangible benefits and appreciated cultural gains to be had from these ephemeral clusters of modern tents of unsurpassed (retro) design. First and foremost, as noted, they make it far more likely that entire families, even those with small children, will attend corralling events. Nowadays, with the helicopter to transport a modern tent able to hold a fire, the reach of young families seems to have increased. Even tiny children with small lassos or homemade toy snags can follow close behind their parents in distant corrals. Considering the expense of helicopter transport for families to distant corrals, togetherness can be costly. With a shorter summer season in the mountains, however, time for acquiring herding skills becomes all the more precious.

How one lives, in which kind of dwelling, where and when, have become matters governed also by issues of culture, enskillment, indigenous politics and conscious identity formation. Assuredly such matters have influenced choices since the dawn of time. For the contemporary herding family in Sweden, however, the alternatives have quickly come to span a vastly more globalized array of choices than ever before, and choosing a path of Sámi modernism, traditionalism or revitalization makes statements about questions which previously were hardly asked. The new social geography of the new Sámi (Moskosel) *laavo* serves both economic restrictions and identity building. Families experience a kind of Sámi village feeling of togetherness even if it is very ephemeral. If the eyes from the early *goattii* (both the old double-arch tent and the first turf dwellings) looked to the mountain, and then from the turf *goattii* to the lake, now eyes look inward into a revitalized community.

Conclusion

This chapter has examined seven specific Sámi dwellings which have been put into use at various times over the past 100 years: (1) a mobile conical double-arch tent *goattieh* (used mainly in the days of intensive herding); (2) a permanent turf *goattieh* (once built to face the mountain, but later built by the lakeshore and oriented to face the lake); (3) a modernized *goattieh* (with a stove and with different flooring); (4) a traditional conical *laavo* (with wooden poles); (5) a Moskosel conical *laavo* (with aluminium poles); (6) backpacker tents; and (7) a Swedish frame house.

When considering dwelling constructions *per se*, it is common for social scientists to speak in terms of 'revitalization' and 'devitalization' when referring to degrees of traditional structural forms or degrees of use. I have presented two traditional Sámi dwellings, the permanent turf *goattieh* and the mobile tent *(laavo)* as caught in a cycle of 'devitalization' and 'revitalization'. However, these terms highlight a problematic point: the 'devitalization' of a traditional construction form might occur in order to 'revitalize' a traditional relationship to the landscape. When speaking of 'revitalization', for example, one might be unconsciously focusing on building form, when so much more is actually involved. For example, the chapter by Andrews in this volume illustrates a 'revitalization' of a rare Dene caribou-hide-covered tent dwelling found in a museum collection. In a cooperative effort by museum staff and Dene community elders, the building techniques, and material procurement and preparation, were brought back in the (re)making of such a dwelling – a new generation became enskilled in the process, and a wealth of traditional lore extending far beyond the tent construction itself was revived.

In the case of the Sámi tent, described here, revitalization did not focus on the recreation or repatriation of a specific old dwelling, in material, in traditional structure or in lore. Enskillment of traditional tent construction was not the issue here. The term 'revitalization' was applied to these tents (albeit perhaps naïvely) because of the temporary social life their use at the corrals afforded, the 'feel' of the old-time smoking tent villages, and the enskillment they facilitated of very young children in herding work, rather than in tent making. Actually, it can be argued that the possibility of purchasing the modern Moskosel tent, with the advantages of its conical form and inside hearth, has made it all the less likely that the truly traditional Sámi *laavo* will be revitalized for anything more than a museum project. The Moskosel tent has the traditional conical form, but its materials and internal structure are significantly different from the Sámi *laavo*. Use of the Moskosel tents is not conducive to the enskillment of Sámi youth in traditional *laavo* construction.

Similarly, in this chapter the term 'devitalization' was invoked to illustrate the transition from use of the permanent turf *goattieh* to the Swedish-style modern cabin. The comparative opposition of the terms devitalization and revitalization was to be found, again, in the realm of ensuing social effects: the transition to cabin living promoting (and reflecting) a shorter season of summer work in the mountains and further distancing from active herding. Yet, as we have seen, the transition to cabin use was to some extent occasioned by legislation, which enabled the children of herders to inherit property (and thereby have a better chance of remaining) in their traditional mountain landscapes. From this perspective, the transition to cabin life might be regarded as a revitalization effort.

In effect, on both counts we find that revitalization and devitalization cannot be conceived of as mutually exclusive. Even in the case presented by Andrews, with a focus on the recreation of a traditional material artefact and the reawakening of knowledge and processes of intergenerational learning, there are obvious, unavoidable aspects of the context of the tent recreation project which are far from traditional and revitalizing of former enskillment processes – even when creativity is acknowledged in past works and fostered in contemporary revitalization efforts. In the end, nothing can be more traditional than the attempt to survive in the place one calls home, pursuing a livelihood one desires, and to achieve this one must be willing and able to change in all kinds of ways. When cultural politics enter into the equation and influence one's success in this venture, for example when majority perceptions of what is traditional for an indigenous minority becomes enmeshed with the power of the majority to change indigenous life, it is then that concepts of revitalization or devitalization take on meanings as significant as they are overly simplified. The how, when and where of dwelling become fraught with political ramifications, and the care devoted to accepted or overly static categories of revitalization swells. My own experiences among the Sámi lead me to believe that appropriate dwelling for them is in essence governed by pragmatism, and when conscious efforts at traditional preservation, revitalization or, for that matter, devitalization of dwelling are manifest, it is because these also have pragmatic sides.

Notes

1. 'Staloluokta' means 'troll inlet' in Sámi and is the name both of an inlet of Lake Virihaure and of the Sámi village by its shore.
2. *Sameby* (sing.). and *samebyar* (pl.) are Swedish terms meaning Sámi 'villages', but these so-called 'villages' in fact designate the ca. 50 territorially defined grazing zones for reindeer herding in Sweden. The term is also used when referring to the social group of Sámi who traditionally inhabited these areas, but in contemporary legislation is limited in reference to

those allowed to exercise their reindeer herding rights there and who thereby form a business enterprise and judicial entity.

3. The term 'permanent' in the sense used here among transhumant reindeer-herders is, of course, not meant to indicate that the herders reside there permanently, but rather that the dwellings are fixed in the landscape to the extent their materials of construction last. Hence they are permanently situated in contrast to mobile, tent dwellings. Of course, the 'permanent' home of a family might relocate should the old structure burn down, be in need of total repair, or be poorly situated with respect to mountain slopes encumbering good smoke flow. Relocation of any dwelling, permanent or mobile, can also occur to bring peace to the spirit of one who had died there, a death accruing to the place in the landscape more than to any shelter, which might have surrounded it.

4. Actually there are a number of permanent Sámi dwelling forms, and hybrids thereof, all of which might come under the term *goattieh*. Those in Staloluokta are of the northern Sámi turf-covered variety whose dome-like inner construction of birch timber is notably supported by four curved birch timbers put together so as to form two arches, in Sámi called *biellie* or 'ears'. Hence these are *biellie goattieh* as discussed in chapter 5.

5. The term 'caravan' in the sense of a string of reindeer hauling sleds can conflate many meaningful distinctions. Naturally, one must distinguish between caravans pulling basic provisions for a work team of herders moving between fixed cabins along a migration route, and one hauling not only provisions but also the entire herding family along with the double arches and poles with which to set up a tent dwelling for encampment anywhere on route.

6. Herders from one *sameby* are permitted by the Reindeer Herding Act to build small, simple (no water, no insulation) shelters for use during herding operations on the territory of another *sameby*, but a *sameby* can prohibit the building of living accommodation (i.e. a cabin) for a herder who is not a member of the *sameby* in question.

7. It is extremely rare that a herder can obtain any sizeable loan, since his reindeer property according to law cannot be used as collateral.

8. Based on my own field experience over the years at innumerable corrallings, I believe the development of helicopter expertise today for work in summer calf markings to be a consequence of previous enskillment over the years when working with the corrallings of the more volatile pre-rut bull reindeer in the autumn. Skill in use of the helicopter for a herder (who almost never has a flying license and who is a passenger in the seat beside the pilot) involves such things as how low to fly, how hard to 'push' and from what angle to approach a herd to move it in the desired location. The herder must work in three dimensions, and a wrong or too aggressive approach can scatter the deer. Most likely he forms a skilled team together with a pilot who has 'flown many corrallings'. Assuredly, helicopter skill for work with reindeer can be acquired in a variety of practical ways, but for the Sámi in the Jokkmokk mountain area I think it is fair to claim that it grew from its role in the critically timed autumn bull slaughters. The helicopter had been used for the transportation of herders, families and equipment, as a more flexible alternative to the seaplane, long before it was used as a vehicle to drive a herd – something a plane can never do – but it came to be used in this way, as a 'flying dog', for the first time when the bulls had to be corralled in the autumn for pre-rut slaughter. In the old days, large-scale pre-rut slaughter was unlikely, as the bulls were too far west, up in the mountains where there were no roads by which to move the meat into cold storage. Rising hormone values in the bulls makes the window of opportunity for this slaughter very critical. Use of the helicopter provided a way for herders to bring the bulls together swiftly to a mountain corral for slaughter and also to transport the carcasses with speed down to the lowlands where mobile slaughter units waited at the end of the road.

CHAPTER 7

Family Matters

Representation of Swedish Sámi Households at the Turn of the Nineteenth Century

Isabelle Brännlund and Per Axelsson

Western nations have long used censuses to gain detailed information on the people residing within their administrative borders. These demographic records are very informative and are used extensively in decision making and when drawing up policies and projections. At the same time, Benedict Anderson and others have argued that statistical records and the identity categories they create are important devices employed by the colonial state to impose a totalizing, classificatory grid on its territory, allowing claims of total control. This has been displayed as the most basic of powers: a power to name, to categorize and thereby to create social reality (Anderson 1991: 184; Kertzer and Arel 2002: 20, 36; Urla 1993: 837).

Scott (1998) argues that through the application of population statistics, the nation state strives to reduce people into categories that are easy to administer and monitor. A growing body of academic literature convincingly shows how these identity categories are political and social constructions that are neither natural nor objective, but have been treated as a fact within the administration of nation states. Furthermore, these categories shape racial/ethnic discourses. Even if, for instance, indigenous people might have difficulties accepting the statistical portraits that arise from these demographic sources, these categories have affected the identity processes of the groups they seek to describe (Axelsson et al. 2011; Mullaney 2011).

It is not straightforward to undertake indigenous research using censuses. The understanding of a geographic area implicit in demographic material, its listed occupations and the societal structures it references will not necessarily mirror conceptions used by the indigenous people themselves or what is known from the ethnographic or anthropological literature. Questions of identity, classification and representation are crucial within the field of indigenous demography, and scholars within this field face three critical challenges. The first is to deal with and somehow integrate qualitative and quantitative methods and data. The second relates to obtaining a thorough understanding of the relationship between historical and contemporary contexts. The last is to address the differences between the internal understandings of indigenous peoples and the understandings developed by administrators, surveyors and census-takers (Axelsson and Sköld 2011: 4–5).

Bearing these critical challenges in mind, this chapter will make use of a newly digitized demographic source – the Swedish 1900 census (NAPP 2012) – in order to analyse the representation of Swedish Sámi households at the turn of the twentieth century. We triangulate quantitative and qualitative sources to highlight discrepancies in understandings and to identify new ways of analysing the material.

The study is divided into three parts. In Part I, we examine the concept of household in the Swedish population registers in general, and in the 1900 census in particular. We analyse the implications of this discourse by performing a descriptive demographic study using the 1900 census material. In Part II we explore the conceptual relationships between Sámi reindeer-herding households and the traditional Sámi reindeer-herding community *(siida),* and show that the concepts of household and *siida* have many similarities that merit further investigation and elaboration in a demographic context. Finally we use some of the concepts of social organization discussed in Part II and merge qualitative and quantitative sources to discuss the ways in which they depict the social nexus of the Sámi reindeer-herding society.

Our intention is to highlight some of the advantages of using interdisciplinary approaches in studying the demographic history of indigenous peoples. For that reason, this chapter combines traditions by mixing methods and concepts that are both qualitative and quantitative in nature (Johnson and Onwuegbuzie 2004; Johnson, Onwuegbuzie, and Turner 2007). We believe the current chapter will be helpful to scholars interested in using census data, especially those who want to study representations of indigeneity/ethnicity.

Reindeer herding in northern Sápmi

The Sámi are one of the few recognized indigenous peoples of Europe, and the only one in Sweden. Reindeer pastoralism is what most people outside of the Sámi society recognize as the most important characteristic of the Sámi culture and is the focus of this study. However, it is important to underline that Sámi society is and has always been diverse and complex, with other important occupations including hunting, fishing and trade. Reindeer management has never been the sole livelihood of the Sámi and it is estimated that only one tenth of the Sámi people herd reindeer today (Sverige 2005).

This study focuses on the mountain reindeer herding culture in Karesuando and Jukkasjärvi parishes in Sweden. This area has been singled out because of the availability of supplementary sources, which have helped us to highlight the strengths of combining materials. Reindeer pastoralism has been a way of life in this area since at least the sixteenth century, and is defined by individual ownership of the animal and seasonal movements between pastures. The reindeer herders in Karesuando and Jukkasjärvi were nomadic and commonly moved their herds over long distances according to the seasonal cycle. In spring, they would take their herds towards the mountains and down the Norwegian coast, while in autumn the reindeer were reorganized into smaller herds and moved down to the lichen-rich forests in the northernmost inland areas of Sweden.

The pastureland was legally a common resource for all herders to use, but its usage was regulated by cultural institutions within the Sámi community. When the Swedish state introduced the reindeer grazing laws of 1886 and 1889, it connected the administration of Sámi land use to reindeer herding districts *(lappbyar)*. However, the preexisting systems governing land use and work cooperation continued to be applied through the old cultural institutions of the *siida*. The Sámi *siida* served many purposes and has been described in terms of a cultural institution for cooperation, a working relationship (Bjørklund 1990: 80; Nordin 2007: 65), and an 'extended family system' (Kuokkanen 2009: 499). It served to organize and exercise knowledge and control within the herding community and ensured that the workforce, the size and composition of the herd, and the availability and quality of pasture were in balance (Bjørklund 1990; Ingold 1978; Lehtola 2002).

At the turn of the nineteenth century, major changes occurred in Jukkasjärvi parish due to the establishment of the mining industry in Kiruna (founded as a town in 1900). The census data show that due to workforce migration, the Sámi had become a minority within the parish by 1900. In relative terms, Karesuando parish could have been considered a more coherent Sámi area at the time. However, the closure of the Finnish/Russian–Swedish border in 1889 had unfavourable consequences for the local herders, who had traditionally used migration routes and pastures on both sides of the border. Consequently, the closed border reduced the amount of pasture available to them (Brännlund and Axelsson 2011; Turi 1987). In the tables, the registered herders from Karesuando and Jukkasjärvi are included in both the 'Sámi' and 'Reindeer herders in Karesuando/Jukkasjärvi' categories.

Sources

This study is based on a variety of sources, all of which were produced outside the Sámi society. The Swedish 1900 census data has recently been incorporated into one of the most ambitious international databases in existence, the North Atlantic Population Project – an archive of census data for historical populations (Sverige 1900). The Swedish 1900 census data registered individual information on the sex, age, birthplace, place of residence, occupation and 'ethnicity' of all citizens, as well the compositions of their households and the relationships between household members. We have encoded and harmonized the census data to convert it into a standard format that allows for international comparisons.[1] While doing this, we found that markers of ethnicity had been registered in various columns, and that different vicars and parish priests used different terms to denote people of Sámi origin. All ethnic markers were therefore assembled under one Nappdata variable ('origin') and we performed subsequent calculations based on this modified data set.[2]

INDIKO (2012) is a tool to search the POPUM, a database of registered and linked parish records provided by the Demographic Database (DDB) of Umeå University, and provides easy access to a pool of relevant information. For the period after 1900, parish records stored on microfiche were used to complement the digitalized material.[3] The use of these demographic sources made it possible to trace household members in the comparative study discussed at the end of this chapter.

The Swedish–Norwegian Reindeer Grazing Commission report of 1907 was analysed because it contains reports on the compositions of *siida* groups in Jukkasjärvi and Karesuando parishes. The main purpose of the commission was to examine the Swedish reindeer herders' migration routes. The report consists primarily of the responses to 172 questionnaire interviews conducted by state officials with nomadic reindeer-herders and settlers. The interviews record the herders' names and ages, how many reindeer they owned, if they had any hired hands working for them, and with whom they migrated (Renbeteskommissionen af 1907). From these interviews, we were able to identify individual herders and *siida* groups and to compare these data with other demographic sources.

Theories of historical household structure

The field of historical demography has long been devoted to the study of family and household structure. However, although the concepts of hearth and home are commonly discussed within the disciplines of archaeology and anthropology, their conception among circumpolar peoples has been given relatively little attention. As shown by Hammel and Laslett, the concepts are closely related to the family and household.

> That is to say: it was at home, within the house itself, where the family carried out those economic tasks which could not be done in the open air, and these tasks were not few, even in agricultural societies. (Hammel and Laslett 1974: 76)

The principal pioneers within the field of historical demography were French: le Play in the nineteenth century, and Louis Henry in the mid-twentieth century. In the 1960s and early 1970s, the work of two British scholars, John Hajnal at the London School of Economics and Peter Laslett with his group in Cambridge for the Study of Human Population, became the starting point for international comparisons. Laslett in particular worked towards developing an understanding of how the family group had evolved under the pressures of societal and economic change, such as industrialization and urbanization. Much time was invested into further defining what constituted a household. The Cambridge group formulated the null hypothesis that the nuclear family should be considered dominant unless the contrary could be proven. Ever since this hypothesis was proposed, it has stimulated research and debate within the area. Based mainly on English material, the Cambridge group further defined certain types of households: the simple (or nuclear) family household (in its full form comprising a married couple and their children); the extended (or complex) family household (adding other kin to the nuclear family); and the multiple-family household (Kertzer and Barbagli 2002: xxxi; Laslett 1972: 1–89).

In their seminal text, Laslett and Hammel showed awareness of the fact that 'the vocabulary for family and kinship is very differently developed' and that this 'itself betrays different familial structures and attitudes, and invites systematic comparison' (Hammel and Laslett 1974: 74). Furthermore, these authors stress that their theory of household structures has an Anglocentric or Eurocentric bias that cannot be considered valid in a wider international context. Nevertheless, it is clear that the transformation from agriculture to industry was fundamental to the formation of a structure that could be broadly compared in a European context.

The work of Laslett and his colleagues has not gone unchallenged. For example, David Kertzer argued in 1991 that Laslett's early work had been transformed into a new sociological orthodoxy that overshadowed the many various family systems that had existed in preindustrial Europe, and that French scholars had never 'joined this revisionist bandwagon' because they knew France to have a wide diversity of household systems. Kertzer drew on convincing evidence from northern, southern and eastern Europe concerning, for instance, the common occurrence of stem-family households or other forms of complex non-nuclear family systems (Kertzer 1991: 159). Wally Seccombe (1992) has also rejected or added nuance to the Cambridge group's hypothesis, and Martine Segalen (2002) concluded that, as elsewhere, there were ecological and economical constraints that affected residential choices and family formations, and that household patterns in northern Europe varied considerably during the nineteenth century.

The peasant household, and its transformation during the nineteenth century, has been the dominant issue in studies of European households. We argue that this is especially valid when it comes to western European households. The prevalent dichotomy has been that of 'rural–urban' where 'rural' has been considered equivalent to the peasant household. Even though the field of historical demography has continued to develop new concepts and methods, such as 'life event analysis' in the late 1970s, the definitions of household structures stated above have remained intact. These traditional concepts have continued to occupy historical demographers in their quest to elucidate how family systems have changed through history.

This 'rural–agricultural setting' has proven problematic in studies of indigenous demography, as noted by Morphy (2007: 179). Borrowing a metaphor from Adams and Kasakoff (2004), Morphy stated that the categories chosen in western censuses created 'bounded containers' that were poorly suited to highly mobile populations with extensive and overlapping kinship networks connected by 'nodal points in space'. Morphy argued that 'categories are not simply "statistical" but also culturally embedded. It is doubly problematic when categories appropriate to one social reality have been used to obliterate those of another' (Morphy 2007: 179). Although Morphy examined a twenty-first-century Australian census, the same reasoning can be applied in other past and present scenarios. Bearing this in mind, we will now investigate the representations of Sámi households in the Swedish 1900 census.

Part I: Swedish population registers

Swedish censuses of the early twentieth century commented that Sweden was privileged to 'host a very homogeneous population within its borders' but that the 'Lapps and Finns' were the main exceptions to that rule. Census data on 'tribal' peoples was also perceived to be a specific branch of national statistics, in which Sweden had a long history (Sverige 1907: XXXIf). That history goes back to the seventeenth century, when a law that mandated the practice of keeping parish registers was introduced in

1686. The purpose of the church law was to enable clergymen to monitor parishioners' Christian beliefs as well as their moral behaviour and literacy (by means of keeping catechetical records). However, these records also provided the Swedish state with demographic information for purposes of taxation and military service. Ethnic markers such as 'lapp' were not mentioned in the law but can be found in the parish registers from this time on (Axelsson 2010: 266).[4]

In the wake of mercantilism, the Swedish state established 'Tabellverket' in 1749, the world's first continuous national population statistics. The resulting data were non-nominal and based on the parish registers, and were presented at an aggregate level. The primary reason for their establishment was to monitor population growth and to increase the number of farms and farmsteads, since it was believed that this would improve the welfare of Swedish society as a whole and thus help to expand its population. In the Tabellverket of 1760, a category of 'Lapps-prisoners-paupers' was introduced and in 1805, a small section for 'Lapps' appeared on the population form. There were three subcategories: reindeer herders, non-reindeer herders, and itinerants/hired hands (Axelsson 2010: 266–70). However, there was no scope for self-reporting of ethnic identity. Instead, people were assigned to one category or another by the local clergy.

In 1858, the state decided to establish a statistical bureau, Statistics Sweden. When the first official census was taken in 1860, it was done under the auspices of this organization. It is important to note that the Swedish censuses were conducted using methods that were relatively unconventional and markedly different to those used in other countries at the time. There were no census takers travelling the country with a questionnaire, interviewing people in their homes. Instead, the census forms were filled out by vicars and parish priests, in part based on preexisting catechization registers (1860–1890) and parish books (1900–1945). While there was some discussion about performing a de facto census of the entire country in 1860, the parish registers, and especially the catechization registers, were deemed to be reliable sources and were believed to cover almost every aspect of the census forms then used in foreign countries. It was therefore decided that it would be more cost-efficient to use an already established organization that was set up to deal with population statistics (Berg 1857: 6, 46). The cost of the process was discussed in the 1900 census:

> The cost for the whole 1900 census would amount to approximately 70,000 kronor, or less than 1.5 öre per inhabitant of the counted population. Compared to the costs in other countries – for example Norway with 15 öre per inhabitant – the Swedish method of registering the populations appears to be superior in regards to cost-efficiency. (Sverige 1902: ix)

There were also arguments that it would be difficult to find and register Sámi nomads who were moving their herds. Evjen (2011) has noted that this was also a concern for Norwegian census takers. The great majority of Norwegian reindeer herders with winter pastures in Sweden were away when the Norwegian census was taken and were therefore excluded from enumeration.

The household concept and the Swedish census of 1900

The instructions given to the clergy when they registered households in the Swedish 1900 census read as follows:

> a) Within the column called 'Household or consumption unit' persons belonging to the same household or consumption unit should be kept together with a bracket and a one (1) before each person. People living by themselves should only be marked with a one (1). …
>
> d) The list of persons should contain the full name of every person, with the given name before or after the last name according to the custom in the parish book. There should also be a note about the person's position within the family, for example wife, son, daughter, the husband's son in his first marriage etcetera. Appropriate abbreviations may be used. (Sverige 1907)

The instructions indicate that the parish book was used as the model for registration and that the traditions of registration used in the parish provided relevant answers regarding the customs of registering persons in a household. The instructions in the church law of 1894, on how to enlist a household, state as a rule that if a son or daughter living in their parents' household marries, 'a new family will be separately enlisted from the old family, even if the families share a dwelling' (Beskow 1894: 31).

Consequently, when examining the 1900 census data, it can be difficult to determine whether two or more families share the same dwelling. Moreover, the use of the word 'family' rather than 'household' in the statement that 'There should also be a note about the person's position within the family' indicates that the concepts of family and household may have been considered to be intertwined and that it may therefore be difficult to make a clear distinction between them when analysing the census. The officials working on the 1900 census affirmed the household as 'the basis for society' and much effort was spent comparing household formations between different geographical areas and over time (Sverige 1902: xxii). When Statistics Sweden commented on the results of the 1900 enumeration, they gave more information about their concept of a 'household'.

> The people who form the household or the consumption unit *[matlag]* are the actual family members, parents, children and other relatives. Hired hands, assistants or servants whether employed for the family for domestic work or for busi-

ness, should be included in the household if they usually live together and receive their daily bread from the head of the family. (Sverige 1907: xxi)

It appears as if the household was considered a closed unit where the members depended on the head of the family to provide for them. We now examine the implications of these conceptions of the household by performing a statistical demographic study of household structures using the 1900 census.

Sámi households in the Swedish 1900 census

In this section, we present results based on the 1900 Census of Sweden, using the concepts defined by its administrators. We find that Sweden had around 5.2 million inhabitants registered at the turn of the twentieth century, of whom almost 7,000 were recorded to be of Sámi descent. We identified a total of 1,903 Sámi and 1,415,813 non-Sámi households listed. The average household size among both Sámi and non-Sámi was 3.6 persons. However, the reindeer herders were recorded to have slightly larger households, averaging 3.8 persons.

As shown by Table 7.1, the 1900 census listed more multiple-family households (identified here as extended, multiple and full households) within non-Sámi society than within the Sámi community. Such households were even more common among the non-Sámi residents of the studied parishes – Karesuando and Jukkasjärvi.

Households have been characterized as having divided responsibilities for decision making and control over property and capital. One cannot be certain that the person reported as the head of the household was the one in whom control was actually vested (Posel 2001: 652). However, the notion of household representatives speaks to the conception of household

Table 7.1 *1900 census data on household structure*

	Ethnicity		
	Non-Sami	Sami	*Reindeer-herders in Karesuando/Jukkasjärvi
Individuals	5,193,264	6,847	1,375
Total number of households	1,415,813	1,903	357
Multiple-family households	258,927 (18.3%)	210 (11.0%)	26 (7%)

Source: Sweden 1900. Census available at www.nappdata.org
* The category is not withdrawn from the Sámi group.

Table 7.2 *Male/female head of household by ethnicity*

	Ethnicity		
	Non-Sami	Sami	* Reindeer-herders in Karesuando/Jukkasjärvi
Female	317,369 (22%)	429 (25%)	72 (20%)
Male	1,098,365 (78%)	1,474 (75%)	285 (80%)
Unknown/ Missing value	79	0	0
Total	1,415,813	1,903	357

Source: Sweden 1900. Census available at www.nappdata.org
* The category is not withdrawn from the Sámi group.

leadership among officials at the time. As Table 7.2 indicates, a male was recorded as the head of the household in the vast majority of cases for all groups. In this respect, there are only slight differences between the groups.

We know from earlier studies that the ethnicity registered in the 1930 census was strictly gendered. If a woman registered as Sámi married a Swede, she was to be removed from the Sámi category. However, this was not the case for Sámi men (Lundmark 2002). This method was clearly stated in the Swedish 1930 census but we are unable to find it the instructions for the 1900 census. We are therefore unable to tell if the instructions of 1930 simply reflect the institutionalization of a preexisting 'modus operandi' or if it was a new regulation that would have new effects on the census data. If this procedure did date back to 1900, it would mean that women previously registered as Sámi or widowers to non-Sámi husbands would have been registered in the 1900 census as heads of 'non-Sámi' households. Another interesting factor that merits elaboration is the effect of the 1864 law that gave legal majority to unmarried or widowed women in Sweden (Hirdman 1992: 110f.; Widerberg 1980: 70f.). A longitudinal study could trace what effects this 1864 law had on the registration of household heads and the mode of registration of Sámi ethnicity among women.

The census states that the single householder was the most common household, both for the registered Sámi and non-Sámi citizens, as well as for the selected reindeer-herding communities. Table 7.3 shows that among the different groups, single householders accounted for between 20.8 per cent and 26.5 per cent of the households in the census.

Households with between one and four persons accounted for more than half of the total households in all of the groups, while households

Table 7.3 *Number of individuals in households, non-Sámi, Sámi and reindeer-herders, Sweden 1900*

				Ethnicity					
	Non Sami			Sami			*Reindeer-herders in Karesuando/Jukkasjärvi		
House-hold size	Number of households	Percent	Cumulative Percent	Number of households	Percent	Cumulative Percent	Number of households	Percent	Cumulative Percent
1	374,047	26.4	26.4	504	26.5	26.5	74	20.8	20.8
2	214,884	15.2	41.6	269	14.1	40.6	49	13.8	34.6
3	195,985	13.8	55.4	242	12.7	53.3	47	13.2	47.8
4	173,106	12.2	67.7	241	12.7	66	51	14.3	62.1
5	142,639	10.1	77.7	196	10.3	76.3	41	11.5	73.6
6	111,119	7.8	85.6	171	9	85.3	49	13.8	87.4
7	81,872	5.8	91.4	108	5.7	91	20	5.6	93
8	54,053	3.8	95.2	84	4.4	95.4	17	4.8	97.8
9	32,474	2.3	97.5	50	2.6	98	7	2	99.7
10>	35,633	2.5	100	38	2	100	1	0.3	100
Total	1,415,813	100		1903	100		356	100	

Source: Sweden 1900. Census available at www.nappdata.org
* The category is not withdrawn from the Sámi group.

with more than six persons represented less than 10 per cent of the total household units. When examining the size and composition of the households, we find no major differences between the Sámi and non-Sámi groups. Among the reindeer herders, we see slightly fewer single householders, and the highest proportion (40 per cent) of households being registered as having four to six people. Among the non-Sámi group, households of this size accounted for 30 per cent of the total.

Tables 7.1–7.3 show that there are no significant differences between the groups in the census, even though their livelihoods were seemingly diverse. This raises the question of why there should be no difference. Although it might simply be that there were in fact no differences, this seems unlikely given the social and cultural diversity that existed between the groups. An alternative explanation might be that the household concept, as assumed and defined within the enumeration procedures, actually fostered this uniform outcome.

By combining qualitative material with the 1926/7 Soviet Polar Census, David G. Anderson has convincingly shown how social networks among Evenki reindeer herders stretched beyond the demographic unit of the household (Anderson 2011b). It is therefore necessary to investigate more closely the nature of reindeer management, while focusing on the social structure that surrounds and supports it. We will analyse the concept of household and *siida* using the analytical framework formulated by Wilk and Rathje (1982). According to these authors, the household can be defined as a social component that exists to meet the productive, distributive and reproductive needs of its members. This corresponds to definitions of the Sámi household proposed by previous researchers (Nordin 2007; Paine 1970). The analysis of households can be further refined to focus on three aspects: (1) the behavioural (i.e. activities performed by the group); (2) the material (i.e. the residence and also the area of activity and the possessions of the members); and (3) the social (i.e. the demographic composition of the household, its number of members, and the relationships between them) (Wilk and Rathje 1982: 618).

Part II: The household and *siida* compared

By relating the household and *siida* to the behavioural, social and material elements defined by Wilk and Rathje (1982), we can see in Table 7.4 how the two concepts are connected to two different aspects of reindeer management: herding and husbandry.[5]

The household was the area for husbandry activities. Questions concerning slaughter and castration, and the physical condition of individual reindeer, were discussed and enacted within the household (Nordin 2007;

Table 7.4 *Aspects of social organization*

	Household	Siida
Behaviour	Husbandry	Herding
Social	Family	Extended family
Material resources	Reindeer herd	Authority over pastureland

Fellman 1910; Beach 1981). The household was primarily concerned with 'the growth of herd capital and the formation of profit' (Paine 1970: 53) whereas activities within the *siida* focused on aspects of herding, i.e. 'the control of nurture of animals in the terrain' (Paine 1970: 53). Questions concerning pasture utilization, migration and the guarding of the herd were resolved jointly within the *siida* (Beach 1981; Fellman 1910; Nordin 2007). The *siida* also served to organize and exercise knowledge and control within the herding community. It was used to resolve conflicts relating to land and water rights and to ensure that a balance was maintained between people (workforce and consumers), reindeer and pasture (Bjørklund 1990; Ingold 1978; Lehtola 2002).

The average reindeer-herding household consisted of a set of family members, and the presence of persons unrelated by blood or marriage within a household was rare. This is consistent with the findings obtained from the quantitative analysis of households discussed in Part I. The formation of a new household, adulthood, marriage, and holding the status of a sovereign herder were all interrelated. Adult status was rarely obtained prior to marriage and manifested itself when a person could make independent decisions about their own reindeer (Fellman 1910; Nordin 2007; Paine 1970; Sara 2002). Although a married couple with young children could use hired hands to help with daily chores, these were never considered to be part of the household on the same terms as family members. The same applies to hired workers who only stayed with the household for a short time during the most labour-intensive part of the season (Nordin 2007; Whitaker 1955).

Research on the Sámi *siida* has suggested that the composition of the grouping depended on several factors, of which the most crucial were the sizes of the herds and households, and also the nature of the pastureland. A *siida* commonly consisted of more than one household, although in some cases a single household could manage their herd separately. Kinship played a vital role in the formation of *siida* groups, which usually comprised parents, children, siblings and cousins (Bergman et al. 2008; Bjørklund 1990; Ingold 1978). The Sámi society has been described as having a tradition of equal status between women and men in various areas (Kuokkanen 2009). *Siida* groups and households could be formed on both the mothers' and fathers' side (Ingold 1978; Whitaker 1955).

The importance of kinship in the formation of *siidas* opened up opportunities in selecting pasture areas, working groups and social contexts. The husband usually represented a household in the *siida* when decisions were to be made, while an older, skilled and competent herdsman with many reindeer and kinsmen typically held an informal leadership within the *siida* (Ingold 1978). Even though a *siida* could consist of the same households over many years, it often regrouped depending on the season. The system was dynamic in nature and usually changed over time, with households often having alternatives available to them and never being obliged to stay within the same *siida*.

Each household had material, social and cultural resources. The reindeer herd and the rights to use traditional pasturelands and fishing waters were particularly important material resources. These were passed on from one generation to the next and were constantly developed, changed and adapted over time. The right to inheritance separated family from other persons in the household, such as hired hands. Within the household, members had their own individual reindeer, which bore the owner's mark. At an early age children acquired their own reindeer, which they tended as an important part of their training. The reindeer herd however, belonged to the household, together with the tent and all the tools needed to carry out the full range of daily tasks (Nordin 2007; Paine 1970). Newly married couples often quickly established their own household, including their own separate tent and kitchen supplies (Nordin 2007; Whitaker 1955). Even though the custom was for every household to have its own tent, they were often shared with other kin, an elderly parent or an unmarried sibling (Whitaker 1955). The *siida* held formal authority over the pasturelands. While the *siida* lands were not owned in the Western sense of property ownership, every *siida* had traditional pasturelands defined by borders that were respected within the community (Korpijaakko-Labba 1994). Disputes between individual reindeer owners over land and water resources were resolved within the *siida,* and the group's strong connection to the land fostered a stability and continuity within the *siida* system that complemented its fairly flexible and informal structure (Sara 2002).

Merging qualitative and quantitative sources

This section demonstrates the scope and limitations of using qualitative and quantitative material simultaneously, by analysing different aspects of households and *siida* groups. We illustrate the discussion in Figure 7.1 in order to clarify the results.

The Reindeer Grazing Commission report of 1907 contains writings about households and *siida* groups in separate parts of Sápmi. By reviewing the report, we were able to identify a *siida* belonging to Könkämä lappby, in Karesuando parish. Two male reindeer herders were questioned about various aspects of their work, and we interpreted the record of their responses. Elisa Persson Hurri,[6] a 38-year-old herder from Könkämä lappby, stated that during both winter and summer he always moved his reindeer together with Jon Nilsson Kitti from Könkämä lappby. Kitti, at 57 years of age, was the elder of the company and he was also registered as the foreman of the herders in the ninth district.[7] Kitti left detailed information about the *siida*'s lands and herding activities. For example, he stated that the *siida* moved down to the lands near Karesuando village at Christmas time. If the winters were harsh, with ice and hard snow crusts on the pastureland, the *siida* stayed in this area throughout the winter. In good years, however, they continued southeast down to Muonionalusta near the Finnish border. We found no information on the size of Kitti's household, but he declared that they owned 150 reindeer. Hurri's household, on the other hand, apparently contained at least three members (brothers or sisters), since Hurri reported that he and his siblings owned 250 reindeer (Renbeteskommissionen af 1907).

Since the report contains no information on any other members of the two households (and thus of the *siida*), we were unable to obtain information on the demographic composition of the group. Neither were we able to get any insight into the husbandry decisions enacted by the households, since these questions were not of interest to the commission. This is generally the case for historical official state material regarding Sámi

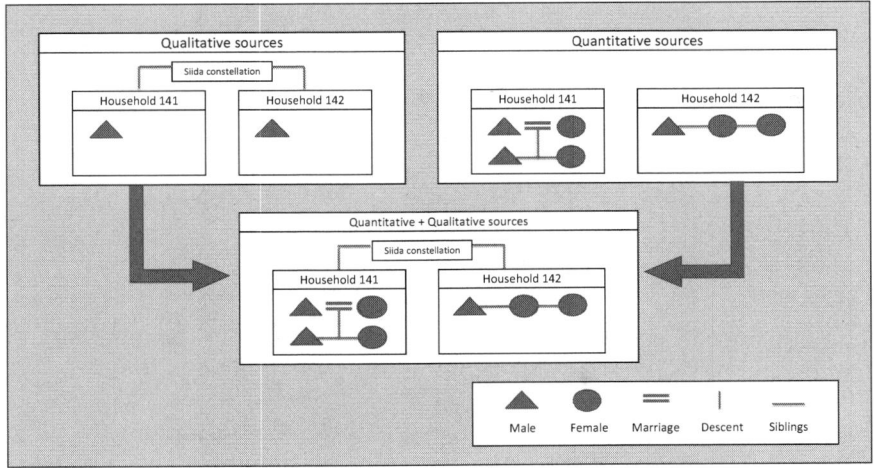

Figure 7.1 *The* siida *constellation.*

issues in Sweden: most sources record land use and migration patterns, since the state was primarily interested in land use in relation to the settled population, or in transnational migration between the Nordic countries.

By identifying Elisa Persson Hurri and Jon Nilsson Kitti in other demographic sources, namely the 1900 census and the parish records for Karesuando between 1896 and 1910, we were able to gain information that was not available in the interview responses. By searching in the parish records and censuses, we were able to identify the dates of birth of an Elisa Persson Hurri and a Jon Nilsson Kitti in years corresponding to the reported ages of the interviewed herders. In the 1900 census, Jon Nilsson Kitti (born in 1851) was registered in a household in Rommavuoma lappby together with his wife and their two children. Hurri was listed as the youngest child of a family and had three siblings – two sisters and one brother. His mother had passed away that same year and his eldest brother was recorded as the head of the household in the census. At the time of the interview in 1907, the eldest brother was no longer listed in the household index and Hurri had taken his place as the head of the household (UUL 1896–1910 A23486: 3; Sverige 1900).

By combining the sources, we were able to identify a *siida* consisting of two households, one nuclear family and one family of siblings, to form a company of seven people that moved and worked together throughout the year. Using the demographic record alone, there would have been no way to identify the extent of any cooperation between these households. However, by tracing such information in other records, we were able to learn much more about household structure than would have been possible by considering qualitative sources alone (UUL 1896–1910 A23486: 4; Sverige 1900).

Tracing kinship in a siida

Using the interviews conducted by the Reindeer Grazing Commission of 1907, we identified a larger *siida* consisting of four households. Nils Olsson Partapuoli aged 51, Jon Persson Omma aged 69, Nils (senior) Persson Nutti aged 64, and Per Persson Parffa aged 36 stated that they moved together as a group through both Norway and Sweden and that their reindeer were kept together (Renbeteskommissionen af 1907). All of these men were originally from Saariovuoma lappby in Jukkasjärvi parish. They did not share a family name and therefore did not appear to be related by familial ties. In both the census and the parish records, their households were listed separately. However, the demographic sources indicated a possible connection between three of the households. The wives of Partapuoli, Omma and Parffa all had the same maiden name in the 1900 census. By using the POPUM database and its INDIKO search tool, we were able to determine that Parffa's first wife, Margaretha Tomasdotter Skum, was recorded as the sister of Partapuoli's wife, Karin Maria Tomasdotter Skum. Margaretha Tomasdotter Skum passed away in 1902 and Parffa was remarried two years later to Ella Omma, the daughter of Jon Persson Omma (UUL 1900–1910 A26263: 9, 8). Demographic sources have enabled us to identify a *siida* connected by sisterhood and the tie between father and daughter. Although the formation of *siidas* using female familial linkages has been described by previous scholars, it has not previously been analysed using demographic sources (Nordin 2007: 65f.). It is evident that qualitative and quantitative materials reveal different aspects of family and household structures and have different strengths and limitations. As Figure 7.1 shows, combining multiple sources can change established pictures of household structure.

Concluding remarks: challenges and possibilities

In this chapter we have highlighted discrepancies in discourses concerning households and shown their implications in a demographic study. One could argue that the presentation of Sámi households in the 1900 census mirrors the conceptions of households within a Sámi reindeer-herding context (consisting of a single family unit). However, we believe that the census provides a representation of simple family households (Laslett 1972: 1–89) detached from the crucial wider context of social organization: the *siida*. The household in pastoral societies was not a closed production and consumption unit. Instead, as argued by Morphy (2007), we see the concepts of household used and applied in the 1900 census as a 'bounded container' that does not represent the social, economic and cultural organization within Sámi reindeer-herding society.

We have shown that in the context of reindeer pastoralism in the north of Sápmi, the household was not considered a solitary socio-economic unit but was seen as an important part of the *siida*. As a unique form of social organization, the *siida* had no counterpart in Swedish society. While there were some cases in which Imperial Russian census data perhaps better reflect pastoral society, this does not appear to have ever happened in Sweden (Anderson 2011c). This could be attributed to a lack of interest from the state in capturing the social organization within the Sámi community in the census, or to a lack of knowledge concerning the functioning of pastoral society. We believe that officials were unable to translate and understand the concept of a *siida*; had they done so, they may have found it interesting and worthy of being registered. We identified three major discrepancies between the household and the *siida* as methods of social organization. These relate to informal hierarchies, multiple providers and dynamic structures.

The structure of the *siida* relied on both cooperation and control, with informal leadership and unevenly distributed authority. However, the households were autonomous and there was not one official 'head of the household' to which all other persons were related. Conversely, in the Swedish nuclear-family household, there was only one person with the legal status of majority – the husband. If a son remained in the household until he reached adulthood, he would still be related to his father until the father could no longer provide for the family. The concept of 'a single provider' for the household also appears to have been important to the officials. This was certainly not the case within the *siida,* where every household was the master of its own reindeer herd.[8]

Finally, the dynamic structure of the *siida* was not reflected in the Swedish notion of a household. The census provides no information on how temporary hired hands were regarded. However, it would be interesting to use demographic sources to analyse the loose outer boundaries of the household, in which certain people had partial membership for short periods of time. The *siida's* lands were also dynamic and did not have a counterpart in the society of the majority. Referring again to the opening Laslett quotation, 'at home' was not merely 'the house' in a nomadic reindeer-herding context; home was also the land over which they moved, which in some cases stretched from the Norwegian to the Baltic Sea. Home included the mountains, fjords, boreal forests, swamps and lakes. During the course of a year, the household gathered a number of different social constellations, and its composition in terms of family, household, kin and hired hands was fluid and subject to change.

It seems easy to pass judgement on demography or demographic sources for trying to capture a 'reality' that is impossible to confine, and to criticize the Swedish administrators' understanding of the socio-economic organization of Sámi reindeer herding. The census was basically performed using a preprinted form at the desk of a clergyman, who 'decided' the ethnicity of his parishioners. When the census form was drawn up, it was not constructed to fit the idea of a Sámi *siida*. Although it has not been proven in this chapter, we believe that the economic unit under scrutiny was probably a farmer and (his) household. This might explain why we ended up with similar results for household composition in rather different groups.

In keeping with the conclusions of Anderson (2011b), we found that the *siida* is not very evident in census material. However, by using qualitative sources from the early twentieth century we were able to distinguish *siida* groups and the sizes of reindeer herds at the household level. The picture of the households and *siida* changed when information from the demographic sources was added, and we believe this is an interesting way to analyse the historical material. However, we have identified some problematic issues using this method. If the demographic material is used to gain information about members of reindeer-herding households, one must consider the dynamics and loose outer boundaries of social organizations within the herding community. Taking an example from our own study, we do not know whether the two sisters listed in the household together with Elisa Persson Hurri in 1907 were the only people included in 'the reindeer-herding household', i.e. the only ones who shared the reindeer herd. It is entirely possible that a sibling might have moved away from the family to earn a living elsewhere. A longitudinal study of the household over time could help to answer these questions. Furthermore, focusing exclusively on kin linkages when analysing *siida* structures might place excessive emphasis on such relationships, overshadowing other vital aspects of *siida* formations.

Even though we have revealed certain weaknesses embedded in the demographical material, we want to underline the possibilities that are presented by the digitized Swedish population statistics. The censuses and parish records undertaken by the clergy were meant to include the entire Swedish population. The material gives researchers a chance to make comprehensive surveys and to perform regional, local and longitudinal studies of individual data. Because censuses are based on nominative extracts from the ecclesiastical registers, they can further be linked to longitudinal datasets such as the Demographic Database at Umeå University, thereby offering the ability to investigate tendencies and processes. The census provides exceptional information that cannot be obtained from qualitative sources since it identifies men, women, children, the elderly and infants, and records their mutual relationships. With the help of demographic data, we can portray families and households, study migration patterns, or analyse the proportion of elderly individuals in a society.

Notes

1. The work with encoding the 1890 and 1900 censuses was funded by 'Encoding and linking Swedish Censuses (SweCens)' VR – Swedish Research Council. Dnr 2010-5921.
2. Further documentation on the Swedish 1900 census and the ethnicity variable can be found here: http://www.riksarkivet.se/default.aspx?id=26406&refid=26414.
3. UUL 1900–1910. Archival classmarks: Jukkasjärvi AIIa: 1 1900–1910 A26263: 8–9; UUL 1896–1910 Karesuando 1896-1910 AIIa: 1 A23486: 3–4.
4. The increasing focus on monitoring the Christianizing of the Sámi become evident in 1746 when the first Sámi parish (Lappförsamling) was formed (Axelsson 2010).
5. For a discussion of the concepts of herding and husbandry see Paine (1970).
6. We have decided to use the full names of the people as they appear in the commission reports. This was done to highlight the individuals discussed in the texts, which is often neglected in demographic work.
7. The summer pastures on the Norwegian side of the border were divided into pasture districts in 1883. This regulation reduced the herders' flexibility in terms of pasture utilization. It

also stated that the herders in the same district were collectively responsible for 'damage' the reindeer caused to land belonging to the settled population.

8. One can also question how well this statement applies to agricultural households, but that is not the focus of this chapter.

CHAPTER 8

The Life Histories of Intergenerational Households in Northern Norway 1865–1900

Gender and Household Leadership

Hilde L. Sommerseth

Since the early 1970s, there has been a broad consensus among family historians that the nuclear family was the dominant way that people organized themselves in western Europe and the United States. These historians assumed that when the children grew up and became independent they would establish their own 'independent' households.[1] They thought that the elderly would continue to live in their own homes as long as their health permitted. Then, when the aged were too frail to remain independent, they were thought to be 'reincorporated' back into the household of one of their adult children (Laslett and Wall 1972; Laslett 1977; Hareven 1982; 1994; Kertzer and Laslett 1995; Alter, Cliggett, and Urbiel 1996, Guinnane 1996). These definitions of 'independent households' and of the 'headship' perhaps say more about the dominant social and political models of how society should be constructed and less about the way that actual historical people structured their lives.

This chapter is based upon the detailed survey of several different types of historical records of rural households in the two most Northerly districts of Norway. These Arctic districts, which hosted a mixed Sámi, Norwegian and Kven (Finnish immigrant) population, at times seem to confirm some of the assumptions of what came to be known as the 'nuclear reincorporation theory'. However, the same records suggest a number of paradoxes, which both make these northern householders exceptions to these general rules, and go further in challenging the assumptions of these models. In this chapter I will analyse detailed census data from the region, as well as reconstructed household registry data, to show the overlapping concerns that may have motivated Norwegian and Sámi people to gradually change the way that they structured their households at the start of the twentieth century.

These data suggest that rather than seeing themselves as 'independent', families in northern Norway used a variety of different strategies to guarantee the continuity of their farms across generations. In line with the chapters in the volume, one could say that often the data show the continuity of 'homes' rather than the rise and fall of independent households. However, the continuity of 'homes' did not necessarily mean co-residing with kin. Towards 1900 we see a significant increase in elderly people registered as lodgers in households with other people to whom they were not related. Further, I will use qualitative data on pensions and property law to query the 'direction' in which incorporations occurred when the older generation was recorded as being co-resident with the younger generation. The unique history of peasant pensions and informal mutual aid in this region suggests that, if multigenerational households were disbanded and reformed, often it was a child and their family that moved back in with the parents, rather than the other way around.

These data also suggest that gendered divisions of labour and patrilineal biases in the legal structure better explain why men continued to serve as the heads of intergenerational stem families in their senior years. These observations are reinforced by differing gendered population structures between the coastal Sámi and Norwegian populations. In contrast to the ideal of a nuclear household, gendered roles are shown to be a stronger predictor of household structure such that, for example, an unmarried daughter would assume the labour of a deceased matron – again reaffirming the local priority on maintaining the homestead. The chapter suggests that while it may be meaningful to search for nuclear families in these data, it is necessary to interpret the numbers carefully to detect local nuances, at least in these northern Arctic districts.

The region examined in this chapter is the northern corner of Troms *fylke* (district) and the district of Finnmark, abbreviated here as the NTF region. This region is located at the very north-eastern tip of Norway against the Barents Sea and well above the Arctic Circle. The population in this area is primarily Norwegian and Sámi, although there are large pockets of a Finnish speaking population, the Kvens. In line with Scandinavian legal practice, the Sámi populations are often divided into nomadic reindeer Sámi populations and sedentary coastal Sámi populations. In 1865 the population of this diverse region was about 31,000 people. By the turn of the century the population had nearly doubled. Despite a significant migration to the area because of its easy access to property and free admittance to fisheries, it was a birth surplus that was the main cause of population growth between 1865 and 1900 (Drivenes et al. 1994: 88–104). Although there are some difficulties in assigning ethnicity to households at this time,[2] it is reasonable to assume that one third of the population was Sámi during the three censuses of 1865, 1875

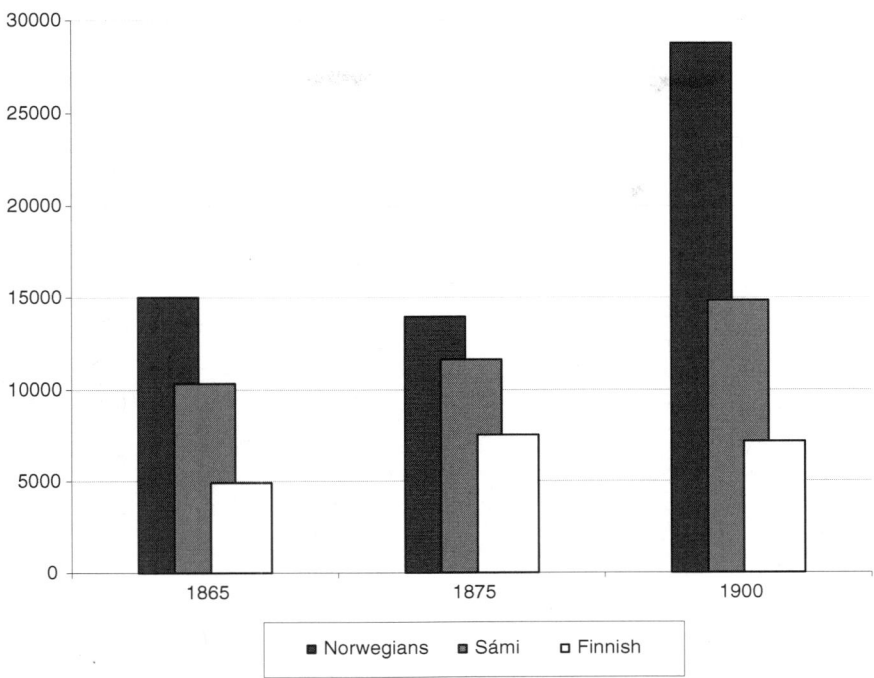

Figure 8.1 *Absolute numbers of inhabitants in the NTF region, according to the 1865, 1875 and 1900 population censuses, by ethnic group.*

and 1900 (and that of these roughly two-thirds were coastal Sámi).[3] The proportion of the Norwegians in the population tended to increase from 48 per cent to 55 per cent during the period (Figure 8.1).

The most common economic strategy in the region was a combination of fishing and farming (Bratrein 1992: 217–26). The family fed itself by raising domestic animals and by catching fish from local stocks. Most households kept on average one cow, some sheep, and in some cases one goat, pig or reindeer which provided milk and meat. The participation in the seasonal fisheries for cod was used primarily to generate cash to allow the purchase of goods. It is important to note that these economic spheres were strictly divided by gender in most households. Women were expected to take responsibility for the subsistence farming and for domestic tasks while men fished both locally and in the lucrative seasonal fishery. The gendered division of labour was not as strict, however, in Sámi households where women might also be responsible for local subsistence fishing while the men went out on the seasonal fisheries along the coast (Niemi 1983). The gendered division of labour on these homesteads was so strong that, as we shall see, many thought a household could not

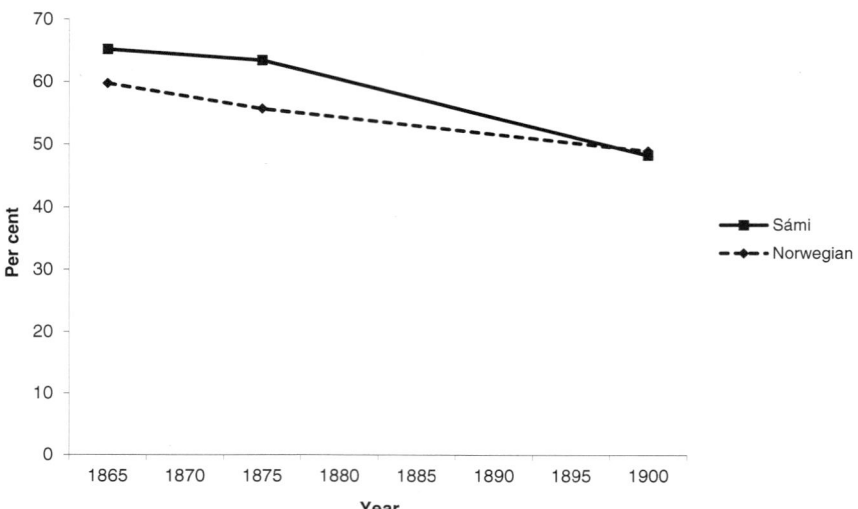

Figure 8.2 *The percentage of elderly people residing with their own adult child, by ethnic affiliation and census year. NTF region, 1865–1900 (population censuses from 1865, 1875 and 1900. Minnesota Population Centre, Norwegian Historical Data Centre (NHDC), Digital Archives, NAPP).*

survive without a woman present. The need for a women in the house, I will argue, heavily influenced inheritance and marriage strategies, and therefore the structure of the household.

Geographically, fishing was most pronounced in coastal settlements, while agriculture came to be more important as one moved inland along the more fertile fjords. Away from the coast, most settlements could be found along rivers and lakes where people would fish for salmon, care for goats and sheep, or herd reindeer (Falch 1994; Storli 1996; Berg 2001; Hansen and Olsen 2004; Gauslaa 2007). Salmon fishing was primarily a Sámi activity (Solbakk 2007). Farm animals were raised by all three ethnic groups: Norwegians, Sámis and Kvens. Towards the end of the nineteenth century, many men in some specific municipalities could also find work in mining (Drivenes et al. 1994: 285–94). However, the consensus among historians is that the majority of the population never gave up their traditional fisherman–farmer economy. Mining just became part of a diversified household economy (Drivenes 1985: 153; Drivenes et al. 1994: 293).

Despite these long-term continuities in economic strategy and in geographic specializations, the data suggest that towards the end of the nineteenth century people began to reorganize their households. Gradually, fewer and fewer elderly people resided with their own adult children. This change is illustrated in Figure 8.2. Until 1875 approximately two-thirds of all elderly Sámi resided with an adult child, which was higher than for Norwegians. However, by 1900 fewer than half of the elderly in both populations lived in so-called intergenerational households. Although it is difficult to find an unambiguous reason for this sharp change, an analysis of the census data and other sources suggests that by 1900 a lucrative market in fish weakened the interest of the youth in maintaining the farm, and thus the intergenerational household that was its heart.

The data for this study come primarily from digitized census records which are available online from the North Atlantic Population Project (NAPP).[4] With reference to three censuses, I analysed records for 6,707 individuals aged 60 years or older who were or had been married (assuming that elderly people who had never been married could not reside with their own children). These households were defined as multigenerational if the elder blood relative (60 years or older) lived with a younger family member aged 18 or older. Despite being highly detailed, these separate records of individuals across three different censuses cannot be easily linked, although work is continuing on this.[5] Therefore many of my generations have been constructed as so-called 'synthetic cohorts' wherein the rules defining each age-cohort in each census is the same, but each census shows an array of different, unlinked individuals (Palmore and Gardner 1994: 36). To compensate for the lack of longitudinal data, I examine some typical life-courses of some 20 households where the census records were linked together by cross-referencing archived baptismal, marriage and burial records.[6]

The question of 'independent households'

Most European census data assume the existence of independent households, and the Norwegian censuses are no exception. The unit of analysis in all three censuses was the household. Enumerators were instructed to number each household (Norge 1872: xxx). Every household member was then designated by their relationship to each other with labels such as 'Housefather, Wife, Son, Daughter, Parents, Servants, Boarders, Visitors, etc' (Figure 8.3).[7] According to the instructions, the labels were supposed to reflect a person's position relative to the head of the household. These protocols were reasonably consistent for all three censuses.

The fact that people were assumed to live in independent households by the state is not unusual. A model of a state made up of settled and fixed households makes it easier for a government to understand its resources and to formulate policies. However, people might have a different way of perceiving this situation. As Brännlund and Axelsson discuss in their chapter in this volume, nomadic Sámi who travelled across national

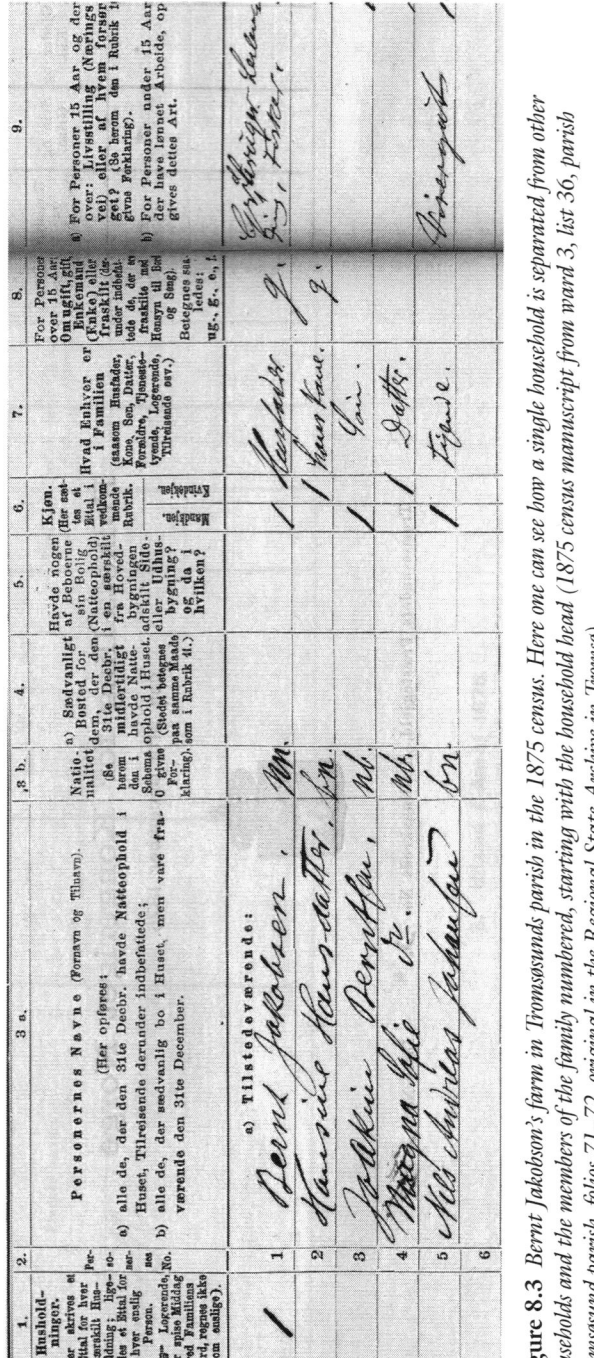

Figure 8.3 *Bernt Jakobson's farm in Tromsøsunds parish in the 1875 census. Here one can see how a single household is separated from other households and the members of the family numbered, starting with the household head (1875 census manuscript from ward 3, list 36, parish Tromsøsund parish, folios 71–72, original in the Regional State Archive in Tromsø).*

borders often challenged these tidy schemes and appeared on paper as paradoxes or outliers. Within farming communities, local strategies might be focused on how to ensure that a farm continues to be viable and thus reflect not an independent household but one that is rolling between generations.

Family historians are aware of the difficulties of assuming that household forms are universal, and have developed a body of theory to account for dynamism and change in human relationships which are reflected in static census records. For example, Kertzer (1995) developed the 'nuclear reincorporation theory', which argued that it was logical to assume that adult children would move out of their parental home once they married, creating two independent households. However, these two households would collapse together again when one of the parents lost their spouse, or when they, for various reasons, were disabled. It this event, he assumed, they were reincorporated back into the household of one of their adult children.

The 'economic development theory', developed by Steven Ruggles (2007), argued, by contrast, that non-nuclear, multigenerational households were the norm in pre-industrial societies. He argued that before economies became commoditized, the older and younger generations were economically dependent on each other. As industrialization and urbanization created new markets, the younger generation was able to break away from their dependence on their parents, leading to the dissolution of intergenerational households (Ruggles 2007: 984–7).

Both theories identify nuclear families as the norm, but one stresses demographic and the other socio-economic circumstances to explain their dynamics. I will argue that the dramatic change captured by the census data in 1900 from the NTF region tends to favour the second theory, but I will question if the newfound economic opportunities really gave the young as much freedom as Ruggles implies. Further, I will show that in order to explain the statistics from earlier periods we have to look more carefully at gendered structures of labour within the multigenerational family.

Norwegian family historians have tended to focus on the multigenerational family, which seems to have persisted much longer in Norway than in other countries in Europe. Many scholars have focused on a family form known as a 'stem family', which was considered rare across western Europe. The concept of a stem family originates with the work of the French social scientist Frédéric Le Play (1806–1882), who defined *la famille souche* (stem family) as a system in which at least one married child remained with their parents (Silver 1982: 261; Jåstad 2011c). On a national level, the 1801 census shows that every tenth household was organized as a stem family, and that 27 per cent of farmers preferred this

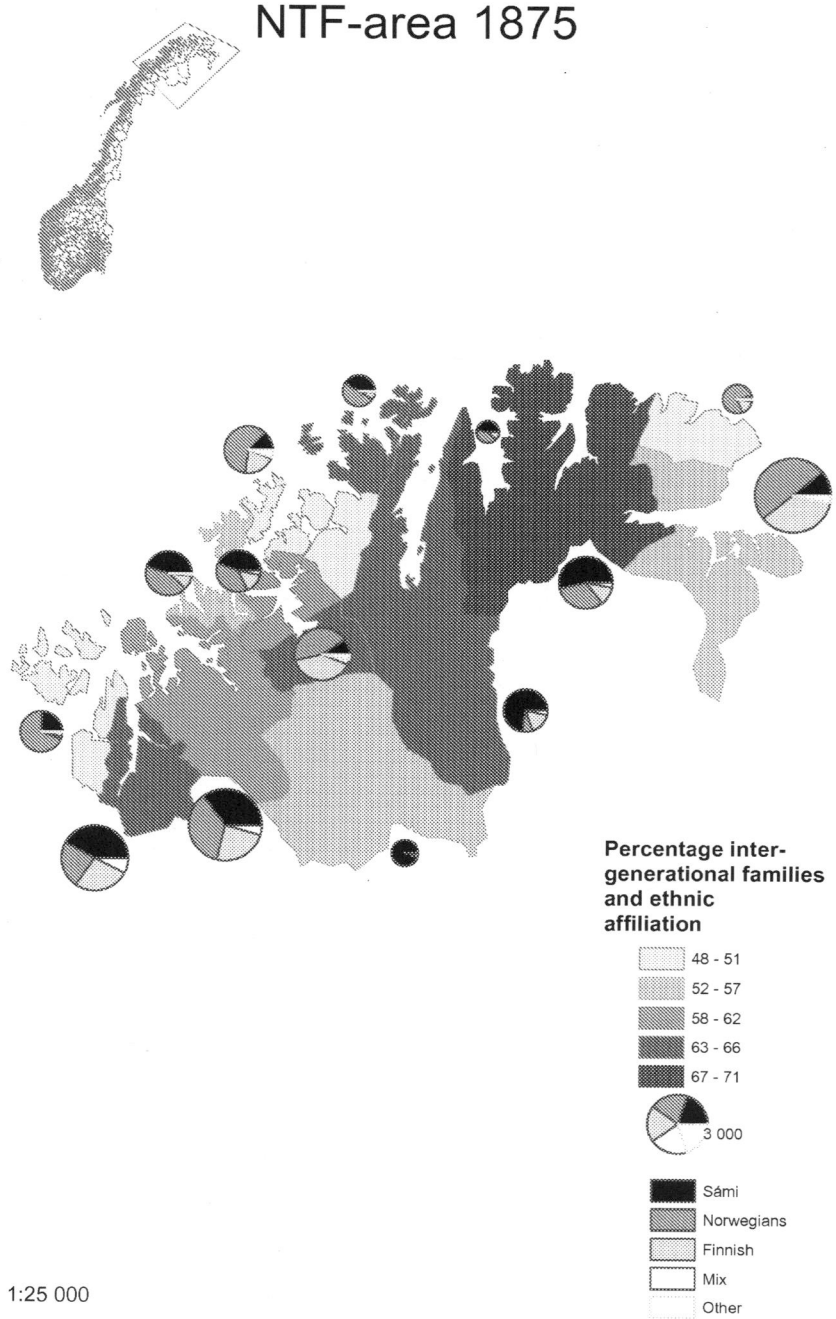

Figure 8.4 *The percentage of intergenerational families by ethnicity in municipalities (1875). Map design: Hilde L. Sommerseth.*

model (Solli 1995: 84). The high number of intergenerational families in northern Norway during the 1875 census is illustrated in Figure 8.4. Research has shown that stem family systems existed to a greater extent among the farmers than among the crofters (Sogner 1978: 708; Fure 1986: 35; Sogner 1990: 36–9; Solli 1995; Bull 2000: 97–9). Further, Ståle Dyrvik argued that fishermen–farmers were more likely to favour stem family systems, while pure fishermen would favour nuclear families (Dyrvik 1993).

These historians often argue that the prevalence of the stem family across Norway was supported by the unique Norse allodium inheritance system, wherein a single heir (usually the eldest son) had preferential rights to inherit the family estate.[8] A clear example of how primogeniture supported intergenerational household arrangements can be found in Eli Fure's (1986) study of Asker municipality in the first part of the nineteenth century. Fure argues that the legal guarantee on the inheritance rights of the oldest son meant in fact that the older generation, usually the eldest male, never surrendered his title as head of household. Instead of a 'nuclear reincorporation' as envisioned by Kertzer, the adult son simply moved back into the parental home before finally receiving his title. This pattern was more evident among farmers than among the crofters (Fure 1986: 35).

It is important to add, however, that inheritance systems were not the same across ethnic groups. Both nomadic and coastal Sámi families tended to favour a system of ultimogeniture, wherein the youngest child – preferably a son – inherited property (Solem 1928: 300). Primogeniture – the right of the eldest child – was the dominant quality of the Norwegian system. Both systems tended to favour male children.

All of these examples tend to suggest that there could be multiple paths by which an intergenerational strategy of ownership might be maintained, which at the time of certain censuses might first appear to be the creation or dissolution of separate households. This complexity is an important element in trying to understand the above mentioned shift in the household structure in the 1900 census.

Age cohorts and co-residence

Much of the statistical analysis used to test theories of nuclear reincorporation or economic development depends on the analysis of age cohorts in census data. Age cohorts are certain sociological groups which are thought to come into existence when a person reaches a certain age. For most of Europe, the age of 60 is thought to be the boundary after which a person is considered to be elderly. Therefore, definitions of intergenerational

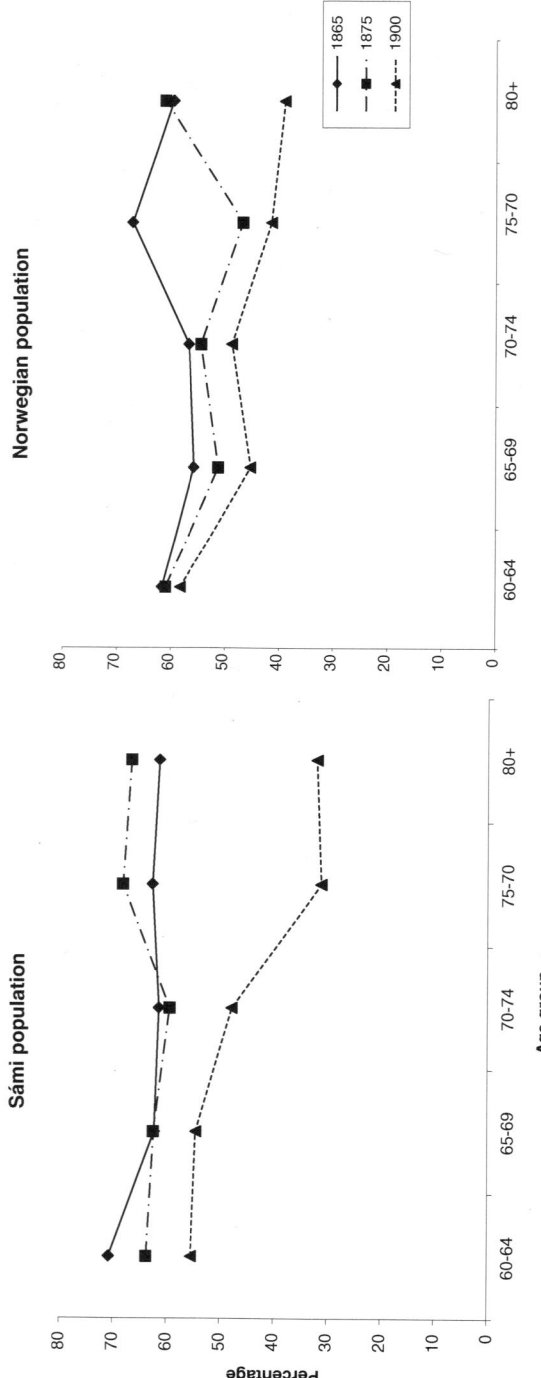

Figure 8.5 *The percentage of elderly people residing with their own adult child, by ethnic affiliation (5a and 5b), age and census year: NTF region, 1865–1900 (population censuses from 1865, 1875 and 1900. Minnesota Population Centre, Norwegian Historical Data Centre (NHDC), Digital Archives, NAPP).*

households are often defined by the statistical co-presence of parents over the age of 60 and children above the age of 18.

Figure 8.5 shows the percentage of different age cohorts of elderly persons living with their own adult children in the NTF region for Sámis and Norwegians for each of the national censuses. The figure gives a more detailed overview of the data previously discussed in Figure 8.2. It is assumed that where elders were reincorporated into their children's households the data on age-cohorts will be U-shaped (since as parents get older they will be increasingly likely to move into their children's homes). This pattern is not evident at all for Sámis, and slightly evident for Norwegians (especially for the 1875 census). When compared to the Norwegian population, age seems to have less effect on Sámis.

As mentioned above, the 1900 census shows very different and much more radical results for both groups. As parents became older, the proportion that was co-resident declines sharply, with the largest change recorded among the Sámi population. In 1900, only 30 per cent of the Sámi older than 75 years lived with one of their adult child. Twenty-five years earlier, between 60 and 70 per cent did so.

A possible explanation of the different age pattern between Sámi and Norwegians, especially during the 1865 and 1875 censuses, may be related to different inheritance practices. The youngest son's right (ultimogeniture) was described by Solem (1928) as a Sámi tradition. Not only did the youngest son inherit his parents' farm or business, he was also given the responsibility of caring for his parents until their death. With this type of system it would not be expected that age would have any effect on co-residence since one would expect the youngest son to remain in the household of his parents. The data confirm this practice both among coastal and reindeer-herding Sámis (although these data are not presented here (cf. Jåstad 2011a: 63).

The marital status of the elderly also reveals an important preference for co-residence between these two groups (Figure 8.6). Generally speaking, similar predictions regarding the number of elderly people who would live with their own adult child in both the Sámi and Norwegian populations could be made on the basis of marital status. The proportion of married elderly people living with their own adult child was relatively constant over time. In 1865 and 1875, elderly widows were more likely to reside with their own adult child than was the case for married couples. In 1900, however, we see that the probability for widows living with their own adult child was far less when compared to elderly married couples. A similar shift occurred for widowers as well, but less dramatically. The most significant decline occurred for Sámi widows living with their adult children. In the case of Sámi widows, the analysis shows that nearly 70 per cent of widows lived in intergenerational families in 1875 compared

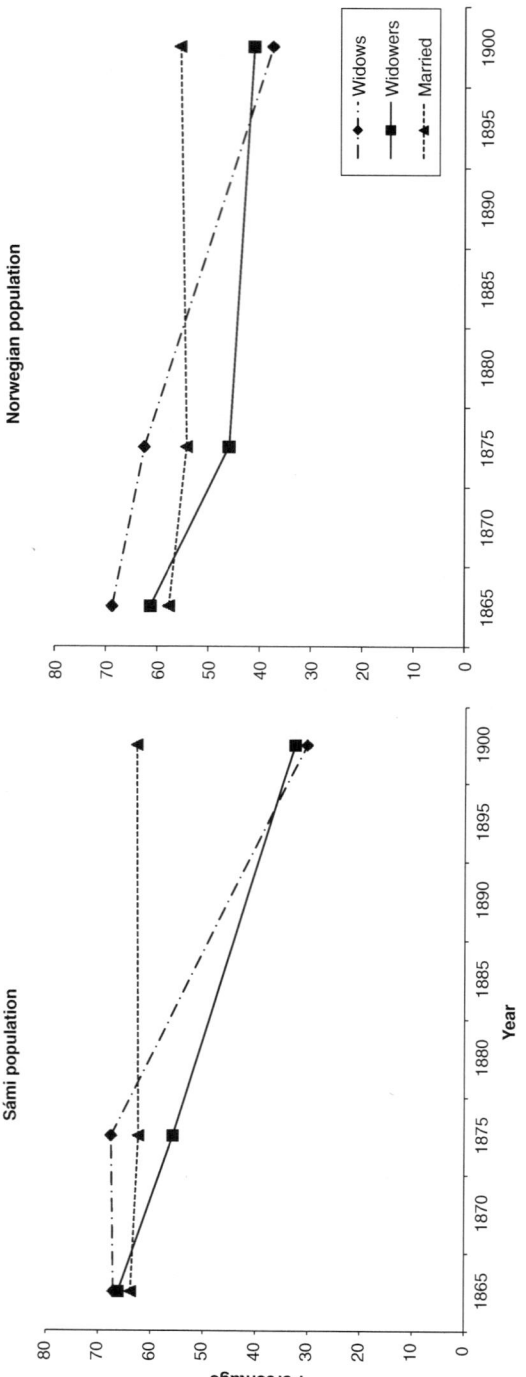

Figure 8.6 *The percentage of elderly people residing with their own adult child, by ethnic affiliation (6a and 6b), marital status and census year: NTF region, 1865–1900 (population censuses from 1865, 1875 and 1900. Minnesota Population Centre, Norwegian Historical Data Centre (NHDC), Digital Archives, NAPP).*

to 30 per cent in 1900. These data suggest that the gender of the parent is a significant factor in how households are described legally in these three censuses. This particular chart, however, does not tell us who moved in with whom. As we shall see, it seems that in many cases young people may have also moved back into their parental home after the death of one of the parents.

In Figure 8.7 we see the percentage of intergenerational co-residence in which the older generation held the position as the head of household. In all intergenerational families where elderly fathers were present (the upper line) the fathers tended to keep their leadership position. This is evident in both the Sámi and the Norwegian population, although strongest in the Sámi population. This pattern seems to contradict the nuclear reincorporation theory. To explain this pattern, it is far more reasonable to assume that the younger generation remained in their parents' households after reaching adulthood, or that they – after a period of independence – returned to the parental home (Ruggles 2007). The middle line shows the percentage of intergenerational families where both parents are present. Even this line shows that most intergenerational families were still headed by the older generation. The bottom line shows the percentage of widows who remained as household heads when living with their own adult child. The relatively low proportion of widows as household heads can be explained by the patrilineal inheritance rules. Upon the death of the father, the status as household head was most likely transferred to the son or son-in-law. This patrilineal rule, however, does not necessarily imply that the widow moved in with one of her children, as the nuclear reincorporation theory predicts. Most likely the widow transferred the headship position to the son or son-in-law in the household, while she remained physically on the same homestead she once established together with her husband. It is interesting to note that Sámi women were more likely to remain as household heads. These results suggest that in this region, at this time, the practice of 'nuclear reincorporation' never occurred and that any change in co-residence was the result of children moving back into their native homesteads. To confirm these findings, I wish to present other historical data on inheritance practice to describe how intergenerational households were conceived by people in this region.

The 'European marriage pattern' and the peasant's pension system

Family historians have often observed that there is a close relationship between the age at which the younger generation marries and when property transfers from the older generation. In many cases, due to the way

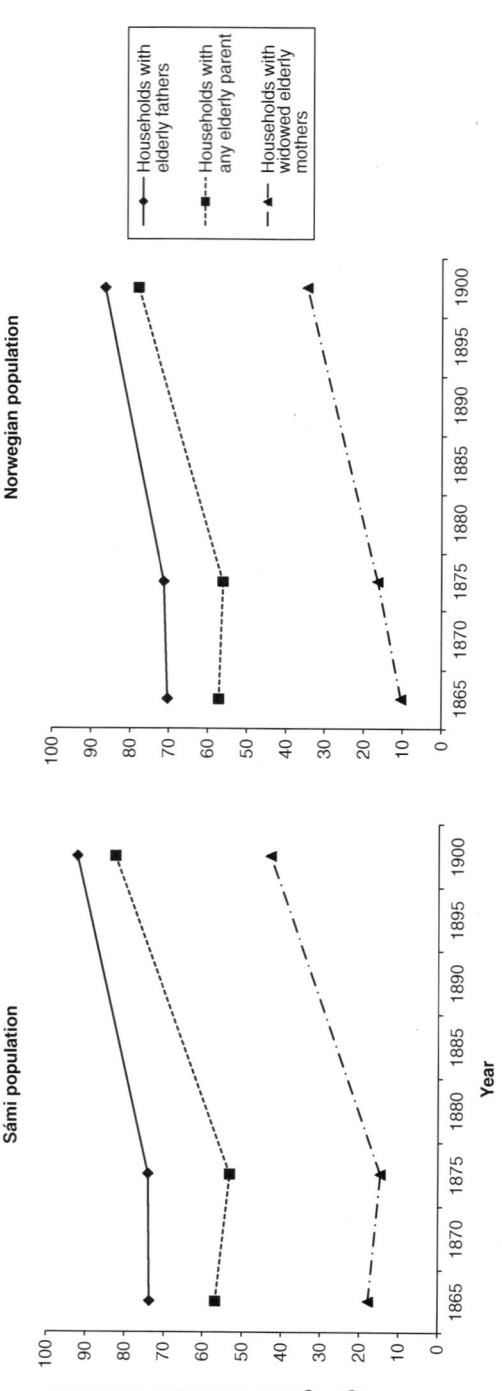

Figure 8.7 *The percentage of intergenerational households in which the older generation heads the household, by ethnic affiliation (7a and 7b), marital status and census year: NTF region, 1865–1900 (population censuses from 1865, 1875 and 1900. Minnesota Population Centre, Norwegian Historical Data Centre (NHDC), Digital Archives, NAPP).*

that property ownership was structured patrilineally, a male child could not marry without first acquiring the family property by inheritance. According to Ruggles (2003), this meant that rather than focusing on the life cycle of the elders, it was better to study the changes that occurred in family structure at the time that the children married. He hypothesized that changes in household leadership would often be linked to the death of a parent, usually the father. In this case, as long as the father was still alive, be he married or widowed, the adult son could not yet inherit the property. Taking this idea one step further, Ruggles argued that we should expect to find a similar association between elderly widowers residing with an unmarried adult child and elderly married men residing with any unmarried adult. The statistical pattern across the NTF region in the second half of the nineteenth century shows that this was not the case.[9] This implies that there is something more complex going on than a simple nuclear reincorporation.

This close connection between marriage and property transfer has even been formalized as the 'European marriage pattern' (Hajnal 1965). While at first glance this rule seems to support the 'nuclear reincorporation' thesis by specifying the traumatic moment when reincorporation occurred, the direction of movement of widows (or widowers) into the household of their children, or the reverse, is still an open question. Property transfers in particular historical contexts was never a simple affair. In most Norwegian rural communities it has been almost always linked to obligations put upon the heir to care for the surviving parent or parents, which in turn complicated the way that 'headship' was understood.

In Norway, inheritance has been historically linked to two kinds of formal old age maintenance systems: *føderåd* and *fletførsel*. Helland-Hansen (1997) defined the *føderåd* – the peasant's pension – as the simultaneous transfer of the farm property and the headship of the household to the younger generation, with the caveat that the elderly would receive support in their old age. In this arrangement, the elderly retained a claim on the future wealth of the new household. *Fletførsel*, by contrast, specified a legal arrangement wherein the elderly moved into the household of another caregiver, who may not in fact be a kinsman. They would not be able to maintain a claim on household wealth generated from that date forward, but only could claim certain benefits of care which were stipulated by law. In comparison to peasant pensioners, a recipient of *fletførsel* was in a weaker position.

Since *føderåd* was not defined by law, its provision varied from place to place, even within a single neighbourhood. Although the institution could be found among both large and small farms, as well as rich and poor farms, it tended to be limited to agricultural households. In most cases the motivation behind the system was the desire to keep sons working

on the farm, a hope to avoid disputes about succession to property, and
the goal of keeping the farm within the family. The elderly retired on the
farm they themselves had established. In the cases of multiple heirs, there
are examples of the elderly living for certain periods in the household
of each heir. Within these general principles there were also some small
differences that are important for understanding family structure.

Helland-Hansen, in his monumental work *Føderådsordningens historie i Norge* (1997), distinguished three main types of old-age support
contracts: *vinningskår, varekår* and *brødkår*. *Vinningskår* was defined as
a situation where the retired elderly person maintained an independent
household and reserved a garden plot (or some similar productive asset)
for their own use throughout their remaining life. Maintaining an independent household was also the norm for the elderly living under *varekår*.
However, here, it was explicitly stated in the contract that the heir was
responsible for food and other necessary supplies for the elderly. The
last peasant's pension system, which was perhaps the most widespread,
was *brødkår*. In this system the elderly person was a part of the heir's
household, and shared meals with the heir. Unlike *varekår* and *vinningskår*,
brødkår was not a formal written agreement. Hence, the consequence
was often a gradual transition between property and household transfer.
Brødkår was more common on smaller farms and especially among crofters (Helland-Hansen 1997: 466). For the purposes of my argument, it
is important to note that although all three systems defined the transfer .
of household property, they each tend to blur the transfer of household
leadership, making it difficult to say who 'moved in' and who 'moved out'.

Within the NTF region, Finnmark had a relatively high proportion of
fletførsel when compared to other parts of the country (Helland-Hansen
1997: 261–98).[10] In northern Troms, we have no examples of *fletførsel;*
however, peasant's pensions were common. Further, in 1875 Helland-
Hansen reported 892 cases of *føderådshovedpersoner* ('representatives
receiving a peasant's pension') in Troms, and that 14.9 per cent of these
were recorded to be separate households (*kårhus*) (Helland-Hansen 1997:
540). It is difficult to know how to interpret these household units represented by a single person. It is possible that these 892 cases conceal
spouses or other elderly people subsisting on the same pension paid to the
single pension representatives.

Why was the relative proportion of *fletføringer* (people practising *fletførsel*) greater in Finnmark than elsewhere in the country? Helland-Hansen
has argued that Finnmark had no tradition of either peasant's pension or
fletføring before the nineteenth century. The late introduction of this old-
age support system therefore blindly followed legal norms. Although *fletføring* had been formally defined by Norwegian law since 1687, owning
land in this region was a new phenomenon, and this, in combination with

a weak peasant's pension tradition, resulted in a situation where it may have been easier for all parties to use the legal text and offer themselves and their goods at the district court (Helland-Hansen 1997: 279, 282).

For the purposes of my argument, it is important to note that even formal *fletføring* was not a simple crisp transfer of wealth in Finnmark but entailed numerous long-term social obligations. For example, in 1867 Kirsten Pedersdatter from Talvik in Finnmark transferred her property and assets to E. Olsen (a non-relative). In return he provided a place for her to stay, gave her food, clothes, room, light, heating, care and attendance. She also reserved milk from one cow and wool from two sheep. E. Olsen made a promise to pay all her debts, and the annual value of the contract was set to 50 speciedaler [currency] (Helland-Hansen 1997: 292). In that she transferred all her assets, this contract may be regarded as a *fletførsel* contract. However, the fact that she had the opportunity to earn money by selling wool and knitted products indicates that this was a more complicated arrangement. This subtlety would not be visible, however, in census records where she would be recorded as being 'incorporated' within a household.

It was common across Norway that both peasants' pensions and *fletførsel* contracts would specify that food and drink, clothing, housing, light, heating and, in most cases, also a decent burial, should be given to the elderly. However, what was the fate of the approximately 90 per cent of the elderly who did not have any formal legal contract for their care? Is it reasonable to assume that they were neglected? It is much more likely that there was an informal care system in place which also did not leave its trace in formal census records. In the words of one man from Trondenes in southern Troms:

> If the farm wasn't especially large, which was common in northern Norway, the old folks did not take out a peasant pension. They managed with an oral agreement that stated that they could be a part of the household (*brødkår*). It was considered natural that parents should have their livelihood together with the younger generation. (Helland-Hansen 1997: 320)

Brødkår was, as previously mentioned, regarded as the most common peasant's pension system and was probably a generic term for all old-age support where no written contract was drawn up. To 'go with bread' (*gå i brød*) carried a hint of a type of subordination. Your position as head of the household was finished, and the 'bread' was supplied by others, hopefully by one of your own adult children. It is extremely unlikely that we can apply this informant's literal words to 90 per cent of the elderly population in the NTF region in the second half of the nineteenth century. As previously mentioned, more than 60 per cent of all elderly resided with an adult child in 1865, and of these 75 per cent were still headed

by the older generation. Therefore, it seems that the few formal contracts, which found their way into census documents, were quite rare in
the NTF region, but that intergenerational co-residence and cooperation
nevertheless continued.

It might be tempting to assume that only 25 per cent of the elderly who
lived with an adult child were actually living on *brødkår*, given that they
were not recorded as being household heads. Thus, derived from the above
discussion, one obvious question should be whether Norwegian family
historians have been defining the position of the elderly too formally.

Because there are no available local or regional studies of the peasant's
pension system in the NTF area, it is difficult to determine exactly the
relationship between retirement contracts and marriage by members of
the younger generation, and thus how likely it was that marriage occurred
after the death of the father. However, it is reasonable to assume that the
death of a parent triggered a discussion and action on the future division
of labour on the farm. This is primarily due to a fairly rigid division of
labour according to gender. First, one cannot exclude the possibility that
the death of a parent affected the probability that the oldest son married
and/or was given the position as head of the household. Second, if there
were no sons of marriageable age available, it is reasonable to assume that
a daughter stayed and took the work that traditionally was in the hands of
the housewife.

That the future division of labour on the farm may have been crucial
for the generation change is shown in a study of the eighteenth- and
nineteenth-century village of Rendalen in the eastern part of Norway.
The study demonstrates a strong association between inheritance practice
and the timing of marriages among the younger generation (Bull 2006).
Furthermore, the same study shows that the pressure on the eldest son to
marry gradually diminished throughout the nineteenth century. A senior
son could increasingly choose when he should marry without risking his
future inheritance of the farm. This was most evident in families where
the father died and no daughters were available. In these cases, the widow
retained her position as mistress of the house and her son postponed marriage (Bull 2006: 20). In the nineteenth century it became more common
that the oldest son was given the farm when he was still unmarried. If he
ever got married it happened after the death of the father.

Rendalen was a prominent agricultural village, and it may therefore be
difficult to draw parallels to the NTF region. Nevertheless, if one assumes
that all households at this time placed a value on self-sufficiency, where the
most important thing was to secure the labour force at the farm, then this
pattern could be used to query the census records from the NTF region.
Given that written peasant pension contracts were rare in this area, it is
reasonable to assume that a majority of the farms were transferred into the

name of the younger generation at the time that one or both parents died, and that until this time (as Figure 8.7 shows) the older generation (and especially the father) remained registered as the head of the household.

Steven Ruggles (2003), on the basis of his research into nineteenth-century families in the United States, has devised a statistical test to determine whether the death of a parent is linked to property transfers. According to him, if there was a connection between the property transfer and the marriage of the younger generation, we should expect the proportion of widowers residing with an unmarried adult child to be equal to the married fathers residing with an unmarried adult child. Figure 8.8 shows the percentage of married sons and daughters who lived with parents, by sex, ethnicity and marital status of the parents in the NTF region. It indicates the contrary trend, that married parents, regardless of ethnic affiliation, were residing with unmarried children to a greater extent than is the case for elderly widows.

The difference is striking. How can this be explained? These large proportions, which hold for both Sámi and Norwegian widowers, indicate that the transfer of property may not be directly connected to the father's death.[11] Nor can we rule out that the difference may be an expression of 'nuclear reincorporation'. However, we are still left with the paradox that most of the elderly in intergenerational households were recorded as being household heads (Figure 8.7), which makes this explanation unlikely. Neither does it explain why widowers increasingly lived with unmarried daughters rather than with unmarried sons.

A possible explanation for the differences may be found in the fairly rigid division of labour by gender. We know from previous research that farming was considered a woman's occupation (Balsvik 1991: 640). Thus, households needed women in order to persist. If an elderly man with an unmarried adult daughter in the household became a widower, he was far less likely to encourage his daughter to marry. As long as he was fit to perform the male tasks, the household could survive with an adult male and an adult woman whether that adult woman was his wife or daughter.

When an old mother was widowed, there was a greater probability that she would reside with a married daughter than an unmarried daughter, but we also see that widows, more than widowers, were residing with a married child, irrespective of the child's sex. One obvious reason for this may be the tendency that mothers, upon the loss of a husband, no longer continued as head of the household (Figure 8.7). However, when a father became a widower, the probability of him continuing as head of household was high, especially in cases where the oldest son was not ready to take over, and where an adult daughter could take over working tasks originally done by the late housewife. This explanation is supported by

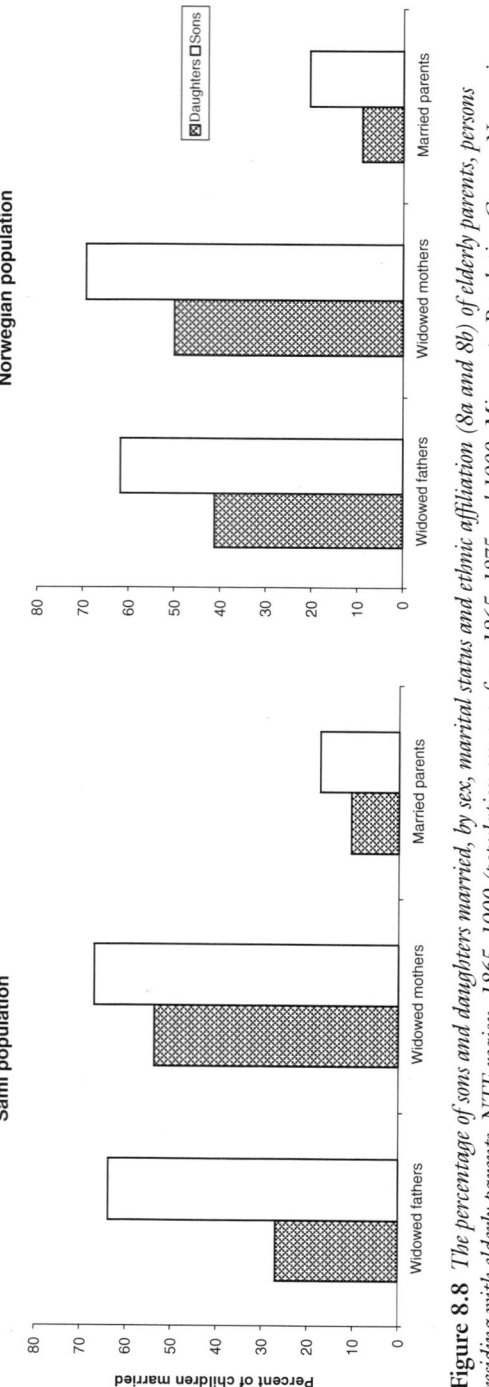

Figure 8.8 The percentage of sons and daughters married, by sex, marital status and ethnic affiliation (8a and 8b) of elderly parents, persons residing with elderly parents. NTF region, 1865–1900 (population censuses from 1865, 1875 and 1900. Minnesota Population Centre, Norwegian Historical Data Centre (NHDC), Digital Archives, NAPP).

the high proportion of elderly fathers who held the position of head of household (Figure 8.7).

Life histories and the demographic shift

As discussed above, the census records a sharp, sudden drop in intergenerational co-residence between 1875 and 1900. This change occurred for elderly people who were not household heads, and the change over time was equally dramatic for the married as for widows and widowers (cf. Jåstad 2011a: 64). In 1865 and 1875, approximately 60 per cent of all elderly people without a position as head of the household resided with their own adult child. In 1900 this was reduced to 25 per cent. In other words, if intergenerational households persisted, the elderly would remain as household heads. This leaves the question of when the children in these remaining intergenerational households chose to marry.

The associations between the child's marital status and their relationship to intergenerational households are presented in Figure 8.9. While close to 35 per cent of the elderly in intergenerational households resided with a married child in 1865, there were only 10 per cent Sámi and 13 per cent Norwegian elderly who had such living arrangements in 1900. This low level was a result of a sustained decline over time. It seems that the above mentioned decline in intergenerational co-residence tracks a decline in the number of married young families who chose to remain within the intergenerational stem family in both the Sámi and the Norwegian population. If we go further and look at the sex of the co-residing child, the analysis shows that the overall decline in the Norwegian population was solely due to a reduction in the elderly residing with their own married sons. If an elderly person lived with an adult son in 1865 and 1875, the probability of doing so with a married or an unmarried son was equal. In 1900, however, the percentage of the elderly residing with married sons was reduced to 10 per cent while co-residing with unmarried sons still remained at a level slightly above 20 per cent.

In Sámi intergenerational households in 1865 and 1875 it was somewhat more common for the elderly to live with married sons: over 20 per cent, compared to 18 per cent residing with unmarried sons. In 1900, this level dropped to 7 per cent. At the same time there was a decline in intergenerational co-residence with married daughters, from 7 to 2 per cent. Common in both the Norwegian and the Sámi intergenerational households, however, was the fact that the child's marital status through the whole period had a greater significance in intergenerational households with daughters. If the elderly resided with an adult daughter, they preferred unmarried daughters in over 60 per cent of the cases, a tendency

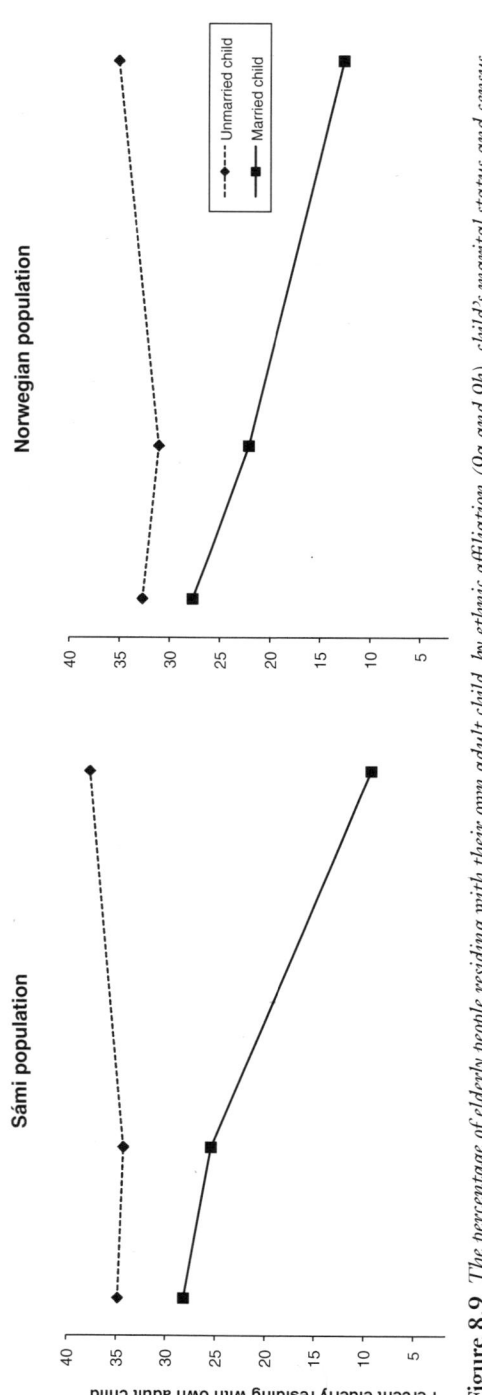

Figure 8.9 *The percentage of elderly people residing with their own adult child, by ethnic affiliation (9a and 9b), child's marital status and census year: NTF region, 1865–1900 (population censuses from 1865, 1875 and 1900. Minnesota Population Centre, Norwegian Historical Data Centre (NHDC), Digital Archives, NAPP).*

which increased towards 1900. The marital status of sons only began to be significant in 1900.

What was the reason for older widows and widowers without a position as head of household to live less often with their children in 1900 than they did previously?

One way to approach the question is to identify important events in the lives of selected elderly people in order to assess whether there were structures in the families' or households' life cycles that conditioned the changes. To construct these life histories, I have linked records concerning elderly widows or widowers in the 1900 census to baptism, marriage and burial records, and the censuses from 1865 and 1875. This led to a sample set of 11 households tracked longitudinally from 1865 to 1900. The baptismal entries show that the widows had, over time, given birth to an average of 2.6 children, which is lower than expected. Twenty-seven per cent of the sample had only girls. Sixty per cent of the sample had an occupation listed in 1900, while one-third were registered as paupers. Half were listed with a different residence address in 1900, but in the same municipality as in previous censuses. One-third of the sample had the same municipality of residence in all three censuses, but only three people were given the same address in the funeral protocol. However, information about residence is missing for more than half of the sample.

In order to try to answer the question of why the long-standing practice of intergenerational co-residence dropped so significantly in 1900, I will analyse the life story of one family. Table 8.1 illustrates the life cycle of widower Morten Larsen, registered as a single lodger in 1900. Morten's story illustrates well the different options he had to try to keep his household together, although in the end he did not succeed.

In 1865 and 1875 Morten was the household head on the farm Hugnes at the southern end of the 276 square-kilometre island Arnøy in Skjervøy parish. He was a Sámi fisherman–farmer with a farm operation consisting of four cows, ten sheep and 14 reindeer in 1865; slightly less in 1875. He married for the first time in 1849, at the age of 22, but the marriage was short-lived. His wife, Marit Nielsdatter, died in 1857 leaving two children. In 1859 Morten married again. His new wife Elen Kristine brought four children from her marriage to the late Niels Peersen. Three of them lived in the household at Hugnes in 1865. Elen Kristine and Morten had four more children together. In 1887 Elen Kristine died, and Morten did not remarry. In 1900, at 73 years old, he still lived at Hugnes, still registered as a fisherman–farmer, but the position of head of household had been transferred to Ole Arnesen and Beret Olsdatter. There was no kinship relation between these young newcomers at Hugnes and Morten. Morten Larsen died on 22 June 1914 as a pauper with residence in Langfjord to the north of Hugnes.

Table 8.1 *The life course of Skjervøy residents*

	49	51	52	53	54	57	58	59	61	63	Census 1865	67	Census 1875	80	84	87	88	89	Census 1900	1914
Morten Larsen (b. 1827)	M							M			Sámi farmer and fisherman. 4 cows, 10 sheep, 14 reindeers. 1 servant Haugnes in Skjervøy		Sámi farmer and fisherman. 2 cows, 14 sheep, 6 reindeers Haugnes in Skjervøy						Sámi farmer and fisherman, widower. Solitair lodger in the household of Ole Arnesen and Beret Olsdatter Haugnes in Skjervøy	† Pauper residence in Langfjorden
Marit Nielsdatter (1. wife)	M					†														
Inger Eline													helps her mother (24 years old)		†					
Peder Martin								M								†				
Elen Kristine Andersdatter (2. wife)																		M		
Inger Maria (Elen K's daughter)																				
Per Andreas (Elen K's son)																				
Mathias (Elen K's son)																				
Peder Anderas (Elen K's son)													helps his father (21 years old)							
Elen Bergithe														M						
Marith Kristine													child care of younger siblings (12 years old)							
Ragnhild Catharina																				
Nille Johanna													†							
Serine Inger Anna (Inger E's daughter)																				

Peder Martin was Morten's only biological son and it was likely that he would take over the farm from his father. In 1875, Peder Martin was 18 years old and still living at home. In 1888, one year after Morten lost his wife, he lost Peder Martin as well. Unmarried and 31 years old, he died when his boat capsized on the way home from the Finnmark fisheries. In the funeral protocol, his place of residence was given as Hugnes.

Peder Andreas, who was Elen Kristine's son from her first marriage, lived in the parental home in 1875. He was 21 years old and by profession 'he helped the father'. Like Peder Martin, Peder Andreas eventually became an active fisherman. In 1900 he lived as a single lodger in the household of his sister, Elen Bergithe. Unmarried and with failing health, he died of kidney inflammation at the age of 53.

Both of Morten's sons chose lives as bachelors and fishermen, and an obvious question is whether they had been at all interested in taking over the farm. During the last part of the nineteenth century, we know that participation in fishing increased, giving young men more choices than ever before. It no longer went without saying that a son stayed behind and took over the farmstead. As a consequence the older generation had to look for others to take on the farm.[12] But what about their daughters?

Out of Morten's four daughters, it has been possible to track three. The youngest daughter, Nille Johanna, died at age 17 from diphtheria. Ragnhild Catharina married and moved far north on the island, to Årvik. In 1880 Elen Bergithe married a neighbour, Nils Andreas Arnesen, and settled nearby in Haugnesbukta. In addition to a husband and seven children, her stepbrother lodged with them. Rather than move to his daughter's, 73-year-old Morten chose to remain as a lodger in the household he had established 51 years earlier, although this was apparently not with close family.

The story of this one family illustrates several themes which are hinted at in the census statistics across the region. First, we can see quite strongly in this story of early death and remarriage that it was important to have a woman on the homestead, at least up until the turn of the century. Second, the choice of the two sons to take to sea and not to remain on the farm might indicate a disinterest in supporting the family homestead. On the other hand, their sudden deaths at sea might instead point to an unsuccessful attempt at managing the great risks attached with North Sea fishing to bolster the household. We cannot know whether, if the two sons had been lucky enough to return, one would have taken up the farm. But, thirdly, the most important conclusion is that the assumption that the elderly always 'reincorporate' themselves into the households of their children is negated in this story. Here each of the men (Morten, his biological son, and his stepson) remains as an independent actor along their respective life paths.

It is difficult to generalize from this one example to the other 11 cases. However, one trend is interesting to highlight. It is striking that this small group has two elderly people without children, and a total of seven who only had one or two children each. Given the changing economy of the time, and the differential distribution of risk in the North Sea fishery, having a small number of children also increased the risk of being alone in one's old age and of having no one to pass the farm onto. Rather than conclude that economic opportunity in northern Norway condemned the long-standing stem family system, it seems that economic risk and low fertility made the intergenerational household vulnerable in the period between 1875 and 1900.

Conclusion

The main purpose of this study was to try to read the strategies of house-holders in the documentary records for the unique multicultural region that is northern Troms and Finnmark in northern Norway. The NTF region, made up of Norwegians, Sámis and Kvens, challenges received models about how pre-industrial households behaved. Given that the bulk of our records for this region are from a series of censuses from 1875 to 1900, there has been a tendency for historians to track the career of independent households. This study has shown that certain paradoxes in the data, especially the tendency for the elderly to remain in their positions as household heads when co-residing with the youth, suggest that there were multiple, intersecting, household-building strategies in the region.

Traditionally, it was thought that the intergenerational stem family was the norm in this region, with the added complexity of there being different inheritance systems for Sámis and Norwegians and a perceived need for there always to be a woman to manage the onshore farm. The intergenerational stem family is often thought to be supported by formal Norse inheritance law. However, this study has shown that formal contracts of this nature were rare. The vast majority of the population used verbal contracts to manage the transfer of their estates and the care of the elderly. My cross-sectional analysis focused on how the position of head of household shifted in intergenerational households. The data suggest that in nearly three-quarters of cases the headship remained with the older parent, and this proportion even increased over the period (even while the number of intergenerational families dropped). These data suggest that the elderly never moved out of their farms (as the 'nuclear reincorporation theory' predicts) but that instead the older and younger generation moved in to maintain the homestead.

During the period of study, and especially after 1875, there was a dramatic change in household structure in the NTF area, characterized by a marked decrease in co-residence: (1) with increasing age among the elderly; (2) for elderly widows and widowers; and (3) with married sons

These changes were common to all ethnic groups (and even more extensive in the Sámi population). The sharp decline in intergenerational households towards the end of the 1800s can be most simply understood as the dissolution of the traditional stem family system. However, other traditional features remained. Unmarried daughters, even during this change, still contributed to the maintenance of the remaining intergenerational household. As sons brought in fewer daughters-in-law, unmarried daughters became a good substitute to take on the chores of the house-wife. Further, the longitudinal case data that was reconstructed for this project also suggests that the dissolution of the traditional stem family was not purely due to the attraction of new economic opportunities. Rather, it seems that new opportunities in commercial fishing put sons at greater risk, which in turn put the traditional family at risk. This finding puts a sharper edge on theories of 'economic development'. Here residents in this Arctic district responded to market opportunities that drove different generations apart, but the fatal change for intergenerational households and farmsteads came from the differential risks associated with these choices.

Acknowledgements

This chapter is a revised version of a Norwegian-language article published in *Historisk tidsskrift* (Jåstad 2011b). The research for this chapter took place as part of a doctoral fellowship financed by the Research Council of Norway. I am especially grateful to my supervisors Lars Ivar Hansen and Gunnar Thorvaldsen for their excellent follow-up throughout the project. I started working with Gunnar during my master's thesis, and I am deeply thankful for his encouragement and the way he has mentored my career as a researcher over the past ten years. I would also like to thank my colleagues at the Centre for Sámi Studies for interesting discussions at the seminar or coffee table. Special thanks to my colleagues in Tromsø: David Anderson, Bjørnar Olsen, Sven-Donald Hedman and Ivar Bjørklund.

Notes

1. An independent household is formally defined as a unit of one or more people who share a living space and meals (Laslett and Wall 1972; Dyrvik 1983: 184; Solli 2003).

2. For further discussion on the possible flaws in the registration of ethnicity see Hansen and Meyer (1991); Lie and Roll-Hansen (2001); Evjen and Hansen (2009); Thorvaldsen (2009); Jåstad (2011a).
3. The dataset consists of 6,707 cases: 2,604 Sámis, 2,623 Norwegians, 1,372 Kvens, and 108 elderly with a mixed ethnic marker. Approximately one-third of those interpreted as Sámis lived in municipalities where the main economic occupation was reindeer herding. The total sample size per census is: 1865 (n = 1,537), 1875 (n = 1,885), 1900 (n = 3,285).
4. The population censuses from 1865, 1875 and 1900 were processed by the Digital Archives and the Norwegian Historical Data Centre (NHDC) and extracted via the North Atlantic Population Project (NAPP), which is available from the Norwegian Historical Data Centre, the Digital Archives, and the Minnesota Population Centre (cf. www.rhd.uit.no; www.digitalarkivet.no; www.nappdata.org). The main advantage of the NAPP data is their regularly constructed family interrelationship variables. These variables identify the location within the household of each individual's spouse, mother and father, and thus provide essential building blocks for the constructing measures of household and family structure.
5. In 2009 2 million NOK was granted from the Norwegian Research Council to plan a national, historical population register where one of the aims was to plan a longitudinal register for the last couple of centuries. The project is headed from the Norwegian Historical Data Centre (NHDC) at the University of Tromsø and will make use of already established databases that will, over the following years, be merged into a complete national database. For a comprehensive overview of the planned register, see Thorvaldsen (2011).
6. The linked data were constructed for widows or widowers who resided in Skjervøy, Nordreisa, Kvænagen or Kautokeino municipalities during the 1900 census and who were also registered in the 1865 census. Five cases had to be dropped when the cross-referencing revealed that they lived with their adult children in 1900. Of the remaining sample, nine persons were Sámi, five were Norwegian and one was Finnish.
7. Copies of the entire original census enumeration forms can be viewed at http://nappdata.org/napp/enum_materials.shtml
8. The allodium law in Norway featured a number of complex changes over the nineteenth century (Dyrvik 1983; 1993; Fure 1986; Sogner 1990; 2009; Solli 1995; 2003; Bull 2000; 2006;). At the beginning of the century the chosen heir enjoyed a period of ten years wherein he could invalidate the sale of an estate to outsiders. In 1857 this was raised to 20 years. An additional provision *(åsetesrett)* gave the oldest son the right to inherit the farm, and in 1863 it was determined that he could take over the farm at a price below the appraised value (Johannessen 1999: 490).
9. 10 per cent of elderly married couples resided with married daughters and 19 per cent with married sons. By contrast, 66 per cent of widowed elderly resided with married sons.
10. It is difficult to understand how widespread *fletførsel* was in Finnmark, since Helland-Hansen provides only percentage proportions in his statistics (Helland-Hansen 1997: 278). Helland-Hansen states that he found 29 peasant's pension or *fletførsel* contracts for the year 1865, and if we see this number in relation to the total number of elderly people (above the age of 60) in Finnmark for the same year, we can assume that approximately 3 per cent of all the elderly had a peasant's pension or a *fletførsel* contract. If we examine the family relation codes carefully in the three censuses from Finnmark, we can hypothesize that 8 per cent of all elderly people who were coded had a peasant's pension in 1865; 3 and 4 per cent in 1875 and 1900. Using the same method for northern Troms, we can estimate that 15 per cent of the elderly above the age of 60 who were coded were registered with a peasant's pension in 1865, 15 per cent in 1875, and 19 per cent in 1900. The true results for both regions should be much higher, since approximately 40 per cent of all the elderly in northern Troms and 50 per cent in Finnmark were not coded with any occupation by the enumerators.
11. A preference for married sons is also evident among the married elderly: the probability of residing with a married son is close to twice as high as that for residing with a married daughter. This dominance, which is a pattern we see regardless of parents' marital status

and ethnic affiliation, may therefore be an expression of either the primogeniture system or ultimogeniture system that favoured sons.

12. Increased participation in fisheries involved an increased risk of death by drowning. Official Norwegian statistics shows that the mortality among men in their twenties was higher than men in the age group 30–40 during the whole period from 1860 to 1920. This trend was most evident around 1890. In addition, the mortality was higher among men than women in this age group (Norge. Statistisk Sentralbyrå 1961: 117–22). An interesting question for further research is to evaluate how much the death of young men affected the decline in inter-generational co-residence that is shown in the above study. Such research needs longitudinal data, and the population register project that is described earlier in Note 5 will give such an opportunity.

CHAPTER 9

Hunters in Transition

Sámi Hearth Row Sites, Reindeer Economies and the Organization of Domestic Space, 800–1300 A.D.

Petri Halinen, Sven-Donald Hedman and Bjørnar Olsen

Introduction

During the Viking Age and the Early Medieval Period, Sámi settlements over the vast interior region of northern Fennoscandia were extensively restructured. Habitation sites were established in areas that were rarely used for settlements previously. These new sites began to display new and distinct features in terms of the organization of domestic space. Hearth row sites are the most conspicuous expression of this new settlement pattern. They consist of large, rectangular hearths organized in a linear pattern (Bergman 1989; Hamari 1996; Hedman 2003; Hedman and Olsen 2009). This restructuring of settlement patterns, which also included the establishment of the so-called Stallo house sites in the northwestern alpine region (Storli 1994; Liedgren and Bergman 2009), took place alongside other pronounced changes: Sámi burial customs became geographically more unified and grave goods more elaborate and varied (Schanche 2000), while sacrifices and other ritual practices intensified significantly (Olsen 2003; Hansen and Olsen 2004; Fossum 2006).

These comprehensive and remarkably unified changes form the background to the current chapter. Focusing on the hearth row sites, our overall aim is to understand why this restructuring of Sámi settlement and domestic space took place and how it relates to other changes in subsistence, settlement and society during the Late Iron Age and Early Medieval Period. Our point of departure is the archaeological investigation conducted during the years 2007–2009 of hearth row sites in the north-easternmost parts of Norway and Finland, in connection with the project Home, Hearth and Household in the Circumpolar North

(HHH). These investigations shed new light on the questions addressed in this chapter.

Sámi hearths and Nordic archaeology

Hearths are the most common surviving elements of Sámi habitation sites from the Late Iron Age to modern times. Even in recent Sámi reindeer-herding sites, the stone-built hearth constitutes the most persistent and visible feature – pertinently so, given the central role the hearth played in the lives of Sámi hunter-gatherers and herders. In the dwelling, the hearth was the focal point of social life and subsistence activities, the place around which they gathered to prepare and consume food, to tell stories, to be warmed and to sleep and rest. Carrying strong religious significance, the hearth also provided an essential spatial node for the socio-religious division of domestic space (Ränk 1949).

Although Sámi hearths have recently become an object of interest to northern archaeologists, their inclusion into Nordic archaeological discourse has been a long and reluctant process. The study of the Sámi past has been strongly affected by national discourses and disciplinary research agendas. The long-held argument of the Sámi as originally 'foreign' to the Nordic landscape, and as lacking the dynamic complexities of the majority populations, contributed to a general acceptance of their past as primarily a matter for ethnographic description; in other words, the concern of a discipline dedicated to the study of distant, isolated, 'primitive' peoples (Olsen 1986; 2000; 2007; Hansen and Olsen 2004; Ojala 2009). Despite the fact that archaeologists and historians throughout the post-war era became increasingly engaged with the Sámi past, the conceptual and interpretative framework was long restricted by this 'ethnographic image' of a primitive culture exhibiting a limited and static repertoire of diagnostic traits.

The early studies of Sámi settlement sites typify this attitude. The ethnic classificatory term 'Lappish hearths' was introduced during the first systematic investigations in northern Sweden in the 1950s. Defining Sámi hearths as either circular or oval in shape, and with a chronology not predating the seventeenth century (Hvarfner 1956; 1957; Meschke 1979), the discovery of the first hearth row sites in the late 1960s created a serious conceptual challenge. Because of their age, shape and size, the large, rectangular hearths 'set themselves apart from the hearths of the Lappish type' and led to an immediate questioning of their Sámi origin: 'Their arrangement along an almost perfectly linear row is also peculiar with regard to Lappish hearths, which normally lack any orderly organisation' (Sundqvist 1973: 56, our translation; see also Christiansson and

Wigenstam 1980: 167). In Norway, the same parameters led to the conclusion that the hearth rows sites excavated at Juntavadda and Assebakte
in interior Finnmark in the late 1960s were cremation burials (Simonsen
1979). In fact, the term Assebakte graves became canonized as the most
common classificatory concept for the hearth row sites in Norway. In
Finland yet another – 'neutral' – term, 'rectangular stone settings', was
implemented, despite the overwhelming data speaking in favour of them
as hearths (Hamari 1996: 131).

The confusing naming and interpretation of this site type clearly reflects
how national borders and research traditions have hampered and bewil-
dered research on what is actually the same archaeological phenomenon.
As such, the fate of the hearth row sites accentuates one of the most crucial challenges facing the study of the Sámi past: to overcome its modern
political economy of national (and territorial) compartmentalization. The
research grounding of this chapter will hopefully set a new agenda by
bringing together Swedish, Norwegian and Finnish scholars in the study
of rectangular hearths.

Hearth row sites

A hearth row site is defined as a set of three or more equally oriented and
regularly interspaced hearths organized in a linear pattern. The sites normally consist of four to eight hearths, although sites with as many as 14
hearths have been recorded. Some of the sites exhibit staggered or uneven
hearth rows, constituted of what may be two (or more) smaller hearth
rows aligned one behind the other. The hearths are large, normally rectangular, and may measure as much as 2.6 × 1.3 m. They are usually very
solidly built, consisting of large frame stones and stone packing inside. It
should be emphasized that these large, stone-lined hearths are much more
substantial stove-like structures than the simple firepits that one finds in
many other sites across the taiga zone of the circumpolar north. They do
find their parallels in the High Arctic in Alaska, Canada and Greenland
(Odgaard and Kanal 2003). At some sites the hearths lack the internal
stone packing (cf. Sundqvist 1973), suggesting possible functional or
seasonal variations. The hearths show traces of intense firing and were
probably used inside a dwelling structure (Hamari 1996; Hedman and
Olsen 2009).

Hearth row sites are found over most of the interior region of northern
Fennoscandia that includes northern Finland, northern Sweden and northern Norway. They are yet to be discovered in the Russian north; however,
the north-easternmost hearth row localities known to date are located just
a few hundred metres from the Norwegian–Russian border (Hedman and

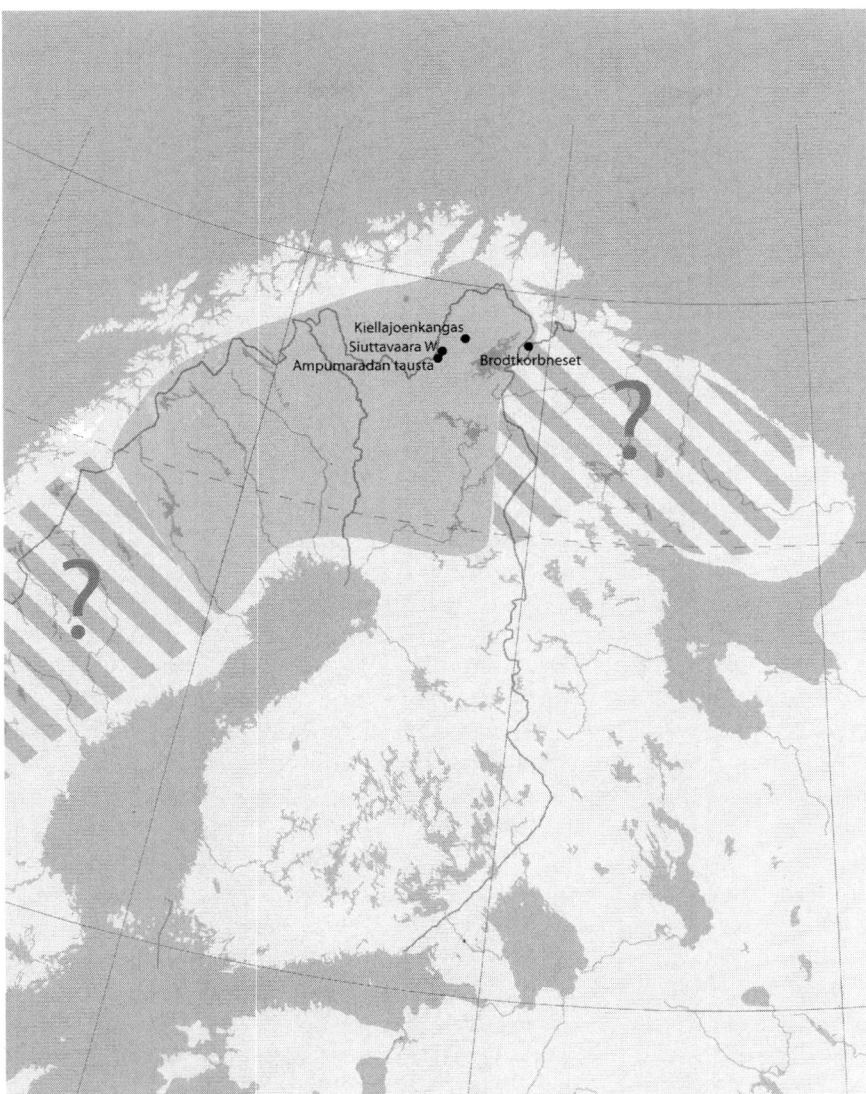

Figure 9.1 *The distribution of hearth row sites in Sweden, Norway and Finland.*

Olsen 2009). Since there is no plausible reason to believe that this modern state border has any relevance to their distribution, it is probably just a matter of time before they are found on the Kola Peninsula (Figure 9.1). More remarkable is a recent find of a hearth row site at Aursjøen, Lesja, Norway, which suggests that their distribution may even have included the mountain areas of southern Norway (Bergstøl 2008: 141–2).

The hearth row sites started to emerge around 800 A.D. They became especially numerous and widespread during the late Viking Age and Early Medieval Period,[1] while around 1300 A.D. their use seems to have discontinued rather abruptly. Their chronology thus coincides with a period of extensive cultural, economic and socio-political transformation in neighbouring Nordic societies. As briefly mentioned in the introduction, this period also brought a number of changes to Sámi communities that in several material respects are remarkably analogous to those represented by the hearth row sites.

Environmental setting

Northern Fennoscandia can be divided into four main environmental zones: (1) the arctic coastal zone, (2) the treeless high mountain zone, (3) the low mountain birch forest zone, and (4) coniferous woodland. These zones are intersected and connected by the numerous larger and smaller rivers and lake systems characterizing these northern landscapes. Hearth row sites are found in several of these environmental zones. They appear within the mountain birch forests as well as in the lower woodland, and some sites have also been discovered in areas near the coast in Norwegian Finnmark. Their main distribution, however, is within coniferous woodland away from the coast and below the high mountain areas. The most typical hearth row habitat is pine forest with rich sources of reindeer lichen. Such lichen woodland has for millennia formed important winter pastures for wild as well as domesticated stocks of reindeer.

The environmental setting of the hearth row sites differs from those considered typical for earlier prehistoric settlements, and suggests that a change in location preferences took place during the Late Iron Age (Hedman 2003; Hedman and Olsen 2009). While the earlier sites are found along the shores of lakes and larger rivers, the hearth row sites normally appear in what may seem more marginal forest areas away from the major bodies of water. The hearth row sites are typically situated on dry moraine outcrops in marsh areas, on forested terraces, or next to small creeks and tarns often surrounded by heathland rich in reindeer lichen (Hedman 2003: 50). Such areas are ideal for pastoral winter habitation and also afford good conditions for storing food in cold caches during summer. While access to water is still important for site location (see Hamari 1996: 129), immediate proximity to lake and riverbank areas seems less imperative.

In terms of paleo-ecological conditions, the general picture of fauna, flora and climate history of northern Fennoscandia is fairly well documented. A number of studies have also provided more detailed knowledge concerning the conditions in the region dealt with here (Zetterberg et al. 1994; Korhola et al. 2000; 2002; Helama 2004; Kultti 2004; Ukkonen 2004). While the fourth millennia B.C. was characterized by gradual climatic cooling and withdrawal of pine forest, the Iron Age provided other changes. Based on the analysis of sub-fossil Scots pine tree rings (Zetterberg et al. 1994: 115–18; Eronen et al. 2002: 678–9; Helama et al. 2002: 683–6; Kultti et al. 2006: 387–8), it is suggested, with some exceptions, that there were two warmer periods: – (i) 865 to 1260 A.D., and (ii) 1480 to 1600 A.D. – with an intermediate period of cooling.[2] Other regional studies have dated the Medieval Warm Period variously as 900 to 1300 A.D. (Korhola et al. 2000: 291), 950 to 1350 A.D. (Kultti et al. 2006: 388–9), and 300–400 to 1300 A.D. (Seppä and Birks 2002: 197), which in general fit well with the local data situating the hearth row sites within the first warm period.

The most important terrestrial animal for past Sámi livelihood was the reindeer (Aronsson 1991; Storli 1991; 1993; Mulk 1994; Hedman 2003; 2005; Halinen 2005). Wild reindeer populations had summer pastures in mountain or coastal areas and winter pastures in forest regions. The herds migrated in spring to the mountain or coastal areas and in autumn back to the forest regions (Halinen 2005). These migrations may to some extent have been modified by the climatic changes. Today the northernmost coniferous forest areas are concentrated mainly in the river valleys, but during the Late Iron Age and Medieval Warm Period the pine forest areas were more extensive. The tree line was situated around 100 m above the current limit in Sweden, and 100–140 m higher on the Kola Peninsula (Kultti et al. 2006: 388). This probably made the lower mountain areas less suitable for wild reindeer during summer and may have decreased the wild mountain reindeer population. The Medieval Cool Period and the subsequent Little Ice Age (1550 to 1850 A.D.) (Korhola et al. 2000: 291), reversed this situation.

The HHH investigations

Four hearth row sites were investigated as part of the project. Three of these sites (Kiellajoenkangas, Siuttavaara, Ampumaradan tausta) are located in Finland, while the last one is situated in Norway (Brodtkorbneset). Since the late 1960s a number of hearth row sites have been excavated in Finland, Norway and Sweden (cf. Simonsen 1979; Bergman 1989; 1990; Furset 1995; Hamari 1996; Hedman 2003). However, these excavations have more or less exclusively been confined to the hearth structures themselves, yielding little information about what may have taken place in the areas outside and between the hearths (see, however, Sundqvist 1973).

In order to achieve a more comprehensive picture of the organization of domestic space at the sites, including activity areas and possible traces of dwelling structures, we chose to excavate a substantial area outside each hearth, varying in size between 20 and 49 square metres. During the excavations we applied a range of environmental archaeological techniques, providing evidence with which to interpret the specific activities that may have occurred at each site.[3] This was complemented by systematic sampling for soil chemical/physical analyses (phosphorus, pH and magnetic susceptibility). At Brodtkorbneset the sampling grid covered the entire site area and samples were collected at intervals of two square metres, while the more detailed sampling at the Finnish sites (0.5×0.5 m) was confined to the trench areas.

The stratigraphy of the area around the hearths was rather uniform at all sites and mostly consisted of natural podzol layers common to this northern woodland zone: a thick organic top soil (layer 1) followed by thin (3–6 cm) leached, grey-white subsoil (layer 2) and red brown, iron-rich soil (layer 3). Most of the finds occurred in the upper part of layer 2, or in the interface between layers 1 and 2. The hearths were treated as separate stratigraphic units and contained layers not observed outside of them (see below).

The Brodtkorbneset site

The Brodtkorbneset site in Pasvik, Finnmark, is situated right on the Norwegian side of the Norwegian–Russian border (Hedman and Olsen 2009). The site is the most north-eastern hearth row site currently known – although, as mentioned above, it is more than likely that the distribution of such sites continues on the Kola Peninsula. The site consists of seven linearly organized hearths placed at intervals of 8–15 m (Figure 9.2). The hearth row is oriented approximately east–west on a sandy terrace between the Brodtkorbneset promontory (and the Pasvik River) in the east, and moraine slopes in the west. The terrace is covered with lichen, moss, heather and pine trees, and prior to the excavation the hearths appeared only as vague moss- and heather-covered elevations.

All the hearths are rectangular and oriented perpendicularly in relation to the overall linear outline of the site. The length of the hearths lay within the range of 1.5–2.4 m, their width varies between 1 m and 1.2 m, and they reach a maximum height of 0.4 m above the surface. All seven hearths were excavated (trenches varying in size between 20 and 36 square metres), making this the most extensive and complete investigation of a hearth row site hitherto conducted. The excavation exposed well-preserved

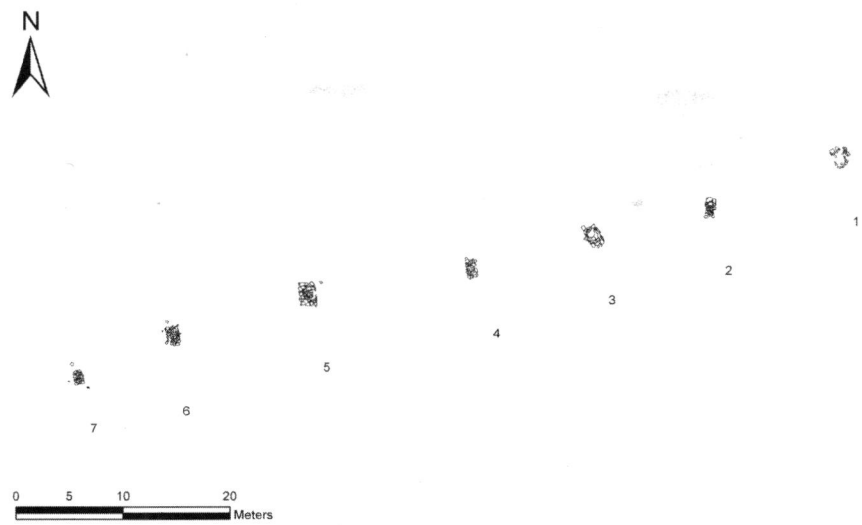

Figure 9.2 *The hearth row site at Brodtkorbneset, Norway.*

rectangular constructions composed of packed and partly layered stones confined by larger frame stones. The only exception was H1, which was severely disturbed by tree-root activity. Some of the hearths (especially the two largest hearths, H3 and H5) contained an upper, covering layer of very compact, sintered soil ('hearth concrete') rich in fragments of burned bones (Figure 9.3). Otherwise all hearths contained a layer of dark brown, fatty soil intermixed with the stones, and a red bottom layer formed by the release of iron oxide during the firing. Another common feature, though most manifest for the largest hearths, was that the northern end was built higher using larger stones, creating a platform-like impression (Hedman and Olsen 2009: 9).

   The faunal material was very rich compared with other interior prehistoric sites in the region, and contained more than 10 kg of bones (11,362 fragments). Most of the bones were uncharred and were found outside the hearths. Their distribution was very distinct and systematic, being almost entirely confined to the north side of the hearths (Figure 9.4). The largest amounts of bones were found at the three central hearths, H3–H5: for example, 7.6 kg of bone (5,240 fragments) were found in association with H3. Reindeer (*Rangifer tarandus*) is by far the most dominant species (c. 90 per cent), but a small but significant component of sheep/goat bones (*Ovis/Capra*) were also identified (Vretemark 2009). Other mammal species represented (in very small numbers) are arctic fox (*Alopex lagopus*), wolf (*Canis lupus*), duck species and grouse. Fish is well

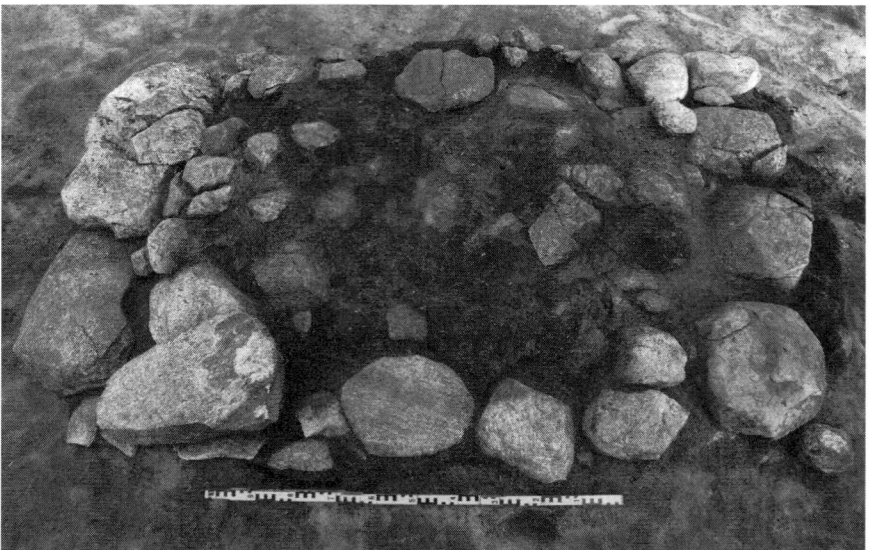

Figure 9.3 *Hearth 5, Brodtkorbneset, excavated to expose the hearth (photo Bjørnar Olsen).*

represented in the charred material that primarily stems from the hearths themselves. The most frequent species are pike (*Esox lucius*) and common whitefish (*Coregonus sp*) (Vretemark 2009). The presence of cod bones (*Gadus morhua*), albeit in very small quantities, indicates contact with the coastal area, most probably through summer residence at the coast (Hedman and Olsen 2009; cf. Tanner 1929; Olsen 1984).

A total of 225 artefacts were recovered, the majority of which consisted of cut pieces of bronze or copper alloy (20 per cent) and (tinder) flint (32 per cent). The finds were concentrated at the hearths and the areas immediately surrounding them. Their even distribution around the hearths differs remarkably from the spatially confined bone distributions (see Figure 9.13: p. 177). The flint debris is that characteristic of firestrikers used to produce sparks and fire. Thin pieces of cut bronze or copper alloy are very commonly found at both Sámi sacrificial sites and dwelling sites in northern Fennoscandia and Russia, and have a wide chronological distribution from the Late Iron Age to early modern times (Serning 1956; Carpelan 1975, 2003; Zachrisson 1976, 1984; Odner 1992; Hedman 2003). As raw cut pieces, their function remains uncertain. One suggestion is that they were used as a kind of trade 'currency' (Odner 1992: 131). Their local importance is witnessed by the fact that they are often worked into ornaments such as trapezoid- and axe-shaped pendants (Serning 1956; Zachrisson 1984). A total of ten of these locally produced pendants were found at Brodtkorbneset, in addition to two other bronze ornaments probably originating from the Ladoga area in Russia (cf. Makarov 1991; Ovsiannikov 1993). Among the other artefacts were four arrowheads, two firestrikers, an axe, a hide scraper, a knife and a fishhook, all made of iron. Bone/antler artefacts were very rare, although a fragmented composite comb was found and the iron knife contained a partially preserved bone shaft. In addition to tinder flint, the stone implements included hones/whetstones and a hammer stone. As with the bones, the artefacts were unevenly distributed among the hearths, with the central hearths being the richest. It is interesting that a 'mundane' artefact such as a tinder flint, while numerous in the deposits from the central hearths, was completely lacking from the two hearths at the extreme (H1 and H7) (Hedman and Olsen 2009).

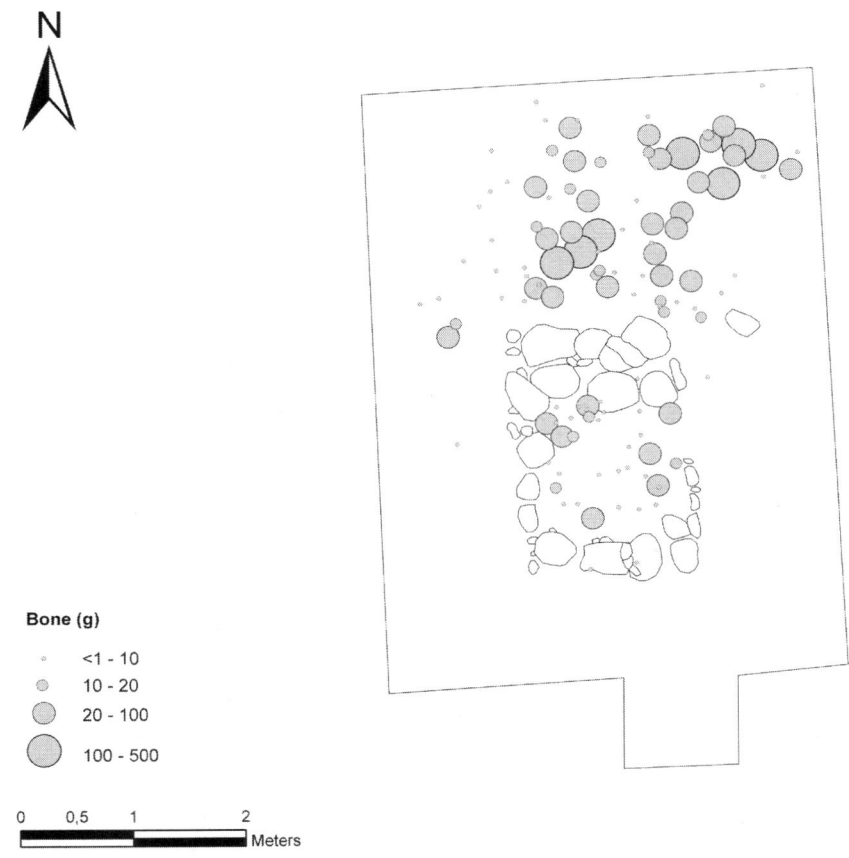

Figure 9.4 *The distribution of bones (weight units) in the area around Hearth 5, Brodtkorbneset.*

So far radiocarbon dating has been conducted on 29 bone and charcoal samples from Brodtkorbneset. The bone samples consist of burned and unburned reindeer bones, while the charcoal samples stem from selected branches and outer growth rings of pine, the only tree species present in the material. With a few exceptions, the dates cluster rather nicely and suggest that the sites were most likely to have been in use sometime during the twelfth or thirteenth centuries.

The Kiellajoenkangas site

The Inari Kiellajoenkangas site is located between the mountain area in the east and the lower lake region and the Lake Inari basin in the west. This intermediate foothill environment is characterized by mixed bog, rivers and lakes. The site is situated on a sandy heath intersected by small lakes and in a mixed forest area of pine and birch. The ground vegetation consists of reindeer lichen, crowberry and lingonberry heather. The site contains nine rectangular hearths organized linearly along a ridge constituting the isthmus between two small lakes.

As with the other sites, the hearths are oriented perpendicularly in relation to the overall direction of the row. The distance between the hearths varies from eight to 21 metres, and it cannot be ruled out that the site is an aggregation of two or more smaller hearth rows (Figure 9.5). At the south-western end of the hearth row there is a circular hearth that is an exception to the otherwise rectangular hearth form. This hearth has not been investigated and it thus remains uncertain how it relates chronologically to the hearth row. The length of the hearths varies from 1.8 to 2.6 m, their width varies between 1.1 and 1.5 m, and their maximum height is 35 cm. Three of the hearths, H4, H7 and H9, were excavated (for the three Finnish sites the excavated area varied between 47 and 49 square metres).

The excavated hearths at this site are very large, measuring as much as 2.6 m in length. As with Brodtkorbneset, they contained bigger and more solid stones at one end – in this case the south-western end. The stratigraphical situation matched that described for Brodtkorbneset, and the fact that fire-cracked stones were present only in the top layer indicates that the hearths were not built piecemeal or rebuilt. Some internal detailed differences could also be observed: inside H7 and H9 there were slab stones under the fire-cracked stones, but not in H4.

The faunal material was much poorer than at Brodtkorbneset. The only identified mammal species is reindeer. Identified fish species are pike *(Esox lucius)*, in addition to unidentified *salmonid (Salmonidae)* and *cyprinid (Cyprinidae)* fish species. The recovered artefacts were also quite few, and included six pieces of cut bronze or copper alloy and seven tinder flint

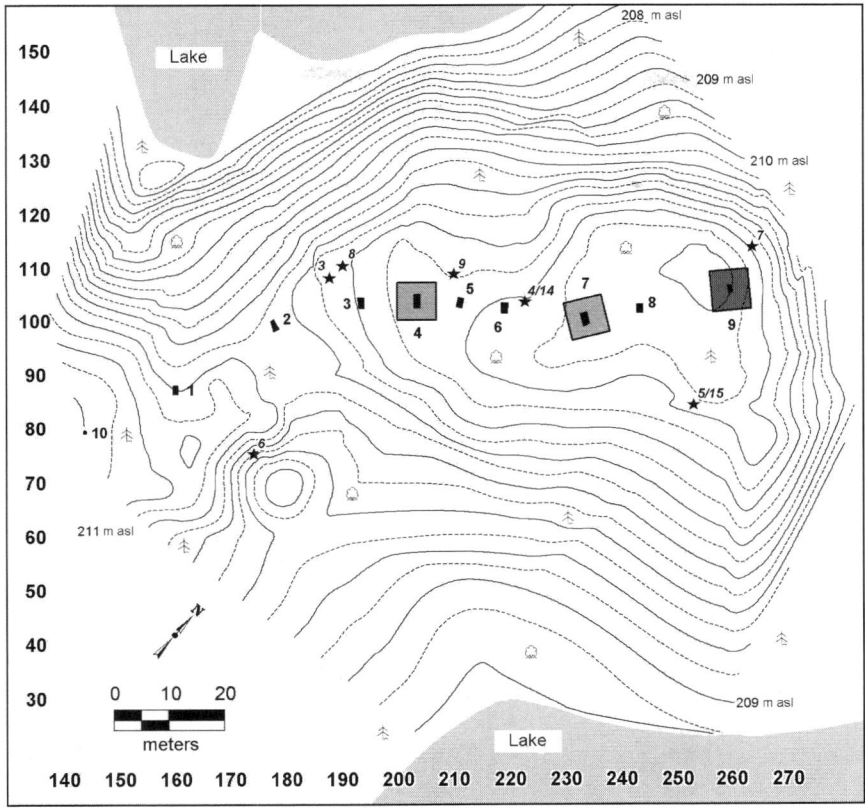

Figure 9.5 *The hearth row site at Kiellajoenkangas, Finland.*

pieces. An iron knife was found in association with H9. The most 'exotic' finds were three intact glass beads and a fragment of a fourth. Compared to bronze and iron implements, glass beads are quite rare in Sámi contexts. We are not aware of any typological parallels to Kiellajoenkangas beads in the Scandinavian and Finnish material, which may suggest that they originate from somewhere in the Novgorodian area of influence (cf. Mulk 1994: 185).

All three excavated hearths have been radiocarbon dated, and a total of five dates are currently available, all based on charcoal. Deciduous tree samples were obtained from H4, while only pine was present in the charcoal samples from H7 and H9. The dates range from the end of the tenth century to the beginning of the thirteenth century. The most likely dating of the hearths is from the end of the twelfth century to the beginning of the thirteenth century, which coincides well with the dating of the Brodtkorbneset site.

The Siuttavaara W site

The Inari Siuttavaara W site is situated on a terrace on the east side of the Inarijoki River. The terrace is flat and situated 15 m above the riverbed. From the terrace the terrain rises gently towards the east, but breaks off quite suddenly into a steep slope towards the river in the west. On the northern side of the site there is a ravine with steep slopes. The dominant tree species is pine with ground vegetation consisting of lichen, crowberry and lingonberry heather.

The site consists of six rectangular hearths organized in a linear pattern. The row is oriented perpendicularly to the terrace edge and the river, which indicates that the river was not a determining factor in its orientation. The hearths are spaced at intervals varying from 8 to 14 m on the remarkably flat site area. Near the hearth at the eastern end of the row (H1) there is a large hunting pit, which was excavated in 1995 and has been radiocarbon dated to the third millennium B.C. (Halinen 2005: 154). About 500 m to the south there is another, larger, hearth row site – Siuttavaara. This site contains 25 hearths in two rows arranged one behind the other with only a short break between the larger and smaller groups. Beside the hearth row there are three hunting pits and a Stone Age/Early Metal Period activity area, which is not properly dated. Four of the hearths have been excavated, and radiocarbon dates indicate a time range from the tenth to thirteenth centuries and on to the Late Medieval Period. The contexts of the charcoal samples, however, were not reliable in every case, which caused a wide range of dates. The hunting pits are radiocarbon dated to the first millennium B.C. The hunting pits clearly predate the hearth row sites, providing evidence for the use of this area for hunting and other activities since the Stone Age.

Two hearths at the Siuttavaara W site were excavated as part of the project, and for each an area of 49 square metres was investigated. The first hearth, H1, was situated in the eastern end of the hearth row and measured 1.8 × 1.2 × 0.15 m. A remarkable feature was that it was mainly constructed of worked stones that had been given an angular shape (Figure 9.6). Both end sides of the hearth contained two bigger stones, though those at the south-western end were higher and more visible. The frame stones were longish in form and clearly bigger than those inside the hearth, which were fire-cracked and tightly packed. The finds were very sparse: only four fragments of unburned bone, two pieces of cut bronze or copper alloy, and one tinder flint. They were found mostly outside the hearth, in a zone which may have constituted the wall area of the dwelling. None of the finds were datable or had characteristic features for cultural interpretation. The only identifiable bone was an astralagus (ankle bone) from a reindeer.

The second hearth, H2, was situated as number three in the row from the east.[4] Its present size was $1.3 \times 1.1 \times 0.15$ m; the short length is at least partly due to the fact that the stones from the northern end of the hearth had been removed. The stones used in its construction were stones that had been shaped naturally. On the northern side of the hearth there was an area of discoloured sand, which included burned bone fragments and a lot of fire-cracked stones. When it was observed, we did not know whether it was what remained of an earlier fireplace or refuse from H2. The bones were reindeer and unidentified mammal bones (probably reindeer as well). Its radiocarbon date, 3844 ± 33 BP (Hela-2155), clearly indicates that it relates to the earlier activity documented in this area, making it almost contemporary with the dated hunting pit nearby. The finds from H2 were very few: a piece of cut bronze or copper alloy inside the hearth, two tinder flints beside it, in addition to some quartz and burned and unburned bones. The unburned bone fragments consisted of two pieces of reindeer bone found on the south-eastern and western sides of the hearth. Most of the burned bones were found in the hearth and in the Stone Age refuse area on the northern side.

The two radiocarbon dates, one from each excavated hearth, are almost identical and suggest a likely dating to the end of the tenth century or to the beginning of the eleventh century. This makes the Siuttavaara W site earlier than the two previous hearth rows described. However, caution

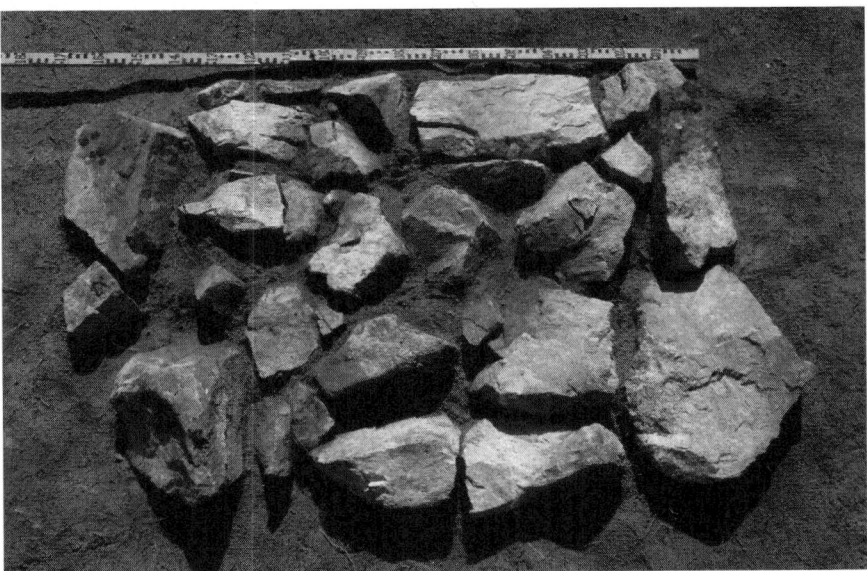

Figure 9.6 *Hearth 1, Siuttavaara (photo Petri Halinen).*

must be taken due to the low number of dates and the fact that they are based on charcoal from pine, which máy skew the dating to produce a slightly older result.

The Ampumaradan tausta site

The Inari Ampumaradan tausta site is situated on a flat, elevated terrace on the eastern side of the River Inarijoki. The flat terrace ends in a steep and deep slope towards the river in the west while the terrain rises gently on the eastern side of the terrace. The vegetation is similar to that of the two previous sites. It is important to note that despite the fact that both this site and Siuttavaara W are located close to the Inarijoki River, they are not located at the river bank but on high terraces above the river bed. The steep slopes down to the river suggest that access to the river was not the crucial issue but rather the terraces themselves and what they 'afforded' in terms of settlement space and proximity to fuel, pasture and migration routes.

In contrast to the previous sites, the Ampumaradan tausta site is small and contains only three hearths, organized in a semi-linear pattern. An additional hearth is situated about 200 m to the north. Compared to the other sites the hearths are also quite small, 1.5–1.7 m long and 1.0–1.2 m wide. The distances between the hearths are 10 and 14 m. At the site there are also 25 hunting pits, of which one (hearth five) was excavated in 1995 (Halinen 2005: 154) and yielded a radiocarbon date to 2905±75 BP (Ua-10446). Traces of earlier sites are also present in terms of quartz residues to be spotted on the surface.

The hearth in the middle of the row, H2, was selected for excavation. Its size was 1.7 × 1.2 × 0.08 m. The excavation exposed a rectangular hearth with its western corner disturbed and the original stones dispersed towards the west. Apart from a few larger frame stones, the hearth is peculiar in that it consists of packed small, rounded stones, probably originating from the riverbed (Figure 9.7). The hearth was low as it contained only one layer of these stones. Most of the stones inside the hearth were fire-cracked and the reddish sand layer underneath them confirms intensive firing. The finds only consisted of two fragments of cut bronze or copper alloy. No bones were preserved.

One radiocarbon dating of charcoal (pine) provided a dating that corresponded well to those from Siuttavaara W. This suggests, taking into consideration the caveats already noted, that these two sites belong to a slightly earlier phase than the Brodtkorbneset and Kiellajoenkangas sites – and were probably in use by the end of the tenth century or to the beginning of the eleventh century.

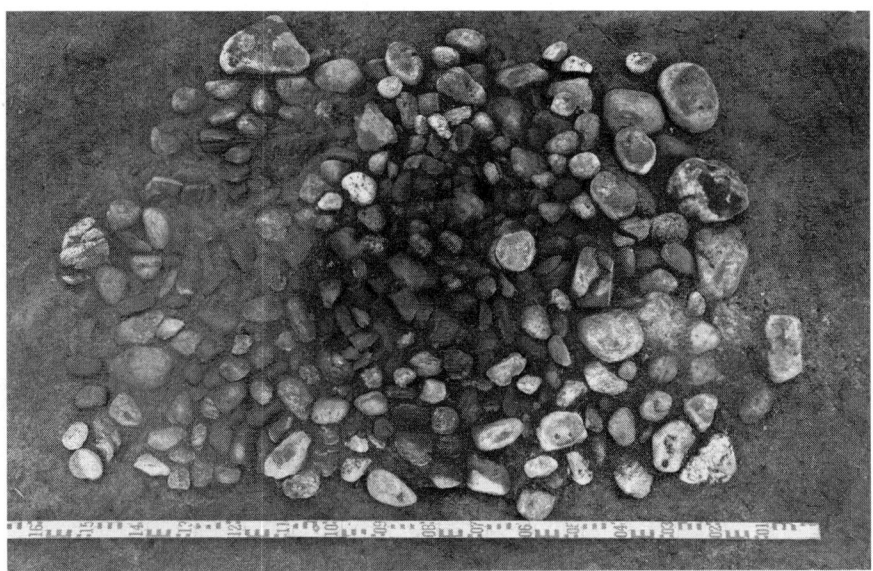

Figure 9.7 *Hearth 2, Ampumaradan tausta (photo Petri Halinen).*

Hearths and dwelling

The basic question is: 'What do the hearths at these sites represent in terms of dwellings and domestic entities?' Despite the substantial area excavated around each hearth, no clear traces related to possible dwelling super-structures – for example, post holes were not found. This negative result resembles earlier investigations, although their limited scales prevented them from reliably scrutinizing this issue. The question thus remains as to whether the hearths represent dwellings or not, but it seems rather unlikely that they do not, for several reasons. The hearths are normally very solidly built, and even in 'lighter' cases such as the Ampumaradan tausta site the amount of stones suggests that heat storage is an important rationale for their construction. Used in an outdoor context, most of the heat would escape into the air and large amounts of fuel would be needed to maintain the heat.

At Brodtkorbneset, the clustering of artefacts around the hearth suggests activity and disposal patterns more in compliance with a dwelling than an open-air site (cf. Olsen 1998: 116ff.). Although the artefact distribution may be claimed to go well with Binford's 'drop and toss zones' for outdoor hearths (Binford 1978: 339), the artefacts recovered here are less likely to be subjected to such 'drop and toss' behaviour. In addition, the systematic distribution of bone refuse clearly suggests spatial patterns

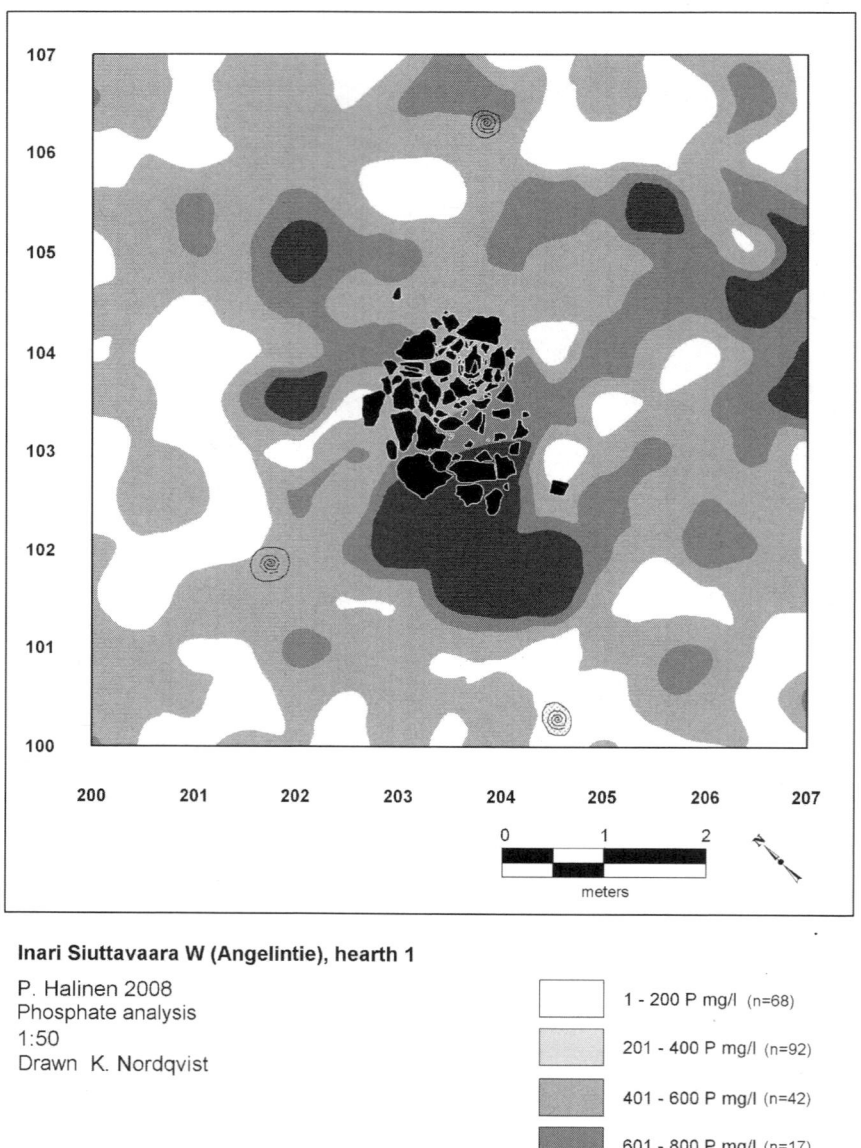

Inari Siuttavaara W (Angelintie), hearth 1

P. Halinen 2008
Phosphate analysis
1:50
Drawn K. Nordqvist

☐ 1 - 200 P mg/l (n=68)

▨ 201 - 400 P mg/l (n=92)

▨ 401 - 600 P mg/l (n=42)

▨ 601 - 800 P mg/l (n=17)

Figure 9.8 *The distribution of phosphate at Hearth 1, Siuttavaara W.*

in accordance with dwelling and entrance structures. At the sites with less favourable preservation conditions, the spatial signatures of the phosphate analyses provides patterns clearly in accordance with what is expected from the confined space of a dwelling and also with historical information concerning the spatial structuring of Sámi dwellings (Figure 9.8, see also Figure 9.11: p. 175).

Given these depositional spatial signatures and the lack of solid building structures, it seems most likely that the hearths were part of a circular tent dwelling with a highly transportable superstructure of light poles and hides or rugs. This type of dwelling was used by the Sámi during both summer and winter. However, there is a significant difference between the light, conical *lávvu* used during summer and seasonal migrations and the more solid winter tent *(goahti)*. The latter was constructed using a framework of paired curved poles *(baeljek)* and was in recent centuries covered by woven wool rugs. The *baeljek* construction also gave the winter tent a more oval floor outline that would even fit large hearths (Figure 9.9). Thus, it seems more likely that the rectangular hearths were used as part of a *goahti* rather than inside a conical tent of the *lávvu* type (see Bjørklund, Chapter 5, in this volume for a detailed description of Sámi dwellings).

From what can be inferred from the intensity and distribution of finds, faunal material and soil chemical signatures, the human groups associated with each hearth were rather small, probably consisting of nuclear families. The hearth lines may thus be seen as representing co-residing households.

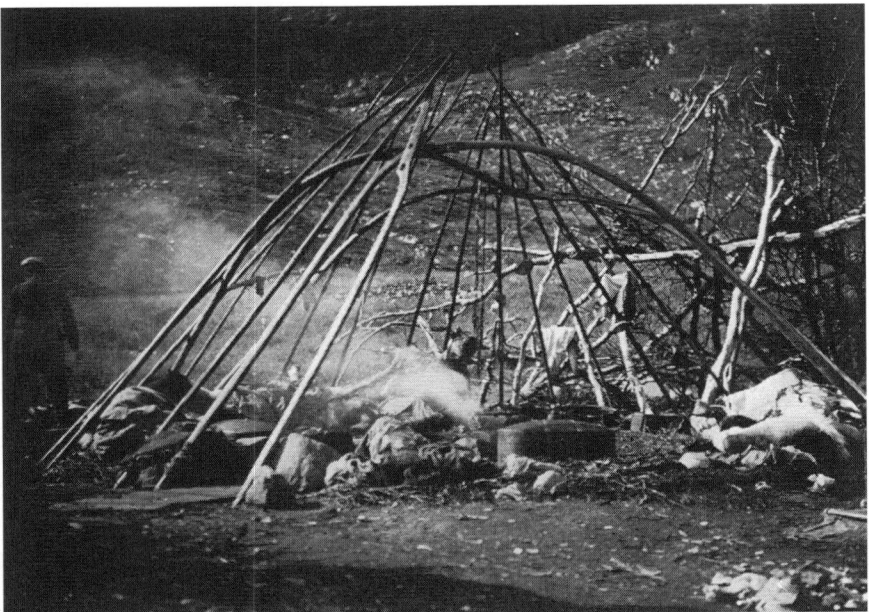

Figure 9.9 *The uncovered frame and* baeljek *of J. Pingis' goahti in Rautasjaure, Sweden, 1909 (photo Gustaf Hallström/Photo c690 Forskningsarkivet, Umeå universitet).*

Seasonality, settlement pattern and economy

All the investigated hearths are large and contain an assemblage of packed stones, normally kept inside a frame of larger rim stones. This design creates good heat radiation and also provides an effective heat reserve. Although by no means identical, the size, solidity and constructional features of the hearths suggest that they were used during the colder part of the year – as also implied from their inferred *goahti* superstructure.

Ethnographic material from the eastern Sámi, and the Skolt Sámi in particular, may be used in support of an interpretation of the hearth row sites as winter settlements (Tanner 1929; Nickul 1948; cf. Tegengren 1952). The winter villages *(talv-sijd)* were used from December to April and they served as aggregate sites for the entire community *(siida),* which dispersed into family-based units during other seasons. The winter village was commonly located alongside smaller lakes or tarns and thus away from the major waterways (Keilhau 1831; Tanner 1929). This was a 'relaxing' site characterized more by social reproduction and networking than subsistence activities. The community mostly lived on stored resources, and access to reindeer pasture and firewood were the main factors that determined the location of the winter site. These very same factors caused the winter village to be moved at intervals of 5–30 years (Tanner 1929: 104–6; cf. Nickul 1948: 54–6).

In a number of ways, the settlement system of the east Sámi *siidas* provides a plausible model for interpreting the seasonality and settlement patterns of the investigated hearth row sites. For example, the fact that in the vicinity of the Brodtkorbneset site there are two more hearth row sites, also with seven hearths, fits well with the pattern of 'moving' winter villages. More generally, the new environmental preferences indicated by the location of the hearth row sites also comply with the location of the historical *talv-sijds*.

Archaeological materials, however, often resist being matched harmoniously to ethnographic examples. Also, in this case the retrieved material urges some caution. While the amount and variety of finds from the Brodtkorbneset site may fit well with a communal site occupied throughout a substantial part of the year, the material from the three other sites is meagre and less conclusive. Much of this is probably due to poor preservation conditions. However, the variation in hearth morphology, size and the number of hearths at these sites may be indicative of other seasonal or socio-economic conditions. The faunal material adds further nuances to the ethnographically derived models of the winter villages.

While the preserved bones from the Finnish sites are far too few to support any firm conclusions, the Brodtkorbneset assemblage allows for some interesting modifying interpretations. Several features indicate a settlement involved in subsistence activities rather than living on stored resources, as assumed by the winter-village model. The cut marks on pike jaw bones indicate the possible procurement of freshly caught fish for drying[5] and the recovered pike vertebrae were all from near the tail part of the spine, suggesting that the fish-rich (and dried?) parts were produced for consumption elsewhere (Vretemark 2009: 10). The same can be said of the pike bones of the Kiellajoenkangas site, which also suggest processing for storing/drying (Halinen 2009). Lake and river fishing were predominantly carried out during spring and fall (when drying also took place), although fishing for pike with nets under the ice during winter is known as well (Tanner 1929: 125, 134–7; Nickul 1948: 21–53). The reindeer bones show an even spread of body parts including meat-rich limb bones, as well as less meat-rich bones such as crania, ribs and vertebrae (Vretemark 2009: 5–6). This suggests that the reindeer consumed were not stored products brought in from other seasonal sites, but had been slaughtered on or near the site, either by killing domestic ones or by hunting from the site. Hunting and slaughtering would most likely take place during autumn, although less extensive late winter snow hunting is also known historically among the Skolt Sámi (Tanner 1929: 116; cf. Tegengren 1952: 105–6). Taking these mixed material suggestions into consideration, it cannot be ruled out that the Brodtkorbneset site was used during fall or late winter/early spring, or that it was used biannually during different seasons. Returning to the same site during other seasons was not uncommon among the late Skolt Sámi (Tanner 1929: 127–9, 216–20).

Having said this, most data still speak in favour of the hearth row sites as primarily cold-season settlements, which in addition to the winter months proper may have included late fall and spring occupation (as suggested by the pike bone remains from Brodtkorbneset and Kiellajoenkangas). Moreover, the organization, frequency and morphology of the hearths make us inclined to believe that the majority of these sites were aggregate sites where the local community gathered and which separate them from family-based sites. Caution, however, must be taken when considering smaller sites such as Ampumaradan tausta, which may represent smaller units cooperating for short-term hunting or herding purposes.

Hunters and herders?

Reindeer is overwhelmingly dominant in the faunal material, which triggers the question as to whether they were of domesticated or wild stock. Pitfalls for trapping wild reindeer are found in the vicinity of all the investigated sites, which, while clearly predating them, suggest that the hearth row sites were located in areas that provided excellent hunting grounds. The presence of arrowheads at Brodtkorbneset is clear evidence that hunting took place (Hedman and Olsen 2009). That reindeer hunting still was a very important part of the Sámi economy is also reflected in the fact that by far the greatest quantity of iron arrowheads known from the Sámi settlement areas date to the very time of the hearth row sites (Serning 1956; Wegraeus 1973; Hedman 2003; Sommerseth 2009). In fact, the collective hunting of wild reindeer is recorded among the Skolt Sámi as late as the early nineteenth century (Rathke 1907: 159), and even later among the Sámi in northern Finland (Tegengren 1952:101–4).

Thus for a long period, hunting was practised alongside reindeer herding among the Sámi, by the very same groups. Although pastoralism did not become a dominant mode of production among the eastern Sámi before the nineteenth century and early twentieth century (Tanner 1929; Tegengren 1952), the keeping of small stocks of domesticated reindeer is clearly older. However, when this small-scale herding emerged is uncertain, as is the extent to which its economic significance has fluctuated in the more distant past. The fact that the location of the hearth row sites differs from the typical location of earlier inland sites may be indicative of a new economic adaptation. Although some of the investigated sites are situated quite close to large rivers (Inarijoki, Pasvik), their location on elevated terraces above the actual riverbanks, making the river difficult to access, suggests that it was not the immediate 'affordances' (Gibson 1979) of the river that were decisive. One possible interpretation is that access to reindeer pastures, and thus the importance of domesticated reindeer, had become imperative to the location of the sites (Hedman 2003). It cannot be ruled out, however, that this new settlement pattern reflects intensified hunting (due to increased trade and taxation), and/or changes in hunting practices.

The age composition of the individuals represented in the faunal material from Brodtkorbneset shows that predominantly adult reindeer were slaughtered, which has been read as an indicator of the hunting of wild animals rather than the killing of domesticated ones (Vretemark 2009: 2). This, however, is inferred mainly from modern patterns of commercial reindeer production, where calves are more commonly selected for slaughtering. In small pastoral herds, the slaughtering of old animals may be considered advantageous, and age composition is hardly a reliable means to determine whether the reindeer in the past were domesticated or not. In all likelihood, small herds of reindeer were kept for transport and decoy purposes, while hunting maintained its importance.

What may be seen as a surprising clue that domesticated reindeers actually were kept at Brodtkorbneset is the presence of sheep/goat bones, which in itself is rather unique in such an early Sámi context. These bones stem from both meaty and less meaty parts of the body, indicating that the animals were slaughtered at the site (Vretemark 2009: 7). In modern times the Skolt Sámi primarily kept sheep for their wool, and since these animals are not well suited for moving long distances in snow, the animals were transported from the winter to spring sites in sleds pulled by reindeer (see Figure 9.10, and Nickul 1948: 67). Consequently, and given that this was not a sedentary site, the documented presence of sheep (and goat) implies the need for a draft technology that involved domesticated reindeer. The fact that only young individuals are represented (Vretemark 2009: 8) may indicate the wool-producing importance of older animals not selected for consumption.

The intriguing concurrence between the Medieval Warm Period and the time of the hearth row sites may have been advantageous for the introduction of domesticates other than reindeer into the Sámi economy. To what extent this climatic warming also played a role in the possible introduction of reindeer herding, albeit on a small scale, is far more uncertain. On the one hand it probably reduced the extent of mountain summer pastures due to forest growth; on the other hand, it may have increased the pasture productivity and lichen growth in the woodland areas. This was probably disadvantageous for the wild reindeer stocks migrating to the mountains, and possibly made traditional reindeer hunting less productive in some inland areas. This, and increased productivity in the woodland area, may have initiated a closer relationship to more stationary populations of forest reindeer and in turn stimulated the introduction of herding (cf. Tegengren 1952: 106–9).

Hearth row sites and the organization of domestic space

The most conspicuous feature of the spatial organization of the sites is of course the linear organization of the hearths. Another remarkable spatial feature, most obviously observed at Brodtkorbneset, is the repeated pattern in bone refuse disposal. The spatial distribution of the bones shows a clear and systematic clustering to the north side of the hearths. The lack of comparable faunal material from the three other sites prevents direct comparison, but the phosphate analyses (mainly reflecting bone disposal) have produced soil signatures in remarkable spatial concordance with those observed for Brodtkorbneset (Figure 9.11, see also Figure 9.8).

An immediate interpretation of this spatial patterning is that it reflects refuse clearance and butchering activities structured by the orientation of the entrance and thus the front and focal side area of the dwellings. Due to the shared orientation of the hearths at each site, the entrances to the dwellings all faced in the same direction and thereby led to a systematic

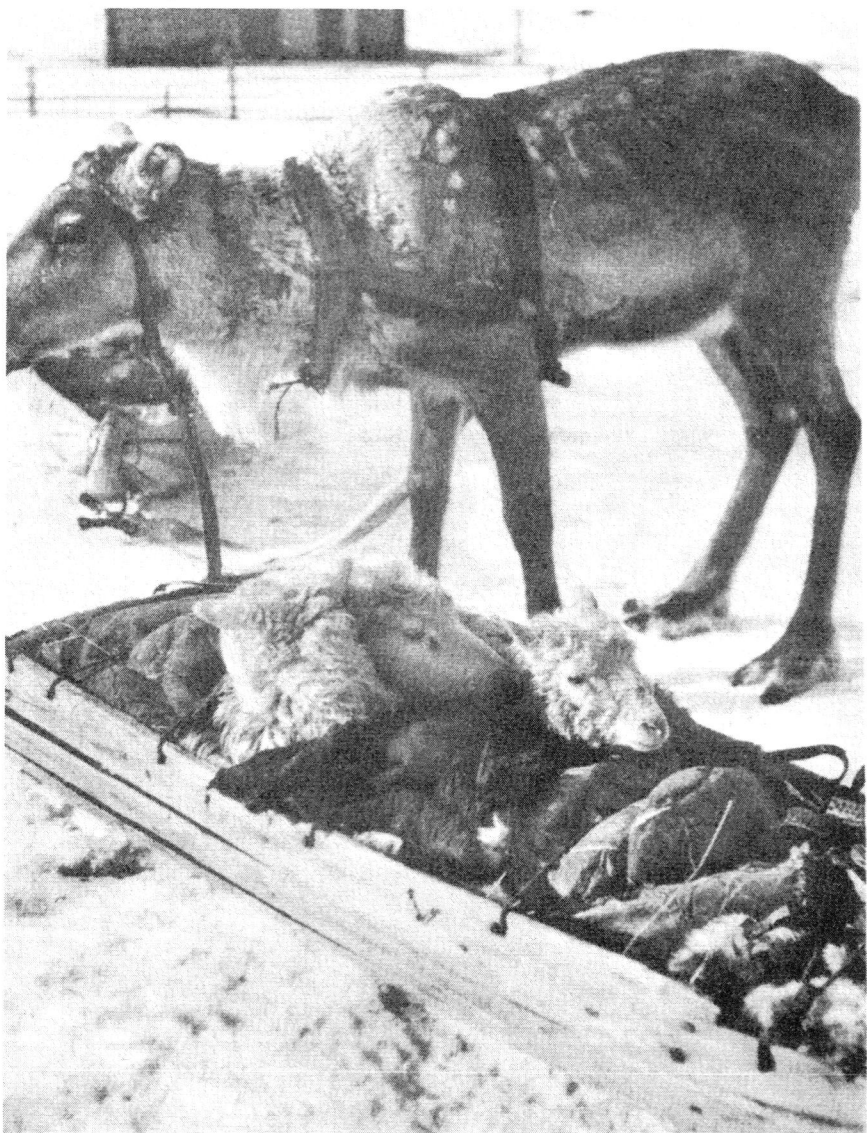

Figure 9.10 *Moving from the winter village: sheep on sledge in Suenjel 1938 (after Nickul 1948: 166, plate XLVII).*

spatial patterning of activities and refuse disposal. This assumption is complicated by historical and ethnographic information regarding the Sámi organization of domestic space (Figure 9.12). As summarized by Gustaf Ränk (1949), the hearth mediated a basic social and cosmological dualism between the front and back spaces in the *goahti,* as also reflected by its two opposite entrances. The inner part of the dwelling (the *boassu* area) was the male area, leaving the front part as the female (and common) domain. The *boassu* was considered sacred, as was the attached back entrance. Sacred objects and hunting weapons were stored here, and as with the slaughtered wild animals, they could only enter the *goahti* through the second doorway (cf. Yates 1989). However, the *boassu* area also served as the kitchen area of the dwelling, the place where meat and fish were cut and prepared for cooking. Thus, according to the ethnographic schemata, it may well be the back side of the dwelling that leaves the most visible imprints in the archaeological and soil chemical record.

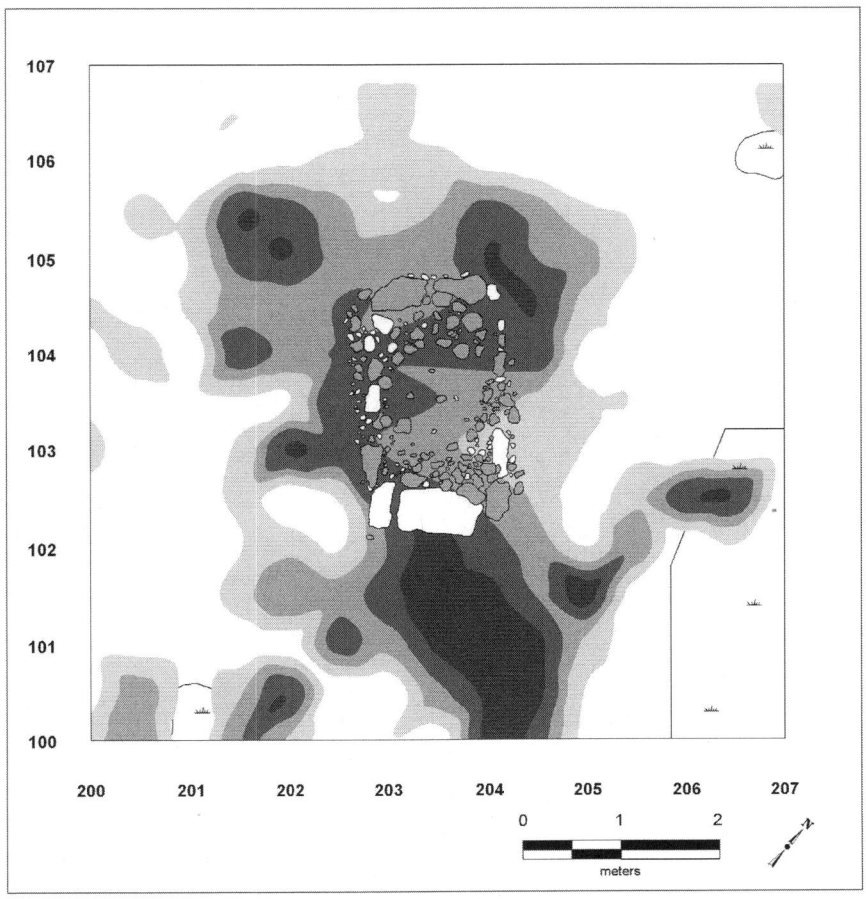

Figure 9.11 *Distribution of phosphate at Hearth 4, Kiellajoenkangas.*

It is interesting to note that the clear spatial patterning of bone refuse is not matched by the artefact distribution at Brodtkorbneset (Figure 9.13). Artefacts are found evenly distributed around the hearth, with most of them next to the long sides. These divergent patterns of distribution could indicate that the bones were more likely to be deposited in accordance with the prevailing social and cosmological schemes. The proposed rules for how and where to handle meat and food within and next to the dwelling (cf. Ränk 1949; Mebius 1968; Edsman 1994; Grydeland 2001) may have been decisive for the discrepancy. However, as mentioned, the generated pattern of bone disposal may simply be the result of a dwelling with just one entrance that determined the direction and spread of refuse disposal. Moreover, according to the dualist interpretation, domestic products such as milk, and also domesticated animals such as goats and sheep, should be kept separate from game and 'wild' products, and should enter the house through the front entrance (Yates 1989). The fact that the bones of goat and sheep are found in the same 'back' areas (and same deposits) on Brodtkorbneset as reindeer and wild animals provides another cautionary tale about being too overenthusiastic in the reading of the ethnographic record into archaeological analysis. Nevertheless, it is still intriguing that the bones of these species were found in the same deposit with a rare iron axe and two trapezoid pendants – and that all the arrows were found in what corresponded to the northern section of the dwellings.

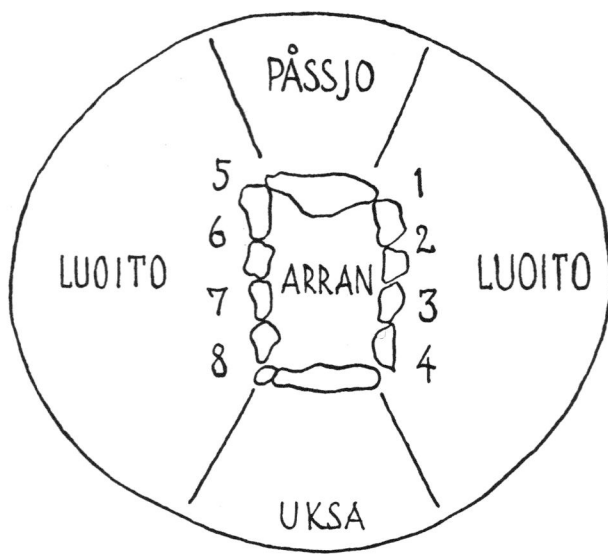

Figure 9.12 *A model of the division of Sámi floor space (after Ränk 1949).*

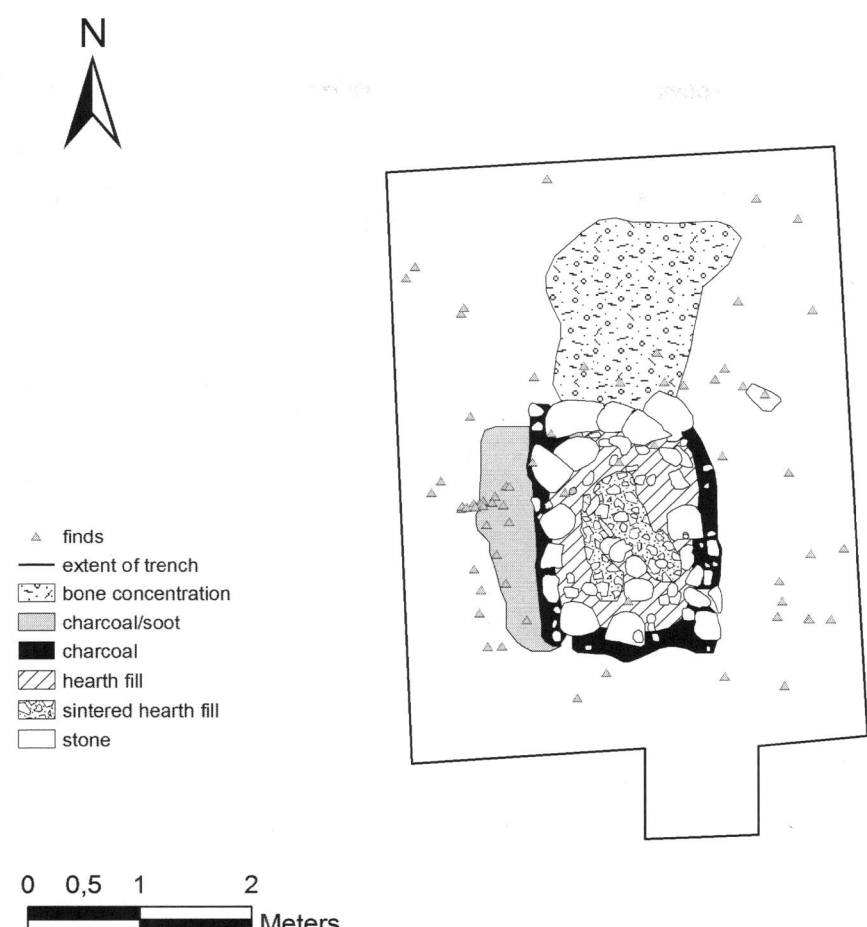

N

finds
extent of trench
bone concentration
charcoal/soot
charcoal
hearth fill
sintered hearth fill
stone

0   0,5   1   2   Meters

Figure 9.13 *Artefact distribution in the Hearth 5 area, Brodtkorbneset.*

Linearity and difference

The most conspicuous spatial feature of the hearth row sites is nevertheless their formalized linear organization. The significance of this spatial
pattern should be considered both on a site-specific and more wide-
ranging regional level. Although we cannot say for sure that all dwellings
associated with the hearths were occupied at the same time (although
most of them probably were), the organization of the site nonetheless testifies that it was constructed and conceived of as an entity. Even if a hearth
row had emerged in an accumulative manner, by subsequent hearths
being added to abandoned ones, those added must have been constructed

and arranged according to the order of those previously built. Possible ancestral hearths would thus have acted as effective members of a hearth row site, also suggesting a more liberal and inclusive conception of contemporaneity than the one normally guiding archaeological chronologies (Olivier 2001: 66; Olsen 2010: 126–8). This possibility notwithstanding, it is important to emphasize that a hearth row site was something more than a number of co-residing units of people. As with all settlements, it was a hybrid site also entailing a number of other inhabitants, including animals and things.

How then should we interpret the linearity so constitutive for the identification and naming of these sites? As with the principle of symmetry, a linear settlement pattern has been associated with egalitarianism (e.g. Levi-Strauss 1979: 133–9, 291–2). By arranging each hearth next to the other, emphasis is placed on the commonality and equality among the people and families occupying the site. This, however, does not mean that we are dealing with a society that actually was egalitarian or without social differentiation beyond that associated with age and gender. As a number of studies have convincingly argued, there is no direct fit between social relations and material manifestation (i.e. Hodder 1982; Schanche 1994; Hayden 1995; Osborne 2007). For example, in his discussion of hearth rows and communal longhouses in the Late Dorset culture of northern Canada, Max Friesen argues that 'this evidence for overt signalling of equality may indicate the presence of the exact opposite: longhouses and hearth rows may have been constructed as acts of resistance to a growing tendency towards inequality or incipient hierarchies' (Friesen 2007: 207; see also Olsen 1984: 105–6; 1994).

Although the row-organized hearths at first glance may look similar to each other, they actually exhibit clear distinctions. These differences include the construction, size and morphology of the hearths themselves, which also, as witnessed at Brodtkorbneset and Kiellajoenkangas, covariates with the amount of bone refuse, as well as the richness of the finds. It should also be noted that the linear outline of the sites is occasionally erratic, modified or broken. Although such variation may be caused by a number of factors, including post-depositional processes, there are still ample reasons to suggest that this also signifies differences between households. Studies of Sámi burials, sacrificial sites and settlements elsewhere in Sápmi have suggested emerging social differentiations within the Sámi societies during the Late Iron Age and medieval period (Odner 1992; Storli 1994; Zachrisson et al. 1997; Schanche 2000; Hedman 2003; Hansen and Olsen 2004; Halinen 2009).

Such emerging differences may be related to the status and prestige ascribed to successful hunters or herders, and/or to a successful involvement in trade networks (Hedman 2003; cf. Hayden 1995). An emerging reindeer pastoralism may possibly have caused tensions in relation to property rights versus common access to resources. Such internal inequality may even have been related to the control of fire. To be able to light and keep the fire in the hearths was vital to survival during the Arctic winters, and to be dependent on others a possible sign of inferiority. It is possible that the uneven distribution of flint and firestrikers at Brodtkorbneset site indicates such differentiated access and dependency. The two firestrikers were found at a central hearth (H5), and the central hearths also contained numerous finds of tinder flint. In contrast, the two most peripheral hearths (H1 and H7) were curiously lacking flint finds.

As already argued, in discussing the potential social significance of the hearths we should be careful in seeing the material side as somehow epiphenomenal or residual to the social side. Things and material structures do not just reflect or mirror a society existing behind the material, but are themselves indispensable parts of this very social fabric (Latour 2005; Olsen 2010). In other words, the hearths were not just expressions of households and communities; they formed integral parts of these collective and composite entities. Taking the hearths seriously as social constituents also implies being attentive to their material characteristics. Despite the impression of equality and sameness imbued by their shape and organization, the hearth rows do also exhibit differences (Hedman and Olsen 2009). The hearths themselves (and associated assemblages) may therefore have contributed to both creating and masking social differences, and as such, played a key role in mediating the opposition between equality and difference, stability and transition.

Hearth row sites, ethnic consolidation and the socio-economy of the North

As previously mentioned, hearth rows became a common feature of Sámi settlement organization during the Viking Age and Early Medieval Period. Given the vast areas affected by this change in settlement organization (cf. Figure 9.1), a proper understanding of it necessitates that the hearth row sites are seen in a wider, interregional context that includes both Sámi and neighbouring societies. Seen from this perspective, their standardized spatial outline may be seen as part of a greater process of formalization and unification of Sámi material culture that took place during this period (Hansen and Olsen 2004: 125–41; Fossum 2006).

In terms of the settlement outline, the same linear pattern is reflected in the organization of the so-called *stallo* house sites that spread throughout the northern Norwegian/Swedish alpine zone (Mulk 1994; Storli 1994; Liedgren et al. 2007; Liedgren and Bergman 2009). Ritual and religious practices also became formalized and unified over larger areas, as manifested in sacrificial practices (Serning 1956; Zachrisson 1984), bear burials (Myrstad 1996) and the spread of the scree-grave burial custom (Schanche 2000; Fossum 2006). Also, with regards to implements and ornaments, the Sámi material repertoire at this time appears as something distinct due to its mixture of foreign (primarily eastern) and local products and styles (Serning 1956; Makarov 1991; Wallerström 1995).

In general, these processes of unification and formalization led to a new 'visibility' of Sámi material culture. From being rather anonymous and regionally patterned during large parts of the Iron Age, Sámi material culture snaps into focus in the late Viking Age as something distinct and widespread, making its recognizable imprint on the vast territory ranging from the South Sámi area to the Kola Peninsula (Hansen and Olsen 2004: 140–41).

These processes of interregional material formalization and unification may be seen as responses to ongoing social and economic processes which took place within neighbouring societies; processes that seriously affected interethnic relationships and thus Sámi societies themselves. The Norse societies become Christianized during the late Viking Age, local chiefdoms gave way to kingdoms and state formations, and in the east the emerging Novgorod trade empire subsequently started to spin its extensive trade network throughout the North.

The effect of all this was an interethnic situation that was under more tension. While earlier interaction was mediated by locally redistributed economies and shared religious values (Odner 1983; Price 2002; Olsen 2003; Hansen and Olsen 2004), the new regimes created a less symmetrical and less predictable sphere of interethnic contact. The intensification of the fur trade (and possibly taxation), particularly (although far from exclusively) as effectuated by Novgorodian interests, put the Sámi economy under pressure, causing a far more direct interface between the 'local' and the emerging European 'world system'. One archaeological signature of this trade is the ornaments of eastern origin found at sacrificial sites (Serning 1956), in burials (Schanche 2000) and at hearth row sites (Simonsen 1979; Hamari 1996; Hedman 2003; Hedman and Olsen 2009). As briefly mentioned, there are ample reasons to suggest that the surplus of this trade acted to create or accentuate processes of social differentiation within Sámi societies.

Within such a turbulent context, the formalization of settlement organization, as reflected in hearth rows and linearly organized *stallo* house sites, together with the unification of religious and ritual practices, may be seen as a way of responding to and coping with this new situation (cf. Olsen 2000; 2003). While also playing a role in terms of negotiating local social processes as suggested above, on a grander scale this material mobilization may have acted to consolidate identity and values and to manifest rights to land and resources. While Sámi ethnic identity was previously meaningful in a primarily local way, and thus differentially manifested, the new material utterances helped to create this identity as something relevant and distinctive on a larger geographical scale. Probably for the first time, Sámi culture and identity emerge as something relatively unified and recognizable within most parts of what is today considered Sápmi. Hearth rows contributed to this process of ethnic consolidation and unification. Moreover, by being constructed over increasingly larger areas, their presence may have reminded travelling traders and tax collectors of the people to whom this land belonged (see also Wishart and Loovers, Chapter 4, in this volume,). Against the backdrop of state economies and trade networks competing over Sámi resources, the hearth rows may have thus also acted as a mutually comprehensible if tacit statement of Sámi rights to pastures and hunting grounds.

Conclusion

The large rectangular hearths, with their peculiar linear organization, were long considered as displaying 'non-Sámi' features. Stereotyped conceptions of Sámi culture as static and spatially disorganized clearly grounded such opinions. On a par with Sámi material culture more generally, the extensive repertoire of hearth row sites brought to archaeological attention over the past 30–40 years clearly challenges these and other prejudiced concepts. In this chapter, we have argued that the order and symmetry implied by the row-organized hearth sites were probably related to both the role they played in internal social dynamics and in negotiating regional processes of change. As such, their conspicuous design and spatial order were clearly historically contingent, responding to transitional processes in one of the most decisive epochs of Sámi and northern history.

The material also provides a thought-provoking supplement to narratives based on the ethnographic record. Although there may be significant commonalities with settlement patterns and subsistence practices, as depicted for the Skolt and eastern Sámi societies from the late sixteenth century to the early twentieth century (cf. Tanner 1929; Tegengren 1952), the material also suggests ways of dwelling and organizing domestic space that do not conform to the historical and ethnographical information. Nor does it comply well with basic socioeconomic taxonomies separating hunters from herders, or 'simple' from 'complex' societies. Those who tented at the hearth row sites nearly a millennium ago may well have been both reindeer hunters and herders, and their pastoral skills were not restricted to just reindeer.

Acknowledgements

The research for this chapter was funded by the Academy of Finland and the Norwegian Research Council. The authors wish to thank Björn Hatteng for producing the geographical map, Radoslaw Grabowski for producing site and distribution maps for the Brodtkorbneset site, and Kerkko Nordqvist for the maps from the Kiellajoenkangas, Siuttavaara and Ampumaradan tausta sites. Maria Vretemark conducted the osteological analysis of the faunal material from Brodtkorbneset, while Eeva-Kristiina Harlin and Kristiina Mannermaa analysed the bones from the Finnish sites.

Notes

1. The Viking Age is commonly dated to c. 800–1050 A.D. and the Early Medieval Period to 1050–1200 A.D.
2. Due to the low sample size covering the period from 1200–1430, it has presented two different temperature curves – a cooler one and a warmer one (Zetterberg et al. 1994: 115), and cooler periods c. 1260–1320 (i), 1440–1480 (ii) and 1781–1850 (iii).
3. We applied phosphorus, pH, and magnetic susceptibility analysis. The phosphorus tests were used to develop phosphorus concentration diagrams which give an impression of the distribution of organic matter, and in particular the concentration of wastes from food processing and the concentration of domestic animals. The magnetic susceptibility tests allow one to make generalizations on which rocks had been disturbed.
4. During the initial survey and recording of the site one hearth situated between H1 and H2 was missed and has later been added to the record. To be consistent with the official heritage record the old numbering is used here.
5. Cutting the front jaw section of the pike head was done prior to splitting the fish along its spine to facilitate better/faster drying (cf. also Itkonen 1921: 65).

CHAPTER 10

Building a Home for the Hearth
An Analysis of a Chukchi Reindeer Herding Ritual

Virginie Vaté

Numbering today about 15,800, Chukchis live in the Arctic reaches of north-eastern Siberia, a region of open tundra bounded to the east and north by coastline. For about three centuries (Vdovin 1965: 4, 14), Chukchis, taking advantage of this environmental diversity, have been split between two distinct socio-economic groups, comprising inland reindeer herders *(Savsu)*[1] and coastal sea-mammal hunters *(Aŋqal'yt)*. This complementary 'dual model subsistence' (Krupnik 1998) has enabled the Chukchi to specialize in different activities, while maintaining access to maritime and terrestrial products through regional exchange networks.

Despite the effects of collectivization during the Soviet period, the division of the Chukchis into reindeer herding and sea-mammal hunting communities still exists. It may in fact have been reinforced by Soviet-era reorganizations, which institutionalized this division (see Kerttula 2000: 81–120). Nevertheless, the Soviet policy of creating permanent settlements (of various sizes) for nomadic peoples has complicated the organization of Chukchis in two types of activity. Today, Chukchis live in Anadyr, the capital of Chukotka, in the smaller cities of the region, in villages dominated by sea-mammal hunting, or in villages dominated by reindeer herding – or, if they are reindeer herders, they move back and forth between the tundra and the village. Members of herding families no longer live permanently and exclusively in the tundra, in mobile tents; rather, they all have a flat or a house in the village, where they have access to manufactured goods and where their children go to school. In this chapter, however, I focus on life in the tundra.

In the areas where I did my fieldwork, although not in all parts of Chukotka, people still live in nomadic tents when they are in the tundra. These tents, which are crucial to reindeer-herding life, are called *iaraŋy* or, in Russian, *iaranga*.[2] As I have shown in previous publications, the *iaranga* is not only a home for herders living in the north-eastern Siberian tundra; it also plays a central role in the way people define their identity through several levels of belonging (see Vaté 2011). Family units are defined in terms of the *iaranga,* so that newborn children belong to the *iaranga* in which they are born or to which the mother belongs when the child is born (which may be her husband's or her parents', depending on whether or not she is married). Each tent is also associated with the name of a group that some authors call 'ethno-territorial' (for instance, Nuvano 2008), since many of these names are affiliated with a topographic space (for instance, the *ŋésqél'yt* are the people from Neshkan – today, a village located on the northern coast of Chukotka). But in particular through its hearth and the representations linked to it, the *iaranga* establishes bonds among the key elements of Chukchi herding life: reindeer, the family and the land (Vaté 2007; 2011). Therefore, in the Chukchi herding context, home, hearth and households are intimately linked (much as Wishart notes with reference to other settings in the introduction to this volume).

Among the Chukchis, the intricate relationship between home, hearth and household finds its optimal expression in ritual context. *Ḓênrir"un,* which occurs in autumn, is the Chukchi reindeer herding ritual par excellence, insofar as it encompasses and puts into play all the elements of herding life. It is what Hamayon defines as a 'totalising ritual' ('rituel totalisateur' – Hamayon 1990: 733): a ritual 'that governs the internal organisation of the society and its relation to the world'. In the course of *Ḓênrir"un,* the hearth, home (the *iaranga),* herders, reindeer and the land (and also ancestors and even plant-life, although I have largely neglected these dimensions in this chapter) are integrated in an elaborate scenography involving multiple levels of symbolism and representations. Therefore, this chapter offers an ethnographic account of parts of *Ḓênrir"un,* supplemented with reference to some aspects of another, now rarely performed, ritual sequence called *Myŋik* or *Mŋêgyrgyn.* As shall be seen, the *iaranga,* including the space around it, is not merely the location where these rituals are performed; rather, it is the centre of ritual organization, both physically and symbolically.

After some brief introductory remarks about the *iaranga* and the structure of the encampment, I will present the ritual *Ḓênrir"un* in general, and then give a more precise description, focusing on some of the main 'actors' and the roles that they play in the ritual: people, reindeer, various ordinary or ritual objects, the hearth and the *iaranga* itself. Finally, I will give some insights into the *Myŋik* ritual and the connection that it builds between the *iaranga,* its inhabitants and their reindeer.

The *iaranga* and the encampment

The *iaranga* is a movable dome-shaped tent, approximately seven metres in diameter, with a covering made of reindeer hides that is stretched over a wooden frame (Figure 10.1). The interior of the *iaranga* consists of two parts. The first part, the *ërony*, is a small inner tent of about two by two metres, built against the back wall of the *iaranga*. It is just large enough for approximately five people to sleep in, and it is well sealed to retain body heat and the heat of candles (in the past oil lamps were used). The second part of the *iaranga* is the *sottagyn* (literally 'what is beyond the pillow', the *sot-sot*), which is the larger, unheated part. This is where many everyday activities occur (e.g. cooking, softening hides, etc.).

When viewed from the perspective of a person sitting at the back of the *iaranga,* in the *ërony* or inner tent, and facing the entrance, the right side of the tent is called *aivas'yn* and the left side *éigysqyn*. In dictionaries, these terms are often translated as 'north' and 'south', but fieldwork conducted in two different regions (Amguema and Kanchalan) revealed that, although the vernacular terminology for the sides of the tent was similar, the compass orientation of the tents varied. In Amguema, the *aivas'yn* was indeed to the south, but, in Kanchalan, it was to the west; correspondingly, *éigysqyn* lay to the north in Amguema but to the east in Kanchalan. In the same way, in Amguema, the entrance of the *iaranga* faces the east (or, more precisely, the south-east), while in Kanchalan it faces the south (or, sometimes, the south-west).

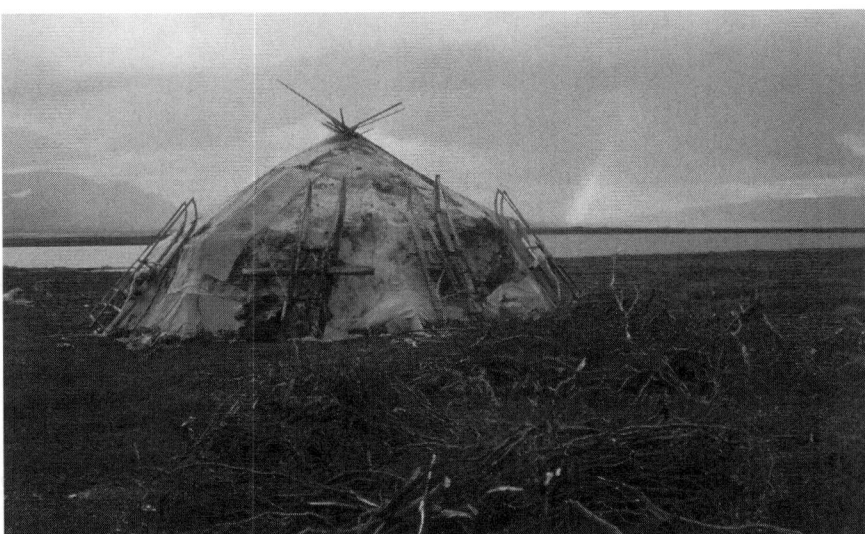

Figure 10.1 *The* iaranga *(Amguema 1999, photo V. Vaté).*

People explained that, in Kanchalan, the strongest winds usually come from the east, therefore the door of the tent could not face in that direction. Indeed, for the terms *éigysqyn/aivas'yn,* Bogoraz gives the following translations: 'side that is in the wind'/'side that is protected from the wind' (Bogoraz 1937: 2, 24). Therefore the orientation of the tent may differ according to the winds prevailing in the region, even if the standard ver- ·
nacular terms denoting direction are applied (on orientation and its relation to the environment – see Oetelaar et al., Chapter 12 in this volume). In this chapter, I will refer to the compass orientation of the tents, as I observed them during fieldwork in Amguema and its vicinity. However, it is important to know that, even though the compass orientation of the tent may differ by regions, the principles governing the organization of the tent and the designation of its space remain constant (for sketches and more detailed descriptions, see Vaté 2005–2006).

The encampments that I visited during my fieldwork were made up of three to ten *iaranga,* depending on a number of variable circumstances. *Iaranga* are usually built in a line, and their sequence in this line reflects the hierarchical position of the tent, or of the corresponding family, in the encampment (about the importance of linear patterns in another context, see Halinen et al., Chapter 9 in this volume). Prior to the Soviet era, the northernmost *iaranga* was that of the owner of the herd (called *érmés'yn* or 'the strong one') or, in the case of an association of herders who had pooled their individual herds, of the one who had the biggest part of the conglomerate herd (see also Vaté 2005–2006, 2011). The position of any given *iaranga* also has something to do with the length of time that a particular family has spent taking care of the herd and living in its proximity. During fieldwork in 2005, for instance, I observed that newcomers from another encampment built their tent on the southern end of the line.

Presentation of *Dênrir''un*

Most of the regular herding rituals are linked to the main events in the life and reproductive cycle of reindeer. Their performance coincides with events in the life cycle of the reindeer and is intended to promote the welfare of the herd. When rituals are performed, it is necessary to feed all of the 'natural' entities and spirits (e.g. tundra, animals, rivers) so that the herd will remain healthy.

Carried out at the end of August, prior to the rutting period, *Dênrir''un* is the main festival in the reindeer herding ritual cycle (on another herding ritual, held in spring, see Vaté 2005). This is when the men return to the encampment with the herd from the big summer pasture (*qoral'atyk* or *bol'shaia letovka* in Russian), where they have been since about mid-July.

Dênrir''un may be understood from several points of view. From a material perspective, it is necessary to get skins for clothing and meat for consumption, and the reindeer slaughtered during the ritual provide for these needs. At the same time, it is important for reindeer herders to take these products in a ritualized manner that will help to strengthen the trustful relationship and agreement between humans and reindeer (Polomoshnov 1991: 32–3). The ritual is also intended to renew the bonds between humans, reindeer and the tent – bonds that may have been distorted during transhumance – and to reintegrate the herd into the protective domestic space, the *iarên:* an area of about three kilometres around the tent and its hearth (see Vaté 2005–2006, 2007, 2011). Lastly, the reproductive potency of the male reindeer seems to be one of the central foci of this ritual, as is, more generally, the reproduction of the herd as a whole. In Kanchalan, this ritual is called *tykyl'yqaanmatgyrgyn* – *tyrkyl'yn* is the male reindeer.

In fact, there are a number of alternative designations for this ritual. In Russian, it is called 'festival of the young deer' *(prazdnik molodogo olenia),* because young deer are sometimes slaughtered, in particular for their light thin skins. This reference to young deer is, however, misleading, as the ritual is concerned especially with male potency and the forthcoming rutting season. Perhaps as a result of Soviet policy, people tend to emphasize pragmatic over symbolic aspects of the ritual (e.g. getting certain kinds of skins and meat according to the season), especially in an urban context. In his classic ethnographic texts, Bogoraz (Bogoras, 1975) refers to this festival with the term *vylgyqaanmatgyrgyn* ('festival of the reindeer with short hair'). But this is confusing, because Bogoraz actually combines two festivals under this single heading. The first is a festival which people in Amguema call *Ulvev* and which I call 'summer festival', since it usually occurs in July. Bogoraz considers this summer festival to be the most important of the two, but in Amguema the second, to which I refer with the term *Dênrir''un,* is evidently more significant. My observations confirm those of Kuznetsova (1957: 282), who did fieldwork in the same region at a much earlier date (from 1948 to 1951).

Today, *Dênrir''un* usually lasts three days, and the activities are distributed roughly as follows.[3] The first day and the third day of *Dênrir''un* start very early, usually at around three o'clock in the morning: a large part of the ritual has to be performed before sunrise. On the first day, men are occupied with the slaughtering of reindeer, after which women are busy butchering. The second day is less regulated, being devoted mainly to cooking the meat for its preservation and preparing the ritual food that will be used on future occasions (such as sausages called *rorat* (m) or *sorat* (f)). Ritual performances dominate on the third day.

In an encampment where *Dênrir''un* is performed, each *iaranga* performs the same series of rituals independently of, but in coordination with, the others. On the first day, the first *iaranga* in the north/south alignment of the encampment begins, and the others follow, with some delay, one after another. On each day, each *iaranga* completes the full cycle of designated ritual practices, ideally in the same sequence in which they began.

I had the opportunity to attend the *Dênrir''un* festival twice in its entirety (in 1997 and in 2005) with two different brigades (each brigade corresponding to a separate encampment, made up of a group of families). I have witnessed the events of the first day five times (three times with three different brigades in 1997 and twice in 2005 with two different brigades). Only a very few differences set the performances of one family apart from another. Through their distinctive practices, family members make collective rituals into familial ones – that is to say, each family perpetuates its own practices, its own marking, within the same framework.

In the following paragraphs, rather than attempting to give an exhaustive presentation of the ritual, I present some of the main 'actors' and show how they are involved or represented in this ritual.

Who is involved in the ritual?

Members of the tent are at the heart of the organization of the ritual, headed by the master and the mistress of the house (in Chukchi *étyn*; in Russian *khoziain, khoziaika*). Members of the tent are usually the father, the mother, the children, and perhaps the wife and children of an older son. But familial situations are very diverse, particularly in the post-Soviet context, and tent-based familial structures can vary.

The activities in the ritual are distributed according to gender. This gendered division of the roles recalls the division in everyday life: men are in charge of everything that is connected to the herd (mostly catching reindeer, slaughtering the animals and feeding the spirits while kneeling in front of the herd and the sunrise), whereas women fulfil all the tasks related to the tent and the hearth (which includes butchering the carcass of the reindeer, preparing the food and feeding ritual objects and other spirits). While men are also involved in rituals, women are given most of the responsibility in their organization, and this had led me to conclude that women bear an indirect responsibility for reindeer herding, which they fulfil through the performance of rituals and in the observance of prohibitions and prescriptions in everyday life (see Vaté 2003, 2011; Povoroznyuk et al. 2010).

Although the family members who reside together in a particular *iaranga* are the active participants in the ritual, the presence of guests is also required. Guests are considered to be necessary for the successful unfolding of the ritual. Rituals are announced by radio so that friends and relatives living in the village or in neighbouring encampments can join. Usually the different brigades, corresponding to a number of different encampments, try to stagger the dates for the performance of *Dênrir"un*, so that their members will be able to visit one another. Guests like to take part in festivals hosted by others, since such events provide an opportunity for enjoying special dishes, prepared only on such occasions, and also for receiving gifts from the hosts (e.g. reindeer or dog skins, whole reindeer, quarters of meat, sledges, etc.). These rituals are, of course, occasions when people can gather together and meet. But this is not the only reason for the presence of guests: they are also expected to share the considerable workload, for example by offering a helping hand in butchering the reindeer slaughtered during the ritual.

In and around the *iaranga:* the place for ritual

On the day before the ritual, the women sweep the *iaranga* carefully with tree branches. Once gathered, dust and other detritus are thrown outside. Housekeeping is not only a preparation for the festival; it constitutes an integral stage of the ritual itself. As Chichlo states with reference to the Yuit (Eskimo) in Chukotka, 'cleaning presents itself as a preliminary rite, which opens the passage to prosperity' (Chichlo 2000: 21, my translation; see also Vaté 2005: 41–2).

During *Dênrir"un*, part of the ritual is performed inside the tent but most of it takes part in front of the *iaranga* – whereas, as we will see, during *Myŋik* it takes place behind the *iaranga*. As is the case with most Chukchi rituals, movements are regulated during *Dênrir"un*. One must circulate around the *iaranga* from north to south, always in the direction of the sun, never the other way around. Elaborate designs and strict rules of movement and orientation help to turn the area around the *iaranga*, where everyday life is lived, into a ritual space (see also Vaté 2005–2006).

Objects
Objects of everyday life

During *Dênrir"un*, many aspects of everyday life are brought into play. Tools that are necessary for everyday activities are involved in the ritual organization of the festival. For instance, on the first day of the ritual a

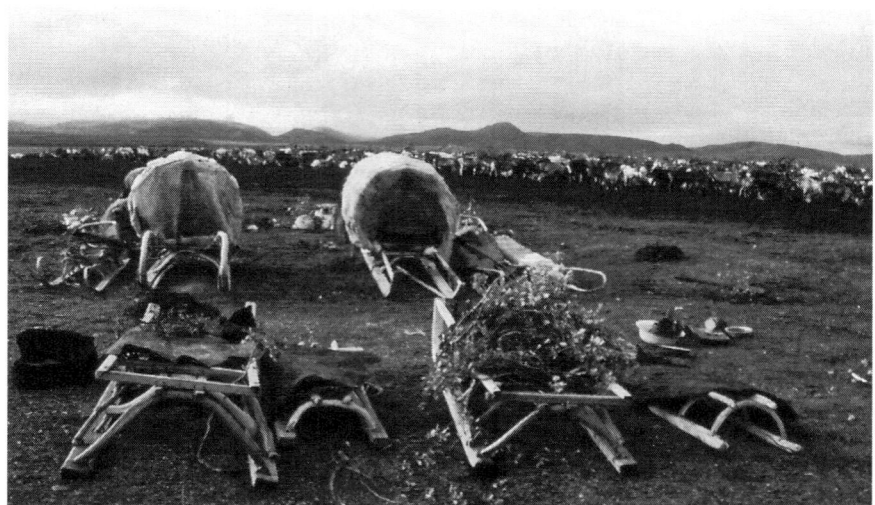

Figure 10.2 *Placement of the sledges during the first day of the ritual* Dênrir"un *(Amguema 1997, photo V. Vaté).*

piece of turf is placed on the wooden board that is used to tan the reindeer skins *(vivyr),* and then it is ignited and thrown in the direction of the reindeer. Also on the first day, the hearth at the front of the tent is lit, and a number of sledges, usually five, are placed in two rows facing each other and the hearth. Sledges, which represent the mobile aspect of the household and which mediate between humans and reindeer, come in different varieties, each of which is positioned accordingly (Figure 10.2). Close to the *iaranga* are placed the *rêpalqolgyn,* or heavy-load sledge, and the *rêlqiinéŋ* – the little sledge with which the central tripod of the tent is transported during migration. Also in front of the *iaranga,* but closer to the herd, one can find the male sledge *(êseêttik),* the female sledge *(ŋav"anorvoor)* and, next to it, the covered sledge for children *(kaaran).* Different ritual objects are placed on the sledges. Once the sledges are in place, the slaughtering of reindeer begins.

All the kitchen utensils that are used in the ritual are first 'washed' – that is, rinsed with water, or scraped clean in the case of wooden objects. The daily dishes are thereby symbolically washed of their secular usage to mark the passage to the register of ritual.

Ritual objects

Ritual objects are handed down from generation to generation – in principle to the eldest son of the family; they are sometimes extremely old. They bear a strong relation to the *iaranga* to which they belong, just as the people born in the *iaranga* have a strong symbolic attachment to it. Categories of ritual objects may vary from one *iaranga* to another, since these objects are closely linked to the history of the family, but the principal objects include wooden offering cups *(koiŋyqagté)*, wooden anthropomorphic fireboards *(milgyt)*, ritual strings *(taiŋykvyt)*, animal skulls *(levyt)*, drums *(iarar)* and ancient weapons (bow, arrows, sheath for arrows, spear) (for more details see Vaté 2005–2006: 44–6; Vaté 2011).

The reindeer

Reindeer are at the centre of the ritual. During the ritual, reindeer are slaughtered and butchered, and parts of reindeer carcasses are either prepared as food or displayed in particular ways and for particular purposes. Several reindeer are slaughtered during the festival. On the first day, after several initial ritual sequences have been performed, the slaughtering starts between four and five o'clock. Each family decides how many reindeer it will slaughter, but usually at least one whole reindeer 'family' is slaughtered – that is to say, a male *(tyrkyl'yn)*, a female *(rêkvyt)* and a young deer born in spring *(qêiuu)*. One of these reindeer, which is called *iitriir*, is slaughtered behind the sledge called *kaaran*, the sledge for children. The *iitriir* is usually a male or a young spring-born deer (which explains, in part, why the ritual is known in Russian as the 'feast of the young deer').

After the slaughtering, the *iitriir*'s body is treated in a special way. For example, the way in which it is placed in the ritual space is quite particular. In a previous article (Vaté 2005–2006), I showed that the orientation of the body of slaughtered reindeer says something about its destination. When, for example, a reindeer is placed along a north–south axis, this means that it is being offered to the deceased and will be consumed at a special place during a rite commemorating the deceased (in Chukchi *iinêniiryk*, in Russian *pominki*). However, when placed along an east–west axis, the reindeer has been slaughtered for living people. The *iitriir* reindeer is also placed along this axis but, during *Dênrir''un*, instead of facing east, as is usual under other circumstances, its head faces west. When it is placed inside the *iaranga*, however, the body of the reindeer must 'look' towards the door (east in Amguema).[4]

The *iitriir* reindeer is usually killed by stabbing it in the heart with a knife, as is also the case in practices of everyday life. However, some families kill it with a spear, thus emphasizing its particular ritual status. Before skinning and butchering the reindeer, the mistress of the house draws signs on the face, armpits, knees and feet of each family member with blood taken directly from the animal's wound (the signs and exact location of the drawings on the body vary in each family). She also uses this blood to paint parts of the *kaaran* sledge (the covered sledge used for children). These drawings are a way of reasserting the bonds existing between humans, the *iaranga* and reindeer. They affirm the link between reindeer and the different members of the household – that is, all the persons clearly related through the hearth of the *iaranga*. Ideally, the mistress of the house paints the markings on her husband and her children, and her husband in turn paints her.

After the family members are adorned with the blood markings, the reindeer is butchered step by step. In this context, I shall mention only those aspects of this process that are relevant for our purposes. The skin of the reindeer is taken off together with the head and placed either in the front part of the *kaaran* or in the front part of a sledge in front of the *kaaran*. The head of the reindeer is put on anthropomorphic fireboards, and ritual objects, such as ritual strings, are draped on the wooden parts of the sledge that sit on the runners. The deer's legs are then placed on its skin, with the front legs in the front and the hind legs in the back. These ritual objects are subsequently 'fed' with marrow from the left leg *(nyqymlëqénat)*. In some families, the big stone *(kysesev)* that serves to secure one of the *iaranga*'s entry pillars, also receives a piece of marrow.

A fuller description of the ritual would have to include many other sequences, but here I restrict myself to explaining what happens to the remains of the *iitriir* reindeer. After some parts of this animal are placed on the sledge, as described above, other parts are put inside the *iaranga*, where they are attached to one of the main pillars of the tent, which is in the shape of a T and located near the hearth (the T-pillars are called *tsytsétsét* (f) *or ryvineŋ* (m) – *tsyvineŋ* (f)) (Figure 10.3). In fact, the lungs, heart, tongue, trachea and antlers of all other slaughtered reindeer are put inside the upper part of the T-pillar, while the right leg of the *iitriir* reindeer is attached to the bottom of the T-pillar with a sprout made of willow[5] *(ëmrottoot)*, a little bit of long grass (called *v"égti*) and white arctic mountain heather *(kênut, Cassiope tetragona)*. The *iitriir*'s antlers are also placed on the ground in front of the leg. The reindeer parts and the leg will stay attached to and on top of the T-pillar until the third and last day of the ritual. On the third day, the treatment given to these parts of the body of the reindeer will involve the hearth, and are explained in the following section.

The hearth

The hearth of the *iaranga* serves to mediate relations among humans, reindeer, the land and the tent itself. Actions affecting the hearth are said to have consequences for the welfare of both humans and reindeer. This is

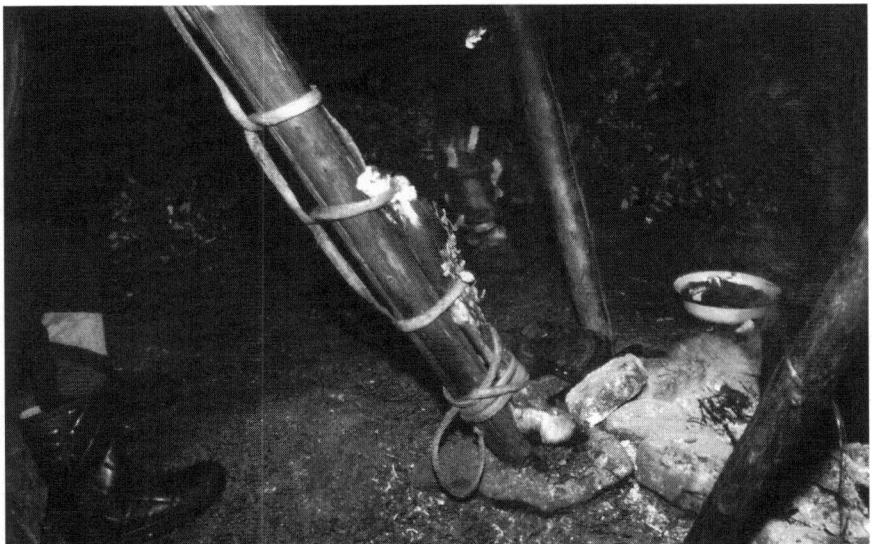

Figure 10.3 *The leg of the* iitriir *reindeer, attached during two days to one of the main pillars of the tent and next to the hearth, at the ritual* Ðênrir"un *(Amguema 1997, photo V. Vaté)*

why the hearth is subject to numerous regulations, prohibitions and prescriptions. For instance, contact with other hearths (or with anything that is liable to come into contact with another fire, such as cooking utensils) is said to bring misfortune and disease to the families of the respective hearths (see also Vaté 2011). It is also forbidden to let a pot hanging from a chain move over the fire, since the movement of the pot is thought to influence the movement of the herd: following the swinging of the pot, the reindeer may run away. Through the hearth, herders believe that they can affect the herd's behaviour in a positive way and promote its health. In this respect, I have argued elsewhere (Vaté 2011: 151) that the fire of the hearth and its smoke play a symbolic role in perpetuating domestication – an issue that is of special concern to Chukchi herders since, generally, reindeer are considered to represent a 'borderline case' in the domestication process (Digard 1990: 151, my translation) and Chukchis, unlike some other herders, do not have a close relationship with their reindeer (with the exception of a few trained animals).

During the *Ðênrir"un* ritual, the hearth occupies a central position. A day before the ritual, the hearth, like the tent and other objects, is 'cleaned'. The mistress of the house removes the ashes thoroughly and takes them outside to the back left side of the tent *(êigysqyn)*, where an older hearth is located (prior to the summer festival *Ulvêv*, the encampment remains on the same location, but each *iaranga* is moved forward slightly in the direction in which the tent entrances are facing; thus, remnants of the hearth that was used previously come to be located behind the *iaranga*). After the hearth is cleaned, it is strictly forbidden to put any rubbish in the fire. Generally, the hearth should always be kept clean, but this general rule is applied more strictly during *Ḓênrir''un* and during the rutting season.

The ritual fire should be ignited exclusively through the use of anthropomorphic fireboards *(milgyt)* – blocks of wood with a 'head' and a 'body' that are used together with a leather bow and a wooden drill to create fire by means of friction. Anthropomorphic fireboards are considered to be the symbolic or 'supernatural' herders of the reindeer (Bogoras 1975: 351–2; Ragtytval' 1986: 171). During the *Ḓênrir''un* ritual the fireboards are activated in order to recharge the capacity of the fire to protect family members and to perpetuate the domestication of the herd (see also Vaté 2011: 153–6).

The fire and the smoke are present throughout the *Ḓênrir''un* ritual. Even before the ritual begins, herders and reindeer are welcomed back from the summer transhumance with fumigations. When the men arrive at the encampment, a few days before *Ḓênrir''un,* the women pass burning branches of white Arctic mountain heather *(kênut; Cassiope tetragona)* in front of them. Each man receives smoke from a branch that has been lit from the hearth of his own *iaranga*. The reindeer, on the other hand, are led into the encampment only on the first day of the ritual. The first act of the ritual involves making a fire with the fireboards and throwing the fire and shooting arrows that were dipped briefly in the fire in the direction of the herd. In fact, fumigations happen throughout the first day, and the hearth, which is fed regularly with ritual food or used to grill ritual foods, occupies the central position in the ritual.

In rounding off this selective review of *Ḓênrir''un,* let us return to the carcass of the *iitriir's* reindeer and the special treatment to which it is subject. On the third day of the ritual, one of the first things that the mistress of the house does upon waking[6] is to take the pieces of meat and the leg that is on the T-pillar of the *iaranga* and put them in a skin bowl *(taqanaŋ)* lying on top of the *rélqiinéŋ,* the small sledge that is used to transport the *iaranga's* tripod when the herding families are moving camp. Then, the mistress of the house makes a fire with fireboards in front of the *iaranga,* where the fire had been made on the first day of the ritual (also with fireboards). On this fire, the mistress of the house burns the bones (e.g. the ribs) of the reindeer that have already been slaughtered and eaten.[7] Then, she grills the hooves of all the slaughtered reindeer, including the hoof of the leg that had been attached to the T-pillar. The hooves will later be put in blood in preparing a food that is one of the most appreciated *(vilmutlymul,* soured blood). In the meantime, the bones of the leg from the T-pillar are broken in order to extract the marrow, which is used to feed the ritual objects once more. When all the hooves are grilled, the ash of the burnt bones is crushed with a hammer *(rypéŋy)* and reduced to dust.

After burning and crushing the bones and grilling the hooves, the mistress of the house goes behind the *iaranga,* where she continues away from the encampment for a short distance. When she stops, she takes two pieces of compact tundra turf (a first one may have already been gathered on the day before the start of the ritual). This tundra turf is laid on top of the ash, two or three layers deep. Then, the remains of the reindeer leg and the willow sprout that were attached to the inside of the tent two days earlier are placed between two layers of turf. This construction is nothing other than a miniature *iaranga,* called *mélgynvyn* ('the place for the fire' from *milgyn* – fire). While making it, the women watch over it carefully to make sure it looks 'like a real *iaranga*' (as I was told). This miniature *iaranga* has stones placed around it, just as the summer *iaranga* has stones around it that serve to hold down the reindeer-skin roof. These stones are said to represent the sledges, which are usually placed around the *iaranga* in winter.

The mistress of the house (dressed in ritual attire) also collects tiny stones, which she puts on top of the miniature *iaranga*. In so doing, she thinks to herself that it is 'as if they were reindeer calves' *('kak budto teliat'* in Russian). Pieces of boiled bone *(taliat)* are laid out near the small *iaranga* as a way of symbolizing the herd. These bones (notably, leg bones and vertebra) have been crushed with a heavy hammer *(rypéŋy)* – very difficult work that the women perform on the second day of the ritual. Then they are boiled on the third day (the fat that is won in this way is later used to make sausage for future rituals).

Finally, other small stones are added to the construction: the *qaŋokvyŋalvyl* or 'herd in stone'. These small stones were gathered by children earlier in the year, when the herders first settled in the summer encampment. 'Find the nicest stones', their parents told them, 'so that we can build a stone herd'. When children are reluctant to fulfil this request, the adults say to them 'so then, will we have no herd this year?' Having the function of a ritual game, the construction of a stone herd is thought to have a symbolic impact on the real herd.

In sum, during the three-day ritual, many objects of everyday herding life are deployed, the end result being the building of a miniature *iaranga*. This *iaranga* contains and protects the main elements of the ritual performance. Taken as a whole, the ritual is a metaphor of Chukchi herding life and, through the construction of a small-scale representation, symbolizes the links established between hearth, reindeer, the *iaranga* and people (Figures 10.4 and 10.5).

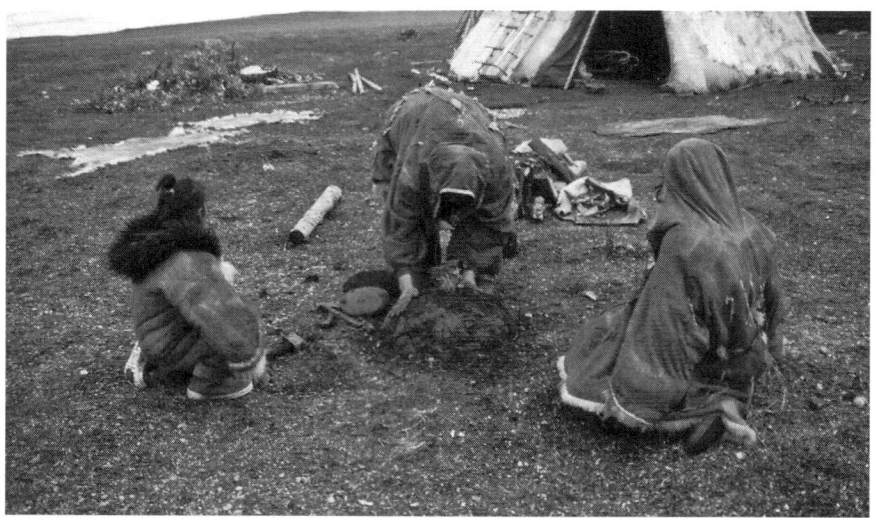

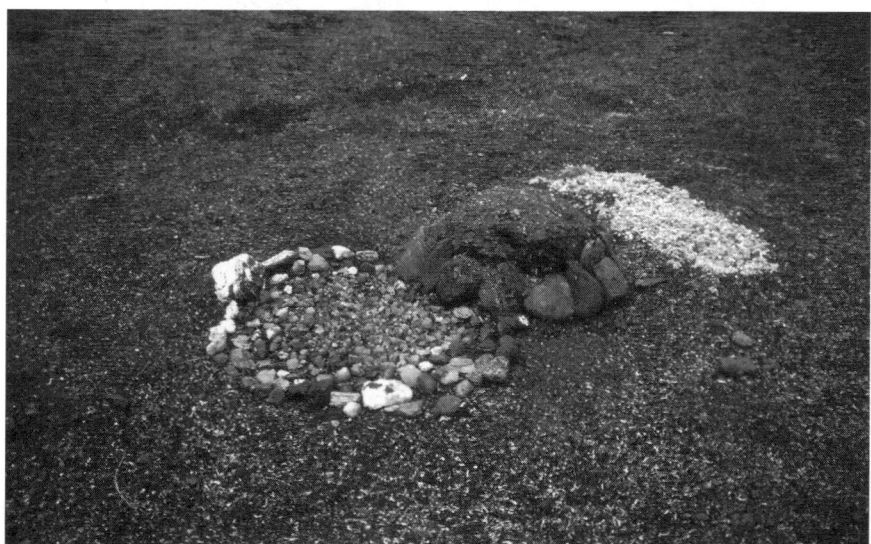

Figures 10.4 and 10.5 *Building the* mêlgynvyn *(miniature* iaranga *made of tundra turf) during the last day of the* Ɖênrir"un *ritual (Amguema 1997, photos V. Vaté).*

Myŋik: a ritual sequence inside of and involving the *iaranga*

Myŋik (also called *mŋêgyrgyn*) is a ritual sequence that can be performed either on the second day of *Ɖênrir"un* or after the spring festival, *Kilvêi*. Bogoraz and Kuznetsova classify *Myŋik* as a 'thanksgiving ceremonial' (Bogoras 1975: 381; Kuznetsova 1957: 314). They also use this terminology to refer to hunting rituals (Kuznetsova 1957: 314). According to these authors, *Myŋik* is performed in the wake of a successful hunt or in response to a dream (Bogoras 1975: 382; Kuznetsova 1957: 315). Indeed *Myŋik* is also performed by sea-mammal hunters, though in a variable form (see Golbtseva 2008).

One particularity of this ritual is that it takes place, in part, inside a hermetically sealed *iaranga*. To the usual roof that is used in summer, the winter one is added with the skin side up, in order to close the hole on the roof from which smoke escapes. This is why local people call this feast *dymnyi prazdnik* in Russian – 'the smoky feast'. This is another example of the symbolic importance of the hearth and fumigation in this ritual system.

Ideally, *Myŋik* is performed once every two or three years. It might have occurred more frequently in the past: according to Bogoraz (Bogoras 1975: 381) it was performed once or twice a year. Today, it seems to be disappearing: in my field site, if I have been correctly informed, this ritual sequence has not been performed since 1998 (I was told this in 2005 – I don't know if it has been performed since then). Unluckily, although my first stay in the area dates back to 1997, I could not be present at *Myŋik*. The following description is based on what an elderly woman, named Raia Kovragyrgina, told me in August 2005. Once again, rather than trying to be exhaustive, I will emphasize only a few aspects that illustrate the role of the *iaranga* in the ritual sequence.

When performed at *Dênrir"un*, I was told, *Myŋik* usually takes place after all the reindeer have been slaughtered on the first day. At this time, yet another reindeer is slaughtered; but while all other reindeer were slaughtered in front of the *iaranga*, this one is slaughtered behind it. Reindeer are slaughtered behind the *iaranga* in only two cases: during the *Myŋik* sequence and when a wild reindeer is caught and ritually slaughtered.

The reindeer that is slaughtered behind the *iaranga* is called *rymŋéën* (m) or *symŋéën* (f). As is the case during the *Dênrir"un* ritual, the blood that is taken from the wound of the slaughtered animal is used for drawings, although this time not on the human body but on or around the *iaranga* itself. People move around the tent several times, starting from the north side and following the movement of the sun. First, the inside of the contents of the slaughtered animal's stomach (*zheludok*, in Russian) are poured around the *iaranga*. Participants to the ritual circumambulate around the *iaranga* while singing 'ho, hoj, ho, hoj' and playing the drum (not with the usual drumstick but with a stick of wood picked up in the tundra before the feast for this purpose). The master of the house must be at the front of the procession. After having made a circumambulation around the *iaranga*, men throw ritual food to the spirits (*inénintytkuk*), beginning in the north. In the meantime, women dress the *rymŋéën* or *symŋéën* reindeer inside the *iaranga*. Its skin, together with its head, is placed in a way that is reminiscent of the *iitriir* reindeer of *Đênrir"un*. The skin lays near the 'pillow' of the inner tent, with the head on the fireboards, 'looking' towards the door. Fireboards and also the lower pillars of the *iaranga* are fed with marrow.

Many details of the procedures within the hermetically sealed *iaranga* must be omitted here. Suffice to say that, when the *rêtêm* (the cover of the tent made out of skins) is opened, women and men located on both side of the *iaranga* beat the pillars with drumsticks and with drums.

Conclusion

In this chapter, I have attempted to show how, for Chukchi reindeer herders, the link between home, hearth and household finds expression not only in everyday life but also in ritual performances characterized by creative symbolism and an elaborate concern for details (only parts of which have been presented here). This symbolism finds its ground not only in the centrality of the tent, the hearth and the family in the life of herders, but also in the fact that home and hearth build connections to the environment and the reindeer, which are central to the life of Chukchi herders.

The ritual plays with different dimensions of articulations and scales of representation: the *iaranga* is the place for the ritual, which occurs either ahead of it, behind it or inside it; and the *iaranga* is also an 'actor' in the ritual by being physically involved in it. Lastly, the construction of a miniature *iaranga*, closes the three-day performance, protecting the fire around which most of the ritual action was centred – building a home for the hearth.

Revealing a complex worldview where all elements are in interaction, these rituals show us that, for nomadic Arctic peoples, home is not only a place where people live, and the hearth is important not only because it provides warmth. Home and hearth are given a central role in ritual and a central function in the life of people that is simultaneously material, social and cosmological.

Acknowledgements

I am grateful to John Eidson for commenting on and editing this chapter, and to David Anderson and Rob Wishart for the work accomplished on the manuscript of this book. I would also like to thank all the reindeer herders of Kanchalan and Amguema tundras who shared their knowledge with me and took care of me.

Notes

1. I use a modified version of the transliteration of the Library of Congress both for Russian and Chukchi languages, as I explain in Vaté (2007: 221, Note 6). Vernacular terms that appear in the text are usually in Chukchi. Chukchi language sometimes differs for male and female speakers. In this chapter, I give some examples of such gendered terminology, indicating male and female version with an (m) or an (f).
2. I will use this term in the text, as it might be easier to pronounce for the reader.
3. During the 1940s, *Ŋênrir"un* could last anywhere up to six days (Kuznetsova 1957: 280). Seventy years ago, presumably, slaughtering was more extensive, so that the workload related to butchering and preparing the meat would tend to make the ritual last longer.
4. Despite the fact that practices may differ according to places, this ethnographic material casts some doubts on Willerslev's statement that blood sacrifices 'made in honor of the dead constitute the main feature of all major festivals' (Willerslev 2009: 695). One can see here that 'sacrifices' for the dead are distinguished from other forms of ritual slaughter, depending on the positioning of the reindeer carcass.
5. Willow *(ëmrottoot, Salix sp.)* plays a central role in rituals. Slaughtered reindeer are butchered on willow branches and willow leaves constitute an important component of ritual dishes. As one of the favourite reindeer foods, willow (along with some other plants) may be used as a substitute for reindeer meat in making offerings. Consumption of willow in a festive context is said to establish a link between humans and reindeer (see also Plattet 2005 and Gorbacheva 2004, in the Kamchatkan context).
6. On this day, the women again wake up before sunrise. Most of the time men do not take part in this ritual action, something that has already been noted by Kuznetsova (1957: 280).
7. As everywhere in the world, eating is an important aspect of the festival. Women have taken care to boil most of the bony parts of the reindeer, which are quickly eaten by the guests. These bony parts are usually the first to be consumed, because they are the heaviest and, therefore, most difficult to carry when moving camp.

CHAPTER 11

The Perception of the Built Environment by Permanent Residents, Seasonal In-migrants and Casual Incomers in a Village in Northwest Russia

Maria Nakhshina

This chapter explores the population dynamics of the village of Kuzomen'
in the northwest of Russia with respect to the attitudes people from the
village hold towards their homes. I examine the centrality of houses in
people's everyday interactions with the built environment and I demonstrate that these interactions differ between permanent dwellers and
various incomers in the village.

Apart from the social club and few shops, people's houses are the only
built spaces in Kuzomen' where interaction with the wider community
takes place. Kuzomen' is thus typical of what Wilson (1988: 4) calls a
domesticated society, which 'relies to a great extent on the house as both
a dominant cultural symbol and a central rallying point and context for
social organization and activity'. The following excerpt from my fieldnotes provides a glimpse of how I learnt about the role of the house in
Kuzomen':

> It is a clear summer day and the time is approaching 1pm. There is a queue outside
> the *kolkhoz* shop as always, because bread is brought from the bakery at 1pm. The
> weather is warm and people are out in the sun chatting. My ear catches part of two
> women's conversation:
> It is Sasha,[1] don't you know him?
> I don't quite understand whom you mean.
> Well, his house is near Andrew's, straight behind.
> Oh, now I see.

It took me a while to realize that to make sense of people's conversations,
I should learn where everybody's house is located. When chatting, people
take great pleasure in investigating, defining, reconfirming and arguing

about which person belonged to which house, or to which house a person used to belong. It took me much longer actually to learn the correspondence between people, houses and their location. And this is despite the fact that houses in Kuzomen' are laid out in a rather straightforward way. There are three streets in the village and four rows of houses situated along them. One row is beside the river, two rows stretch along the main street, and the last one is on the edge of the settlement that opens towards the sea.

The village of Kuzomen' is located on a cape between the river Varzuga and the Terskii Coast of the White Sea in the Kola Peninsula[2] (Figure 11.1). The Terskii Coast is a historical rather than geographical name in the sense that it does not appear on contemporary maps of the region. As several waves of settlers arrived on the White Sea coast at various times, the coastline was consequently divided into seven parts, or Coasts, each of which received its own name.

All the villages along the Terskii Coast belong administratively to Terskii district *(raion)* and Umba is the district centre. Terskii district is one of five districts that comprise Murmansk Province *(oblast')*. About 7,000 people live in Terskii district, with 6,000 residing in Umba and 1,000 in the other villages. Varzuga, which is the closest neighbouring village to Kuzomen', is the biggest among them and currently has 400 people. There are approximately 80 people registered in Kuzomen' as permanent residents.

Russian people first came to the White Sea coast in the first half of the eleventh century, attracted by fishing and hunting opportunities. They reached what was later called the Terskii Coast around the middle of the twelfth century. The first travellers were mainly traders, hunters and fishermen. Later waves of settlers also included peasants, who were especially attracted by vast empty lands and a lack of serfdom in the area compared to the agricultural regions of Russia from which they had escaped (Ushakov 1972: 23–4). Gradually they settled in different areas along the coast, including the southern part of the Kola Peninsula. These people have been traditionally referred to as *Pomory* (singular for 'a person' is *Pomor)*. The name comes from the Russian *po moriu* which means 'by sea'.

At the beginning of the twentieth century around 800 people were living in Kuzomen'. By January 2009, just 80 people were registered there as permanent population.[3] However, the number nearly doubles in the summer. In the second half of the twentieth century, Kuzomen' experienced significant out-migration of villagers to cities. Around the late 1980s many of them started to come back to their rural homeland in the summer. So, like many places in the circumpolar north, Kuzomen' is characterized by a history of a high degree of population fluctuation that is both long term and seasonal.

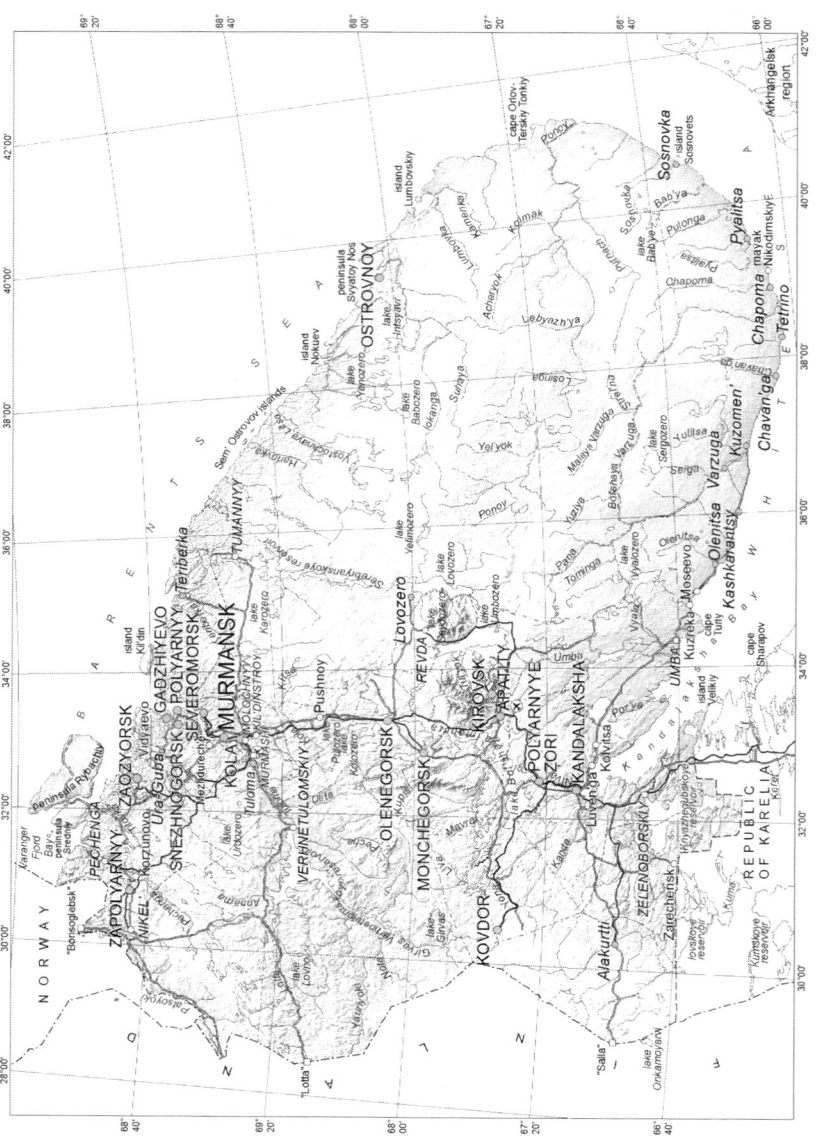

Figure 11.1 *Map of the Kola Peninsula. The villages Umba, Varzuga and Kuzomen' are located in the south-west. The map is based on a digital topographic map developed by the Main Scientific Research, Information and Computer Center of the Russian Ministry of Natural Resources (GlavNivts MPR), 1998. This map was designed by joint-stock company 'Kola geological information laboratory center' (JSC 'KGILC') in 2011.*

I came to Kuzomen' for the first time in late May and stayed for two and a half weeks. This turned out to be the right period for me to capture two different states of Kuzomen': from empty streets with lonely villagers on a busy trip somewhere to a lively settlement full of idle strollers of different ages. As I spent more time in Kuzomen' on subsequent fieldwork, I came to be fascinated with the extent to which its population fluctuated throughout the year. Hardly a day passes without somebody visiting or leaving the place. People come for a day, week, fishing season, summer, half a year, or move in for good.

Permanent dwellers and various visitors generate different types of interactions in Kuzomen'. In particular, people share different perspectives on local architecture. In this chapter, I look at how houses in Kuzomen' are perceived differently by people depending on the length and regularity of their stays in the village.

Outline of the argument

Life in Kuzomen' is largely centred on houses. Other buildings in the village include several utility structures, such as the medical post, the school building, the library, the social club and a few shops. In this chapter I show how the house is central for people in several ways, such as in processes of orientation, measurement and remembering. Another aspect that I consider is how houses are perceived differently by permanent dwellers, summer visitors and short-term incomers. The comparison will be made at two parallel levels: between locals and incomers, and between permanent residents and summer visitors. I want to develop three main arguments in this respect.

The first is that locals' understanding of houses is volumetric, while that of short-term incomers is rather flat. Local people gather information by walking around buildings as well as actually dwelling in them, which together give depth and volume to their perception. As for incomers, they usually know houses only from the perspective of the main street and their experience of dwelling is often very limited. The second argument is related to this, namely that incomers perceive houses through observing achieved forms whereas local people are aware of houses' histories and the processes of their creation. These two modes of engagement with local architecture generate two distinct perceptions of its features.

The third argument is that people who come to the village only for the summer tend to treat their houses as museums; they try to preserve tradition and culture, whereas permanent residents dwell in their homes following mundane comings and goings of things and habits. Summer

visitors are also much more active in collecting and formalizing historical
and genealogical data about their families and Kuzomen'. I argue that for
summer visitors this serves as compensation for their separation from the
place once they moved out, whereas permanent villagers, being constantly
in place, have no need for it.

This chapter develops the general theme of tracing a correlation
between the length and regularity of people's stays in Kuzomen' and
their ways of engaging with it. Before I discuss the perception of architecture in Kuzomen', I would like to situate my approach within the
broader context of anthropological approaches to the built environment
in general.

The built environment in anthropology

Wilson regards domestication as a major cultural innovation in human
history. He argues that people's adoption of 'the built environment as their
context for living' (1988: 4) has had impacts on their interactions with
one another and with the environment. Houses have provided people
with a basic spatial structure, which in turn has influenced social organization. Furthermore, the house has served 'not simply as a dwelling,
shelter, and spatial arrangement of activities but also as a central instru-
ment through which people record and express their thoughts' (ibid: 66).
Anthropologists have since elaborated on the nature of the connection
between people's ways of approaching the world and the built environment they inhabit. In this respect, I would like to draw attention to some
recent developments in this field.

Allerton (2013) argues in relation to studies of the Indonesian built
environment that they are dominated by symbolic and structuralist
approaches, according to which houses are treated separately from the
everyday activities of their inhabitants. This observation can also be
applied to studies of the built environment elsewhere. Many profound
works on architecture that are outstanding in terms of aspects of structure, symbolism, aesthetics and physical properties of the built environment that they cover, at the same time lack accounts of experiential and
mundane experience of engaging with houses (see Johnson (1993) on
traditional English architecture; Permilovskaia (2005) on the northern
Russian house; and Waterson (1991) on south-east Asian architecture).
These works speak extensively of what houses mean and symbolize for
people and provide details of how they are structured to meet people's
needs, but they are often silent about the ways that these aspects cor-
relate with how people actually dwell in their houses on a day-to-day
basis.

In her own work in Manggarai in eastern Indonesia, Allerton (2013) takes an approach that incorporates the totality of people's everyday dealings with their houses. This brings together structures and economies, conversations and whispers, conviviality and lament, as houses in Manggarai are highly permeable to flows of sound and substance. In my research, I approach the built environment along similar lines, looking at how one's perception of the house is shaped in the course of ordinary everyday practices. This stance views the built environment as an entwinement of the materiality of things and the sociality of subjects, or as a merging of each dimension with the other. I develop ideas advanced by Morton (2007) on the way in which the materiality of the house is implicated in processes of memory, and by Telle (2007) on how buildings can mediate people's actions. These authors advocate an experiential approach to houses that incorporates people's engagement with built architecture in a variety of ways, particularly on the level of the most mundane practices.

Carsten and Hugh-Jones (1995a) also look at houses and people as brought together in one whole through their mutually constituting and ongoing relations. This approach has been called 'holistic' or 'rounded', in so far as it looks at the interrelationship between houses, people and environment. According to Morton, this view of the built environment sees the house as 'playing a central role in social life; not just as a backdrop to social activity, but as an active process within it' (2007: 158). As Carsten and Hugh-Jones (1995b: 3–4) note, houses (and architecture more generally) have been neglected in anthropology: 'one reason for this neglect is that houses get taken for granted. Like our bodies, the houses in which we live are so commonplace, so familiar, so much a part of the way things are, that we often hardly seem to notice them'. Another reason, however, lies in the way the study of the house has been fragmented between various sub-disciplines. The authors want to develop

> an 'alternative language of the house', one not based on the assumed priority of kinship or economy but which enables us to escape some of the constraints of conventional analysis of these areas, and to bring together aspects of the house previously treated separately. (ibid: 2)

In my contribution to developing an alternative language of the house in this chapter I look at how the centrality of the house in Kuzomen' is played out in people's everyday engagements with it. In this endeavour, I focus on the perceptions of both permanent residents and various incomers, and the differences between them, which have received scant attention in existing works on the built environment.

The centrality of houses in Kuzomen'

Houses as a means of orientation

I began this chapter with an example of a conversation outside the *kolkhoz* shop, which demonstrated that houses are often substituted for their inhabitants by the local people. It is possible to simply tell these people the location of somebody's house without mentioning the owner's name, and they will understand who is being discussed. While locals understand the location of houses in the village through the totality of relations of buildings and their inhabitants, the perception of incomers is limited by the particular relations that they have managed to establish in the village. As a result, their spatial knowledge of the place may be more partial compared to that shared by locals.

I happened to talk to a group of tourists who came to Kuzomen' from Saint-Petersburg for the fishing. Soon after we began our conversation, they asked me where I was staying – a standard question to any incomer in Kuzomen'. At first, they could not get it from my description. I then decided to relate my description to a man called Zhora, as I knew that the tourists often socialized with him. Zhora is portrayed by everybody in the village as quite a character; he sticks in the memory of anyone who has visited Kuzomen' and met him there. When I said to the men that my place was one building further down from Zhora's house, they became even more perplexed as they thought that there were no houses beyond that point at all, and that Zhora's was the last in the village. In fact, nearly a quarter of the village's houses are beyond that building. The reason why the tourists perceived the village as they did lies in their relations with Zhora. During their stay they got to know him quite well. They also remembered him from their previous visit to Kuzomen' a year ago. They did socialize with some other people in the village but not with anybody living beyond Zhora's house. And so they were unaware of any houses beyond his.

In the course of fieldwork, I 'discovered' houses in Kuzomen' a few times. Quite often, I would find out that there is a house in a place which I previously considered to be empty, after I got to know a person who lived there. The acquaintance could take place in the house of a person whom I had already known and who happened to have a guest during my visit. After being introduced to the person, I would usually ask where they live in Kuzomen'. It happened a few times, that when people tried to describe the location of their houses to me I had difficulties imagining it because I had not known anybody living in houses nearby. When I walked past that place next time, I paid attention and a house would suddenly 'appear' in a location I had not noticed before.

Houses as a measuring tool

Houses in Kuzomen' are central for villagers in the way they provide an always-at-hand basis for various estimations. Throughout fieldwork, I was struck by the range of things that people in the village define by referencing them to houses or their parts. If a conversation takes place outside, and people need to explain how high something is, they may point to a house nearby, saying that the thing in question is equal to the height of the house's windowsill. If people talk inside, they usually refer to the dimensions of a room they are in if they need to estimate things: various objects are as high as the ceiling, and a white whale that came to the river last summer was about the length of the room. I once heard Tania and Tetia[4] Olia discussing how much roofing felt they needed to buy in town in order to renovate the roof of their house. Their final estimate was that they would need slightly less than their neighbour used for his recently covered roof and therefore they could just ask him how much he bought. In a conversation about salmon fishing, a local man complained to me that if someone is caught on the river fishing salmon without a license, he will have to pay 'half a house' of fines. Houses therefore have the capacity to be a measuring tool.

People outside Kuzomen' often ask me how many residents live in the village. What they want to hear in response is the number of inhabitants. When I ask the same question of villagers, they often respond in the following way: 'Alright, let me see ... I will proceed from the upper end of the village: so, there is Ira's house – four people there, then goes Pavel's house, which is one person...' The counting goes through the whole village from one end to the other, until all inhabited houses are taken into account. For Kuzomen' villagers, houses and people constitute one whole. People think in terms of house–dweller associations and not merely numbers of inhabitants. Although they know the approximate number of inhabitants in the village, they prefer to arrive at this number in a more engaging way than to provide bare statistics.

Another example comes from my further conversation with the tourists from Saint-Petersburg. After I managed to specify the location of my accommodation, they asked me to tell them its size in square metres. This put me in quite a quandary. I had neither thought of the house in that way myself, nor had I heard of any local person doing so. To answer the question, I started doing what locals did: I explained the size by comparing the house where I stayed with the room where our conversation took place. The tourists, however, kept pressing me for precise numbers.

Whereas incomers from town might need abstract units such as square metres and numbers to measure things, for local people a house in the village provides all the necessary means for that. This centrality of the house as a measuring tool could be partly due to the peculiarity of Kuzomen's landscape, which lacks any conspicuous objects such as tall trees, hills or rock formations that could provide a context for measuring things. Indeed, houses are the only protruding objects in people's surroundings. When a practical issue arises, people in Kuzomen' attend to things that are readily available to them to solve the problem. This allows them to engage with their surroundings on a level that is not available to incomers from elsewhere. This is a more nuanced and direct engagement. While dealing with numbers implies an abstract scale of measuring, the 'house-based' scale that villagers use is very concrete and fleshed out. It is based on what they see every day and on things with which they can engage directly. Incomers often lack this immediacy of engaging with the village, with consequences for the way they perceive Kuzomen'.

Houses and the process of remembering

The house is also central in Kuzomen' in the way that it structures people's memories. Here I draw on the work of Morton (2007), who focuses on the role of the built environment in social processes of memory. He asks whether the interweaving of memories of the family and memories of the built environment suggests a deeper relationship between dwelling and social life than has been heretofore acknowledged. Particularly, he looks at the dynamic relations between the material home and processes of memory among people in northern Botswana. Through a series of case studies he shows how people use the same idiom whether talking about generations of houses or those of families; how kin are remembered through the processes of building and rebuilding houses; and how dwellings interweave materials, activities and social relations that refer to the wider social landscape. One of his main arguments is that 'the material house can be considered as a crucial generative influence on the way people mentally order and understand the world' (ibid: 159).

In Kuzomen' there is a strong correlation between people, houses and the process of remembering. Whenever somebody is recalled in the village, he or she is placed in relation to a house. Similarly, when recalling the village's past, people often start by saying how many houses there used to be in Kuzomen' and then they go into detail on particular buildings. They tell from memory where a particular house stood, who lived there and who the neighbours were. Such recollections usually come up in conversations with summer visitors rather than permanent dwellers. The former left the village when there were many more people compared to the present situation and their experience of Kuzomen' is therefore grounded in the past. I return to this topic later in the chapter when I talk about different attitudes to houses' interiors among summer visitors and permanent dwellers.

Another function of the house is that it transmits memories of the past into the present. This is a feature that Morton calls the 'othertimeness' of a house when it refers 'outwards to other times, seasons, events' (2007: 166). A good example comes from a house in Kuzomen' that has a particularly complex dwelling history. Dating back to the second half of the nineteenth century, initially it belonged to a clerk. With the beginning of the Soviet era it was turned into a hospital. After a new and bigger hospital was built in the village, the former one was turned into a dormitory for people who were appointed to work in the village for a certain number of years, through the Soviet system of the distribution of graduates. Today the house accommodates two families that rent several of its rooms, and it also contains a library and private shop. People in the village use different names when they refer to this building. For me it has always been 'Olesia's house', because her flat was the first place I stayed during fieldwork. Many people refer to it as the 'house where the library is'. Some call it a 'dormitory'. There is at least one person, a woman in her eighties, who refers to it as the 'hospital'.

Anna Pavlovna lives in town and comes to Kuzomen' every summer. She spent her childhood in Kuzomen' and was there when the house was still a hospital. She remembers it as a very clean place with thoroughly swept floors, tidy rooms and the fresh smell of a well-aired building. When Anna Pavlovna has occasionally to visit it today for shopping, each time it is painful for her to see the present state of the building. She complains about it being so dirty and having an awful smell that comes from a common inside toilet. Anna Pavlovna persistently refers to this building as 'hospital' even though other people do not always understand her. If misunderstood, she would explain what she means and then carry on deploring the fact that what used to be such a nice clean building could turn into something so disgusting. She does not want to reconcile herself to this, and her rejection of the present state of the house is reflected in the way she uses the name from its better past.

Different attitudes towards Kuzomen' among summer visitors on the one hand, and permanent villagers on the other, are generated from their movements in relation to the village. Summer visitors have experienced a movement in space but have remained 'frozen' in time, as they compare the present state of things with how the village looked when they left it. In this light, the past for elderly summer visitors in Kuzomen' is 'a well-known, often visited, and sometimes longed-for second home' (Nadel-Klein 2003: 105).

People–house relations

A house in Kuzomen' also plays a crucial role in people's migration to the village. When I asked Anna Pavlovna how long she plans to continue coming to the village, her answer was: 'I will keep coming as long as my house allows me to do so'. At the same time, houses depend on people to last longer. People in Kuzomen' say that if nobody lives in a house at least from time to time, it eventually dies. Villagers speak disapprovingly of those who own houses in the village but never come there. People and houses in Kuzomen' are thus closely interrelated and the well-being of one affects the other.

In his work with the Sasak people, Telle focuses on people–house relations and how buildings can mediate action. He looks at how material things 'cannot be fully mastered', and in fact often 'stand apart, resisting human desires' (Telle 2007: 202, 215). He explores the case of a Sasak woman who rebuilt her house after she felt it was not compatible with her anymore and that she had lost control over it. Through building a new and bigger house she wanted to express her different status in the society as well as to regain control over her life course, as among Sasak people the house is a focal institution, which is often endowed with human qualities and considered to make the person 'complete' (ibid: 206). Telle urges us to pay more attention to the 'biographical significance of houses, and to the affective ties established between specific persons and houses' (ibid: 214).

In Kuzomen' I often visited Irina Petrovna in her semi-detached house on the edge of the village. She and her sister hired workers from Varzuga to build it. They chose a house for two families because they wanted their aging aunt from another village to move in with them. The construction lasted for several years and the aunt died before it was finished. The second half of the house has stood empty since then. It is occasionally used when somebody comes for a visit and needs to stay overnight. This uninhabited half of the house reminds Irina Petrovna of her aunt and obligations towards her. Irina Petrovna often says that her aunt must have thought that she and her sister dragged out the construction for so long because they did not want her to stay with them. Now Irina Petrovna has to perform some maintenance in that part of the house in order to keep the whole building going. The lives of people and houses in the village are intertwined and each sets concerns for the other.

I once became involved in a conversation with an older man on the bus on the way to Kuzomen'. Upon hearing about my interest in studying village life and people's attitudes to their homes, the man was inspired to talk about his own country house, and eventually gave me a very vivid opinion on the matter:

> A house in the village involves a lot of cares. It should be nursed as a sick person. If you do not take care of it for a year, it gets old and warps. It becomes ill, starts rotting and moaning. In short, if you have a house in the country, it must be inhabited.

The structure of houses

A typical house in Kuzomen' is semi-detached, single-storied, made of wood and with many small windows to let the light in (Figure 11.2). While there is much uniformity in terms of the form and structure of houses in Kuzomen', at the same time, their details vary greatly. Differences can be difficult to notice for short-term visitors, especially as they may reveal themselves only through an actual visit to a house. In fact, on closer inspection, houses in Kuzomen' are very diverse and idiosyncratic. The variety exists especially through added parts such as verandahs and garages, and among small inside rooms such as pantries. There is no rule for either the size or location of these. The height of both outside and inside doorways is generally very low in Kuzomen' but still different in every house, and a visitor needs to adapt each time when paying a visit. It is especially difficult for urban dwellers, who often bang their heads against the posts. The height level varies from door to door even within a single building. Therefore one needs time to become accustomed to a house's anatomy to feel comfortable in it.

Again, the multiplicity of house interiors in Kuzomen' is discovered during actual visits to buildings. When people enter a house, they first

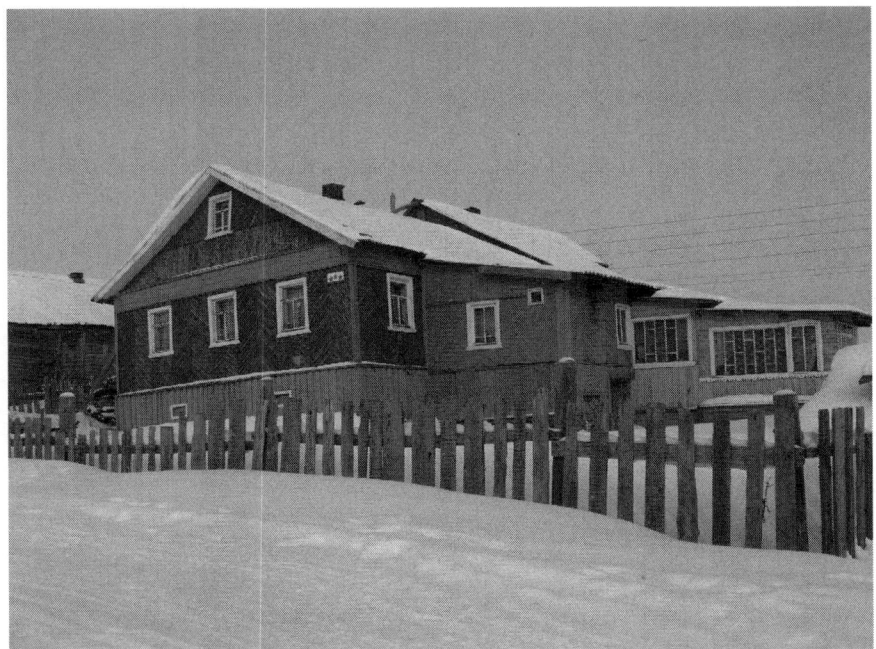

Figure 11.2 *A house in Kuzomen'.*

go through the front door. Then they reach a hallway with several small doors on its sides, and sometimes there is more than one hallway. Here one can face a puzzle. Only one of the doors leads to the lived part of the house and it is on this door that a visitor is supposed to knock. The usual darkness of the hallway makes the situation even worse. Knocking on the front door makes no sense as it is too far away for inhabitants to hear. These moments of shifting from one foot to another often embarrass me as I feel myself having entered someone's house, yet not quite, as the hosts are still not aware of my presence. At the same time, it feels as if some sort of connection with insiders is already being established. Often I would knock on several pantry doors first before I reached the living quarters. My imagination would then immediately picture the hosts' becoming aware of a stranger's presence behind their inside door and waiting for them to reveal themselves.

Similarly, when we had visitors in the house where I stayed, I could often hear when somebody had already entered the hallway and was about to knock on the door. My hosts, however, did not seem to pay attention to these noises and only reacted when they heard a knock. This variety of hallways, turnings and small doors makes any building in Kuzomen' enigmatic and appealing. Every house in the village reflects the idiosyncrasy of its inhabitants, and every new visit to a house is a little discovery, as a visitor becomes acquainted not simply with another building but with the totality comprised by the house and its inhabitants.

Innovations and redecorations in homes of permanent residents are often introduced more easily by people who live in houses that do not belong to their ancestors. Such buildings do not provide a sense of deep history and family tradition. Their inhabitants thus do not have to deal with the load of memory of how it looked when their grandparents were alive. By contrast, those who live in houses which they inherited from their parents or grandparents are reluctant to make profound changes to the interior. Their immediate surroundings provide inhabitants with established ways of how a house should look. When asked about the meaning of some objects inside their homes, these people may reply that 'I don't know. ... It has always been like that' or that 'this is how my grandmother used to do it'. They do not need any explanation of the habitual way of doing things, as their house serves as sufficient justification for the way things are.

When people do not have profound connections with a place or have lost them through time, or when their experience of a place is limited, their engagement with it can be restricted to a perception of what is available on the surface. In the first part of the next section I will talk about this way of perceiving the built environment in Kuzomen'.

Engaging with a house in Kuzomen'

Perception of the exterior

The way that people engage with houses in Kuzomen' affects their perception of architectural features. Unlike locals who are actively involved in making changes in their houses, short-term incomers usually do not have direct access to such practical knowledge and often base their judgements about architecture on observation of surfaces rather than of the 'depth' of the house. Even so, their perception of surfaces is quite different from that of locals. Furthermore, incomers and local people see houses differently due to the ways they move in and around them. The former often come to know houses only from the perspective of the main road, and they have a limited experience of actually dwelling in them. Compared to them, locals move through and around houses a lot in the course of their daily activities. They also have prolonged experience of dwelling in a house in the village. Altogether, this leads to quite distinct ways of seeing a house in Kuzomen'. I illustrate these points with two examples from fieldwork.

Tania and Tetia Olia lived through two house-fires and they now live in a house whose owner resides in a city. The owner is a woman called Margarita. She left Kuzomen' when she was a teenager and never returned. When the second fire took place about ten years ago, somebody in Kuzomen' contacted Margarita to ask whether she could let the family in as they had nowhere to go. She agreed, and did not even ask Tania and Tetia Olia for any rent during all these years.

One Tuesday, when the weekly bus from the district centre came to Kuzomen', I went to the bus stop to meet it. Children gathered at the place long before the bus as usual. They are here for the same purpose as I am, curious to see who is coming and leaving. I try not to miss these Tuesday afternoons as it is always a big event in the village. People from the neighbouring village Varzuga say that nothing significant happens in Kuzomen' and therefore that the arrival of the bus is a big thing there, whereas in Varzuga they pay no attention to it unless they need to meet somebody personally.

The bus arrived; among the crowd I noticed the unfamiliar face of a woman in her fifties. She was rather tall, with dyed blond hair. She came alone and nobody met her. She did not wait at the bus stop and immediately walked away. I stayed for some time at the place, waiting until those who were leaving got on the bus, which then drove off and finally disappeared in the dunes.

When I got back home, I found Tetia Olia talking with the newly arrived woman. I was surprised, as Tetia Olia did not mention that any guests were coming. I sank quietly into a chair. From further conversion I gradually realized that the woman was Margarita and that she had travelled to Kuzomen' from far away in order to sell the house. Margarita and Tetia Olia discussed the matter for some time. As soon as initial agreement was reached, Margarita suggested going out for a walk. She wanted to see Kuzomen', where she had spent her childhood. We set off. Along the way Tetia Olia answered Margarita's questions and comments on the buildings that we passed. We were approaching Volodia and Rita's newly built house which was not yet painted and therefore had the natural grey colour of wood that had been long exposed to rain and sun. The building caught Margarita's eye, and she said that from its look it had to be an old but rebuilt house, as it was very upright. 'Quite on the contrary, it is a new house', said Tetia Olia. Sometime later we passed the house of Petrovy, where I had stayed with Lena before moving to Tetia Olia's place. The house was more than 50 years old. At the sight of this building Margarita suggested that this was apparently a new house. This was followed by Tetia Olia's smiling remark that the house was in fact very old, but was planked and painted.

Margarita's persistent mistakes regarding the houses were caused by the fact that she made her judgements relying on observation of the final result, a completed form. Only the houses' surfaces were available for her to judge from. Like many other incomers she lacked practical knowledge of the processes of house construction, whereas local people had a general idea about how a house was built and how it ought to be further maintained. Not only do they know the general properties of materials used in construction; they are often aware of the individual history of transformation through building for every particular house in the village.

This way of perceiving architecture by people in a place about which they know little is paralleled in the sphere of research on architecture. Regarding indigenous Evenki vernacular architecture in Siberia, Anderson notes that 'descriptions of building among Evenki people, and perhaps other hunting people as well, have tended to emphasize achieved forms rather than the process of marshalling materials to make dwellings' (2006: 4–5). To a large extent, this holds true for literature on architecture in general, in which researchers are often seen to concentrate on how buildings look after they are finished rather than on the processes of their creation (Permilovskaia 2005; Waterson 1991).

My next example will serve to illustrate my second point about the perception of the house: how it is related to modalities of movement.

During my first visit to Kuzomen' with the ecology students, one house attracted our attention each time we passed it on our way to the shop. We found it the most beautiful building in the village. It looked spacious and steadfast to us. Later during fieldwork I realized that the same house evoked frequent comments from other people who were new to the village. Upon the sight of this house people usually pointed out how beautiful it is, how nice and solid. A similar remark was prevalent among those to whom I showed pictures from the village. Local people's opinion of this building, however, is rather different.

Standing in a queue for white bread outside the shop one day in summer, I heard several local women discussing this very house, which is located right next to the shop. One of the women sighed: 'O-o, Ivanovy's house is so neglected. It's going to fall one day'. This opinion was readily taken up by other women in the queue as, together, they discussed the house's miserable condition. When I shared my and others' excited remarks on this house with the women, some of them were surprised and said the house did not look good at all.

In the course of fieldwork I learned that people in Kuzomen' know the history of the occupation of Ivanovy's house and can comment on different owners' attitudes to the building. Thus, its initial owner was famous for being a very handy man. Today the house belongs to his grandson who lives and works in a city. He comes to Kuzomen' for a week or two each year. He is a man of business and keeps to a rigid schedule. When he is in the village, he usually spends time visiting friends or fishing. He comes to Kuzomen' to relax and has little time to care for the house. In addition to this knowledge of the history of the building, local people pay attention not only to its front but also to its sides and roof. Thus, they are aware of some big cracks that can be seen on one of the sides, and talk about a part of the roof being damaged. One could say that locals' understanding of a house is volumetric, while that of incomers is rather flat. Potential depth and volume is added to locals' perception because they have experience of actually dwelling in houses with similar structures.

Dealing with houses' interiors

So far this chapter has dealt mainly with what occurs outside a house in Kuzomen'. In what follows, I would like to look at what happens inside. On the one hand, houses in Kuzomen' are rather similar in terms of their interior. Thus, walls are usually covered with wallpaper, the floor is painted brown and sometimes has carpets or carpet strips on it, and the ceiling is planked and whitewashed. No house in the village has running water. People fetch water from the wells located along the main road. All houses have stoves that require firewood to provide heating, apart from the house of Volodia and Rita who installed a type of central heating system, with a boiler in the cellar and pipes in each room. Most people have gas stoves for cooking, except two elderly women who refused to introduce them because they considered them too dangerous to cope with at their age. Most permanent dwellers and some summer visitors have telephone connections.

On the other hand, interiors may be distinguished at the level of furnishing and general décor. There are two major ways of treating furniture and domestic appliances among people in Kuzomen', depending on their position as either permanent dwellers or summer visitors. The latter are rather conservative in terms of what they have in their homes. Summer visitors admire the historical dimension of their houses. They keep old things and treasure them. Often when I paid a visit, people would display their possessions and encourage me to take pictures. They would tell me what they are called, explain how they work and suggest how old they are. Among these things were a spinning wheel, a samovar, and old utensils. When I visit Anna Pavlovna, she likes to talk about the past of the village. She recalls old words and expressions, and tells about domestic appliances that are no longer in use. From time to time she accompanies her words by demonstrating the actual antiques that she has kept in the house. On one such visit she suggested putting all the old objects that she had on the kitchen table so that I could take a photo (Figure 11.3).

By contrast, permanent dwellers do not seem to care much about antiques. Whenever I asked permanent residents about such things as a spinning wheel or samovar, they often said something like: 'Oh, it is somewhere in the attic', or 'People from a museum came and we gave all that stuff away to them'.

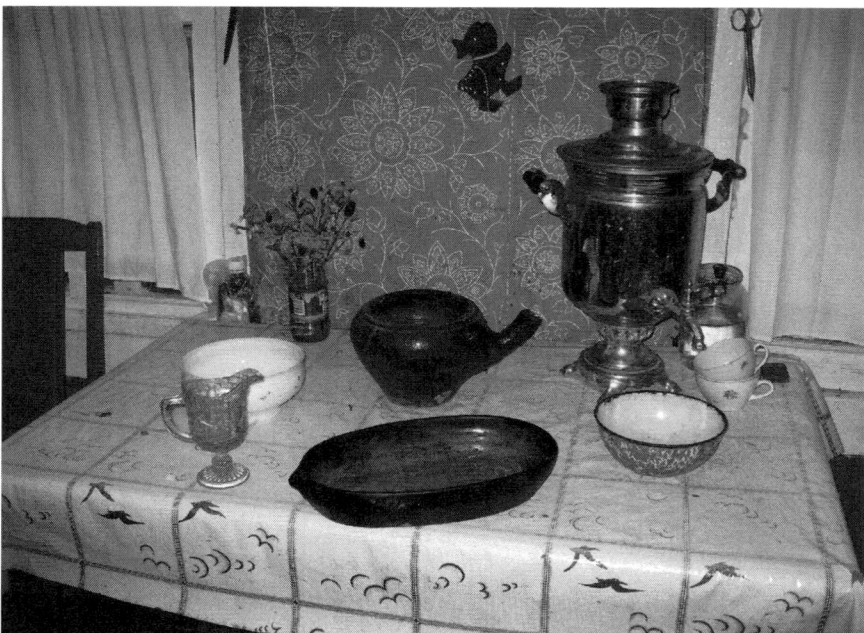

Figure 11.3 *Display of utensils.*

I suggest that summer visitors tend to freeze the culture and tradition inside their homes. I call this the museification of the house. When I visit such houses, the owners often show me around, as if we were on an excursion. They explain and demonstrate things. Women in two summer-houses told me about different parts of the stove and their purpose. This would hardly ever occur in the house of a permanent dweller. A person will take me along to another room only if I ask or if we go there together for some practical reason. Permanent residents simply inhabit their houses on a day-to-day basis. The dwelling process unfolds according to the life of the resident, incorporating new things and shaking off old, unneeded things (Figures 11.4 and 11.5). This is not to say that there are no old things that permanent dwellers would treasure. The most common among such objects are photos of family and relatives, as well as clothes left from parents that have passed away. These clothes would include traditional Pomor dresses that people used to wear on festive occasions. One of the reasons why people are sometimes reluctant to get rid of old clothes is that, compared to domestic appliances, they carry more personal associations with those who have passed away. Another reason is aesthetic, as such dresses are considered to be very beautiful.

There is similar distinction in the way people treat the history of their families and the village. As a rule, only summer visitors carry out research

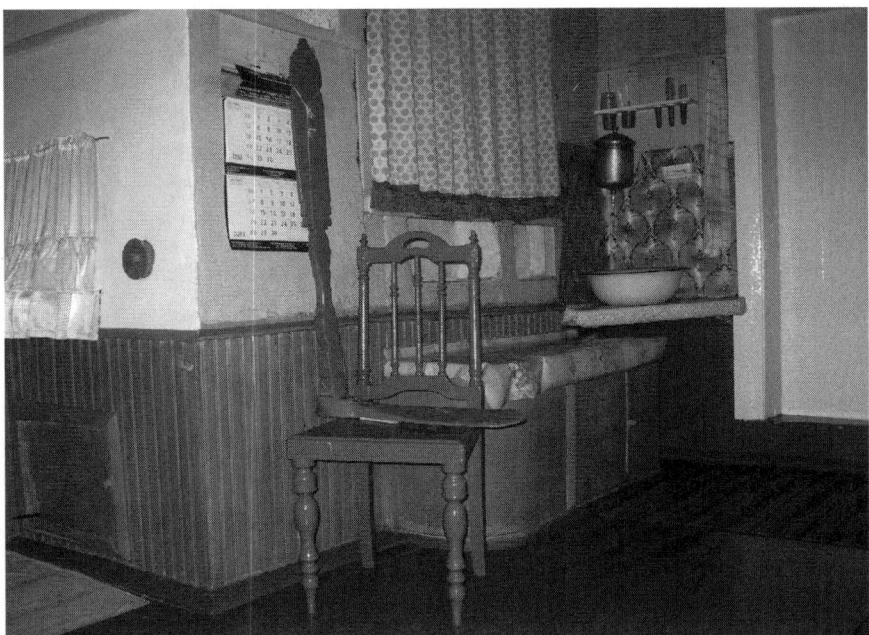

Figure 11.4 *A stove in the house of a summer visitor.*

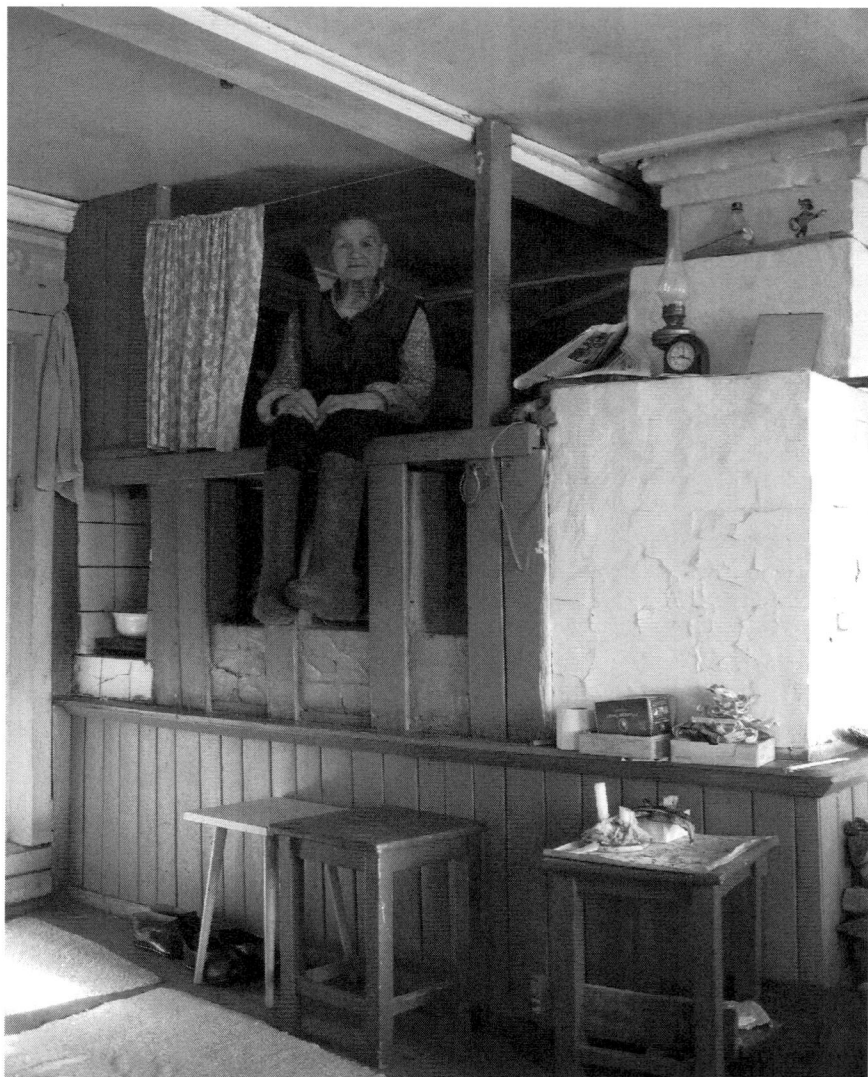

Figure 11.5 *A stove in the house of a permanent dweller.*

on their family trees. They may gather information about their families and the village in archives and literature. They keep clippings from different historical texts and sometimes carry this material with them when they travel in summer from town to village and back. There is an amibiguity in how incomers treat life in the village: on the one hand, they bring in new concerns and attitudes because the experience of living away has influenced their perception of Kuzomen'. On the other hand, they conceive of village life in terms of the past, the way it was when they left Kuzomen'. I call the attitude of summer visitors 'diachronic'. Their perspective is frozen in time. I mentioned earlier that summer visitors enjoy recollecting household histories in Kuzomen'. For them the activity of collecting and formalizing historical data about the village and building genealogical trees fulfils a compensatory function. It serves as compensation for their separation from their home place the loss of a place that is dear to them.

Basu (2007) deals with issues of genealogical research and migrants' identity in his book on people of Scottish descent who live outside Scotland and undertake journeys to their Scottish homeland in order to reengage with relatives and visit sites associated with their ancestors. These journeys are often part of, or lead to, genealogical research where people learn about their family's history. Basu argues that 'through these genealogical journeys, individuals are able to construct meaningful self-narratives from the ambiguities of their diasporic migrant histories, and so recover a more secure sense of home and self-identity' (2007: cover page). Through building genealogical trees, summer visitors in Kuzomen' likewise reengage with their home place and reconnect with their kinsmen.

In contrast, people who live in Kuzomen' permanently do not have a need to reify the village's history and culture, because they are in the place, and this constantly keeps them busy with various everyday concerns. Permanent villagers are interested in local history as well, but they rarely become actively involved in collecting information or giving it any physical form beyond keeping it in their heads. I call the attitude of permanent dwellers 'synchronic'. The difference in attitudes stems from the nature of people's movements in relation to the village. There is a contrast between the high mobility of summerfolks and their static treatment of house interiors on the one hand, and the relatively low mobility of permanent dwellers and the ever-changing interiors of their homes on the other. There is a peculiar interplay between physical and symbolic mobility and immobility in the respective ways in which temporary visitors and permanent villagers perceive the built environment of Kuzomen'.

Parallel distinctions can be found in literature on second homes. Aronsson (2004: 83), in his study of the place attachment of vacation residents on Smögen, an island off the Swedish west coast, suggests that 'permanent residents have a fundamental cultural identity in the place', which vacation residents lack. Aronsson explains this as the difference in the two groups' ways of life: the permanent residents having low levels of mobility and the vacation residents being highly mobile. The former are deeply attached to place, whereas the latter are in search of such attachment. In this context, a second home in the countryside provides an opportunity for fulfilling this goal.

Summer visitors tend to give the history of their homes a physical, tangible and fixed form, examples of which are archival excerpts, paper clippings and genealogical trees. By contrast, permanent dwellers can be satisfied with dreams and images. When I visit Ira and her husband, who are permanent residents in Kuzomen', they often say that they like imagining the way that Kuzomen' used to look when there were more people and houses in the village. They dream of travelling through time just to have a quick glance. This imaginary engagement with the village's history is sufficient and people do not need a tangible material expression of it.

Conclusion

In this chapter, I have looked at the centrality of houses in Kuzomen'. I introduced the distinction between synchronic and diachronic attitudes of people to houses, depending on the type of their engagement with the village. In this distinction, the temporal aspect of one's engagement is especially important. Having experienced a break in their relations with the village, summer visitors tend to perceive houses in a historic retrospective and thus share a diachronic attitude to them, whereas permanent dwellers who have remained in the village for most of their lives are more grounded in the present and therefore share a synchronic attitude to houses.

I would like to conclude this chapter with a suggestion that the way people perceive the built environment in Kuzomen' connects to their opinions about the village's future. In their perception of space people have to deal not only with the presence of things, but with absence as well. There is a distinction between how incomers and locals perceive the empty spaces between houses in Kuzomen'. To incomers, they give the impression of a scarcely populated village. Ruins of former buildings between still-standing houses indicate the village's decay for them. At the same time, for local people both empty spaces and ruins evoke the former prosperity and density of population in Kuzomen'. When they walk through the village they often pause at intervals between houses and say whose house used to stand there. Frequently this is followed by a half regretful, half proudly nostalgic statement about how very many houses there used to be in the village and therefore how many people lived there, which made life much merrier. Locals may treasure empty spaces and ruins; they value the absence of houses as well as their presence. Such a perception is only available to those who can read the local landscape in a way informed by a nuanced knowledge of local history.

The perception of empty space has implications for people's views of the future of the village. To incomers, empty spaces and ruins provide an image of a dying village, with no future beyond a mere tourist centre. At the same time, for locals empty spaces and ruins generate a more optimistic view, bringing back memories of a once prosperous place and hopes that it will rise again one day.

At the beginning of the fieldwork I concentrated on the desertion and abandonment of the local landscape. However, the longer I stayed in the field the more I started to notice features revealing the habitation and history of dwelling in the village. This was made possible through my prolonged acquaintance with the place. As a result, I started to look at houses differently. Incomers who are in Kuzomen' only for a short time have little opportunity to go beyond the static perception of achieved forms. Mundane engagement with houses in Kuzomen' therefore has far-reaching outcomes, as it connects with the way that people perceive the overall development of the village.

Acknowledgements

Many people have contributed to making this chapter a reality. The field-work was funded by the Wenner-Gren Foundation for Anthropological Research, grant No. 7482. I also received some funding from the University of Aberdeen Small Grants Program.

I would like to thank everyone I have met during my numerous field-work trips to Kuzomen' for their varied support. I am particularly grateful to Tat'iana Fedorovna Oleinik and Natasha Abakumova, Anzhela, Vitia and Nastia Dvininy, Ania Moshnikova, Ekaterina Nikolaevna Plotnikova, Galina Ivlevna Pavlova, Gennadii Vlasovich Vishniakov, Larisa Ivanovna Koneva and Ira Dvinina, whose generosity and hospitality helped me enormously throughout my countless visits to Kuzomen'.

I owe a lot to my supervisors Professor Tim Ingold and Dr Jo Vergunst who have consistently provided great support, inspiring advice and general guidance throughout the entire period of my work. I also thank other members of staff at the Department on Anthropology for their comments and advice on my work in progress, in particular Rob Wishart and also my fellow research students in Aberdeen who have provided invaluable advice on the draft of this chapter.

Notes

1. I use pseudonyms for all my informants in the chapter.
2. The Kola Peninsula is situated in the northwest of Russia and is surrounded by the White Sea from the southwest to northeast and the Barents Sea in the north. It borders upon Norway in

the northwest, Finland in the west and the Republic of Karelia, which is part of the Russian Federation, in the south.

3. I received this data from the Statistical Department of the district administration by phone communication.

4. In Russian the term *tetia* means 'aunt', but it is also a polite way to talk to people who are older than you.

CHAPTER 12

The Hearth, the Home and the Homeland

An Integrated Strategy for Memory Storage in Circumpolar Landscapes

Gerald A. Oetelaar, David G. Anderson and Peter C. Dawson

The structure and symbolism associated with the home, the hearth and the landscape often serve as key metaphors within a people's cosmology. Conversely, the cosmology provides the interpretive framework for understanding the landscape and a blueprint for designing and constructing the home and the camp. In this way, the identity of the group and its association with a particular homeland is constantly reinforced through ideological threads extending from the home to the camp, the landscape and the cosmos. Using examples from two societies in the circumpolar north, we will attempt to illustrate how the cosmology and social organization of Inuit in the Canadian Arctic and Evenkis in the Siberian taiga are imprinted in the design of the house, the location and orientation of the camp, and the perception of the landscape.

In this comparative account we build upon Keith Basso's (1996) pioneering description of the story-telling in Apache society. He saw the Apache landscape as being covered with 'mnemonic pegs' – motifs – each of which could remind an attentive listener of one or more stories documenting the history of relationships of that place. Mnemonic pegs are classically thought to be the memory aids a person uses when trying to reassemble a large list of details such as a list of place names. Here we would like to take the metaphor one step further to suggest that certain key features in the land are also repeated on a smaller scale within the confines of the settlement, the home, or even around the hearth. Thus at least between these two northern societies we would like to show how certain qualities, such as ideas concerning water and orientation, are memorable on a number of different scales.

The people in these two societies, those of Evenkis and of Inuit, live on opposite sides of the circumpolar Arctic and inhabit radically different landscapes. Evenkis are one of the most widely dispersed hunting and reindeer-herding peoples in Eurasia, living predominately in the taiga zone. Inuit are widely dispersed along the northern coast of North America, living a hunting lifestyle reliant on sea and land mammals, but also facilitated with domesticated dogs. Despite these great differences there are strong similarities between how their lifestyle is mirrored within their dwellings and activities. In particular, both use water and aquatic images to frame their cosmological ideas. Through the examples of these two peoples we provide an account that looks more broadly to the circumpolar North as a whole.

In order to give a sense of coherence to these accounts – to make them representative of Inuit or Evenkis everywhere – we take advantage of several attempts to distil a unified folklore for each people. This somewhat nationalist project has been acclaimed most highly in John Bennett and Susan Rowley's (2004) compilation of Inuit oral history *Uqalurait*. We rely heavily upon this text, as well as recent oral history work done with the *Paatlirmiut* Inuit; one of nine subgroups referred to by ethnographers as Caribou Inuit. Although a lot of energy has gone into fashioning a single literary dialect for Evenki and with it a set of official school books which follow a standard pattern, those books until recently have tended to rehearse pan-Soviet themes (such as stories of Lenin's childhood). Nevertheless, Grafira Vasilevich's (1936) early folklore collection in the old orthography stems from a similar, if less smoothly edited, idea. Her short article on 'Early Conceptions of the Universe' (1959; 1963) provides a similar summary. More recently, a volume in a recent book series on epic stories of all Siberian peoples (Myreeva et al. 1990) has renewed this tradition. Our intention in using these collections is to refer to a body of stories told by elders while the fur trade was central to their lives, with the hope that the motifs point further back to a time before the creation of fur-trade society.

Part I: Inuit

Cosmology

The myths and stories shared among Inuit in the Canadian Arctic indicate a common cosmology, and a collective Thule culture ancestry. Yet variations in the narratives occur and stem largely from the belief that Inuit belong to the land. Thus, the geographical locales of shared stories, including those of the widely known Inuit cultural hero *Kiviuq*, tend to vary somewhat by region (Figure 12.1). Still, the overarching themes of these myths and stories reflect values common to all Inuit (Bennett and Rowley 2004: 120).

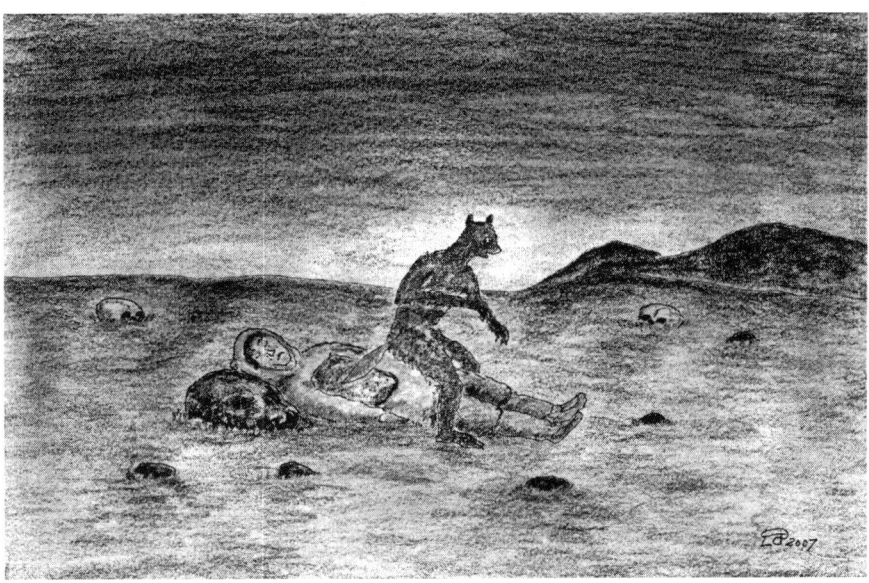

Figure 12.1 *The Inuit culture hero Kiviuq attacked by a malevolent being, as depicted by Paatlirmiut Elder Mark Kalluak in this illustration. The creature's attempts to pierce the sleeping Kiviuq with his stinger are thwarted by a flat slab of rock placed by the hero over his chest (Mark Kalluak, Department of Education, Govt. of Nunavut).*

In these stories, as in life, spirits control the wind, the weather, the seasons and the animals. These spirits maintain the balance in nature and ensure the renewal of the land, the resources and the people. Human beings play a critical role in maintaining this equilibrium through their daily practices and rituals. Each individual in each community carries the responsibility of maintaining this balance in the home, the camp and the surrounding landscape. Moreover, these obligations extend beyond the living community to the spirits of past and future generations of Inuit. This world view structures the lives of individuals in the dwelling, in the camp and on the landscape. To remind people of their responsibilities, the house, the camp and the landscape include mnemonic pegs designed to elicit the appropriate narratives, songs and rituals. For the Inuit, then, as for Evenkis, the world of the spirits permeates every aspect of life and affects all social and ecological relationships (Kemp 1984: 473). As a result, Inuit experience the real world of places and things through their negotiations with the associated incorporeal elements.

The wisdom to negotiate social and ecological relationships through spiritual intermediaries derives from narratives such as the story of

Nuliajoq. In the many versions of this narrative, *Nuliajoq* – also known as *Takatuma, Sedna, Uinigumasuittuq, Takannaaluk, Kannaaluk, Taliilajuq,* and *Arnakapsaaluk* [Bennett and Rowley 2004: 171]) – is lured by a handsome fulmar (seabird) to join him in the land of the fulmars where there is never hunger, where tents are made of beautiful skins, where beds are made of soft reindeer skins, where bedding is made of thick bear skins, where lamps are always filled with oil and where the pots always have meat. When she arrives in the land of the fulmars, her tent covering is made of fish skins with holes through which wind and snow constantly blow, her bed is made of hard walrus skins and her diet consists of miserable fish. *Nuliajoq* cries for her father to take her back and, on his first visit the following spring, the father kills her fulmar husband and escapes with *Nuliajoq* in his boat. Discovering the body of their friend, the fulmars pursue the pair and soon locate the boat whereupon they stir up a heavy storm. In serious peril, the father offers his daughter to the fulmars and throws her overboard. She clings to the edge of the *qajaq* but her father cuts off her fingers at the first joint. As these fall into the water, they become whales, the nails turning into whalebone. Her father then cuts off the second joints, which swim away as seals, and then he cuts off the third joints, which become the ground seals. Believing that *Nuliajoq* has died, the fulmars let the storm subside and her father allows *Nuliajoq* back into the boat. Once they reach the shore, *Nuliajoq* orders her dogs to gnaw off her father's feet and hands. When he awakes, the father curses all of them whereupon the earth opens and swallows the hut, the father, the daughter and the dogs (Boas 1974: 583–5).

In his discussion of this narrative, Boas (1974: 587–8) also implicates *Nuliajoq* in the creation of the caribou and walrus. During a famine, *Nuliajoq* apparently carries a small piece of her abdominal fat (or her boots) to a nearby hill where it is magically transformed into caribou. Frightened by the charging animal, she knocks out its front teeth and then kicks the caribou as it runs by, lopping off its tail. Sometime later, she throws another piece of her body fat into the ocean where it is transformed into a walrus. *Nuliajoq* thus creates the animals of the land and sea before she and her father descend to the underworld or *Adlivun*, which is described as a land with no sun, very cold temperatures, terrible snow storms and ice all around (Boas 1974: 589). This description of the underworld, which is reminiscent of the Arctic landscape during the winter months and the darkest time of the year when life is most precarious (Bennett and Rowley 2004: 172), is in stark contrast to the portrayal of *Qudlivun,* or the upper world, which is depicted as a land of perpetual light, with no snow, no ice and no storms. Evoking the Arctic landscape during the summer months, *Qudlivun* abounds with deer, fish and fowl. In *Adlivun*, *Nuliajoq* and her father live in a house protected by fierce dogs lying in the entrance tunnel. Inside the house, *Nuliajoq* occupies one half of the sleeping platform and her father inhabits the other half. Despite the dismal living conditions, *Nuliajoq* is the mistress of *Adlivun* and controls the availability of marine animals, whereas her father is the protector of terrestrial resources and he, like his daughter, sometimes withholds these animals from the Inuit (Bennett and Rowley 2004: 171–5; Boas 1974: 586).

Dwelling on the landscape

This story sets the stage upon which the Inuit enact their ecological relationships with the resources of the land and sea. The annual sub-sistence round of most Inuit involves a winter occupation along the coast, during which time they rely on marine resources, and a move-ment inland to exploit terrestrial resources during the summer months[1] (Balikci 1984; Kemp 1984; Mary-Rousselière 1984). Although the ringed seal is the most important marine resource, the Inuit also rely on walrus, narwhal, beluga whale, polar bear and some deep-sea fish. During the summer, groups move inland varying distances to collect eggs, capture waterfowl, hunt caribou and fish. Although these subsis-tence strategies display an intimate knowledge of animal behaviours, the Inuit realize that success in any and all of these activities is dependent on the actions of *Nuliajoq*.

Under normal circumstances, *Nuliajoq* and her father release the ani-mals to supply the physical needs of humans. However, when people fail to observe the proper taboos about preparing and consuming marine and terrestrial resources, they withhold the food supply, causing famine and starvation. The most common infractions occur when people ignore the distinction between marine and terrestrial resources, such as cooking caribou meat on the sea ice, cooking products of the land and sea in the same pot, sewing caribou hides after movement to the winter dwellings or sewing sealskin at fishing creeks when the salmon are running.

When minor taboos are broken, *Nuliajoq* can sometimes be convinced to release the animals through offerings. *Paatlirmiut* Inuit elders recall leaving items such as pocketknives, tobacco, cigarettes, coins and flash-lights at special places called *Tunnillarvik* in exchange for wishes, better health or feeling better. One of the most unique examples of *Tunnillarvik* is the *Hiutiru'juaq* offering cave, located on the shores of *Kaminak* Lake (Figure 12.2) (Dawson 2011). Here, large numbers of personal objects have been left behind by visitors as offerings over a period that stretches back hundreds, and possibly even thousands, of years. Large numbers of *Tunnillarvik* sites have been recorded throughout the *Kivalliq* region of Nunavut.

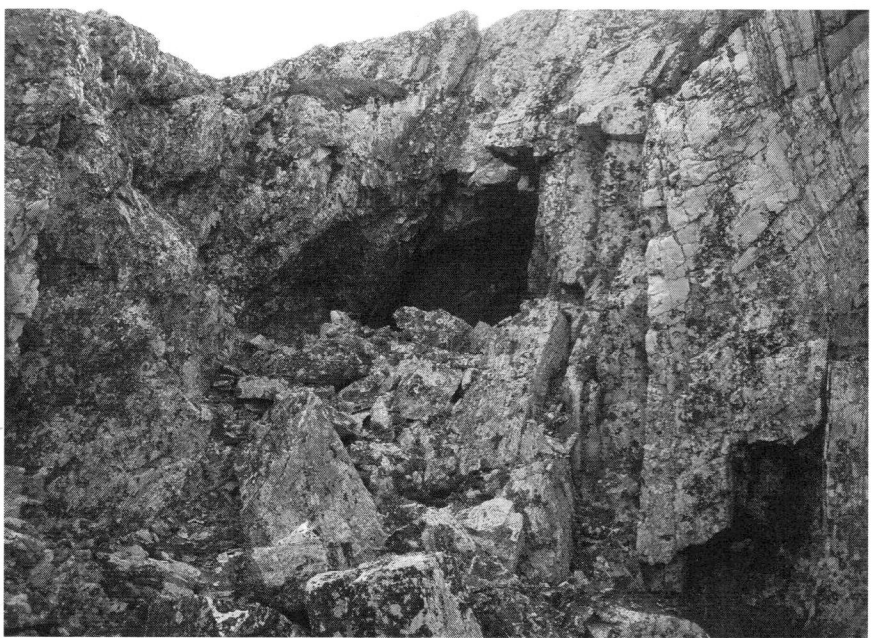

Figure 12.2 Hiutiru'juaq *Offering Cave, on the shore of Kaminak Lake, in the central Canadian Arctic.*

Interestingly, this area is among the most challenging places to live in the Canadian Arctic, and several well-documented and widespread famines occurred here in the early twentieth century (Birket-Smith 1929; Burch 1986). Consequently, the concept of *Tunnillarvik* was an important means of managing ecological uncertainty among the *Paatlirmiut*. Serious infractions required that the shaman or *angakut* travel to the home of *Nuliajoq* in the underworld, carefully move by the angry dog(s) in the entrance tunnel, cross an abyss and eventually liberate the animals by placating *Nuliajoq*. If successful, the shaman would attempt to release the animals by combing *Nuliajoq's* hair, soothing her aching fingers or depriving her of her charms.

The spirits also control the wind and weather and thus affect the movement of people across the landscape. Travel across the Arctic landscape is always challenging, giving the region's susceptibility to sudden storms and strong winds. In the summer, Inuit travel along the coast by *qajaq* (kayak) and *umiaq* but are always aware of the strong currents and countercurrents, the extreme tides and the heavy seas. In the winter, the Inuit traveller follows the same coastal trails using dog sleds but remains alert for patches of thin ice, sudden displacement of sea ice, and blowing snow. To negotiate these challenges, the traveller relies on a succession of named landmarks clearly visible from the watercraft (Aporta 2004; 2005; 2009; Hallendy 1994; 1997), on observations of animal behaviour to tell if ice is landfast or moving out to sea (Bennett and Rowley 2004: 389) and on narratives outlining the appropriate strategies for circumventing such obstacles. The place names and stories also identify the resident spirit whose assistance can be requested in times of real peril. The inland routes, like those along the coast, are bordered with landmarks, which help the traveller avoid rocky ground and follow isthmuses, fjords, frozen lakes and rivers (Aporta 2004).

Even though Inuit are adept at travelling by *qajaq, umiaq* and sled, place names also play an essential role in navigation because they provide insights into how the arctic landscape is conceptually organized (Keith 2004). Among the *Paatlirmiut* Inuit, place names can exist as literal descriptions of geographical elements: for example, *Matugijjat* meaning 'steep hills, an obstacle for going around' (Dawson 2011). Other names can orient a person by referencing river flow or wind direction, such as *Hannirut* meaning 'the island is facing north' (Dawson 2011). Place names can indicate people's activities, as with *Qadgitaqturviit* which means: 'where caribou are caught by digging snow traps' (Chapin et al. 2005). They can also be metaphorical, as when landforms are referred to as animal or human body parts. The name *Nuvuguaiq*, for instance, refers to a cliff at *Arvia'juaq* (Sentry Island), on the western coast of Hudson Bay that resembles a whale flipper (Dawson 2011). Place names can depict historic events, such as skirmishes with First Nations, or ancestors associated with graves. *Himiuttat* refers to a place near *Arvia'juaq* where Inuit and Chipewyan frequently met (Dawson 2011). Finally, they can be associated with supernatural beings and myths, such as *Ijiralik* – a type of creature that kidnaps and hides human beings (Dawson 2011).

Children and young adults, through deliberate instruction and recitation, acquired the cultural information contained in place names during the course of the seasonal round (Keith 2004; Whitridge 2004). Often, these recitations describe movement along the relevant section of the trail as a narrative that presents, in chronological order, the succession of place names and the distance between landmarks in terms of travel time. Travelling songs, which mention the names of places along paths and trails, serve as memory aids (Bennett and Rowley 2004: 120), as do the rhymes which string together place names into tongue twisters for children to repeat. The sequences of names always follow known routes of travel, most of which begin with the home village (Correll 1976: 178). In times of trouble, travellers are advised to remain on the established network of trails because the chances are very good that they will meet another traveller who can offer assistance or inform the person's relatives of their whereabouts. Under these circumstances, the location of a stranded traveller is always described by reference to landmarks and wind direction (Aporta 2004).

To orient themselves on the landscape, the Inuit use a vocabulary based on the location and orientation of the coastline, the boundary line between the land and the sea (Fortescue 1988; Keith 2004; Robbe 1977). The terminology assumes that the individual is standing on the shore facing the open water. Given this orientation, the Inuit use one term to indicate places away from the coast out to sea and its opposite to identify places located inland from the coast. Two additional terms are used to describe orientations, defined as right-along-the-coast and left-along-the-coast. The landscape of the Inuit is thus subdivided into four principal sectors with the coastline serving as the basis for the orientation system.

Another standard set of terms is used in combination with toponyms to indicate exactly where a person or a particular resource is located on the landscape. A person standing on the shore uses a similar terminology to communicate the location of a seal to the hunter in a *qajaq*. In each case, the coastline or the dividing line between the land and the sea serves as the reference point for the system of orientation. Similarly, games also functioned to correctly 'position' people on the landscape. The outlines of 15 stone *qajat* have been recorded at *Arvia'juaq* (Sentry Island) on the western coast of Hudson Bay (Figure 12.3). Oral histories refer to these features as *Qillalugaujarvik* or the beluga *qajaq* game, and their purpose was to train young hunters. The flow of rivers (east–west) and the relative location of the ocean, two important concepts in landscape organization and orientation in the *Kivalliq* region, are reflected in the orientation of these stone *qajaq* features. Beluga whale hunting typically occurs at the mouths of rivers, which flow from land to sea in an eastward direction. The stone *qajaq* outlines are similarly positioned in an east–west direction, correctly orienting players seated in their stone *qajaq* to real life circumstances (Dawson 2011).

The importance of the coastline becomes even more apparent when one examines the Inuit maps drawn for early explorers and traders (Bagrow 1948; Boas 1974: 643–8; Rundstrom 1990; Spencer 1955; Spink and Moodie 1972). Examples of earlier maps are incised in ivory or carved in wood and depict, in sculptural relief, the important features of the coastline (Peterson 1984). Among Inuit, maps are used to convey travel directions and instructions to someone who is unfamiliar with the area. Unlike western European cartography, scale can shift several times within a single map. Such manipulation of scale may reflect an attempt to overcome the deficiencies of a two- or three-dimensional representation

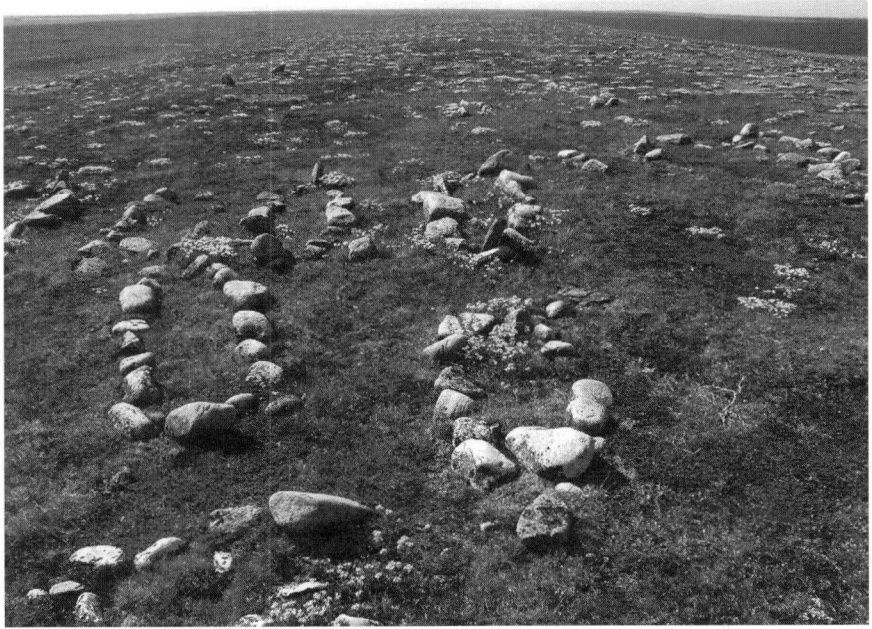

Figure 12.3 Qillalugaujarvik, *or Beluga Kayak* (Qajaq) *Game, found at* Arvia'juaq *(Sentry Island), off the western coast of Hudson Bay.*

of a four-dimensional 'object' – namely a journey (Whitridge 2004: 224).

During the preparation of a map, the cartographer draws the outline of the area in the sand or snow as he explains the most desirable travel route, identifies the important landmarks, indicates the prevailing wind directions by season and describes the snow, ice and ground conditions during a storm. The narrator also piles snow or sand in ridges to indicate landmarks, hollows out sections for lakes, smoothes out beach and ocean areas, draws in water courses and clearly shows all obstacles (Spencer 1955: 46). Of course, the traveller must commit the map to memory, fixing in his mind the names of the important landmarks. Although the Inuit, like all aboriginal groups who rely on oral traditions, are adept at this type of memory storage, they also know that the appearance of each landmark when approached from a particular direction will remind them of the place name and, by extension, the associated narratives.

Dwelling in the camp

Although Inuit groups move inland to hunt caribou and harvest fish during the summer months, they identify themselves based on the names of the winter settlements which are strategically located relative to the favoured habitats of marine resources, primarily seals. That is, winter settlements tend to cluster in areas where seals maintain breathing holes and where the smooth, fast ice allows hunters to capture the animals. At the same time, the residents of these winter settlements are identified geographically using the suffix '*–miut* "the people of" appended to the name of the particular place and socially by use of the suffix complex *–kut* "members of the family of" added to the name of a person' (Kemp 1984: 464). Each individual thus belongs to a social unit and identifies with a place or settlement on the landscape. Most winter camps have a long record of occupation and thus give the members of the community a sense of history and attachment to place. More importantly, the residents of the historical settlements acknowledge their role in the perpetuation of the lineage and the transmission of cultural information from one generation to the next.

In the world of the Inuit, the people associated with a winter camp commit to the reproduction of the social unit and the transmission of the oral traditions. Camps, which consist of an orderly arrangement of houses, festival houses/tents, caches, household and community middens, and burials, contain a myriad of crisscrossing paths, reflecting the repetitive movements of individuals as families visit each other and engage in daily tasks. Most houses, which are reoccupied year after year, become repositories of family histories, whereas snow houses are connected together using passages of ice and snow to reinforce the social and ideological solidarity of the group. In addition to these domestic practices and social interactions, the ideological obligations of the community are met through continued negotiations with the spirits of the ancestors.

The Inuit have two souls, including the breadth of life *(inu'siq)* and the soul proper *(tayniq)*. After death the souls go to *Adlivun* and remain there for one year, during which time they reside in *Nuliajoq*'s dismal abode. While in *Nuliajoq*'s home, the souls lie by the side of her father who constantly pinches them (Boas 1974: 588). During this time, the soul is called *tupilaq* and is looked upon as a malevolent spirit who frequently roams around the villages killing those who touch it and causing illness and mischief among those who see it. After a year, the soul, often with the help of a shaman, finds rest as an *Adliparmiut* or an inhabitant of the country farthest below the world. Thus, after death, the spirit of a deceased member of the community remains nearby and eventually is reincarnated as a new member of the living community. For this reason, a newborn can only be named after a deceased member of the community and, later in life, this individual strengthens the mystical bond by visiting the burial place of her/his namesake. These individuals also refer to each other as *avvariik* or *maliktigiik* meaning 'those who follow each other' (Bennett and Rowley 2004: 6), thus insuring the continuity of the social relationships with the camp.

Community members have similar obligations towards their ecological relationships, particularly the stewardship of resources, and these can only be met through continued interactions with the spirits tied to particular places on the landscape. Like people, animals possess an *inua* or inner soul that must be propitiated lest the animals seek revenge on humans for taking their bodies for food and clothing (Bennett and Rowley 2004: 43). Although the power and authority of supernatural beings such as *Nuliajoq* extend across most of the Canadian Arctic, others are clearly attached to specific places within the acknowledged homeland of individual settlements. Each community is therefore responsible for a very specific store of information shared within a well-defined social network. Further, the residents have an obligation to transmit that information from one generation to the next through narratives, songs and repetitive phrases. Of particular importance is the dense network of place names and associated narratives describing the location and characteristics of landmarks within the geographical homeland of the community. In this way, the residents of individual settlements are able to fulfil their obligations for maintaining ties with the local spirits for the benefit not only of the local community but of all Inuit who might travel through the area.

Dwelling in the home

Just as the landscape and settlement are seeded with mnemonic pegs to remind the Inuit of their role in maintaining the key social and ecological relationships, so too does the house embody the cosmology of the group. Although a number of narratives are associated with the house, the story of the 'Raven and the Whale' is perhaps the best known and most widespread. In this narrative, Raven, who created daylight with his cry, is out at sea in search of land but finds a whale instead. He flies into the whale and there finds a woman sitting on a bench tending a lamp. At regular intervals, she leaves her bench and returns a short while later. She warns Raven not to follow her, but after a while he can no longer resist the temptation. As he follows the woman, she dies and, soon thereafter, the lamp burns out leaving the space in total darkness. Raven later learns that the woman is the soul of the whale, whereas the oil lamp is its heart (Sheppard 1998; Lowenstein 1993). Although this narrative explains the importance of the lamp and the small ventilation hole to the survival of the household, the story also reminds the occupants about the proper treatment of the spirits in the world of the Inuit. Like the whale, all living things have souls which, when treated properly, return to the world of the

Inuit to occupy new bodies, thereby ensuring the continuity of resources and of people.

Although the Thule winter house provides a locus for everyday activities such as playing, sewing, woodworking, cooking and eating (Whitridge 2004: 232), the structural framework of whalebones serves as a metaphor for the whale in the story (Lowenstein 1993). At the same time, the location, orientation and organization of the Inuit house remind the occupants of important social and behavioural taboos, especially those relating to the resources of the land and sea.

Although the snow igloo is often constructed on the sea ice, the winter sod house is typically erected on the shore with the entrance tunnel facing the open water. In this way, the home possesses a fractal-like quality, infinitely reflecting important cosmological principles at varying scales. Movement into and out of the dwelling serves as a constant reminder that survival in the Canadian Arctic depends on the resources of both the land and the sea. At the same time, the terms used to describe the different sections of the house are exactly the same as those used to orient oneself on the landscape (Fortescue 1988). That is, the Inuit orient themselves by standing inside the building facing the entrance. In this position they refer to the entrance using the landscape term for out to sea, whereas they identify the back wall using the word for inland. Similarly, the walls on the right or left of the individual are described using the terms designating the directions of right-along-the-coast and left-along-the-coast, respectively. In this way, movement within the dwelling mirrors travel on the landscape.

Part 2: Evenkis

Cosmology

Evenkis, like Inuit, are a people who occupy a large territory; only in their case their homelands are a boreal, Eurasian territory. There are many Evenki dialect groups and local societies with slightly different histories and subsistence strategies. However, as with Inuit, they share many common stories and have a narrative style which is deeply linked to their taiga landscape. According to one of the most well-respected ethnographers of Evenkis, Grafira M. Vasilevich (one of the only people to have worked with Evenkis in all of their home regions), it is possible to combine their tradition of epic traditional stories – *nimngakan* – as well as their everyday tales into a single cosmological tale (Vasilevich 1959; 1963). Perhaps unlike with Inuit, there is no consensus on how deep the roots of this cosmology go, with both Vasilevich (1959: 189–90) and Sergei M. Shirokogoroff (1926) agreeing that they reflect a relatively recent concern with extensive movement and migration in the present era, and only glimpses of earlier paleoasiatic motifs.

In almost all accounts, Evenkis see the universe as being made up of three coexisting realms, often called upper, 'middle' and lower. These territories do not divide the universe but rather overlap. People and animals as we interact with them typically live in the middle territory, and the upper and lower realms mirror this territory. I have sometimes heard Evenkis speak of 'shadows' that follow people and animals in the here-and-now. All of these interwoven realms are collectively called the universe, or the world *(buga, dunne)* but in specific contexts can be modified with adjectives to signal the realms nearer the sky or under the ground, while the 'middle' realm remains just *buga*.

Vasilevich (1959: 160) argues that the belief in a single universe is older, while the belief in a tripartite overlapping universe is a later phenomenon. These realms are nevertheless ever-present, since people or animals in each sometimes have the ability to act on each other. In cosmological stories, spirit-masters *(dukh-khoziain)* can be encountered by people from the everyday world if they fall through the ice or into a river or, as John Ziker in this volume records, they get lost searching for their reindeer. Similarly, spirits from the other realms can sometimes appear in the 'middle' realm. In most cases, a person out of place causes illness or death in one or both realms, but highly skilled, knowledgeable people *(shamanil)* can move between the world to attract hunting animals or to search for the lost or the dead.

As with Inuit, a healthy taiga and society depends on keeping the agents in each realm in balance and in place. Thus, old Evenki stories tell of a supernatural bear pursuing a supernatural elk in the upper-realm creating the constellations and the ordering of day and night. In the lower realm, a supernatural elk 'gives people their food – their catch – releasing from under the earth a greater or smaller quantity of animals' (Anisimov 1963b: 176). Animals are only released if people observe the established prohibitions towards the hearth, if they do not kill animals unnecessarily and do not dishonour the catch (ibid).

Water plays an important role for some Evenkis in their account of how the different realms fit together. Almost everyone who has travelled with Evenkis notes their superior sense of orientation linked to hydrology – here the hydrology of rivers and not that of the sea. Water also forms the backdrop for one of their primal legends of the origin of today's world. It dates back to a time when today's dry earth was a tiny element amidst a giant watery horizon. People suffered then since they had no place to live, and no place to herd their reindeer. The Mammoth noticed that Man was sad and asked why. 'How can one be happy', the Man replied, 'there is water everywhere and nowhere to travel'. Mammoth decided to help the

Man by drying out the Earth. He sloshed through the water until he met Chzhiabdar the Snake. He proposed to Snake, 'Come along with me, let's dry out the Earth. I'm strong and you're flexible. You can help me out and then lie on the sand afterwards'. Mammoth set his tusks into the depths and brought up sand, clay and rocks. They grew into mountains, plateaus and valleys. Snake wound his way between the hills and valleys and water drained along the road (*doroga*) that he carved with his body (reprinted in Vasilevich 1936: 280 from Marenenok 1933).[2] An interesting small detail of this primal legend is way that the words for road and river are linked and blur together in the body of the snake (cf. Ermolova 2007: 87). This polysemanticism, we will show, is an important aspect in understanding how river imagery works on a variety of scales.

Since the three realms are understood to be imminent – that is, to be still freshly structuring the world – talk of these elements are often linked exclusively to shamanism. It is certain that shamanism would not be what it is without them. However, it is important to distinguish what Khasanova (2007: 197–8) identified recently as the difference between everyday and 'emergency' interactions with the spirit-masters. As an example, she identifies within the folklore of the Lower Amur Tungus peoples a set of daily, almost unconscious rituals, which appeal to the spirit-masters who might attend to the placement of fish. These she distinguished from the rarer 'emergency' rituals conducted to solve a problem with starvation or the loss of a kinsman. The emergency rituals are elaborate and striking, but not entirely interwoven into the fabric of everyday life. The individual rituals, however, she describes in a way that make them look more like a form of common sense, wherein people exercise an unreflective urge to make small offerings or to lower their voice when approaching certain natural features. In this respect, the practical cosmology of Evenkis – or perhaps their 'psychomental complex' (Shirokogoroff 1935) – links most easily with the landscape cosmology of Inuit and other circumpolar peoples. The everyday interlinking of the tangible and implicit recalls a number of traditions of animist thought, where one order is enlivened by another. Roberte Hamayon (1990: 331–2) calls this quality *surnature* – a supernature – where one realm is 'animated' by another but not always by discrete spirits. Evenkis communicate directly with agents in the upper and lower worlds through their actions and through specific rituals (Tugolukov 1978). The actions are normally incorporated into daily practices such as requesting permission to set up camp, feeding the hearth and leaving behind a small offering when abandoning the site. Other rituals are performed at specific places on the landscape, especially openings in the surface of the earth and at the bottom of large bodies of water, which are seen as entrances to the lower realm. Offerings of bright ribbons are placed near dangerous river crossings and near whirlpools. In

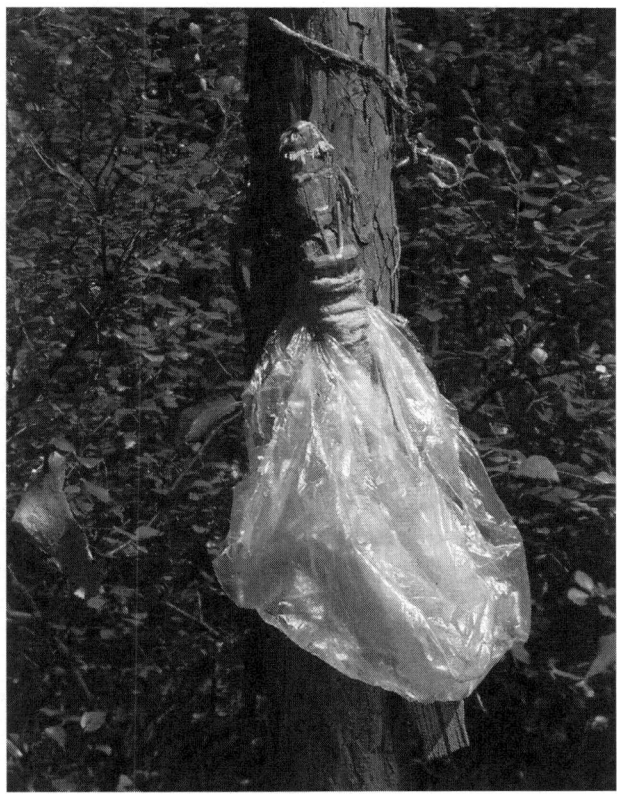

Figure 12.4 *A wooden idol* kunakun inuvun *tied to a larch tree at the boundary between two watersheds. The plastic skirt on the idol was designed to protect the tobacco from the rain.*

addition, prayers and offerings are made in the vicinity of various ritual structures ranging from graves to ritual idols that are scattered throughout the territory (Figure 12.4). In fact, each group seems to have its own objects of veneration – *bugady* – which might be unusual stones, rocks with zoomorphic features or trees of unusual size and form.

Rituals can also be seasonal. During the spring and fall, individual hunters travel into the forest to build a special fire and feed the resident spirit choice morsels of meat, while negotiating the outcome of future hunting endeavours. To ensure success, however, the hunter has to be diligent in his efforts to properly dispose of the bones, skins and skulls of all wild or domestic animals killed and butchered by himself and his relatives (Lavrillier 2000; 2008). Lower Amur peoples made seasonal offerings to rivers before and after the fishing season to ask for a good catch and to offer thanks for the year's catch (Khasanova 2007: 197). The well-known spring *ikenipke* ritual (Vasilevich 1957), recently revitalized in south-eastern Siberia (Lavrillier 2003), reenacts the annual hunting cycle over several days.

The shamanic ceremonies of Evenkis have become extremely well known in Europe through the English translation (Anisimov 1963a) of Arkadii Anisimov's (1952) account of a unnamed shaman's appeal to both a supernatural tree and a supernatural river within a 'shaman's tent' *shevenchedek* (cf. Iampol'skaia 1992). Building on his access to Innokentyi Suslov's partly published description (1936; 1993; Suslov and Menges 1983) of an abandoned shamanic tent along the Podkamennaia Tunguska river valley, Anisimov added his own observations of a shamanic performance in 1931 in the same region.

Although the context of, and reason for, the ritual are extremely unclear in his published text, he provides one of the clearest illustrations of the way that water imagery, and that of the home, can be manipulated power-fully in an evocative ritual. Here, his unnamed Western Evenki shaman built a special conical dwelling which created a microcosmic version of the universe. A special larch – *turu* – was placed to cross the lodge from its smoke opening to the hearth to help the shaman and his helpers ascend to the upper realm. Other upturned larches in the tent symbolized trees within the lower realm. The copious illustrations in the chapter show how the *shevenchedek* was surrounded by carved versions of animal helpers who could transverse several elements (such as the salmon–trout, or the loon). In the shaman's account, he made use of a raft and a supernatural river *engdekit* which flowed through the tent, and which helped him to move between one realm and the other. In a later article, Anisimov (1958: 61) reproduced a sketch of the *engdekit* made by a local informant emphasiz-ing the shoals and the intersecting streams where the shaman could rest on his or her way up to the upper realm, as well as the waterfalls which impeded progress (Figure 12.5).

Vasilevich (1959; 1963) made a subtle critique of these accounts of the supernatural river connecting the three realms, arguing that it was a very recent development confined only to certain western Evenki groups. It might be significant that in Anisimov's own article the *engdekit* was ambiguously described as a 'road-river of water' (*mumengi khokto bira*) and not merely a river. There is a strong argument to be made that the shaman performing this ritual in this troubled period of time (1926–1931) may have elaborated upon it in order to respond to the dangerous political pressures at that time.[3] The link between this type of shaman-izing and domestic architecture is nevertheless strong since similar, less elaborate performances could also take place in an ordinary conical tent. Comparative folklorists, including Anisimov (1951), have commented

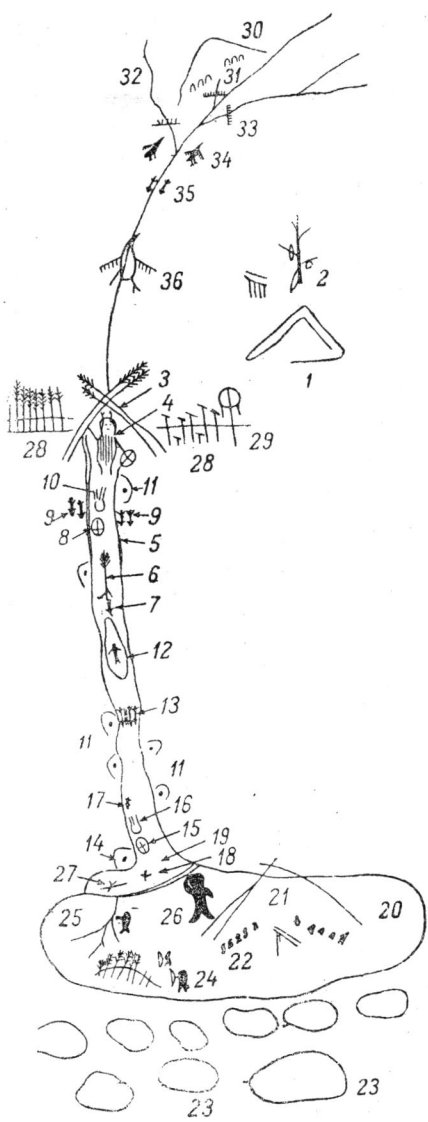

Figure 12.5 *This sketch, published by Arkadii Anisimov (1958: 61), represents the path of a shaman along the supernatural river accompanying a dead relative to the lower realm. The diagram is annotated with 36 features, too numerous to translate here. Image 1 is the lodge of the dead relative. Image 3 is the shaman's tent. Image 11 represents the camps of dead relatives guarding the entrance to the lower world. Image 15 is the shaman using his drum as a boat to cross to the lower realm. Image 23 shows the nine shamanic worlds, the largest of which is inhabited by the master of the lower world. Image 32 represents the headwaters to the supernatural river. The sketch was drawn by Vasilii Sharemiktal with the help of the shaman Katerina Pankagir.*

on the fact that the references to an upended supernatural (vertical) tree and supernatural (horizontal) river inscribe a primeval motif of control over both horizontal and vertical space (Ermolova 2007), making this particular ambiguous account one of the most widely cited.

To understand the extremely practical manner in which rituals animate everyday life for Evenkis, it is important not to mistake the geography for its agents. All Evenkis make offerings both through fire and through water, but often the offerings are presented directly to the agents living within these places. In most cases it was thought that the spirit animating a river was an old man, or sometimes a monstrous fish (often a pike) (Ermolova 2007: 101–4). The hearth was often thought to house an old woman, or as Ziker (this volume) quotes for Dolgans, a grandfather. Certainly, even when reading both Suslov's and Anisimov's descriptions of the *shevenchedek*, the thing that strikes one first is the clutter of carved wooden fish and other animals surrounding the tent in the illustrations (literally, the *shevenchedek* translates as the place of the shaman's helpers – not the shaman's tent).

In a recent, remarkably revisionist collection of essays on the role of rivers in structuring cultures in eastern Siberia, a number of authors take the time to specify the important yet non-central role of river imagery in Evenki folklore. Given that Evenkis first and foremost thought of the welfare of their reindeer (as in the Mammoth and Snake legend), Ermolova (2007: 108) states quite clearly that 'one does not find a cosmological image in the direct sense of [any concrete] river among Evenkis', unlike with other river peoples, such as Khantys.[4] The relation and wonder of rivers, as we shall see below, was linked to the way that they help one orient oneself in the world.

Dwelling on the landscape

The story of the drying and carving of the Earth by Snake and Mammoth illustrates two remarkable qualities of contemporary Evenki taiga adaptation: their desire to travel and the semantic linkage of rivers with roads. River names, directions and the relief that they carve are one of the primary methods by which the landscape is named and described (Ermolova 2007; Lavrillier 2005–2006; Sirina 2006: 80). Evenki terms to describe not only the quality of a river (its size and strength) but also its direction and motion, form part of a unique topographic language that describes relief extremely well.

Evenki map-making also played an important role in an early twentieth-century debate on the perception of the environment of 'primitive' peoples and on the raw ability of the unschooled mind to draw accurate sketch maps (Adler 1910). Indeed, the late nineteenth-century geographer Prince Kropotkin actively participated in discussions at the Royal Geographical Society in London on the design of the very first topographical maps following his field experience working with his Evenki taiga guide in Zabaikal'e (Kropotkin 1873; 1904). However, Evgeniia Alekseenko (2007: 55–6) sounds a note of caution about assuming that the river-landscape language has a very ancient hold on the ideas of central Siberian peoples. She cites the important fact that systems of river orientation were documented by European ethnographers at the exact time when the fur trade dictated how and where people should travel. The result is a creolism of coming to know the landscape in order to participate in a globalizing economy.

Evenki principles of taiga orientation nevertheless start from different principles than those of cartographers. Ethnographers agree that they creatively combine four sets of information: (1) directions relative to one's body ('forward', 'backward'); (2) the movement of the sun ('the place that the sun rises'); (3) the direction of rivers from the point of view of the speaker; and (4) descriptions of the slopes of the mountains that always surround Evenkis (Ermolova 2007: 89–90; Lavrillier 2005–2006; Shirokogoroff 1926; Vasilevich 1971: 225).

The fact that these directions are rooted in the point of view of the speaker, and not from the perspective of an imaginary observer flying above the landscape (as with topographical maps) is an important detail. Alexandra Lavrillier (2005–2006: 121–3) provides a rich set of diagrams and texts showing this system in action, wherein a journey can be described through the alteration of proceeding upstream and downstream, and then crossing watersheds, wherein the relational vocabulary resets and begins again. These elements of sun, slope and position can also be combined in certain topographic words such as *boso,* often translated as the 'northern slope' of a mountain, but meaning literally the slope shaded from the sun. A description like this also carries with it embedded expectations as to whether the forest is thick or thin (as one would expect on the north slope) and therefore what animals might live there.

Both Shirokogoroff (1926) and Vasilevich (1971) noted that pure cardinal directions were absent in the language. Instead, directions might be given with reference to a large river such as 'towards the Enisei'. Nevertheless, Ermolova (2007: 89) observes that general cardinal directions could be abstracted from this relational topography, especially if, as in Zabaikal'e, the major rivers move north–south. However, a somewhat competing collection of essays on practices of orientation in Siberia and inner Asia, edited by Jean-Luc Lambert (2005–2006), places the emphasis on the fact that this language of orientation never sees the world as a flat plane with cardinal points, but instead as a world that is always tipped in one or another direction. This observation overlaps with that of Ingold

(Chapter 2, this volume) on the unsuitability of interpreting space as providing a flat foundation for dwellings or for creatures that dwell on it.

Although the Evenki language of orientation is rooted in a personalized view of the topography, they often translate this perspective into birds-eye paper sketch maps that we would recognize as hydrological maps (Lavrillier 2005–2006; Sirina 2006: 80). When asked to produce a map, the Evenki cartographer always begins by drawing the most important river and the direction of its current as a line extending away from his or her body. Tangents are added to this line in order to indicate the relevant tributaries as well as those of the neighbouring rivers. In this way, they depict the main rivers and the directions of the currents; the relevant tributaries and their sources, and the presence of passes between major river valleys. The number and order of the tributaries is important, not their respective lengths (Sirina 2006: 80). Even though Evenkis have detailed knowledge of the meanders in these watercourses, the rivers are normally represented as straight lines, capturing that ambiguity in the language that links rivers to roads.

Dwelling in the camp

Most taiga Evenkis, like Inuit, also practise a strong seasonal round, although their movements are planned around the needs of their domestic reindeer. There is no universal pattern since the climate and geography across Eurasia is so varied. One can find groups living in the south in thick forest. They move their reindeer, and their camps, to the tops of mountains in the winter to take advantage of the thinner snow. In the spring they move to the bottom of valleys seeking places with a good supply of wood and water where they can construct smudge fires to save their reindeer from insects. In the northern sub-Arctic zones this pattern is reversed, with herders taking their considerably larger stocks of reindeer to the tops of the mountains in the summer where cold alpine winds keep them free of insects. In the winter they seek the shelter of the valley bottoms away from the bitter blizzards of that dark time.

People are nevertheless associated with one set of rivers or often one major drainage basin. Alexandra Lavrillier records how the Aldan-region Evenkis define themselves according to the principal river along which they travel (2005–2006: 115). Ermolova (2007: 96–101) identifies a subtle form of identity management in the way that terms for the lower course or the middle course of a river have been built into what we recognize today as the ethnonyms of fixed peoples such as Dolgan or Solon. When travelling temporarily or relocating to a new watershed, some hunters perform a smudging ritual with smoke to clean themselves before encountering a new master (Figure 12.6). To a great extent this constant

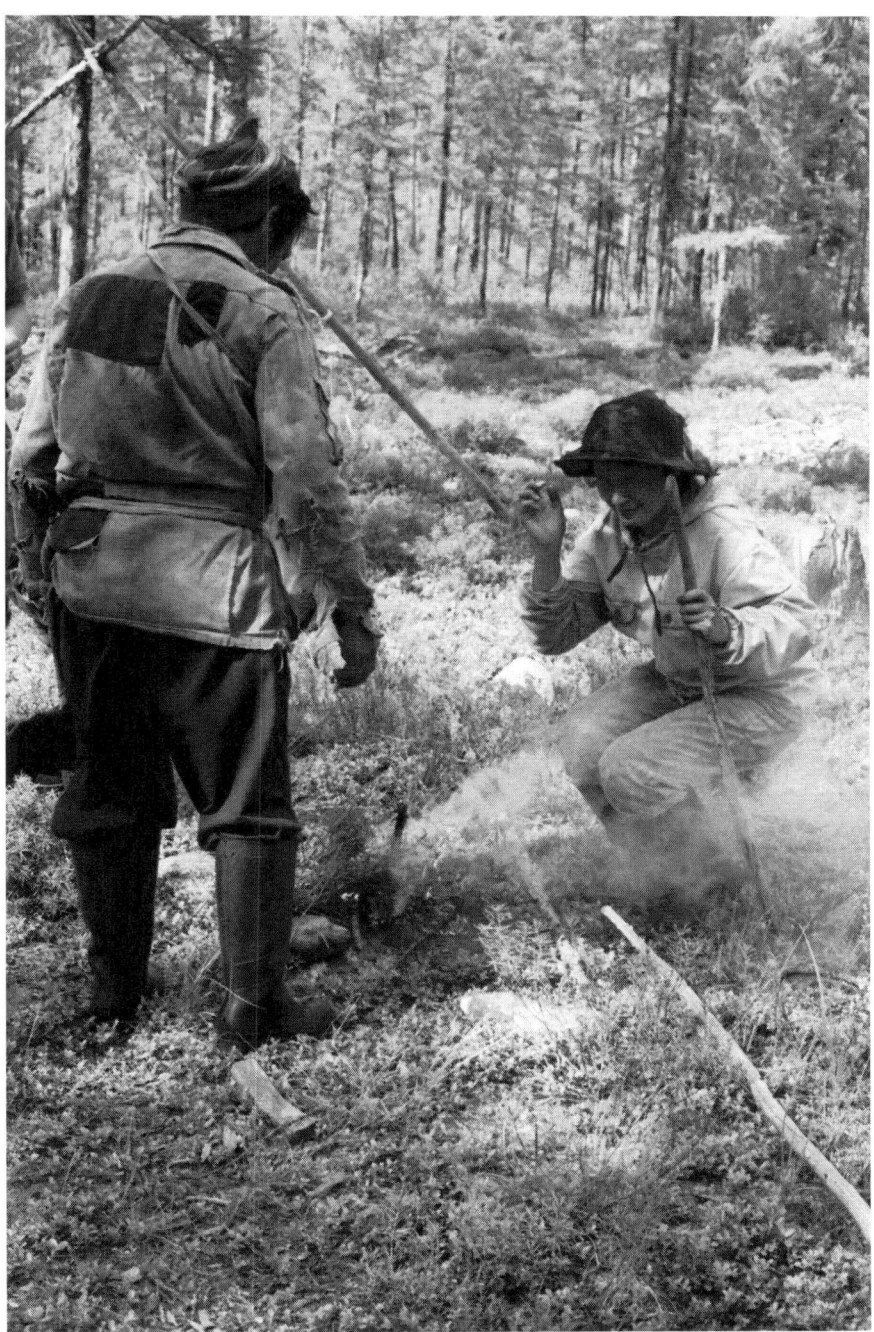

Figure 12.6 *Nikolai Aruneev and Anastasia Pastukhova performing a smudging ritual with* khenkere *[juniper] before crossing to a new watershed.*

movement up and down watersheds harmonizes with the Evenki language of orientation, their perception of certain masters living in specific watersheds, and the cosmology of the upper and lower realms.

In a practical manner, however, as in the legend of the Mammoth and Snake, Evenkis mix together different criteria when selecting a 'good place' to hold reindeer. This can be described by a number of formal criteria such as access to water and wood, or wind and forage (Lavrillier 2005–2006: 106–8). However, more often than not these tend to be places that reindeer themselves choose to live. Donatas Brandišauskas (2009) develops the idea of a *bikit* – 'a place of living' – to describe how Orochen hunters and herders select places for their lodges. This is a type of ecological 'patch' that is recognized as such by significant animals such as reindeer, or squirrels or moose. People have their own *bikitil* which might be selected for their convenient location to both pastures, the places that hunting animals frequent and to a village where on the whole a hunter's kin would live. Or a hunter may choose to be a guest in a *bikit* of a moose or some other animal. Sometimes reindeer and other animals completely avoid certain 'bad places', which on formal botanical criteria might seem like good ecological patches. Here hunters associate the negative influence of some misfortunate death or interaction with some other dark shadow which scares both people and animals away.

Anna Sirina (2006: 111), in her book on Katanga Evenkis, has a beautiful description of a correctly designed camp wherein the conical lodge crowns a vertical cone made up of buildings and the sloping landscape around. Ever conscious of the possible interaction of multiple realms, camps are never deliberately established on top of abandoned campsites. Tents are set on fresh places and hearths established anew, even if only a stone's throw away from a previous camp. Places that have been used before are described as 'soiled' or 'polluted'. One often hears stories of hunters who, in the rush of declining twilight, mistakenly set up a tent on an old campsite and then suffer bad dreams or are disturbed by visible or invisible creatures.

When setting up a new camp, the owner of the tent (classically, but much more rarely now, a woman) requests permission to use the place and, when leaving a camp, she always leaves behind on the abandoned site a small offering such as a piece of cloth, a reindeer hide or a thing no longer used. Without the benefit of this protection, the household members become sick or fail to provide for themselves and their relatives (Anisimov 1963b: 175). Similarly, the artefacts of everyday life are curated appropriately around the camp in special deposit areas or in trees. The bones of hunted animals or reindeer are not thrown into the fire or given to the dogs. They are often collected and hung up on ritual scaffolds upstream of the camp (Lavrillier 2005–2006; 2011). At the same time, any camp might be surrounded by other significant places nearby where offerings are made (Anisimov 1963b).

Dwelling in the lodge

The home of Siberian Evenkis is classically the conical lodge made of a frame of straight poles and a covering sewn from skins (often tanned skins from wild or domestic reindeer or moose). As with many circumpolar societies documented in this collection, the conical lodge has also become a symbol of the cultural strength for Evenkis today. Although some Evenkis still use conical lodges, most use a combination of canvas-wall tents and stationary cabins. Nevertheless, the pragmatics of using these 'modernized' spaces reflect many of the traditions of traditional *d'u*.

It is widely documented that space within a conical lodge is strictly divided (cf. Shirokogoroff 1929: 255–6) into special zones bounded by the central firepit and the circular covering of the tent. Classically, the area opposite the door, behind the hearth, (the *malu*) is made a special place suitable for honoured guests, and also the place where hunted animals, such as sable, may be brought in from under the tent covering. To the right and left of the fire are places reserved for the master and mistress of the tent, with a cooking and storage area closer to the door.

Coupled to the gendered and status patterns of using space are perhaps the more prevalent restrictions on movement, especially 'circling' either the hearth or the lodge itself. Children or naïve visitors are asked to retrace the exact steps they used when entering the tent, since completing a circle is thought to bring bad luck or illness. Most Evenkis do not feel comfortable 'circling', and there are multiple cosmological explanations for this. Some Evenkis speak of walking into one's own shadow – a reference to the other realms that might be present. However, some reassure that one only has to be careful about circling if powerful idols are held in the tent (which from Soviet times onwards were increasingly rare). People are to avoid 'circling' graves or places where powerful spirits, and idols, may lie.

The furnishings inside the lodge also remind people of the proper directions of movement. Two horizontal poles provide supports for pots suspended over the hearth. These architectural elements normally run from the back of the lodge towards the entrance. Given their function, these poles cannot be affixed too high above the hearth, and thus the horizontal supports restrict movement inside the lodge. In essence, these architectural elements constrain movement such that people entering the lodge move to one side or the other of the hearth, and tend to remain on that side of the dwelling. As such, the horizontal supports serve to remind people that walking in a circle around the tent or the fireplace is strictly forbidden.

Comparative folklorists such as Anisimov (1952) associate the division of space within the tent to a microcosm of the universe. In his interpretation, the fire in the hearth symbolizes the middle realm of the living, while the area behind the hearth or *malu* represents the lower realm. Thus, the central axis of the lodge, which consists of the entrance, the hearth and the *malu,* represents the upper, middle and lower realms, respectively. Although the V-shaped configuration of these supports serves a very practical purpose, the orientation of the V towards the rear is symbolic. That is, the two horizontal supports for the pots are concrete representations of the supernatural river, which for some groups can be envisioned within the tent.

The fire is treated with especial respect within the lodge. Evenkis tend to make fires only out of dry larch, avoiding sappy wood that might crack or spark. A 'fire' that speaks is thought to carry messages from other realms. The residents must avoid spitting on the fire, throwing litter into the hearth or quenching the fire with water. Instead, they must periodically feed the fire choice morsels of meat or fat and extinguish the flame with sand to avoid displeasing the mistress of the fire (Tugolukov 1978).

There seems to be no pan-Evenki formula for how the lodge is placed, however the placement of the lodge is often semantically linked to the way that directions are given within the landscape itself. Khasanova (2007: 191–2) notes that eastern Evenkis and other Tungus groups place the door of their tent towards the river. Semantically, then, motions within the tent are described with reference to the 'side of the taiga' (towards the back of the lodge) or the 'side towards the river/river bank' (towards the door). These directions are indicated not with adjectives but with special suffixes attached to verbs, and thus carry easily to other contexts outside of the lodge itself. These phonemic 'pegs' are heard multivocally, and are dependent on the context in which they are spoken. Motion towards an outer wall is simultaneously motion towards the taiga, as it might also be motion up the slope away from the river, upstream, northwards (Ermolova 2007: 106–7).

It may be of interest that Khasanova (2007: 194) places great antiquity to these particles, arguing that they demonstrate that the ancient Tungus dwelling must have had the hearth closer to the door, and not in the centre of the dwelling. Ermolova (2007: 107) makes a structuralist argument that the polysemantic language referring to rivers, mountains (taiga) and the hearth (centre) allows Evenkis to describe any position horizontally and vertically relative to the place that they are speaking about on a day-to-day basis within the tent, as well as ritually in complex rituals. Heonik Kwon (1993), reporting on the time that he spent with Sakhalin Oroks, describes a similar phenomenon more pragmatically. In his ethnography, whenever a conical tent was set up the world and all the words used to describe it were recreated anew.

Conclusion

Although Inuit and Evenkis occupy very different homelands, this overview shows how certain structural elements in the design of their dwellings and the way that they organize space are reflected in their cosmology. A key element in this overlapping of motifs is the way that supernatural features animate the tangible world, making every journey or every interaction with the environment a statement of one's relationship with the universe.

The narrative image of a mnemonic peg helps explain how place names and features can make direct links to powerful narratives which describe how the world came to be. Further, many words and grammatical units are polysemantic, carrying meaning over a variety of contexts which, within a western European language, would be strictly separated. This overlapping quality in the way that Evenkis and Inuit speak about the world makes everyday actions point to the cosmological and vice versa. This comparison has placed a heavy emphasis on water symbolism and systems of orientation involving rivers and coastlines. It is unclear how old, primeval or widespread these images might be, but even if they are rooted in the demands of a fur-trade society they nevertheless show a sensitivity to patterns on multiple scales which a group living in a different place and a different time might also establish with a different ensemble of images.

In a sense, the comparative ethnographic material presented here takes us beyond the idea of a mnemonic logical operation to the suggestion that the landscape itself whispers clues to hunters about how it is best attended to. Whether we understand this to be a land literally animated by spirits, or a land that is metaphorically animated through logical pegs, the way of seeing the land as being repeated in the homespace seems a strong constant in these two societies.

Acknowledgements

The authors wish to thank the Social Sciences and Humanities Research Council of Canada and the Research Council of Norway for their support for the fieldwork that went into this article. The writing and some of the theoretical work on this chapter was partly sponsored by ERC Advanced Grant 'Arctic Domus'.

Notes

1. Exceptions to this pattern are the Caribou Inuit societies of the western Hudson Bay region. Several of these societies appear to have abandoned coastal sea-mammal hunting in favour of full-time tundra hunting, perhaps as early as the seventeenth century (Burch 1978).

2. Vasilevich (1959: 188–9) links the water motifs in Evenki folklore to a deep, ancient level of the culture perhaps dating back to the time that North America was linked to Eurasia. She links it to a landscape that appeared following the melting of the great glaciers. It should be noted that the mammoth here *(khele)* is usually described by Evenkis as an 'underground, watery moose' and not elephant-like. The tusks that one finds belong to one and the same creature – both that known by paleontologists and that thought to live today in the lower realm.

3. In the only published English translation of Anisimov (1952), and in much work citing it, the *engdekit* is often translated as a 'cosmic clan river' *(mirovaia rodovaia rechka)*. Here we have chosen to use the word supernature, following Hamayon (1990), in order to represent the very difficult polysemantic Russian word *mir*. While this word can be used as an adjective to designate both a cosmic river and an earth river, the primary meaning of the word is an overarching order.

   The 'clanness' of the river, we would argue, is a misunderstanding of the original text. The editor of Anisimov's translation removed a large section devoted to denouncing the linguist Marr and framing Anisimov's view of historical materialism. When reading the entire chapter in the original it is clear that Anisimov was assembling, or reassembling, evidence to show that Evenkis could play a starring role in Marxist historical ontology. As demonstrated by the Russian historian of anthropology Sergei Alymov (2008), Anisimov, once having been a devotee of Marr's linguistic theories, had to quickly retune his work in another key. The word 'clan' *rod* is never used to evoke kinship as anthropologists know it today. It is used perhaps like the English word 'primitive' to mark these features as a stage in human history. The shamanic ritual of the chapter is shown to be the work of an elitist 'priest like' ritual specialist who dragged Evenkis to the first stage on the road to class stratification.

   It is significant that Anisimov himself notes that many of the elitist features of the ritual first manifested themselves during the early years of Soviet power (1952: 238; 1963a: 122). This region at this time was one of several battlezones for the establishment of Soviet power. Indeed, it proved impossible to set up Soviet administrative institutions well until 1927, and the district itself was formally called an 'unregulated district' *(bezvolostnaia volost')*. The region was the site of violent conflicts between Bolshevik forces and a group of organized middlemen known as the *Tungusniki*. Evidence of the difficulty of these battles can be found in the archived field notes of Nikolai Sushilin and his one published article (1929). We would suggest that this evocative and extremely atypical ritual might reflect the reaction of an animist tradition to a difficult period in the fur trade, much like Feit (1994) has argued that the organizers of the Cree shaking tent ceremony also responded to adverse historical circumstances.

4. In the same volume Khasanova (2007: 196) concurs that Evens and Evenkis, in contrast to Lower Amur peoples, never maintained a belief in water-spirit helpers 'of a global character'. She further argues that although Evenkis never live far from rivers, cosmologically the river was never deeply associated with the meaning of life (2007: 194).

CHAPTER 13

The Fire is our Grandfather

Virtuous Practice and Narrative in Northern Siberia

John P. Ziker

One man had two sons. The man did not like to communicate with other people, so he and his family lived alone, and he did not allow his sons to visit with neighbours. And so, they lived alone with no neighbours – just their family.

Once, the man went to gather his reindeer. Having rounded them up, he turned the herd in the direction of his *chum* [conical tent]. He started to look at his surroundings and back from where he had walked. He saw that the earth was ripped. A deep cavity appeared where he had just walked on solid ground. He began to walk by the edge of the canyon and he asked himself, 'How is it that I did not notice this? I almost killed all my reindeer.'

At that point the man himself fell into the void. He fell. He fell a long time in the nothingness. He fell until he perceived the ground, solid under his legs. It turned out to be solid earth.

The man saw three *chumy* [plural of *chum*] in the semi-darkness. Farther off in the dusk he saw a big herd of reindeer. The *chumy* were big – gigantic, in fact. Near the central *chum* he saw two people blacksmithing. The man walked up to the camp, approached the blacksmiths, and said, 'How do you do?'

One of the blacksmiths asked the other, 'What happened?' Their fire crackled. The other blacksmith said, 'Why is our fire trying to tell us something? *Ot ähätär.*' [The fire is our grandfather.]

The man from the Middle World said to them in surprise, 'Ah, hey! What happened to you?' And again he said, 'Hello.'

The two blacksmiths did not see the newcomer. One said, 'Something is going to happen. We need to stop working.' They paid no attention to the man from the Middle World. 'Let's go home,' they said. And the blacksmiths went into their *chum*. The man from the Middle World followed right behind.

Okse Bezrukikh (Ust'-Avam, 1996)

The story continues with the man from the Middle World trying to communicate with the Lower World people. When he talks, they hear the fire crackle. The Lower World people make sacrifices to the fire, but these do

not help, and the fire continues to crackle when the man from the Middle
World talks. He sits in their *chum,* hungry, while a Lower World woman
makes soup out of bones. When the Middle World man touches one of
their reindeer, it falls down and dies. When he sits next to the daughter,
she falls ill. The Lower World family observes these ill omens and calls for
a shaman. The shaman arrives and performs a shamanic ritual *[kamlanie],*
but to no avail. The Lower World people search out and find another,
more powerful shaman, who upon arrival to the camp can see the man
and understands their problem. The Lower World family must fulfil several requirements, and the second shaman during a *kamlanie* is able to call
the powerful spirit Ayyi from the Upper World to send the man back to
his world, riding on a great white reindeer. Before he leaves, the shaman
tells the man from the Middle World that he must live near other people.
Upon his return, the man rejoins his community and retells the story of
what happened to him and what he learned.

This chapter discusses how narratives can be used to suggest virtuous
practice in an indigenous community in northern Siberia. The chapter
examines how social norms are established, maintained and modified
through stories with a special emphasis on metaphors of homelands and
of the hearth. Here I will be particularly concerned with certain social
and environmental ethics that are implied in these narratives that many
readers might assume instead to be a result of economic considerations
and to endanger animal populations: namely, killing animals in order to
encourage the land to give more animals. Building on the work of Gell
(1998) and Widlok (2004) I will demonstrate that the best way to understand this paradox is to jettison the deductive logic that is most commonly
applied in Western European philosophy, and to use a non-consequential
type of reasoning. Narratives, and the metaphors communicated, I argue,
are crucial to establishing this type of thinking.

The subject of social norms, and their establishment and maintenance,
has been addressed in anthropology and sociology for more than a century (Durkheim 1982). Social norms are shared ideas and expectations
about how people ought to act in given situations. Norms imply: (1)
a tacit agreement that people ought to adhere to certain standards of
behaviour, (2) that people judge the actions of others according to how
closely actions adhere to those standards, and that (3) people who fail to
follow the standards risk a negative reaction (Bailey and Peoples 2010:
25). Norms are often described in terms of 'rules' that are deduced by
observing behaviour. However, I will argue that this approach cannot
account for the way that people change their practice to adapt to changing circumstances. To understand the flexible way in which best practice
comes about, we have to understand how narratives serve as guides to
action and in turn suggest varied courses of action.

The story of the Lower World, provided by Okse Bezrukikh, who was 93 at the time I interviewed her in 1996, communicates an overt social norm: survival in the Taimyr tundra requires mutual sacrifice and engagement in social relationships. In Okse's story, the protagonist did not follow norms of behaviour, his actions were judged by supernatural forces, and he suffered negative sanctions. The protagonist's experience in this narrative, therefore, serves as a model for others to follow. The form of the narrative does not ask listeners to apply an ideal to all contexts. Instead, listeners are encouraged to match their own experiences with the models provided to them.

The story also brings strong symbolic archetypes into play. Beyond the virtuous ideal of mutual aid, what some locals call the 'Law of the Tundra' (Ziker 2003), the story emphasizes the need to feed the hearth fire with reindeer bone marrow during certain significant social occasions (such as when a woman prepares food, when guests visit or when the fire crackles loudly). This detail frames the fire as a social being who communicates with human persons through crackling, who is thought to be 'our grand-father', and to whom respect is shown through the feeding of fat. Details like this remind listeners that the range of social agents is much wider than simply human agents, and that their actions are being accounted for on another plane of existence. Finally, it is significant that the individuals who the protagonist first sees in the Lower World are blacksmiths. Blacksmiths harness the power of fire to transform raw materials into useful items such as metal arrows, knives and ritual objects that represent the spiritual world.

Background

The research that informs this chapter was conducted within the political boundaries of the Taimyr (Dolgano-Nenetskii) Autonomous Region, Russian Federation, between 1992 and 2007. The region was officially subsumed under the larger Krasnoiarskii Krai beginning 1 January 2007, as the result of a referendum that passed in late 2006. Now the region, which is twice the size of the state of California, is referred to as the Taimyr Municipal District.

The indigenous population of Taimyr includes five ethnic groups: the formerly titular Dolgans and Nenetses, along with Enetses, Nganasans and Evenkis. Dolgans are described as a mixed minority population descended from Iakut and Tungus (Evenkis), along with Russian and Samoedic ancestors (Dolgikh 1960). Nenetses, Enetses and Nganasans are thought to be descended from Iron Age immigrants to the region and speak languages related to the same Samoedic group (Klobystin

2006). Evenkis are one of the most widespread indigenous populations in Siberia, generally living in small taiga communities, and are known for keeping small domestic reindeer herds. Russian industrial expansion and mass immigration to the region began in the 1940s with the development of Noril'sk Alpine Metallurgical Corporation, and the population of newcomers now numbers over 150,000. The indigenous population has come to be less than 10 per cent of the entire population since the amalgamation with Krasnoiarsk in 2007.

The study community, Ust'-Avam, has a population of 550 people and is situated at 71°07' N latitude and 92°49' E longitude on the Taimyr Peninsula, the northernmost extension of the Eurasian landmass. The community is approximately 50 per cent Dolgan, 45 per cent Nganasan and Enets and 5 per cent other various nationalities from the former Soviet Union.

The people of Ust'-Avam have a mixed-subsistence economy in which hunting, fishing and trapping predominate over commercial food production and exchange (Ziker 2002a). Many hold salaried jobs in public-service institutions, the proceeds of which go to purchasing consumer goods and services. After the collapse of the Soviet planned economy, the number of jobs at the state-owned hunting enterprise (Gospromkhoz 'Taimyrskii') was severely curtailed. Dolgan and Nganasan hunters in Ust'-Avam compensated by continuing to hunt wild reindeer, fish, trap and to consume hunted and gathered foods at almost every meal (Ziker 2002b; 2007). The common-pool hunting-and-fishing territory *(liubitel'skaia ugod'ia)* surrounding the village of Ust'-Avam became more important as hunters and other workers were laid off from the Gospromkhoz in the early 1990s. The size of the common-pool territory effectively expanded after the cessation of large-scale caribou hunts at river crossings in 1993.

Dolgans and Nganasans manage the enlarged common-pool territory with a variety of context-specific norms that include and exclude specific people in particular forays at particular spots *(tochki)*. This informal means of regulating access to hunting and fishing spots, particularly during the goose-hunting season and during caribou hunting, regulated potential social conflict and produced an informal body of property rights in the community (Ziker 2002a; 2003). The narratives and aphorisms discussed here are used to support such property relations.

Narratives and logical abduction

The collapse of central state provisioning in the post-Soviet period led to a unique economic and ecological crisis wherein the residents of Ust'-Avam were forced to rethink their relationship to the land. The 'conservationist logic' that the Dolgans and Nganasans adopted, I argue, is not the same as that which is most common in the Western European philosophical tradition. To make this point, I will adapt the argument of Thomas Widlok (2004) who applied Alfred's Gell's (1998) analysis of non-European aesthetic senses to interpret the virtuous practices of hunters in Namibia. I find that Gell's understanding of logical abduction explains both the evocativeness and implicit power relations within narratives and metaphors about the homelands and the hearth.

In contrast to deduction, which is the dominant form of reasoning in European moral discourse, abduction is a 'non-demonstrative' or 'synthetic' inference. In this type of inference, the antecedent is affirmed from the consequent (Gell 1998: 13–14). Paavola (2004) suggests that abduction is similar to hypothesis formation. A common example of an abductive inference is the aphorism, 'where there is smoke, there is fire'. While this is a good rule of thumb, and in most cases this statement is true, there can be other causes of smoke or smoke-like phenomena. Abduction allows us to tap into our rich background knowledge in order to develop hypotheses and to choose the most promising as a basis of action.

I can outline the differences between deduction and abduction using this everyday example. In logical deduction, one begins with an abstraction or rule: 'fire produces smoke' (i.e. combustion necessarily produces energy – appearing as light or flame – plus oxides of the elements in the fuel and contaminants appearing as smoke). Next, a case representing the abstraction is obtained, for example 'a fire is occurring'. And finally, a result is derived from the case – 'smoke is produced'. Abduction, by contrast, assumes a rule and works backwards from the result. Given the rule that 'fires produce smoke', the fact that one has seen 'smoke' is explained by the statement that 'where there is smoke, there is fire'. The statement has the quality of a reasonable guess, since it leaves open the possibility that the smoke may have come from a cause that produces a collection of airborne solid and liquid particulates and gases.

We can also apply this example to a case from northern Siberia. Once, while walking between one house and another, an elderly woman explained to me the best way of managing ashes from the fire. Before, when living out on the land, she mentioned that it was easy to avoid stepping on the ashes, since there were not so many vehicles driving around spreading the ashes as one now finds in the recent, permanent settlements. In her view, this disrespect for ashes from the hearth brings about negative consequences for the community. She emphasized that despite all of the traffic in the village, her household still managed to keep their own ash pile tidy.

If we were to translate this short narrative into the familiar example of logical deduction, it would read as such: 'all persons who respect the spirit of the fire do not walk upon the ashes' *(rule);* 'this person respects the spirit of the fire' *(case);* 'therefore, this person does not trample the ashes' *(result)*. In this kind of logic, one begins with the rule and the case and anticipates the result. Abduction, by contrast, starts from the rule and result to explain the case: 'all persons who respect the spirit of the fire do not walk upon the ashes' *(rule);* 'this person did not trample the ashes' *(result);* 'therefore, this person respects the spirit of the fire' *(case)*. This line of reasoning has the general tenor of a prediction. Given the rule, one would predict that a person exhibiting the trait would also exhibit the minor premise of respect for the spirit of the fire. Abduction leaves open the possibility that people avoiding the ashes do not really respect the spirit of the fire, but may be avoiding the ashes for some other reason, especially if that person does not subscribe to such beliefs. As a rule of thumb in social relations, given particular background knowledge and situations, the logic of abduction provides a model for proper behaviour, but not a necessary one.

In these examples, the formal process of logical abduction makes narratives somewhat open ended: a quality which I argue makes them adaptable to a large number of circumstances. Here I will apply it to examples of conservation practice.

Conservation and virtuous practice

My ethnographic studies among Dolgans and Nganasans began at the time that the local subsistence economy became increasingly important following the collapse of the Soviet planned economy. One strategy followed by some hunters and their families was to pursue land claims with the regional government. These were pursued and issued on a case-by-case basis, and those who were successful tended to be the best 'connected' people in the community (i.e. people living in the city or those whose main form of employment allowed regular visits to the city).

Such land claims, while significant for the native rights activists in Moscow, were not popular in Ust'-Avam and other local communities. Here, hunters evaluated the effort that went into a claim as not being worth the result *(nevygodno)*. Community members also harshly judged claimants for negotiating claims outside the local social network – a clear parallel to Okse's story at the start of this chapter. Land claimants were often referred to derogatorily as renters *(arendatory)*, even into the late 1990s. Almost everyone else in Ust'-Avam either continued to use the lands assigned to them during the Soviet period and/or to use the amateur hunting area surrounding the village (especially if they did not have an assigned territory). The importance of the common amateur hunting area led it to be the focus of moral sanctions in order to extend its viability.

According to Elinor Ostrom (2003), users of common resources need to be able to identify and exclude those who threaten the resource. This right to a negative sanction can also be viewed as protection of a virtue. I argue that authority over such common-pool resources in Ust'-Avam is expressed, accepted and recognized through narratives that include non-demonstrative inferences such as abduction. The acceptance or denial of abductions of proper conduct creates informal micro-social boundaries that provide some controls on access to resources. For example, the above-mentioned 'Law of the Tundra' contains an admonition against mistreating the flora and fauna, and a prescription that people help each other when living out on the tundra. Elders express, and others repeat, such ideas through narratives.

One of the more common narrative genres concerns the proper treatment of animals, which is linked to the idea that proper treatment will ensure that the animals will return again and again. Many hunters in Ust'-Avam mentioned to me that they wanted the animals to be around for the long term, to be healthy and to reproduce for their and their children's future hunting and fishing. They explained that their hunting and fishing techniques satisfied this social goal of conservation. For example, they held that it was not best to hunt a local herd *(mestnyi tabun)* of wild reindeer *(dikie)* during the middle of winter. Hunters stated that the best time for hunting reindeer is in the autumn. They said that since they wanted local deer to return to their territories in future years, they would 'let them roam' *(pust' begaiut)* in the winter. Similar stories were told concerning local and migratory arctic fox (Ziker 2003).

Refraining from hunting local animals in the middle of winter is held up as a virtuous practice in Ust'-Avam. Beyond the obvious proximate goals of hunting and fishing enough to provide benefits for family and community, these virtuous practices were explicitly geared towards long-term conservation, which is seen as a social good. These examples use the familiar abductive logic that virtuous practice in the present will lead to social goods in the future. However, more complex models also abound.

In the Canadian sub-Arctic, Rock Cree hunters say that moose choose to present themselves to hunters to be killed, thus actively contributing to human existence. Doing so in the correct manner, which includes proper treatment of kills in distribution and disposal of remains, contributes to the animals' existence and reproduction (Ingold 2000a: 143, following Brightman 1993: 388). Hunting (and killing) is the essence of reproduction in this view. Similar relationships are reported for the Wemindji Cree with black bear and migratory fowl (Scott 1996) and the Mistassini Cree with caribou (Tanner 1979). A very similar logic is used by hunters in Ust'-Avam when hunting migratory caribou and migratory arctic fox in the autumn. While such statements may appear completely unrelated to conservation, in these cases the social good of conservation is abducted from virtuous practices applied during and after the hunt, and not deduced from a rule that removing animals from the land will lead to a lower population in the future.

The hunters in Ust'-Avam used such abductive logic in a similar way after state-farm procurement plans for rock ptarmigan *(kuropatka)* were cancelled. In the 1970s and 1980s, a hunter was rewarded with the gift of a new snowmobile from the state hunting enterprise if 1,500 rock ptarmigan were turned in. Good hunters could shoot that many in one season. According to one Dolgan hunter discussing rock ptarmigan hunting and trapping with me in 2003, plenty of the birds circulated when hunters paid attention to them. During the Soviet period, the birds were treated with the right amount of respect and interest, and thus such hunting was a virtuous practice. In the 1990s, after state-sponsored hunting collapsed and this incentive programme was abandoned, the rock ptarmigan mysteriously disappeared. The reason given to me for their disappearance was that hunters stopped paying attention to the birds. If one gives credence to the abductive inference above, the statement makes perfect sense, since the animals did not return and we know that birds were not treated with proper respect and hunting intensity (i.e. they were ignored).

Again, the disappearance of a social good was abducted from the failure to apply virtuous practice. The reverse situation was also said to be true. More recently, when food has been short in the spring, young hunters have been setting up snares in a series of routes (trap lines) in riparian areas within walking distance of the village. These hunters have been successfully bringing home rock ptarmigan almost every time they check their traps. Rock ptarmigan are again being paid attention to, and so they have returned in good numbers. Again, the statement shows that people in the community know that they have personal relationships with their environment, that they have a role to play in the local ecological system and that a certain amount of hunting is more virtuous than not hunting at all.

Expressed more formally, the implicit goal of conservation was achieved by the application of a virtuous practice. 'If hunters treat animals with proper respect, then the animals will return' *(rule)*. The observations of the hunters are that 'these animals returned' *(result)*; so, by abduction, 'the hunter treated animals respectfully' *(case)*. A discussion along these lines would reaffirm and emphasize the virtuous practices of the hunters in the community, thus creating positive examples and ideals of behaviour.

Abductive logic and social relationships

Okse's story is a narrative that is more than a simple admonition about proper, virtuous relationships, but it provides a model of social interaction. In Widlok's analysis of 'sharing by default' among San in Namibia, he demonstrates that the so-called generosity documented by hunter-gatherers can arise indirectly through the goal of managing so-called 'basic social goods' to strengthen social relationships: a 'sharing in' instead of a 'sharing out'. The moral 'lesson' of Okse's story is that people need to help each other and that presumably, through mutual aid, everyone will benefit. However implicitly, the story weaves a complex story of social relationships between kin, between people and animals, and between people and the hearth (the interface with the supernatural and ancestors).

Ideas about social relationships with animals are widespread across the circumpolar North and in indigenous societies across the globe. For example, among the Rock Cree of Canada, relationships with animal bosses *(awaken)* and prey are fundamental to their philosophy (Brightman 1993: 93, 187). Colin Scott (personal communication) argues that such philosophies represent a web connecting people, their actions and the cosmos. In his view, the 'web' is both seen (actions, experiences and consequences for human and non-human persons) and unseen (principles, visions and quest for knowledge), and actions are embedded in a process of personalized cause-and-effect. Action and reaction in the world is more a negotiation and less a physics. It is my contention that as part of such negotiations, inferences from such social-exchange rules are communicated and accepted to affirm the virtuous practices of individuals in the community.

In this light, specific events are discussed and interpreted in the community as evidence of deviation from virtuous practice. Social malfeasance is abducted from unvirtuous practice. An example from Ust'-Avam is a story from a hunter who killed nine wolves one winter and was given a prize from the state farm. (Nine wolves was an unusually high number.) Later, the hunter's aunt died at a young age *(result)*. The hunter associated the premature death of his relative with his own actions in the tundra: animals were hunted without proper respect and intensity *(case)*.

Similarly, deaths and accidents are widely discussed within the community, and ultimate causes are often debated among adults. During these desultory conversations, tragic events can become associated with the unvirtuous environmental or social behaviour of an individual who is in some way connected to the individual who suffered the tragedy. Eventually a consensus is reached. The consequence is affirmed through the process of abduction. A similar consequence is associated with abnormally large animal kills in Canada (Scott 1996; 2007). Too much killing and not enough killing are unvirtuous practices, as summarized in certain hunting symbols and rituals, and can result in a hunter's death or impoverishment.

Such narratives that embed tragic events in a wider social-ecological context are a discursive process that bolsters traditional knowledge. When abductions of unvirtuous behaviour are promoted by elders, and accepted by middle-aged and younger people, then that acceptance is a reaffirmation of the community's traditional authority. By accepting these metaphors and abductions about the negation of social contracts with spirit owners of the tundra and its resources, for example, individuals signal their willingness to accept the authority of those communicating these abductions and metaphors (Steadman and Palmer 2008).

Discussions about the causes of tragic events in the home or on the land relate the importance of the given background knowledge and those who contribute to it. Such discursive processes, often depending on logical abductions from virtuous or unvirtuous practices, function to promote social norms, goods and goals, thus encouraging social relationships. The proximate benefits (e.g. social cohesion or protection of ecological balance) of these social goods and goals are promoted through abduction to specific cases. It is not just a reaffirmation of the traditional authority but also about current and future social good.

Many of the aphorisms, concepts and identities that are characteristic of Dolgan and Nganasan social organization are ecological or relational in nature, but some are dealing directly with personal relationships. It is important to understand the relational cosmology in order to make better sense of the use of abductions in attempting to influence the behaviour of others (including descendants and co-descendants) in the community. Galina Gracheva (1983: 52) gives the etymology of the Nganasan terms to describe life cycles – a complex set of concepts meaning 'life continuing itself, sometimes called together (arranged) and placed'. This concept is critical to understanding the Nganasan perspective on their actions in the universe. The life force, or *nilymty,* extends beyond the person. It is in all objects and essences the person touches or connects with, such as clothes, smells, names, inspiration, speech, songs, dances, actions, foraging trails, housing and children. The connections are like unseen threads. The implication is that even if people are not monitoring social contracts, spiritual forces are. Through *nilymty,* the results of virtuous or unvirtuous behaviours can be traced back to the individuals who performed them.

Among the Nganasans, the Earth-Mother *(mou-nemy)* is a predominant supernatural force *(ngo).* The term 'mother' *(nemy)* is a metaphor usually used to refer to a myriad of such supernaturals, although sometimes the gender is switched and they are referred to as father *(diasi).* Gracheva (1983: 27) states that some Nganasans try to differentiate the spirits by gender while others do not. Since the gender is not what is significant, I believe the best translation would simply be 'ancestor'.

In addition to the Earth *ngo*, there are three important generating forces – conceived of as children of the Earth *ngo* (illustrating my point that the Earth mother is an ancestor) – viewed as independent and necessary for human existence: Fire, Water, and Tree *ngos*. According to Gracheva's ethnographic materials (1983: 23), the most essential force for the home-hearth is the earthly fire (in contrast to the Sun *ngo),* since sparks for the hearth fire are created using earthly materials (flint and iron) – gifts of the Earth *ngo*. The Tree *ngo* is friendly with the Fire *ngo*, and Tree also serves as food for the Fire. However, Fire does this only through the Earth. The receptacle of fire is referred to as 'fire rock' *(tui-fali)* or 'day/light-rock' *(diali-fali)* – flint, chalcedony, carnelian – stones from which sparks are extracted with a blow of a flint strike. Such stones and the iron strike are products of the Earth, directly given (sacrificed to humans) from the body of the Earth (Gracheva 1983: 22). Moreover, every species on earth had its own *ngo*, descended from the Earth *ngo*, and in attempts to contact these spirits, it is possible to kill a reindeer or dog so that through their life force the owner's request would go to the appropriate spirit.

The Nganasans use zoomorphic and anthropomorphic idols *(koika)* that embody the *ngo* of the clan, and Dolgans have similar containers called *shaitany* (Popov 1963). A Nganasan *koika*, Maganka-ngo, even includes all hump-shaped, crooked and cross-eyed peoples' *ngo*. It is possible to contact these *ngo* directly, killing a reindeer or dog, feeding the *koika* with smoke from the hearth fire made by burning fat from the animal sacrifice, and preliminarily making contact with the Fire-Mother-Ngo (Gracheva 1983: 28). As is illustrated in these examples, the hearth fire is a mechanism for communication with the spirit world. Like the Dolgans, the Nganasans take actions of symbolic reverence for the hearth fire by feeding it fat as the most symbolic of oblations – the most caloric part of the animal.

Furthermore, the traditional Nganasan funeral procession includes building a small hearth fire to make tea and have one final conversation with the dead. The fire is put out with snow or sand, or left to die out on its own. It is necessary to do it this way so that there would be no fire, or even any smoke, when the entire funeral party departs (Gracheva 1983: 104), as conversations with the dead occur through fire. Additionally, for someone to look back as the funeral party departed (first youth, then elders) is forbidden. Gracheva's informant told her on two different occasions (1983: 105): 'He has gone to the north. If you turn around, you will also turn after him in the direction of the tundra'. And later, 'It's impossible to do. To look back is taboo; it's a sin; otherwise the dead will grab you'. Partly, this taboo makes sense in terms of 'letting go' of the dead; partly, it shows respect to the elders. The hearth fire is powerfully transformative in Ust'-Avam for both Dolgans and Nganasans. Beyond its importance as a prerequisite for survival, the hearth is a mechanism to speak to the dead and a locus of social relations. The fire is a metaphor for, and mechanism to contact, ancestors and other spirits who define virtuous behaviour.

The elders, as representatives of the ancestors, can be shown respect in various ways. Agreeing with the metaphors of the hearth by making the appropriate oblation to the hearth fire at the appropriate time is socially and symbolically important as virtuous practice. Understanding and following the subtleties of the taboo on turning back during the funeral procession puts oneself in agreement with the elders and within a given micro-social boundary of those relatives and co-descendants who also accept and follow the taboo. Disagreement on that point, or on the many other taboos, puts oneself outside the received ancestral wisdom and traditional authority. If something tragic occurs to an individual, then the tragedy is traced back in discourse to their breaking of the taboo. The logical process by which this is done is abduction. In a worldview where everything a person touches is connected back to him or her through spiritual threads, people are encouraged by elders and ancestors to be careful with their actions in their physical and social environment.

Conclusion

In this chapter I have explored ideas about virtuous theories of dwelling in northern Siberia through an examination of the frames of reference and inferences used in relation to people's relationships to the environment and with each other. I argued that what is commonly categorized as traditional ecological knowledge is but one manifestation of the social norms that are communicated, accepted and recommunicated as a process in which social goods are inferred from virtuous practices. Virtuous practices are used as examples of proper or moral behaviour in connection with a place or identity, and these are contrasted with unvirtuous or amoral behaviour.

To circle back to the title of this chapter, the metaphor 'the fire is our grandfather' is an archetypal expression in Taimyr that makes sense in the particular setting and situation for the Taimyr's indigenous people. The cosmological frame of reference is to spirit worlds that interact with the living world, and the social frame of reference is a setting where 'half the village are kith and kin'. Fire is critical to survival in the Siberian Arctic because of the extremely cold climate. When one accepts the metaphor that 'fire is our grandfather', one is providing an index of an important social norm, a sign of respect to the home/hearth and co-descendants.

The metaphor references an important and respected elder kinship relationship. The social good abducted from the virtuous practice of feeding fat to the fire is that the people treat one another like kinsmen, even if fictive kin, since they are accepting the influence of a common metaphorical grandfather. So this virtuous practice – feeding fat to the fire upon being invited to share tea – provides a basis from which the social good of cooperation can be abducted. The negation of the practice – refusing to feed fat to the fire at the appropriate time – would explicitly place oneself outside of the kinship relationship and would provide the basis from which negative consequences are abducted.

Acknowledgements

I am very grateful to the people in Taimyr who participated in the research and hosted my repeated visits. I thank Thomas Widlok, Gerry Oetelaar, Colin Scott and Will Palmer for constructive comments on earlier drafts of this chapter. This material is based upon work supported by the National Science Foundation grant 0631970. Any opinions, findings, and conclusions expressed in this material are those of the author and do not necessarily reflect the views of the National Science Foundation. I respectfully acknowledge the Canada–US Fulbright Commission for the award of the 2009–2010 Research Chair in North American Studies at the University of Calgary and also the Department of Archaeology, of the same university, where I first drafted this chapter. I also acknowledge the Max Planck Institute for Social Anthropology, in Halle, Germany, for support of field research in 2003.

CHAPTER 14

Home, Hearth and Household in the Circumpolar North

David G. Anderson

The title of this chapter, and that of the four-year research project that it represents, is an attempt to draw attention to circumpolar idioms of dwelling within the humanities. The idea of viewing social life through the frame of a house is an old one in comparative ethnology, given new life in anthropology by the influential collection edited by Janet Carsten and Stephen Hugh-Jones (1995a) *About the House*. Building on Lévi-Strauss' (1982) concept of house societies, they argued that an 'alternative language of the house' could reinvigorate comparative anthropological research much in the same way that work on embodiment and practice has. Their ethnographic examples from Latin America and Southeast Asia, when read closely, focus on household dynamics and commensality around the hearth as 'the very heart' of the house (Carsten 1995a: 114) – hence the link between homes and hearths. If there is one idiom that is common all across the circumpolar North, it is the centrality of the hearth in social life and of commensality with the home fire itself.

The inspiration for the project came from this literature, but also from a very different experience. In 2000, at the request of the Canadian Government, I organized a set of exchanges between Cree and Dene First Nations people in Canada and Evenki and Iakut peoples in Siberia.[1] A number of discussions developed out of those meetings, but what captured my attention was a strong feeling of kinship between these taiga peoples who, aside from living thousands of kilometres from each other, were in turn divided by two power blocs during the Cold War. Despite these divisions they spoke of sharing similar problems, having similar dreams and indeed recognizing their 'uncle' or 'auntie' in the face of some of the delegates. Today, circumpolar indigenous activism is not an unfamiliar event thanks to the dedicated work of a number of indigenous non-governmental organizations and special attention from the United

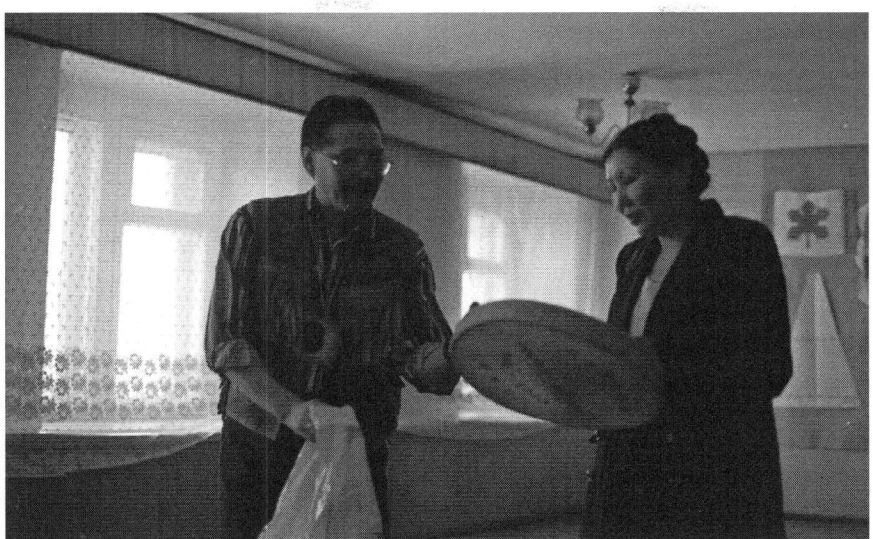

Figure 14.1 *Henry Zoe (Rae Edzo) and Svetlana Ivanovna Karachkova (Tura) inspecting a Tłįchǫ drum during an exchange between Evenki and Tłįchǫ community members in the boarding school in the village of Tura, 2000. The drum was one symbol that tied these communities together. In the background, children from the boarding school had decorated a tableau representing the exchange with a figure of a conical lodge.*

Nations. However, at the turn of the millennium the idea that locally based kin networks could also reach outward to peoples so far away was an unfamiliar idea. During the meetings, these feelings of interrelationship were often expressed through tangible material symbols such as in clothing, song and the image of the conical lodge (Figure 14.1).

It might at first seem strange to place the house at the centre of discussions of local culture and identity in the circumpolar North. Of all regions emerging from colonial administrations, the North had been the most consistently criticized for lacking stable architectural structures that could be recognized as homes. Whether one looks at late Imperial policy in Siberia, the work of 'industrial schools' in Canada, or the post-War rebuilding efforts in northern Scandinavia, circumpolar governments have focused their energy on providing fixed framed structures, and confining people to them. Almost universally, in each colonial setting, locally made portable lodges were described as being smoke-filled, damp and unhygienic – as markers of poverty. If there are any societies that could be classified as the anti-thesis of Lévi-Strauss' *sociétés à maisons* it would be the nomadic hunting and fishing societies of the circumpolar North.

Despite this colonial history, or perhaps because of it, northern design has now captured the imagination of historians of vernacular architecture. Nikolai Kharuzin (1896) exhaustively analysed the conical and circular dwellings of the Turkic and Mongol peoples of Siberia, with a view to understanding how they develop naturally into more familiar and comfortable sedentary forms. Mauss and Beuchat (1979) wrote a perennial anthropological classic analysing how coastal Inuit (Eskimo) society ebbs and flows with the seasons partly reflected in the design of encampments and the iconic snow *iglu*. In his classic global overview of vernacular forms *House Form and Culture*, Amos Rapoport (1969) returns often to the examples of Inuit winter and summer dwellings to encourage readers to abandon their preconceptions of how scarcity or harsh climate forces people to simplify their dwellings. To balance a growing literature on South Asian and Latin American forms of vernacular architecture, there have been an increasing number of works expressing an interest in traditional or pre-contact forms of indigenous architecture in the Americas (Lee and Reinhardt 2003; Nabokov and Easton 1989) as in other parts of the circumpolar North (Hodder 1989; Permilovskaia 2005; Sokolova 1998).

The example of the *iglu* notwithstanding, examples of the vernacular architecture and modes of dwelling of northern sub-Arctic boreal peoples remain sparse. Even Peter Nabokov and Robert Easton (1989: 417), in their authoritative overview of Native American architecture, note that sub-Arctic dwellings are underreported. Further, both Lee and Reinhardt (2003) and Ann Fienup-Riordan (1990) caution us about the way that the *iglu* has become 'cemented in our collective consciousness', eclipsing our view of a variety of other dwellings – timber or tent dwelling types – used by Yup'ik and Inuit peoples. It would seem that even within the fragmented literature on circumpolar dwellings, boreal architecture suffers more than others from the stereotypes held by colonial and post-colonial builders.

If Latin American and Southeast Asian vernacular houses challenge our ideas about belonging – about how people calculate descent and alliance – it seems that circumpolar dwelling patterns challenge our definition of architecture itself. Architects see structures definitively as the 'spanning of space' (Rapoport 1969: 3). Or, among the sociologically inclined, as the element that gives form to amorphous social processes. As Gieryn (2002: 35) notes, 'buildings stabilize social life. They give structure to social institutions, durability to social networks, persistence to behaviour patterns'. As Tim Ingold (2000a: 179) notes in his criticism of what he identifies as the building perspective:

> worlds are made before they are lived in; or in other words, that acts of dwelling are preceded by acts of worldmaking. ... Human beings, then, inhabit the various houses of culture, pre-erected upon the universal ground of nature.

Rapoport (1982: 178) perhaps best represents this architectural determinism where his built environment consists 'of relationships between people, between people and things, and between things'. The building perspective is often best illustrated through a contrast. One classic example comes from Judith Okely's (1983) description of how British traveller Gypsies constantly confront a 'house-dweller ideology'. In her account, all moral and ethical norms by which people were measured in 1970s Britain were indexed to one's attachment to a single fixed dwelling, in contrast to the flexible residential strategies of Travellers. Northern living patterns, be they in the 'pre-contact period' or today, are also extremely flexible, involving strong seasonal movements across space and often breaking apart discrete activities across a number of sites. It would seem that there is no physical structure elaborate enough to span these seasonal rounds, although words, place-names and narratives do exceptionally well in weaving these places together.

To develop this idea of the 'non-spanning' architecture of northern societies, it is useful to review our expectations when studying dwellings. If colonial enumerators are needed to break people into bounded households in order to lend a sense of focus to their analysis of human relationships, it seems that many contemporary researchers are equally inclined to see social activity as entangled within walls, roofs and thresholds. There are understandably powerful interests lying behind these visions of architectural determinism.

As Peter Dawson (2008) pointed out in a recent article, welfare-state planners had a vested interest in supplying specific types of centrally manufactured and 'cost-effective' dwellings to their northern clients despite being well aware that they did not always suit local needs. Caroline Humphrey (1988), in an early position piece, also noted the tendency of disaster relief organizations to express their corporate identities through supplying structures that reflected their own economic and structural concerns. As is often remarked, Soviet centrally planned architecture provided some of the most brutal examples of form usurping practice (Hudson 1994).

Postmodern authors often invest power and agency in particular architectural forms (round vs square; skin vs brick; striated vs smooth) but show a somewhat aloof interest in how Northerners nevertheless make homes for themselves in structures of an unfashionable type. Despite these paralysing examples, what might be called the vernacular architecture movement gains its energy and recruits its enthusiasts from the insight that 'dwellers' can design their own structures to express their own needs without the supervision of architects. To adapt this insight to the North one must first ask: should all practice fit within a single dwelling or for that matter within any framed dwelling at all?

Household archaeologists have been among the most hopeful candidates for finding a structured relation between activity and easily excavated spaces. Among the more evocative models are those of Susan Kent (1984; 1990) who stressed that 'architecture partitions usually are conscious manipulations by humans to create boundaries where they do not exist in nature' (1990: 2). Her comparative research demonstrated a link between what she identified as 'social complexity' and the partitioning and segmentation of space, with complex societies generating more varied, and segmented dwellings. Her findings were echoed in a companion chapter by Rapoport (1990), who encouraged us no longer to look at dwellings as unitary structures but instead to consider that all societies construct 'systems of settings' which, in certain complex settings, might be confined under a single roof divided by functionally specific rooms. For our purposes, what he described as 'small-scale, homogeneous, pre-literate societies' might disperse their activities not among rooms but in several settings dispersed across the landscape. In this manner, an entire cultural landscape might appear to be 'a home' writ large. As the chapters in this volume illustrate, this is by far the most common quality of northern dwelling both today and in the past.

Hugh Beach provides an interesting, revisionist account of the 'revitalization' of vernacular architecture in one landscape known as Staloluokta in northern Sweden. Beach analyses an architectural ensemble which he describes as being created from successive waves of interaction between Tuorpon Sámis and an interventionist welfare state. Here Sámis use a combination of turf huts, industrially produced conical tents and frame cabins in order to 'survive in the place that one calls home'. He portrays this helicopter-mediated collage as successful, if a little frantic, casting doubt on whether one structure can be seen as primeval (the turf hut) and others at best as creolisms (the frame cabin or the canvas *lávvu*). This 'system of settings' is invigorated by the way that people engage with the land and the animals, as well as with the planners, tourists and kin who also maintain an interest in this site.

Rob Wishart and Peter Loovers examine a similarly controversial example in the Gwich'in log cabin – a rectangular, built structure which contrasts dramatically with the domed skin dwellings of the past. The authors argue that despite a superficial similarity between the form of the dwelling and that of dwellings prescribed by modernizing states, Gwich'in cabins stand out both in the detail of how building logs are 'hunted' in the patchy forests of this sub-Arctic landscape and the way that they stand as monuments to self-reliance. These home-built structures grow defiantly beside the government-built flat-packed houses, demonstrating that skills learned on the land can contribute positively to the project of building a centralized community. In this case, the building is a place to live but also a symbol of the larger watershed that defines Gwich'in identity.

On a smaller scale, Halinen et al. draw attention to the ideology of dwelling implicit in the local placement of early Sámi hearth-dwellings in the alpine regions of northern Norway. Here a clear 'linear' settlement plan denotes a formalized concern for equality in a society that may have been struggling over the unequal distribution of resources. The authors directly link the linearity of the hearth-landscape with the affordances of what they interpret as new alpine economy in harvesting migratory reindeer.

Siberian ethnography provides some striking examples that blur the idea of a discrete home that purportedly shelters the person from the landscape. In the early Soviet period, northern Russian and Siberian hunters and reindeer herders confounded early census enumerators with their inability to distinguish a house (tent) from a community of homes. Instead they would produce hybrid regional designations of a *pogost* or *nasleg* – terms which blended kinship, landscape and architecture together – which the enumerators had to artificially dissect in order to fill out their forms (Anderson 2011c).

Classically, as Oetelaar et al. illustrate in this volume, some Evenki hunters developed a polysemantic language of orientation wherein movements around the tent were described linguistically using the same words and particles that one would use to describe a hike up and down a river valley. In a more elaborate example of personality and scale, Halemba (2006) illustrates how Altaian Telengits describe their mountainous homeland as being composed alternately as parts of the body or parts of the house. Fienup-Riordan (1990) documents a strong cosmological overlap between houses and non-human persons wherein the architecture of the home can stand for the openings of human bodies or the breathing holes used by seals in the ice.

A recently completed doctoral dissertation by Vladimir Davydov (2011) describes Kholodnoe Evenkis inhabiting the ruins of Soviet and post-Soviet development projects, one of which is the site of their village itself. He illustrates that temporary residence in an abandoned state-built flat, or in one of a series of self-built cabins, is neither 'nomadism' nor a symptom of being 'homeless' but rather an expression of an old skill of making creative use of existing infrastructure. For him, 'when local people move from place to place, their feeling of home moves with them' (Davydov 2011: 216).

Even if one conducts a close conversational analysis of how people describe a single built structure, as Maria Nakhshina does for conversations about Pomor wooden houses, the very discreteness of that object always fades in and out of view. In her account, northern Russian houses are often in a process of construction and renewal and are never 'built' (past perfect). Moreover, even the boundaries of 'the house' are flimsy, with the 'inside' concealed behind a system of porches and the very location of the house invisible until signalled by one's own conservation in the village. Tim Ingold, in an important series of chapters, describes this fallacy of experiencing a dwelling as complete and discrete as a form of logical inversion wherein life-giving activity is sealed up in a shell disguising its true activity (Ingold 1993; 2000a: 178–181; 2011: 68–9).

These examples arguably stretch the idea of architecture beyond its breaking point. In its place we have an ensemble of practices which happen to engage with the bits and pieces that we are taught to associate with buildings. Just as one can hang a door on a frame to create a division between 'in and out', so can one describe a river's outlet as a 'door' to a particularly productive and vibrant valley. Is it meaningful to roll all these metaphoric meanings into one?

As Oetelaar et al. point out, it is a feature of European languages that they strictly separate the literal from the metaphorical, while in many indigenous languages the transcendent is also always the concrete. This blending of the symbolic and the real does not create difficulties for northern dwellers, but it does seem to challenge university-trained scholars. One way to contextualize these northern lifeworlds is to invent a new language to describe environments, such as that of the earth–sky world promoted by Ingold in this volume and in Ingold (2011: Ch. 9). Another way is to take a closer look at the social actors inhabiting these environments and to question if we might be overlooking the agency of other entities.

If there is one hallmark of northern ethnography it is of the plurality of persons united together in social relationships. As Hallowell (1960) classically noted among Ojibwas, the agents able to act in society might be winds, rocks, caribou, eagles and human persons. If the purpose of architecture is to place persons into a relation, then should we not be first looking for a northern architecture that binds together human and non-human persons?

In a literal sense, non-human persons are bound into many northern dwellings through their frames. As Oetelaar et al. document, Thule houses constructed out of whalebone provide a constant reminder of the fundamental legends that explain the relation between people and animals. The 'revitalized' Tłįchǫ caribou skin lodge presented here by Tom Andrews is physically a structure made of wooden poles and the tanned skins of caribou – the latter being a significant personage in the Tłįchǫ lifeworld. Symbolically, as with the Gwich'in log cabin, the Tłįchǫ lodge is also social project which binds together the memories of ancestors with archived artefacts. These revitalized homes sometimes carry with them undiplomatic memories, such as those associated with the Northern Sámi *bealljigoahti*. Here, the covering on this widely used mobile tent was made of sheep's wool, which it seems once was a common part of a reindeer Sámi's household. Bjørklund points out that the conical lodge today is more of a symbol than a dwelling – and that as a political symbol it aims to distil a vision of reindeer herding (and not sheep herding) as a practice-based line distinguishing communities.

Both archaeological and historical demographic research emphasize that built structures were not only the homes of humans. As Halinen et al. cite in this volume, early Sámi hearth-dwellings were used to transform sheep, fish and reindeer into food, and likely also served as the home for people and sheep. It is only recently that household demographers came to focus on people. Earlier nineteenth-century enumerators tended to survey households – people, crops and livestock – as units.

As Sommerseth argues in this volume, in northern Norway marriage and kinship strategies often focused on maintaining the integrity of the homestead (house plus livelihood) to such a degree that complex contracts were made to transfer the homestead to anybody who would keep running the homestead, even if they were not kin. The home here can be best seen as a hybrid entity enclosing life, albeit one held by a human person. Vesa-Pekka Herva (2010) demonstrates that wooden buildings built in Tornio on the border between Finland and Sweden in the middle ages show evidence of ritual richness that anthropologists usually associate with hunting societies Here she argues that buildings became persons by playing an active role in the regeneration of human life. In this volume we see a similar element in Maria Nakhshina's description of Pomor houses in the far North seaside village of Kuzomen'. Here wooden houses guide people's memories, express their character and express permission on whether or not to allow someone to remain.

The homology between the house and the person was one of the founding insights that led Carsten and Hugh-Jones (1995b: 2) to encourage anthropologists to think of the house 'in the round'. Frustrated with the mathematical strictures of lineage theory which dominated the field at that time, they pointed to the fact that ethnographies often pointed to houses as being entities in their own right – or in Lévi-Strauss' terms, a 'moral person' *(personne morale)* – which would often outlast the people who built them or inhabited them.

While lineage politics surely exists in the Latin American and Southeast Asian societies that they analysed, the house was a place where competing lineages were fused, creating a truly social actor out of competing social interests. This is of course an old idea. Lewis Henry Morgan (1881) anchored his evolutionary examples of 'house-life' in his inclusive – if vague – concept of 'communism in living'. This early representation of what we might call 'reciprocity' today was clearly oriented towards inter-human collaboration against a harsh environment (although he too used few ethnographic examples from the Arctic).[2] He demonstrated how the use of covered space facilitated a communal praxis described as the 'law of hospitality'. My argument here is that the northern dwellings perhaps take these relationships one step further by balancing a 'communism of life' between both human and non-human agents.

Recent criticisms of Lévi-Strauss' twin concepts of the house society and the moral person have focused on the difficulty that anthropologists have had in moving beyond social relationships within houses to speak about the qualities of architecture itself (Gillespie 2000; Sandstrom 2000; Vellinga 2007). Alan Sandstrom (2000), in his analysis of multi-household Nahua, identifies a similar 'non-spanning' quality to the way that Nahuas feel a common sense of belonging. Members of a compound see themselves as nurturing each other through shared labour and through a vital living force. None of these exchanges can be limited to a single threshold or a single hearth, but instead stretch across a dispersed compound made up of many homes. Abiding by the purist interpretation of Lévi-Strauss that characterizes all of the chapters in this collection, Sandstrom argues that Nahuas could be called a house society only if we exchange the 'currency of descent' for a new 'currency of interaction'. His example and reasoning fits well with the circumpolar examples presented here.

In most northern societies, multiple structures and places bind humans and non-humans within a common style of social interaction. There has been little work describing these various currencies of interaction in the North. One exception is Virginie Vaté's (2011) work on the Chukchi *iaranga* house society, which ties its residents together with the experience of being 'of one blood'. The startling exception to her example is that the residents are not necessarily related through sharing the blood of their lineage, as the metaphor is often used in European contexts, but as sharing the blood of their reindeer, without which the *iaranga* could not exist. As Ingold (2011) outlines in his recent book, the task seems not to reduce social life to the containers which confine it but instead to understand how people inhabit their worlds, and in so doing produce structures that reflect their lives. In many cultures this may reflect a unitary framed dwelling, in others in may reflect a system of compounds or a network of places. As many authors in this volume suggest, Northerners may not inhabit a spanning type of architecture at all. However, in all cases the 'ecology of life' will be reflected in the dwellings that people choose to assemble.

Recent ecological theory offers a subtle way to decentre these domestic spaces. Leslie Johnson and Eugene Hunn (2010) identify 'ethnoecological' concepts to enhance the sometimes clumsy terminology often used in landscape ecology. The authors in this collection point to multiple hybrid concepts that blur together plant communities with physical spaces, and with human action. They direct our attention to polysemantic terms such as *tūtsel* (the Kaska word for 'swamp'), which glosses a large number of types of wetland which provide important niches for the reproduction of moose, medicinal plants or springs. Leslie Johnson challenges the negative connotations of the standard word 'swamp' with her retranslation as 'the place where you get your food' (Johnson 2010: 210–14). In another place, Johnson (2000) argues that productive environments might be described morally and aesthetically such as 'a place that is good'. These ideas come close to the way that Halinen et al. in this volume, building on Ingold, identify certain 'affordances' in the Nordic landscape which suggest the place where one might expect to find migratory wild reindeer, and therefore the remains of alpine camps established to hunt them. Zabaikal Evenkis use a special word, *bikit,* to describe these 'living environments' – a place where one might expect animals and territory to fit together in a place that harbours life (Brandišauskas 2009). In this case, spaces where people, animals and landscape can be found can be as simple as a shaded or protected hillside – a type of grown shelter for human and non-human persons that is quite far from what architects might conceive of as a building.

The blending of the dwelling into the land is most radically described in Tim Ingold's perspectivist interpretation of a Tłı̨chǫ conical skin tent. Cautioning the readers about the word landscape itself, Ingold argues that the structure of a conical lodge confounds the stereotypical elements of a building by providing no clear division between wall and floor, foundation and structure, or indeed earth and sky. In his interpretation the conical lodge is 'stitched into the fabric of the earth'. Being neither set upon the earth or sheltering the inhabitants from the sky, he sees the lodge as harbouring both humans and a fire. It not only reaches up to the sky but 'unbinds' and returns material from the forest to the air. His interpretation is that this dwelling is life giving in its own right (although he admits that other common dwellings one finds in the North might not be so evocative).

A second powerful metaphor, never far away from discussions of the home, is that of the hearth. In all ethnographic descriptions of built structures, the commensality of preparing and consuming food is a central definition of how the domestic space is described. As mentioned above, the focal social nature of hearths in general was one anomaly that nudged the authors to Carsten and Hugh Jones to describe forms of social interaction within houses rather than architecture.[3] Northern ethnographers often take for granted that the number one criteria for the design of a dwelling should be the production of heat and light in the winter (and often smoke in the summer). The formula hearth = home is so strong in Scandinavian archaeology that the spectacular raised stone hearths used by Sámi and paleo-Eskimos are used as proxies for identifying the sites of homes, even if it proves impossible to find the outline of the domestic space that these hearths may have heated (Odgaard and Kanal 2003).

The common-sense assumptions that fuel an interest in the hearth stem from a conviction that northern places are harsh and cold – and that there is therefore a 'need' to transform them to make them fit for human habitation. Much as we questioned the ideology of built structures above, it also stands to scrutinize this metaphor of the hearth. Northern hearths are important, but perhaps in their own way. In much the same way that Carsten and Hugh-Jones (1995a) argued for a re-centring of descent theories about the house, the chapters in this collection speak to a need to re-centre descriptions of northern societies 'about the hearth'.

Almost all ethnographic descriptions of northern societies describe the centrality of the hearth. Aside from its perhaps too-often cited function as being a key to survival, the hearth is often clothed with rituals of respect. Dwellers in most Siberian societies feed the fire gifts of food, or of vodka, as a gesture of reciprocity with the 'masters' which are thought to be alive within the flames. It is perhaps an interesting detail that one can make these offerings both to fires in open-pit hearths, as to fires in stoves, or to bonfires outside (not to mention electric heating elements and steam radiators in urban settings). The specific engineered quality of the domestic architecture is not as important as fire itself. As Tom Andrews documents for the Tłįchǫ conical lodge, the fire at the centre of the lodge was used to communicate with ancestors by feeding it offerings of food. Aside from formal reciprocity, the home fire is often not fed refuse or poor quality wood, as Oetelaar et al. cite in this collection. John Ziker gives numerous examples of how Taimyr Dolgans and Nganasans 'respectfully' tend to the ashes from the fire and speak of the fire as a sentient kinsman. In the rituals of First Nations of the Canadian plains, fire is used in a more directed manner to produce cleansing smoke from sweetgrass or tobacco. Perhaps the best way of capturing this mood is through the concept of attending – much as Inuit dwellers attend to their soapstone lamps which double as a source of heat, light and a symbol of life itself (Bennett and Rowley 2004: 297–304). Inuit ethnography achieves a double resonance with the fact that the hearth-lamp was fed fat (and not wood) much like a breathing person itself.

Although hearths 'provide' both heat and light, it is striking that often these are not the qualities that circumpolar peoples stress when describing them. One interesting clue comes from an older survey of settlement architecture by K.C. Chang (1962) wherein he puts an emphasis on identifying 'independent hearths' as a clue to understanding the identity of households. The idea of autonomy and self-sufficiency is certainly a strong element in the way that narratives of hearths are structured. For example, the Inuit oral history collection by John Bennett and Susan Rowley (2004) contains multiple references to how the gift of a *quilliq* hearth-lamp is associated with the coming of age, just as its disposal accompanied the death of a woman. In the words of Zipporah Piungittuq Inuksuk from Amitturmiut:

> We used to have play *quilliq*, which were made from soapstone. We would use them when we were playing in a play tent ... We would get them fuelled and light them up as we played; we were trying to be as realistic as we possibly could. Only when [a woman was] able to get her own side of the bed [would she get her own *quilliq*]. (Bennett and Rowley 2004: 299)

Virginie Vaté's fieldwork on Chukotka reveals a strong interaction with fire and the creation of a 'human' space itself. The *iarên* – the area around the tent – is defined by the relationship of space to the smoke and fire of the domestic hearth itself (Vaté 2011: 142–3).

While hearths are indeed warm and bright, the ethnography seems to insist that they are both personal and often seen as containing persons themselves. To undress this observation it might be helpful to separate the architecture of the hearth from the fire itself. The most elaborate hearths within the North are the raised stone hearths described by Halinen et al. in this volume, or as documented for Thule Inuit (Odgaard and Kanal 2003), which appear more like stone stoves. Ethnographic and cosmological interpretations of these raised stone hearths stress their importance in dividing up and defining domestic spaces (Ränk 1949; Yates 1991). Often, the archaeologically invisible boundaries of the tent coverings can only be imputed by their placement relative to the firm infrastructure of the hearth-stove.

By contrast, most traditional conical dwellings whether in Canada or Siberia tended to have open-pit fires. These also had a subtle architecture, often involving the placement of a gravel base or a stone circle, or the prescribed placement of wood in a certain defined pattern. These firepits were also dressed with accessory equipment such as hanging poles and vertical rods for cooking, as described here for the Evenki lodge by Oetelaar et al. The firepits were often dressed with a skin or canvas covering around them – but not always. There is a remarkable lacuna in the ethnographic record of the different types of open firepits used both inside tents and outside around the camp for various purposes (Anderson 2006). Most accounts, using the logic of inversion, assume that the hearth is a natural object which can be identified by the mark it leaves on the land and the transformations it makes to the soils and rocks that may enclose it.

However, as Tim Ingold reminds us, it is not always that easy to divide an object from its environment. If the conical lodge can be interpreted as being entangled between earth and sky, a hearth it seems is entangled with the cooking supports that hang over it, the stones that dissipate its heat or perhaps the finely tailored skins that surround it. What would circumpolar ethnography look like if we assumed that most hearths were cloaked, and that lodges were more like clothes than buildings?

The parallel between dwellings and clothing can also be traced in the classic literature, but only as a distant subtheme. Amos Rapoport (1969: 20) prominently cites the wind shelters built by the Ona of Tierre del Fuego, only to emphasize that their comfort is guaranteed by (some say) their metabolism and others the fish oil that they rubbed into their bodies. Carsten and Hugh Jones (1995b: 2) also note the homology between the house and the person: 'The house is an extension of the person; like an extra skin, carapace or a second layer of clothes, it serves as much to reveal and display as it does to hide and protect'. They nevertheless move on from this interesting insight to elaborate social structural and cosmological themes. Perhaps the exception that proves the rule is the admission of a prominent evolutionary ecologist in a debate in *Current Anthropology* that 'well-designed clothing' such as that worn by Inuit can be admitted as one means by which *Homo* could modify their 'personal climate' (Leach 2003: 364).

My own fieldwork suggests that the parallel development between clothing and built structures is much broader. Taimyr *tundroviki* (tundra people) often describe how they make use of a 'ptarmigan's tent' when caught unexpectedly by a storm. This describes how a hunter, who is wearing double-layered reindeer fur clothing and a wool poncho over the top, beds himself down vertically into a lightly packed drift in order to survive the winds, as ptarmigan do. Dolgan, Nenets and Evenki tundra clothing is sewn so that one does not need a fire and tent to survive. Indeed, one has to store this type of clothing outside since it spoils if you bring it into a heated space. Young children are dressed in parkas with the ends of their sleeves sewn together (Figure 14.2) so that should they fall off a sled or a reindeer they can lie safely in the snow until someone finds them. This point was driven home when I was drinking tea in Vasillii Trofimovich Elogir's skin-lined caravan *(balok)*. Vasillii had eight children, five of which were living with him and his wife in this single 4-square-metre dwelling. One was an infant who spent most of her time in a hammock strung between the door frame and the small window. I asked, naïvely, where everyone slept. The answer was, 'outside of course!' What I misinterpreted as a dwelling was actually a mobile cooking and cleaning area. Sleeping out on a sled in the winter is perhaps unusual but not uncomfortable. I came to do it several times.

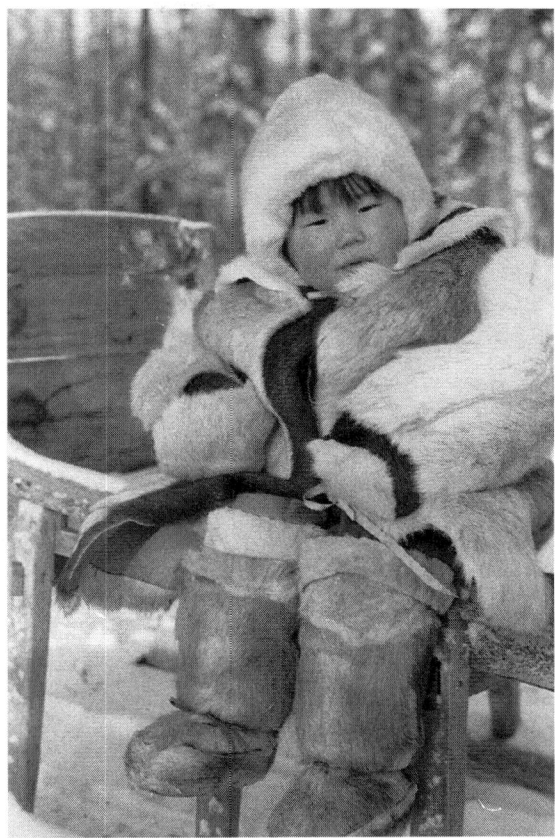

Figure 14.2 *A. Gavrilova with the Number 3 Reindeer Brigade, Surinda, dressed in her winter parka with the sleeves sewn up to give her an autonomous form of personal shelter from the cold.*

There has been a lot of energy spent trying to understand the dynamics of the human use of space within conical dwellings. The same ethnographic data can be used to interpret conical tents, or even *iglus*, as structures that enclose fires. Both a conical tent and an *iglu* have to be designed with proper ventilation so that air channels through the dwelling, removing the smoke but not extinguishing the hearth (cf. Oetelaar et al. and Beach, this volume). Conical lodges are positioned and set with openings that regulate the draught around the hearth (cf. Andrews, this volume). The materials one uses are also important. An interesting counter example of a fire dressed with poor materials was given to me by Taimyr *tundroviki* who described with great humour a bureaucratically designed 'nomadic' circular tent *(iurta)* mobile dwelling made of lightweight aluminium and

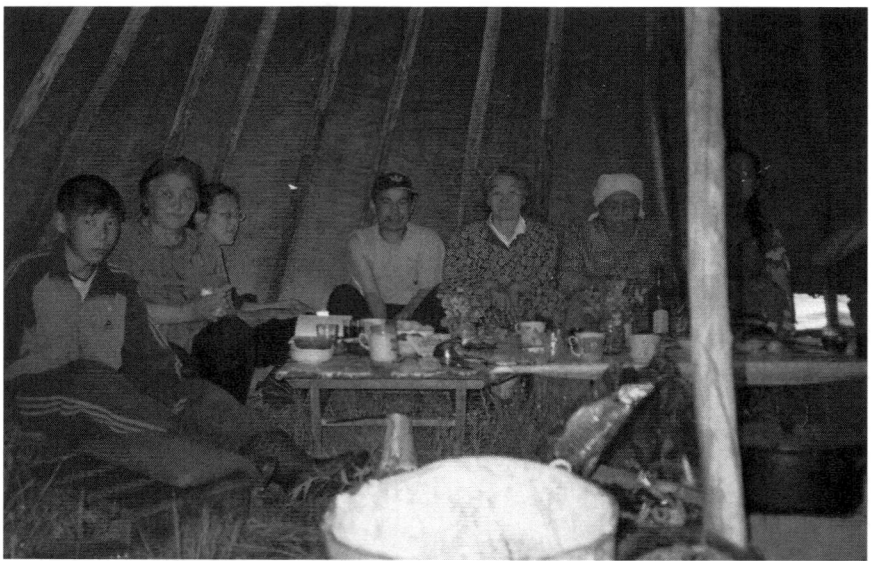

Figure 14.3 *A large communal lodge set up in the Iakut community of Essei for a summer feast. This large lodge was assembled from eight panels designed for individual lodges.*

canvas. The structure was easy to move and easy to assemble, but when it heated up the temperature difference between the inside and the outside interacted poorly with the conductivity of the metal so that it literally rained on the inhabitants. (The reindeer herders continued to use pieces of metal from the *iurta* to make more useful tools.) The skills that one uses to build a lodge are much closer to that of tailoring than that of carpentry, and it is often knowledgeable seamstresses who answer for both lodge coverings and clothing. As Ingold describes in his chapter, lodges are sewn and not assembled as brick buildings are.

An Evenki conical *d'iu* has a modular design which might be an interesting demonstration of these practices (Anderson 2007). The structure is made up of a minimum of four wedge-like patchwork skin panels, any one of which can serve to cover a small one-person tent. The panels are sized so that they can be rolled and packed comfortably on a reindeer. If more than one family meets, the panels can be combined to make a larger covering (Figure 14.3 and 14.4). Moreover, since skins were rare, each panel was often given as a wedding gift to a new family. Thus, each piece of the Evenki lodge can hold a story about which side of the extended family donated it to create a new family. To extend the terms of Tim Ingold, not only are each of the panels made of a patchwork, but the patchworks themselves are patched together. This extremely flexible

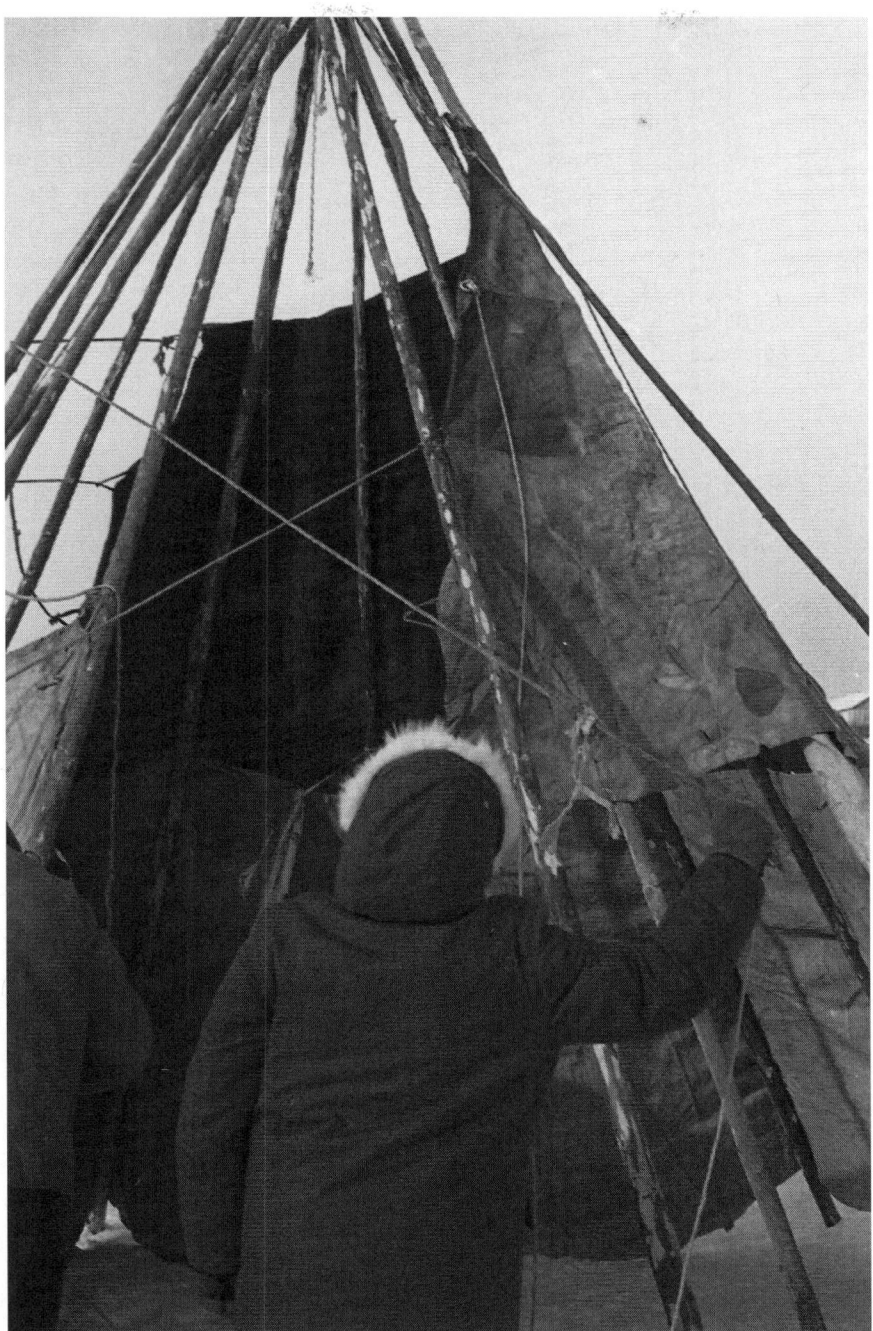

Figure 14.4 *Mary Richardson from Rae Edzo (Canada) helping to assemble the individual panels of a caribou skin lodge for a display in the village of Tura.*

design is difficult to identify as a single discrete built dwelling, since each time it is assembled it could be assembled differently. Nevertheless, each instance is carefully structured so that it provides the draughts craved by the fire.

This collection offers two clear examples of the hearth being clothed by a covering. It is interesting that the Tłı̨chǫ Dene word for a conical lodge is actually an *ewǫ̀ kǫ̀ nı̨hmbàa,* meaning a skin hearth-lodge (from the word for a hearth – *ewǫ̀*). Similarly, in Hugh Beach's account of dwellings in northern Sweden, Sámi do not recognize polyester tourist tents as shelters, given that one cannot make a fire within them.

Interpreting lodge coverings as a way to modify one's 'personal climate', and as a way of clothing a hearth, has the advantage of resituating an old debate in the ethnological literature on the cosmological significance of round and square dwellings. As Vladimir Davydov (2011) points out, the early ethnological literature associates 'roundness' with primitive peoples (Waterman 1927). Square dwellings were rationalized as a type of architecture one used when one settled down since, it was argued, they made it structurally easier to add another room without disassembling the entire structure (Lawrence and Low 1990: 462–3). In this view, log cabins such as those preferred by Gwich'in, or indeed by Evenkis today, might serve to illustrate the assimilation of a culture to a different, sedentary relationship to the environment.

This is clearly not the view of most of the contributors here. If we consider all coverings tailored out of local materials as a way of regulating one's personal climate, be they caribou skin leggings, conical skin lodges or the logs in log cabins, then differences in design imply different ways of approaching a similar problem. Rectangular log cabins are often denigrated as a borderline case of 'pure' vernacular architecture in the North, since they often imprison the ritual fire into a metal box and then even decentre that box to a corner of the dwelling. Yet as both Wishart et al. and Hugh Beach document, this does not make these dwellings any less creative or any less evocative in the way they are woven into the social setting.

Tim Ingold, in his chapter in this collection, goes to considerable lengths to contextualize the architecture of pastoral nomads within the architectural cannon that favours the sceptic, pre-built intuitions of urban architects. He helpfully separates the metaphors of 'striated' and 'smooth' space from the life-enhancing activities that real craftspeople are engaged in. Rather than setting up a simple dualism between urban architects and rural pastoralists, he shows that societies can range along a continuum of craftsmanship, such that Mongolian herdsmen with their felt *iurts* might represent a desirable optimum of a striated engagement with the world, while others stitching tent coverings out of patches achieve the same in a less elegant manner. Farmers do rather badly in his scheme, condemned to trammel the earth along straight furrows, never lifting their eyes to feel the wind or taste the rain. However, the same criticism might also be applied to nomadic pastoralists. People everywhere engage with sentient environments in complex ways.

The classic environment of the nomadic pastoralist might be the sweeping steppe, but even nineteenth-century ethnographers such as Nikolai Kharuzin (1896) recognized that Mongolic and Turkic herdsmen were already keeping herds to please the Imperial regimes that taxed them. Social relations with a tribute-fuelled economy, like a market economy, generates certain regular returns to trading points along trampled trails. To an Evenki reindeer herder, the subsidy-centred lifestyle of Sámi reindeer pastoralism will surely look as optic, regimented and planned as that of a City stockbroker. A wealthy reindeer rancher might survey his or her herds from a helicopter and set up a smooth portable canvas *lávvu* for a brief time at a number of temporary counting corrals over any particular season. But as Hugh Beach suggests, this does not necessarily mean that he or she is no longer investing in the social relations of family and landscape. At best it is a different type of engagement with the world, and perhaps a sadder one, but not necessarily a weaker one. In his account it is certainly 'patched' together out of many different types of structures. The anthropological tradition has already given us a number of rankings of vernacular dwellings according to different hierarchies of form (Kharuzin 1896; Morgan 1881; Ruong 1937). Tim Ingold's discussion of the haptic and the optic guides our attention towards the vibrancy of social life in relation to materials, but it functions a little less sensitively as a guide to social and political relations in general.

If dwellings accentuate a certain social currency (and not a social structure), then the stationary log cabin accentuates relationships which may require a stationary 'spanning of space' as a strategic goal. As Wishart and Loovers, and Andrews, document, the skills that go into building a log reinforced structure always existed alongside those that allowed one to make a skin lodge. In the pre-colonial period, log structures (which were often underground) might have been erected out of necessity or at a certain time of the year when many families gathered together at one place. Today, in order to raise a healthy family, Northerners must develop strong relationships with government agencies and outlets to the global market, both to sell their products and to buy the goods they desire. The welfare-state mediated market places its own demands on the accessibility of the person – and if one wishes to interact with them a less-mobile type of dwelling is necessary at least for some times of the year. However, as Dawson (2008) or Davydov (2011) report, the circulation of people (especially children) between fixed structures in northern settlements quickly dispels the impression that these are unitary house societies. The fixed structure, be it a log cabin or a frame house provided by the state, is simply one form of enclosure within a region that takes its place among tents and proper clothing.

Accepting the fact that settler 'boxed' architecture might have its place in the repertoire of northern enclosures does not need to blind us to the effects of social power on these communities. Most of the chapters in this volume give accounts of people struggling to keep their domestic spaces self-reliant. Whether this be the difficulties faced by the elderly homeowners of Kuzomen' in a remote community on the Kola, or the energy spent by Tłįchǫ Dene to create blueprints of museum-curated dwellings only faintly recalled in memory, Northerners like many other people fight for access for resources and space in order to maintain communities that serve the animals they care for.

Given the demands placed on them by government administrations, often the most elegant solution is a homestead or fixed boxed structure. These adaptations are not always successful. As Sommerseth points out in the sobering conclusion to her chapter, an extremely intricate multi-generational kinship system regulating the relations between extended family members in northern Norway was no match for the real risks associated with the demands of commercial fishing. The longer journeys undertaken by sons in search of fish to sell, and the high mortality rate this implied, generated a situation where only a nucleus of the family survived. In her account, the 'transition' to a nuclear household is no more preordained than that of the 'transition' to a sedentary box structure. Both the single-family household and the rectangular log cabin are lived expressions of the demand of a northern ecology striated by commodities. Stem-families and conical lodges might exist in a material sense today only in museums and archives, but as many chapters in this collection show, the knowledge behind them can be revitalized when conditions shift.

Is there a firm and fast line dividing the people who travel the taiga dressing their hearths with conical lodges and those who sketch and sew 'revitalized' lodges for an audience? The goals of the activities are certainly different. There are perhaps few examples of people inhabiting revitalized dwellings. The Tłįchǫ lodge that frames this collection is certainly venerated as an artefact and is curated in a protected environment. But judging the lodge, or the *lávvu,* as a mere representation of a life that once was is in its own way a logical inversion of living practice. The patchwork activity of reassembling a lodge or a *bealljigoahti* involves not only a mental exercise of imagination and projection, but also a bringing together of skilled craftspeople and hunters to achieve a task. It draws attention to the unfamiliar skills that in turn take their place in the repertoire by which people engage with the world. This is not unlike the life project of Tim

Ingold himself who strives to revitalize anthropology through a careful rereading of old and often forgotten texts, allowing us to experience the social world anew. In a region of the world so regimented by powerful states, and military alliances, the revitalization of dwellings is a strong step towards a more vibrant local engagement with the world. We all hope that this volume will play its role in this movement.

Acknowledgements

I am greatly indebted to all the participants of the multinational project Home Hearth and Household in the Circumpolar North for the ideas and ethnography that formed the basis of this chapter. This project generated a wealth of data but also a wealth of discussions, which are reflected here. I am particularly thankful to my co-editors and the other authors in this collection who offered suggestions and further comparative examples to develop the argument in this chapter. I would also like to acknowledge an Advanced Grant from the European Research Council for the time to bring this theoretical chapter to completion.

Notes

1 These exchanges took place during several projects financed by the Canadian International Development Agency and managed by the Canadian Circumpolar Institute, the Department of Indian and Northern Affairs and the Inuit Circumpolar Congress between 1998 and 2001. A description of the projects can be found in Popkov and Anderson (2002), Anderson (2011a) and Wilson (2006).

2 Morgan collects his examples of vernacular architecture mainly from the 'upper status of savagery' and the 'lower status of barbarism'. This choice gives primacy of place to Iroquois and their multi-family long-houses. The sole Arctic examples he cites are from multi-family Aleut and Gwich'in dwellings, which were used only in a specific seasonal context. There are two fragmentary descriptions of conical tents among Ojibwa and Dakota, but these lack the description of proxemics and 'communism in living' of the other examples.

3 The interlacing of the concept of the hearth with that of the home in Carsten and Hugh-Jones (1995a) is fought out in footnotes and asides. One of their interesting reference is to Stephan Gudeman's and Alberto Rivera's (Gudeman and Rivera 1990) classic comparison of Columbian peasant economies and those of Scottish physiocrats. Pointing out that although the founders of social anthropology would often hear local terms for social relationships, such as that of the 'hearth' among Evans-Pritchard's Nuers, they preferred to represent these relationships as lineages or as corporations: 'the onlooker can only wonder how the history of descent theory might have appeared had the theorists of the 1940s, instead of exporting their own market experience, used a model of the home and the hearth' (Gudeman and Rivera 1990: 184).

Notes on the Contributors

David G. Anderson is Professor of Social Anthropology at the University of Aberdeen. His interests include circumpolar ethnography, ethnoarchaeology, ethnohistory and the history of science. He is the author of a monograph on Taimyr Evenkis and Dolgans, and the editor or co-editor of several collections from Berghahn Books, the most recent of which is entitled *The 1926/27 Soviet Polar Census Expeditions* (Berghahn 2011). He was the project leader of the collaborative research project 'HHH: Home, Hearth, and Household in the Circumpolar North' and the principal investigator of the Norwegian independent project within that network during his tenure as an adjunct professor based at the Centre for Sámi Studies, University of Tromsø. He is presently the principal investigator of a five-year international research project funded by the European Research Council "Arctic Domus" based at the University of Aberdeen.

Thomas D. Andrews is the Territorial Archaeologist with the Prince of Wales Northern Heritage Centre, in Yellowknife, Northwest Territories. He has conducted anthropological and archaeological research in the northern Yukon and in the Mackenzie Valley of the Northwest Territories since the late 1970s and his publications include articles on community-based resource management in the Northwest Territories, Dene traditional knowledge and place names, Tłįchǫ ethnoarchaeology and sacred sites, ice patch archaeology and aboriginal cultural landscapes. He conducted collaborative fieldwork in the Northwest Territories and in the United States within the HHH collaborative research project for both the Canadian and American HHH independent projects.

Per Axelsson holds a PhD in History and is a researcher at the Vaartoe Centre for Sámi Research, Umeå University. His research interests and recent publications focus on indigenous demography, longitudinal studies of indigenous health, effects of colonization on the indigenous Sámi people and medical history. Recent publications are printed in *Global*

Environmental Change, Global Health Action, Ber. zur Wissenschaftsgeschichte and he co-edited the volume *Indigenous Peoples and Demography* (Berghahn 2011). He was the project leader for the Swedish HHH project on historical demography.

Hugh Beach is Professor of Cultural Anthropology at Uppsala University in Sweden. He has lived among Sámi reindeer herders for many years in Sweden, Norway and the Kola Peninsula of Russia. In Swedish Sámpi, his work has been devoted to studying the practical determinants of herding form. He has also worked as a reindeer herder in Alaska with the Inuit NANA Regional Corporation herd, and in general is specialized in the study of indigenous circumpolar peoples. He has led and been engaged in a number of interdisciplinary and international research projects, for example: Managing the Wilderness and the Dilemmas of Cultural Ecology: Laponia – Sámi Landscape and World Heritage Site; the Swedish part of the project Survey of Living Conditions in the Arctic (SLiCA): Inuit, Sámi, and the Indigenous Peoples of Chukotka; Post-Soviet Political and Socio-economic Transformation among the Indigenous Peoples of Northern Russia: Current Administrative Policies, Legal Rights, and Applied Strategies; and the Swedish part of the project The Challenges of Modernity for Reindeer Management: Integration and Sustainable Development in Europe's Subarctic and Boreal Regions. Currently he is Principal Investigator for the American NSF funded IPY project Dynamics of Circumpolar Land Use and Ethnicity (CLUE): social impacts of policy and climate change. He conducted fieldwork in Northern Sweden for the Swedish HHH project.

Ivar Bjørklund is a social anthropologist working at the University Museum in Tromsø. His research interests include pastoral adaptions and interethnic relations in Norway and he has also published on ethnohistory and ethnic revitalization movements. He was responsible for the HHH module on cultural revitalization in museums for the Norwegian independent project.

Isabelle Brännlund is a PhD student in history at the Vaartoe Centre for Sámi Research, Umeå University. Her research focuses on how reindeer husbandry has been affected by, and adapted to, the climatic changes of the eighteenth and nineteenth centuries. Her first article was published in *Global Environmental Change*.

Peter C. Dawson is an Associate Professor in the Department of Archaeology, University of Calgary, and a Research Associate at the Arctic Institute of North America (AINA). His research interests include computer modelling and visualization of archaeological data, circumpolar hunter-gatherers and indigenous knowledge systems. He has conducted archaeological research in many areas of the Canadian Arctic for almost two decades. Examples of recent publications include '"Breaking the Fourth Wall": 3D Virtual Worlds as Tools for Knowledge Repatriation in Archaeology', published in the *Journal of Social Archaeology* (2011). He conducted archaeological fieldwork for the Canadian HHH independent project.

Petri Halinen is a university lecturer and a docent in archaeology at the University of Helsinki. He defended his doctoral thesis in archaeology in 2005, 'Prehistoric Hunters of Northernmost Lapland – Settlement Patterns and Subsistence Strategies'. His research interests are in the archaeology of Lapland, especially the Sámi culture, and in the Stone Age of Finland. He has conducted surveys and excavations for both the Finnish and the Norwegian independent projects within the HHH network.

Sven-Donald Hedman took his PhD in archaeology at the University of Umeå, Sweden in 2003. His doctoral thesis was entitled 'Settlements and Sacrificial Sites: Economic Strategy and Settlement Pattern among the Forest Sámi 700–1600 AD'. His interests include Sámi prehistory and research into early forms of reindeer herding. He held a post-doctoral fellowship at the University of Tromsø in connection with the Norwegian HHH project. Within that project he prepared surveys and excavations in the Kola Peninsula, Russia and northern Norway, Oardujávri and Pasvik.

Tim Ingold is Professor of Social Anthropology at the University of Aberdeen. He has carried out ethnographic fieldwork in Lapland, and has written on environment, technology and social organization in the circumpolar North, on evolutionary theory in anthropology, biology and history, on the role of animals in human society, on language and tool use, and on environmental perception and skilled practice. He is currently exploring issues on the interface between anthropology, archaeology, art and architecture. His latest book, *Being Alive,* was published by Routledge in 2011. Prof. Ingold served on the scientific advisory board of the ESF-funded project 'BOREAS: Histories from the North'.

Jan Peter Laurens Loovers is Research Fellow of the ERC-funded project 'Arctic Domus' at the University of Aberdeen. He was recently the RAI Urgent Anthropology Fellow and Visiting Fellow at Goldsmiths University of London. He is further affiliated with the Gwich'in Social and Cultural Institute. His most recent work with Gwich'in in the Canadian North concerns the relation between poetics, memory, well-being and land. His interests are archaeology, Athabascan or Dene people, circumpolar ethnography, colonization developments and policies, ecological anthropology, ethnohistory, ethnographic filmmaking, ethnopoetics, Gwich'in, indigenous rights, indigenous peoples, literacy, Maya (Quich'é), Namibia, pedagogy, philosophy (specifically Deleuze, Leibniz and Spinoza), politics, resource extraction, San (!Kung), United Nations Permanent Forum on Indigenous Issues, and visual anthropology. He was an affiliated member of the Norwegian HHH project.

Maria Nakhshina is network facilitator for two international research projects based at the University of Aberdeen, one of which is the ERC Advanced Grant Arctic Domus. She was a research fellow at the Max Planck Institute of Social Anthropology, Halle, Germany. She is also a part-time researcher at the Barents Center of the Humanities, Kola Branch of Russian Academy of Sciences, Apatity. She received her PhD in Social Anthropology from the University of Aberdeen in 2011. She has conducted several years of fieldwork in fishing villages on the White Sea coast in the northwest of Russia, among people traditionally called Pomors. Her research interests include rural-urban migration, political economy of mobility, lifestyle and local identity, Pomor identity movement, post-socialist change in resource use and values, management of fishing resources in Russia and the Arctic, sanitation management in rural areas, and ethnographic film-making. She was an affiliated member of the Norwegian HHH project.

Gerald A. Oetelaar is a Professor and current head of the Department of Archaeology at the University of Calgary. His research interests centre on the perception, organization and use of space at the level of the household, community and landscape as well as the evolution of natural and cultural landscapes in North America. He has explored these research interests since 2000 through a Major Collaborative Research Initiative grant and, more recently, the Eurocores BOREAS programme. He has contributed several book chapters, has served as co-editor of *Indigenous People and Archaeology: Honouring the Past, Discussing the Present, Building for the Future,* and has articles in *American Antiquity, Plains Anthropologist, International Journal of Osteoarchaeology, Great Plains Research, Canadian Journal of Earth Sciences* and *Géographie Physique et Quaternaire.* For the HHH research group he led the Canadian independent project on the revitalization of knowledge in museums and ethnoarchaeology in the Canadian Arctic.

Bjørnar Olsen is Professor of Archaeology in the Department of Archaeology and Social Anthropology, University of Tromsø. He has written a number of papers and books on northern and Sámi prehistory and history, museology and archaeological theory. His latest books are *In Defense of Things: Archaeology and the Ontology of Objects* (2010), *Persistent Memories: Pyramiden – A Soviet Mining Town in the High Arctic* (2010) (with Elin Andreassen and Hein Bjerck) and *Hybrid Spaces: Medieval Finnmark and the Archaeology of Multi-room Houses* (2011) (edited with Przemyslaw Urbanczyk and Colin Amundsen). He coordinated the archaeological research for the Norwegian HHH independent project.

Hilde L. Somerseth is Associate Professor in history at Sogn and Fjordane University College. She received her PhD in History from the University of Tromsø, Norway, in June 2011. Her research centres on historical demography. In her PhD she evaluated the effect of cultural and economic dynamics of family living arrangements, explored from the perspective of elderly people co-residing with their own adult children. Her thesis was entitled 'Northern Co-residence across Generations in Northernmost Norway during the Late Nineteenth Century'. Her PhD fellowship was part of the Norwegian HHH project.

Virginie Vaté (PhD Nanterre University, 2003) is an anthropologist at the Centre National de la Recherche Scientifique (CNRS) in France. Since 1994, she has been doing research in Chukotka (north-eastern Siberia), particularly among Chukchi reindeer herders. Working mainly in the field of the anthropology of religion, she addresses issues such as human–animal relations, human relations to 'nature', male and female roles in everyday life and in rituals, conversion to Evangelical Christianity and interactions among various religious practices, especially shamanism-animism and Evangelical Christianity. In 2011, she began to investigate missionary activities coming from Alaska and directed toward Chukotka, in particular native-to-native ministry. Within the BOREAS network, she led a project associated with the collaborative research programme on New Religious Movements in the Russian North (NEWREL). With P. Gray and P. Plattet, she is co-editor of the NEWREL volume, currently in preparation.

Robert P. Wishart completed his doctorate in anthropology at the University of Alberta, Canada, and joined the University of Aberdeen in September 2003 as a postdoctoral researcher, then as an RCUK Fellow, and was appointed lecturer in 2010. His ethnographic work has been on the Gwich'in-Dene of the Mackenzie Delta in Northern Canada, with the Ojibwe of Ontario, and with Scottish fishers. His research is on the political and economic relationships between settlers, development interests and indigenous peoples of the North and how these relationships have been used in various discourses and (mis-) represented in state policy. He led an associated project on vernacular architecture in the Gwich'in settlement area for the HHH research consortium.

John P. Ziker is Professor of Anthropology at Boise State University. His interests include indigenous land tenure systems and their sustainability, demographic health, human sociality, the circumpolar north and post-socialist societies. He is author of *Peoples of the Tundra: Northern Siberians in the Post-Communist Transition,* from Waveland Press. He has authored numerous articles on Siberia for the journals *Science, Human Nature, Human Ecology, Nomadic Peoples,* and *Ecology of Food and Nutrition*. He recently co-edited, along with Konstantin Klokov, a volume in Russian on the 1926/1927 Polar Census in the Russian North and Western Siberia, and in 2011 co-edited with Florian Stammler a volume titled *Histories from the North: Environments, Movements, and Narratives,* published jointly by Boise State University and the University of Lapland. For the HHH network he led the American independent project on historical demography, the revitalization of knowledge in museums, and vernacular architecture in Canada and in Siberia.

References

Adams, J.W. and A.B. Kasakoff. 2004. 'Spillovers, Subdivisions and Flows: Questioning the Usefulness of "Bounded Container" as the Dominant Spatial Metaphor in Demography' in S. Szreter, H. Sholkamy and A. Dharmalingam (eds), *Categories and Contexts: Anthropological and Historical Studies in Critical Demography*. Oxford: Oxford University Press, pp. 43–70.

Adler, B.F. 1910. *Karty pervobytnykh narodov*. S-Peterburg: tip. A.G. Rozena.

Alberti, L.B. 1988. *On the Art of Building in Ten Books*, trans. J. Rykwert, N. Leach and R. Tavernor. Cambridge, Mass: MIT Press.

Alekseenko, E.A. 2007. 'Rechnoi component v kul'ture narodov Eniseiskogo basseina', in L.R. Pavlinskaia (ed), *Reki i narody Sibiri*. Sankt-Peterburg: Nauka, pp. 55–86.

Alexander, C. 1964. *Notes On the Synthesis of Form*. Cambridge, Mass.: Harvard University Press.

Allerton, C. 2013. *Potent Landscapes: Place and Mobility in Eastern Indonesia*. Honolulu: University of Hawai'i Press.

Alpers, S. 1983. *The Art of Describing: Dutch Art in the Seventeenth Century*. London: Penguin.

Alter, G.C., L. Cliggett, and A.L. Urbiel. 1996. 'Household Patterns of the Elderly and the Proximity of Children in a Nineteenth-Century City: Verviers, Belgium 1831–1846', in T.K. Hareven (ed.), *Aging and Generational Relation Over the Life Course: A Historical and Cross-Cultural Perspective*. Berlin: de Gruyter, pp. 30–52.

Alymov, S.S. 2008. 'Tri etiuda o "marrizme" v sovetskoi etnografii', *Etnograficheskoe obozrenie* 6: 79–93.

Andersen, E. and A. Nørgård. 2009. *Et uldsejl til Oselven. Arbejdsrapport om fremstillingen af et uldsejl til en traditional vestnorsk båd*. Roskilde: Vikingeskibsmuseet (available online at http://vikingeskibsmuseet.dk).

Anderson, B. 1991. *Imagined Communities. Reflections on the Origin and Spread of Nationalism*. London: Verso.

Anderson, D.G. 2000. *Identity and Ecology in Arctic Siberia: The Number One Reindeer Brigade*. Oxford: Oxford University Press.

Anderson, D.G. 2006. 'Dwellings, Storage and Summer Site Structure among Siberian Orochen Evenkis Hunter-Gatherer Vernacular Architecture under Post-Socialist Conditions', *Norwegian Archaeological Review* 39 (1): 1–26.

Anderson, D.G. 2007. 'Mobile Architecture and Social Life: The Case of the Conical Skin Lodge in the Putoran Plateau Region', in S. Beyries and V. Vaté (eds), *Les civilisations du renne d'hier et d'aujourd'hui. Approches ethnohistoriques, archéologiques et anthropologiques*. Antibes: Éditions APDCA, pp. 43–63.

Anderson, D.G. 2011a. 'Local Healing Landscapes' in D.G. Anderson (ed.), *The Healing Landscapes of Central and Southeastern Siberia. Patterns of Northern Traditional Healing Series 1*. Edmonton: CCI Press, pp. 1–12.

Anderson, D.G. 2011b. 'The Mystery of the Magnate Reindeer Herders: Household Structure and Economy Among Lake Essei Iakuts', 1926/7 in P. Axelsson and P. Sköld (eds), *Indigenous Peoples and Demography: The Complex Relation between Identity and Statistics*. Oxford and New York: Berghahn Books, pp. 197–218.

Anderson, D.G. 2011c. 'The Polar Census and the Architecture of Enumeration', in D.G. Anderson (ed.), *The 1926/27 Soviet Polar Census Expeditions*. Oxford and New York: Berghahn Books, pp. 1–32.

Andre, A. and I. Kritsch. 1992. 'The Traditional use of Travaillant Lake Area, Using Trails and Place Names of the Gwichya Gwich'in from Arctic Red River'. NWT Report Prepared for the NOGAP Archaeology Project. Hull: Canadian Museum of Civilisation.

Andreassen, L. 2001. 'Arkeologiske utgravninger i Indre og Ytre Sortvik, Porsanger, Finnmark 1987–1989', Tromura 33. Tromsø: Tromsø Museum.

Andrews, T.D. 2007. 'Changing Bone into Stone: Knowledge Repatriation and Indigenous Archaeology in the Northwest Territories, Canada', in A.V. Kharinsky (ed.), *Etnoistoriia i arkheologiia Severnoi Evrazii: teoriia, metodologiia i praktika issledovaniia: Sbornik nauchnykh trudov*. Irkutsk: ISTU, pp. 375–8.

Andrews, T.D. and S. Buggey. 2008. 'Authenticity in Aboriginal Cultural Landscapes', *APT Bulletin* 39 (1–3): 63–71.

Andrews, T.D. and E. Mackenzie. 1998. *Tlicho Ewo Konihmbaa: The Dogrib Caribou Skin Lodge: An Exhibit*. Yellowknife: Prince of Wales Northern Heritage Centre.

Andrews, T.D. and J.B. Zoe. 1997. 'The Idaa Trail: Archaeology and the Dogrib Cultural Landscape, Northwest Territories, Canada', in G.P. Nicholas and T.D. Andrews (eds), *At a Crossroads: Archaeology and First Peoples in Canada*. Vancouver: Archaeology Press, Simon Fraser University.

Andrews, T.D., J.B. Zoe, and A. Herter. 1998. 'On Yamozhah's Trail: Sacred Sites and the Anthropology of Travel', in J. Oakes, R. Riewe, K. Kinew, and E. Maloney (eds), *Sacred Lands: Aboriginal World Views, Claims, and Conflicts*. Edmonton: Canadian Circumpolar Institute, pp. 305–20.

Anisimov, A.F. 1951. 'Shamanskie dukhi po vozzreniiu evenkov i totemicheskie istoki ideologii shamanizma', *Sbornik Muzeia Antropologii i Etnografii* 13: 190–5.

Anisimov, A.F. 1952. 'Shamanskii chum u evenkov i problema proiskhozhdeniia shamanskogo obriada', in L.P. Potapov and M.G. Levin (eds), *Sibirskii etnograficheskii sbornik 1*, pp. 199–238.

Anisimov, A.F. 1958. *Religiia evenkov v istoriko-geneticheskom izuchenii i problem proiskhozhdeniia pervobytnykh verovanii*. Moskva-Leningrad: Nauka.

Anisimov, A.F. 1963a. 'The Shaman's Tent of the Evenks and the Origins of the Shamanistic Rite', in H.N. Michael (ed.), *Studies in Siberian Shamanism*. Arctic Institute of North America, Anthropology of the North. Translations from Russian Sources 4. Toronto: University of Toronto Press, pp. 84–123.

Anisimov, A.F. 1963b. 'Cosmological Concepts of the Peoples of the North', in H.N. Michael (ed.), *Studies in Siberian Shamanism*. Arctic Institute of North America,

Anthropology of the North. Translations from Russian Sources 4. Toronto: University of Toronto Press, pp. 157–229.

Aporta, C. 2004. 'Routes, Trails and Tracks: Trail Breaking among the Inuit of Igloolik', *Études/Inuit/Studies* 28 (2): 9–38.

Aporta, C. 2005. 'From Map to Horizon; From Trail to Journey: Documenting Inuit Geographic Knowledge', *Études/Inuit/Studies* 29 (1–2): 221–31.

Aporta, C. 2009. 'The Trail as Home: Inuit and their Pan-Arctic Network of Routes', *Human Ecology* 37 (2): 131–46.

Appadurai, A. (ed.) 1986. *The Social Life of Things: Commodities in Cultural Perspective*. Cambridge: University of Cambridge Press.

Aronsson, K-Å. 1991. *Forest Reindeer Herding A.D. 1–1800. An Archaeological and Palaeological Study in Northern Sweden*. Archaeology and Environment 10. Department of Archaeology, Umeå : Umeå universitet.

Aronsson, L. 2004. 'Place Attachment of Vacation Residents: Between Tourists and Permanent Residents', in C.M. Hall and D.K. Müller (eds), *Tourism, Mobility and Second Homes: Between Elite Landscape and Common Ground*. Clevedon: Channel View Publications, pp. 75–86.

Asch, M. with R. Wishart. 2004. 'The Slavey Indians: The Relevance of Ethnohistory to Development', in R.B. Morrison and C.R. Wilson (eds), *Native Peoples: The Canadian Experience*. Oxford: Oxford University Press, pp. 178–97.

Axelsson, P. 2010. 'To Abandon "the Other" – Statistical Enumeration of Swedish Sami 1700s–1945 and Beyond', *Berichte zur Wissenschaftsgeschichte* 33 (3): 263–79.

Axelsson, P., and P. Sköld. 2011. 'Introduction', in P. Axelsson and P. Sköld (eds), *Indigenous Peoples and Demography. The Complex Relation between Identity and Statistics*. Oxford and New York: Berghahn Books, pp. 1–14.

Axelsson, P., P. Sköld, J. Ziker, and D.G. Anderson. 2011. 'Epilogue: Indigenous Demography', in P. Axelsson and P. Sköld (eds), *Indigenous Peoples and Demography: The Complex Relation between Identity and Statistics*. Oxford and New York: Berghahn Books, pp. 295–308.

Bær, A.P. 1926. 'Erindringer 1825–1849', in O. Kolsrud (ed), *Norvegia Sacra (1921–1940)*. Kristiania: Steenske forlag, pp. 39–79.

Bagrow, L. 1948. 'Eskimo Maps', *Imago Mundi* 5: 92

Bailey, G. and J. Peoples. 2010. *Essentials of Cultural Anthropology*. Belmont: Wadsworth.

Balikci, A. 1984. 'Netsilik', in D. Damas (ed.), *Arctic,* Handbook of North American Indians 5. Washington, DC: Smithsonian Institution, pp. 415–30.

Balsvik R.R. 1991. 'Kvinner i nordnorske kystsamfunn', *Historisk Tidsskrift* 4: 636–53.

Basso, K.H. 1996. *Wisdom Sits in Places: Landscape and Language Among the Western Apache*. Albuquerque: University of New Mexico Press.

Basu, P. 2007. *Highland Homecomings: Genealogy and Heritage Tourism in the Scottish Diaspora*. London: Routledge.

Beach, H. 1981. *Reindeer-Herd Management in Transition: The Case of Tuorpon Saameby in Northern Sweden*. Uppsala Studies in Cultural Anthropology 3. Uppsala: Acta University Ups.

Beach, H. 1983. 'A Swedish Dilemma: Saami Rights and the Welfare State', in Équipe écologie et anthropologie des sociétés pastorales (ed.), *Production Pastorale et Société*. Cambridge: Cambridge University Press, pp. 9–17.

Beach, H. 1993. *A Year in Lapland: Guest of the Reindeer Herders*. Washington, DC: Smithsonian Institution Press.

Beach, H. 2000. 'Reindeer-Pastoralism Politics in Sweden: Protecting the Environment and Designing the Herder', in A. Hornborg and G. Pálsson (eds), *Negotiating Nature*. Lund Studies in Human Ecology 2. Lund: Lund University Press, pp. 179–211.

Beach, H. 2001, *A Year in Lapland: Guest of the Reindeer Herders*. Seattle: University of Washington Press.

Beach, H. 2008. 'Reindeer Ears: Calf Marking During the Contemporary Era of Extensive Herding in Swedish Saamiland', in Kungl. Humanistiska Vetenskaps-Samfundet i Uppsala (ed.), *Årsbok /Yearbook 2007*. Uppsala: Societatis Litterarum Humaniorum Regiae Upsaliensis, pp. 91–118.

Beach, H. and F. Stammler. 2006. 'Human–Animal Relations in Pastoralism, in Humans and Reindeer on the Move', *Nomadic Peoples* 10 (2): 6–30.

Bennett, J. and S.D.M. Rowley. 2004. *Uqalurait: An Oral History of Nunavut*. Montréal: McGill-Queens University Press.

Berg, B.A. 2001. *Samiske sedvaner og rettsoppfatninger*. Norges offentlige utredninger 2001: 34. Oslo: Statens Forvaltningstjenestestatens trykning.

Berg, T.F. 1857. *Plan för Insamlande af Uppgifterna till Sveriges Befolkningsstatistik 1857*. Stockholm: Norstedt.

Berger, T. 1977. *Northern Frontier, Northern Homeland: Terms and Conditions*. The Mackenzie Valley Pipeline Inquiry Vol. 1. Ottawa: Minister of Supply and Services.

Bergman, I. 1989. *Det samiska boplatskomplexet vid Rackträsk, Arjeplog*. Arkeologi i norr 1. Umeå: Umeå universitet.

Bergman, I., L. Liedgren, L. Östlund, and O. Zackrisson. 2008. 'Kinship and Settlements: Sami Residence Patterns in the Fennoscandian Alpine Areas around A.D. 1000', *Arctic Anthropology* 45 (1): 97–110.

Bergstøl, J. 2008. *Samer i Østerdalen? En studie av etnisitet i jernalderen i det nordøstre Hedmark*. Oslo: J. Bergstøl.

Beskow, W. 1894. *Kyrkobokföringen och dermed sammanhängande stadganden: 1894*. Stockholm: P. A. Norstedt & Söner.

Binford, L. 1978. 'Dimensional Analysis of Behaviour and Site Structure: Learning from an Eskimo Hunting Stand', *American Antiquity* 43 (3): 330–61.

Birket-Smith, K. 1929. *The Caribou Eskimos: Material and Social Life and Their Cultural Position, Descriptive Part*. Report of the Fifth Thule Expedition 1921–24 Vol 5 (1), Copenhagen: Gyldendal.

Bjørklund, I. 1985. *Fjordfolket i Kvænangen. Fra samisk samfunn til norsk utkant 1550–1980*. Oslo: Universitetsforlaget.

Bjørklund, I. 1990. 'Sámi Reindeer Pastoralism as an Indigenous Resource Management System in Northern Norway: A Contribution to the Common Property Debate', *Development and Change* 21 (1): 75–86.

Bjørklund, I. 2004. 'Saami Pastoral Society in Northern Norway: The National Integration of an Indigenous Management System', in D. Anderson and M. Nuttall (eds), *Cultivating Arctic Landscapes*. New York and Oxford: Berghahn Books, pp. 124–35.

Boas, F. 1974 [1888]. *The Central Eskimo*. Toronto: Coles Publishing Company.

Bogoras (Bogoraz), W. (V.). 1975 [1904–1909]. *The Chukchee*. The Jesup North Pacific Expedition. Memoir of the American Museum of Natural History (Vol. VII). New York: AMS press.

Bogoraz, V. 1937. *Luoravetlansko-russkii (chukotsko-russkii) slovar'*. Moskva-Leningrad: Gosudarstvennoe uchebno-pedagogicheskoe izdatel'stvo.

Brandišauskas, D. 2009. 'Leaving Footprints in the Taiga: Enacted and Emplaced Power and Luck Among Orochen-Evenki of the Zabaikal Region in East Siberia'. PhD Dissertation. Department of Anthropology: University of Aberdeen.

Brännlund, I. and P. Axelsson. 2011. 'Reindeer Management During the Colonization of Sami Lands: A Long-Term Perspective of Vulnerability and Adaptation Strategies', *Global Environmental Change* 21 (3): 1095–105.

Bratrein, H.D. 1992. 'Kystkultur og kystsamfunn i Nord-Norge', *Heimen* 4: 217–26.

Bratrein, H.D. 1998. 'Passio Olavi – et kildested om finnmarksfisket på 1100-tallet', *Håløygminne* 79 (1): 117–21.

Brightman, R. 1993. *Grateful Prey: Rock-Cree Human Animal Relationships*. Berkeley: University of California Press.

Bruner, E. 1993. 'Epilogue: Creative Persona and the Problem of Authenticity', in S. Lavie, K. Narayan, and R. Rosaldo (eds), *Creativity/Anthropology*. Ithaca, NY: Cornell University Press, pp. 321–44.

Bull, H.H. 2000. 'Hushold og generasjonsskifter i Rendalen 1762–1900: Ættesamfunnets siste skanse?'. Masters Thesis. Faculty of Humanities, University of Oslo.

Bull, H H. 2006. 'Marriage Decisions in a Peasant Society. The Role of the Family of Origin with regard to Adult Children's Choice of Marriage Partner and the Timing of their Marriage in Rendalen, Norway, 1750–1900'. PhD Dissertation. Faculty of Humanities, University of Oslo.

Burch, E. 1978. 'Caribou Eskimo Origins: An Old Problem Reconsidered', *Arctic Anthropology* 15 (1): 1–38.

Burch, E. 1986. 'The Caribou Inuit', in R.B. Morrsion and C. Roderick (eds), *Native Peoples: the Canadian Experience*. Toronto: McLelland and Stewart, pp. 74–95.

Carpelan, C. 1975. 'Saamelaisten ja saamelaiskulttuurin alkuperä arkeologin näkökulmasta', *Lapin tutkimusseura: vuosikirja* 16: 3–13.

Carpelan, C. 2003. 'Inarilaisten arkeologiset vaiheet', in V.P. Lehotola (ed.), *Inari – Aanaar*. Oulu: Inarin historia jääkaudesta nykypäivään, pp. 29–95.

Carsten, J. 1995a. 'Houses in Langkawi: Stable Structures or Mobile Homes?', in J. Carsten and S. Hugh-Jones (eds), *About the House: Lévi-Strauss and Beyond*. Cambridge: Cambridge University Press, pp. 105–28.

Carsten, J. 1995b. 'The Substance of Kinship and the Heat of the Hearth: Feeding, Personhood, and Relatedness among Malays in Pulau Langkawi', *American Ethnologist* 22 (2): 223–41.

Carsten, J. and S. Hugh-Jones. 1995a. *About the House: Lévi-Strauss and Beyond*. Cambridge: Cambridge University Press.

Carsten, J. and S. Hugh-Jones. 1995b. 'Introduction', in J. Carsten and S. Hugh-Jones (eds), *About the House: Lévi-Strauss and Beyond*. Cambridge: Cambridge University Press, pp. 1–46.

Chang, K.C. 1962. 'A Typology of Settlement and Community Patterns in Some Circumpolar Societies', *Arctic Anthropology* 1 (1): 28–41.

Chapin, M., Z. Lamb and B. Threlkeld. 2005. 'Mapping Indigenous Lands', *Annual Review of Anthropology* 34 (1): 619–38.

Chichlo, B. 2000. 'Sous le toit de la *qaygi* : Folklore et pratique rituelle chez les Yuit de la Tchoukotka', *Études/Inuit/Studies* 24 (2): 7–31.

Christiansson, H. and H. Wigenstam. 1980. 'Nordarkeologiprojektets Arvidsjaursinventering', *Fornvännen* 75: 163–9.

Cooney, G. 2003. 'Introduction: Seeing the Land from the Sea', *World Archaeology* 35 (3): 323–8.

Correll, T.C. 1976. 'Language and Location in Traditional Inuit Societies', in M.M.R. Freeman (ed.), *Inuit Land Use and Occupancy Project, Vol. 2: Supporting Studies*. Ottawa: Department of Indian and Northern Affairs, pp. 173–80.

Cruikshank, J. 2005. *Do Glaciers Listen? Local Knowledge, Colonial Encounters, and Social Imagination*. Vancouver: University of British Columbia Press.

Davydov, V. 2011. 'People on the Move: Development Projects and the Use of Space by Northern Baikal Reindeer Herders, Hunters and Fishermen'. PhD Dissertation. Department of Anthropology, University of Aberdeen.

Dawson, P.C. 2008. 'Unfriendly Architecture: Using Observations of Inuit Spatial Behavior to Design Culturally Sustaining Houses in Arctic Canada', *Housing Studies* 23 (1): 111–28.

Dawson, P.C. 2011. 'Arviat Oral History Project', Unpublished fieldnotes in possession of the author. Department of Archaeology, University of Calgary.

Deleuze, G. and F. Guattari 2004. *A Thousand Plateaus: Capitalism and Schizophrenia*, trans. B. Massumi. London: Continuum.

Digard, J.-P. 1990. *L'homme et les animaux domestiques*. Paris: Fayard.

Dolgikh, B.O. 1960. *Rodovoi i plemennoi sostav narodov Sibiri v XVII veke*. Trudy Instituta Etnografii im. N.N. Mikhlukho-Maklaia, Novaia Seriia, 55. Moskva: Nauka.

Drivenes, E.A. 1985. *Fiskarbonde og gruveslusk*. Oslo: Universitetsforlaget.

Drivenes, E.A., M. A Hauan, and H.A. Wold (eds). 1994. *Nordnorsk kulturhistorie. Det gjenstridige landet*. Oslo: Gyldendal norsk forlag.

Durkheim, É. 1982 [1895]. *The Rules of the Sociological Method*. New York: Free Press.

Dyrvik, S. 1983. *Historisk demografi: ei innføring i metodane*. Bergen: Universitetsforlaget.

Dyrvik, S. 1993. 'Farmers at Sea: A Study of Fishermen in North Norway, 1801–1920', *Journal of Family History* 18 (4): 341–56.

Edsman, C.-M. 1994. *Jägaren och makterna: samiska och finska björnceremonier*. Uppsala: Dialekt- och folkminnesarkivet.

Elbo, J. 1952. 'Lapp Reindeer Movements across the Frontiers of Northern Scandinavia', *Polar Record* 6 (43): 348–58.

Ermolova, N.V. 2007. 'Reka v trekh mirakh evenkiiskoi Vselennoi' in L.R. Pavlinskaia (ed.), *Reki i narody Sibiri*. Sankt-Peterburg: Nauka, pp. 87–126.

Eronen, M., P. Zetterberg, K. Briffa, M. Lingholm, J. Meriläinen, and M. Timonen. 2002. 'The Supra-Long Scots Pine Tree-Ring Record for Finnish Lapland: Part 1, Chronology Construction and Initial References', *The Holocene* 12 (6): 673–80.

Evjen, B. 2011. 'Finn in Flux. "Finn" as a Category in Norwegian Population Censuses of the Nineteenth and Twentieth Centuries', in P. Axelsson and P. Sköld (eds), *Indigenous Peoples and Demography: The Complex Relation Between Identity and Statistics*. Oxford and New York: Berghahn Books, pp. 163–72.

Evjen, B. and L.I. Hansen. 2009. 'One People – Many Names: On Different Designations for the Sámi Population in the Norwegian County of Nordland through the Centuries', *Continuity and Change* 24 (2): 211–43.

Falch, T. 1994. *Bruk av land og vann i Finnmark i historisk perspektiv*. Norges offentlige utredninger 1994: 21 Oslo: Statens Forvaltningstjenestestatens trykning.

Feit, H.A. 1994. 'Dreaming of Animals: The Waswanipi Cree Shaking Tent Ceremony in Relation to Environment, Hunting, and Missionization', in T. Irimoto and T. Yamada (eds), *Circumpolar Religion and Ecology: An Anthropology of the North*. Tokyo: University of Tokyo Press, pp. 289–316.

Feit, H.A. 1988. *Self-Management and State-Management: Forms of Knowing and Managing Northern Wildlife*. Boreal Institute for Northern Studies Occasional Publication 23. Edmonton: Boreal Institute.

Fellman, I. (ed). 1910. *Handlingar och uppsatser angående Finska Lappmarken och lapparne*. Helsingfors: Finska litteratursällskapets tryckeri.

Fienup-Riordan, A. 1990. *Eskimo Essays: Yup'ik Lives and How We See Them*. New Brunswick: Rutgers University Press.

Fienup-Riordan, A. 1994. *Boundaries and Passages: Rule and Ritual in Yup'ik Eskimo Oral Tradition*. Norman: University of Oklahoma Press.

Fienup-Riordan, A. 2005. *Ciuliamta Akluit: Things of Our Ancestors: Yup'ik Elders Explore the Jacobsen Collection at the Ethnologisches Museum, Berlin*. Seattle: University of Wisconsin Press, in association with Calista Elders Council, Bethel, Alaska.

Flusser, V. 1999. *The Shape of Things: A Philosophy of Design*. London: Reaktion.

Fortescue, M. 1988. *Eskimo Orientation Systems*. Meddelelser om Grønland, Man and Society 11. Copenhagen: Nut Nordisk Forlag.

Fossum, B. 2006. *Förfädernas land. En arkeologisk studie av ritualla lämningar i Sápmi, 300 f. Kr. – 1600 e. Kr*. Studia Archaeologica Universitatis Umensis 22. PhD Dissertation. Umeå: Umeå universitet.

Frampton, K. 1995. *Studies in Tectonic Culture: The Poetics of Construction in Nineteenth and Twentieth Century Architecture*. Cambridge, Mass.: MIT Press.

Friesen, T.M. 2007. 'Hearth Rows, Hierarchies and Arctic Hunter-Gatherers: The Construction of Equality in the Late Dorset Period', *World Archaeology* 39 (2): 194–214.

Fure, E. 1986. 'Gamle i flergenerasjonsfamilier – en seiglivet myte?', *Historisk tidsskrift* 1: 16–35.

Furset, O.J. 1995. *Fangstgroper og ildsteder i Kautokeino kommune*. Rapport fra forskningsutgraving 24 Juli–3 September 1994. Stensilserie B nr 37. Tromsø: Institutt for samfunnsvitenskap. Universitetet i Tromsø.

Gauslaa, J. 2007. *Samisk naturbruk og rettssituasjon fra Hedmark til Troms*. Norges offentlige utredninger 2007: 14. Oslo: Departementenes servicesenter, Informasjonsforvaltning.

Gell, A. 1998. *Art and Agency: An Anthropological Theory*. Oxford: Clarendon Press.

Gibson, J.J. 1979. *The Ecological Approach to Visual Perception*. Boston: Houghton Mifflin.

Gieryn, T.F. 2002. 'What Buildings Do', *Theory and Society* 31 (1): 35–74.

Gieser, T. 2008. 'Embodiment, Emotion and Empathy: A Phenomenological Approach to Apprenticeship Learning', *Anthropological Theory* 8 (3): 299–318.

Gillespie, S.D. 2000. 'Lévi-Strauss: Maison and Société à Maisons', in R.A Joyce and S.D. Gillespie (eds), *Beyond Kinship: Social and Material Reproduction in House Societies*. Philadelphia: University of Pennsylvania Press, pp. 22–52.

Gladwin, T. 1964. 'Culture and Logical Process', in W.H. Goodenough (ed.), *Explorations in Cultural Anthropology*. New York: McGraw-Hill, pp. 167–77.

Godelier, M. 1986. *The Mental and the Material*. London: Verso.

Golbtseva, V. 2008. 'The Thanksgiving Ceremony "Mn'in"', in V.V. Obukhov (ed.), *Beringia – A Bridge of Friendship – Materials of the International Scientific and Practical Conference*. Tomsk: Tomsk State University Pedagogical University Press, pp 42–51.

Gorbacheva, V. 2004. *Obriady i prazdniki Koriakov*. Sankt Peterburg: Nauka.

Gracheva, G.N. 1983. *Traditsionnoe mirovozzrenie okhotnikov Taimyra (na materialakh Nganasan XIV-nachala XX v.)*. Leningrad: Izdatel'stvo Nauka.

Grydeland, S.E. 2001. *De sjøsamiske siidaen. En studie med utgangspunkt i Kvænangen, Nord-Troms*. Nord-Troms Museums Skrifter 1. Sørkjosen: Nord-Troms museum.

Gudeman, S. and A. Rivera. 1990. *Conversations in Colombia: The Domestic Economy in Life and Text*. Cambridge: Cambridge University Press.

Guinnane, T.W. 1996. 'The Family, State Support, and Generational Relations in Rural Ireland at the Turn of the Twentieth Century', in T.K. Hareven (ed.), *Aging and Generational Relation over the Life Course: A Historical and Cross-Cultural Perspective*. Berlin: de Gruyter, pp. 100–19.

Hail, B.A. and K.C. Duncan. 1989. *Out of the North: The Subarctic Collection of the Haffenreffer Museum of Anthropology*. Bristol: Haffenreffer Museum of Anthropology, Brown University.

Hajnal, J. 1965. 'European Marriage Patterns in Perspective', in D.V. Glass and D.E.C. Eversley (eds), *Population in History: Essays in Historical Demography*. Chicago: Aldine, pp. 101–38.

Halemba, A. 2006. *The Telengits of Southern Siberia: Landscape, Religion, and Knowledge in Motion*. New York: Routledge.

Halinen, P. 2005. *Prehistoric Hunters of Northernmost Lapland – Settlement Patterns and Subsistence Strategies*. Iskos Suomen muinaismuistoyhdistys 1. Helsinki: Finnish Antiquarian Society.

Halinen, P. 2009. 'Change and Continuity of Saami Dwellings and Dwelling Sites from the Late Iron Age to the 18th Century', in T. Äikäs (ed.), *Máttut – Maddagat – The Roots of Saami Ethnicities, Societies and Space/Places*. Oulu: Giellagas Institute, pp. 100–16.

Hallam, E. and T. Ingold (eds). 2007. *Creativity and Cultural Improvisation*. Oxford: Berg.

Hallendy, N. 1994. '*Inuksuit:* Semalithic Figures Constructed by Inuit in the Canadian Arctic', in D. Morrison and J-L. Pilon (eds), *Threads of Arctic Prehistory: Papers in Honour of William E. Taylor, Jr.*, Archaeological Survey of Canada, Mercury Series, Paper 149. Ottawa: Canadian Museum of Civilization, pp. 385–408.

Hallendy, N. 1997. 'Places of Power', *Canadian Geographic* 117 (2): 42–8.

Hallowell, I. 1960. 'Ojibwa Ontology, Behavior, and World View', in S. Diamond (ed.), *Culture in History: Essays in Honor of Paul Radin*. New York: Columbia University Press, pp. 19–57.

Hamari, P. 1996. *Taking a Look at a Sámi Way of Life – Rectangular Hearths in Finnish Lapland or: A Periphery Reconsidered*. Kontakstencil 39. Umeå: Umeå universitet, pp. 127–35.

Hamayon, R.N. 1990. *La chasse à l'âme: Esquisse d'une théorie du chamanisme sibérien*. Paris: Société d'ethnologie.

Hammel, E.A. and P. Laslett. 1974. 'Comparing Household Structure over Time and between Cultures', *Comparative Studies in Society and History* 16 (1): 73–109.

Hansen, L.I. and B. Olsen. 2004. *Samenes historie fram til 1750*. Oslo: Cappelen Akademisk Forlag.

Hansen, L.I. and T. Meyer. 1991. 'The Ethnic Classification in the Late 19th Century Censuses: A Case Study from Southern Troms, Norway', *Acta Borealia* 2: 13–56.

Hansen, L.I. and B. Olsen. 2004. *Samenes historie fram til 1750*. Oslo: Cappelen Akademisk Forlag.

Hareven, T.K. 1982. *Family Time and Industrial Time: The Relationship between the Family and Work in a New England Industrial Community*. Cambridge: Cambridge University Press.

Hareven, T.K. 1994. 'Aging and Generational Relation: A Historical and Life Course Perspective', *Annual Review of Sociology* 20: 437–61.

Hayden, B. 1995. 'Pathways to Power: Principles for Creating Socioeconomic Inequalities', in T.D. Price and G. Feinman (eds), *Foundations of Social Inequality*. New York: Plenum Press, pp. 15–86.

Hearne, S. 1958. *A Journey from Prince of Wales Fort in Hudson's Bay to the Northern Ocean in the Years 1769, 1770, 1771, and 1772 [1795]*. R. Glover (ed.). Toronto: MacMillan.

Hedman, S.-D. 2003. *Boplatser och offerplatser: Ekonomisk strategi och boplatsmönster bland skogssamer 700–1600 AD*. Studia archaeologica universitatis Umensis 17. PhD Dissertation. Umeå: Umeå universitet.

Hedman, S.-D. 2005. 'Renskötselns uppkomst i Övre Norrlands skogsområden' in O. Andersen (ed.), *Fra villreinjakt til reindrift – Gåddebivdos boatsojsujttuj*. Árran lulesamisk senter Skriftserie nr. 1. Drag: Árran lulesamisk senter, pp. 13–32.

Hedman, S.-D. and B. Olsen. 2009. 'Transition and Order: A Study of Rectangular Hearths in Pasvik, Arctic Norway', *Fennoscandia archaelogica* XXVI: 3–22.

Heidegger, M. 1971. *Poetry, Language, Thought*, trans. A. Hofstadter. New York: Harper and Row.

Heine, M., A. Andre, I. Kritsch, A. Cardinal, and the Elders of Tsiigehtchic. 2007. *Gwichya Gwich'in Googwandak: The History and Stories of the Gwichya Gwich'in as Told by the Elders of Tsiigehtchic*. Tsiigehtchic and Fort McPherson: Gwich'in Social and Cultural Institute.

Helama, S. 2004. *Millennia-Long Tree-Ring Chronologies as Records of Climate Variability in Finland*. PhD Dissertation. Helsinki: Yliopistopain.

Helama, S., M. Lingholm, M. Timonen, J. Meriläinen, and M. Eronen. 2002. 'The Supra-Long Scots Pine Tree-Ring Record for Finnish Lapland: Part 2, Interannual to Centennial Variability in Summer Temperatures for 7,500 Years', *The Holocene* 12 (6): 681–7.

Helland-Hansen, K. 1997. *Føderådsordningens historie i Norge*. Riksarkivaren skriftserie 3. Oslo: Riksarkivet.

Helm, J. 1972. 'The Dogrib Indians', in M.G. Bicchieri (ed.), *Hunters and Gatherers Today: A Socioeconomic Study of Eleven Such Cultures in the Twentieth Century*. New York: Holt, Reinhart and Winston.

Helm, J. 1980. 'Female Infanticide, European Diseases, and Population Levels among the Mackenzie Dene', *American Ethnologist* 7 (2): 259–85.

Helm, J. 1989. 'Epilogue: Women's Work, Women's Art', in B.A. Hail and K.C. Duncan (eds), *Out of the North: The Subarctic Collection of the Haffenreffer Museum of Anthropology*. Seattle: University of Washington Press.

Helm, J. 1998. Personal Communication. Letters and notes in the Author's possession. Yellowknife.

Helm, J. (MacNeish) 1956. 'Leadership among the Northeastern Athasbascans', *Anthropologica* n.s. 2: 131–63.

Helm, J. and T.D. Andrews. 1999. 'Chief's Lodge Comes Home', *Anthropology News* 40 (4): 19–20.

Helm, J. and N.O. Lurie. 1966. *The Dogrib Hand Game*. Ottawa: National Museums of Canada.

Herva, V.P. 2010. 'Buildings as Persons: Relationality and the Life of Buildings in a Northern Periphery of Early Modern Sweden', *Antiquity* 84 (324): 440–52.

Hirdman, Y. (ed.). 1992. *Kvinnohistoria: om kvinnors villkor från antiken till våra dagar.* Stockholm: Utbildningsradion.

Hodder, I. 1982. *Symbols in Action*. Cambridge: Cambridge University Press.

Hodder, I. 1989. *The Meanings of Things: Material Culture and Symbolic Expression.* London: Unwin Hyman.

Hoffmann, M. 1974. *The Warp-Weighted Loom: Studies in History and Technology of an Ancient Implement*. Oslo: Universitetsforlaget.

Hubka, T. 1979. 'Just Folks Designing: Vernacular Designers and the Generation of Form', *Journal of Architectural Education* 32 (3): 27–9.

Hudson, H.D. 1994. *Blueprints and Blood: The Stalinization of Soviet Architecture, 1917–1937*. Princeton: Princeton University Press.

Hultblad, F. 1968. *Övergång från Nomadism till Agrar Bosättning i Jokkmokks Socken.* Acta Lapponica XIV. Lund: Nordiska Museet.

Humphrey, C. 1988. 'No Place Like Home in Anthropology: The Neglect of Architecture', *Anthropology Today* 4 (1): 16–18.

Hvarfner, H. 1956. 'Rapport over kulturhistoriska undersökningar inom Ume älvs källområden, Lappland 1954–1955 Storuman till Juktåns infall i Ume älv. Storuman, Steselse, Långsele, Barsele, Grundfors m.m.', Del I: text och fotografier. Unpublished research report. Stockholm: Swedish National Heritage Board.

Hvarfner, H. 1957. 'Endast före eller även under järnåldern? Om det norrländska inlandets stenålderskultur', *Västerbotten 1957*: 70–115.

Iampol'skaia, I.A. 1992. 'Shamanskii chum evenkov: istoriia otkrytiia, rezul'taty issledovanii, gipotezy', in V.A. Popov (ed.), *Etnosy i etnicheskie protsessy. Pamiati P.F. Itsa*. Moskva: Vostochnaia literatura, pp. 107–18.

INDIKO 2012. Demografiska databasen, Umeå universitet. INDIKO – kyrkböcker på nätet (available at http://www.ddb.umu.se/tjanster/indiko/ [accessed 20 July 2012]).

Ingold, T. 1978. 'The Transformation of the Siida', *Ethnos* 43 (1–4): 146–62.

Ingold, T. 1980. *Hunters, Pastoralists and Ranchers: Reindeer Economies and their Transformation*. Cambridge: Cambridge University Press.

Ingold, T. 1993. 'The Art of Translation in a Continuous World', in G. Pálsson (ed.), *Beyond Boundaries: Understanding, Translation and Anthropological Discourse*. Oxford: Berg, pp. 210–30.

Ingold, T. 2000a. *The Perception of the Environment: Essays in Livelihood, Dwelling and Skill*. London: Routledge.

Ingold, T. 2000. 'Making Culture and Weaving the World', in P. Graves-Brown (ed.), *Matter, Materiality and Modern Culture*. London: Routledge, pp. 324–32.

Ingold, T. 2007a. *Lines: A Brief History*. London: Routledge.

Ingold, T. 2007b. 'Materials against Materiality', *Archaeological Dialogues* 14 (1): 1–16.
Ingold, T. 2011. *Being Alive: Essays on Movement, Knowledge and Description*. London: Routledge.
Ingold, T. and E. Hallam. 2007. 'Creativity and Cultural Improvisation: An Introduction', in E. Hallam and T. Ingold (eds), *Creativity and Cultural Improvisation*. Oxford: Berg, pp. 1–24.
Itkonen, T.I. 1921. *Lappalaisten ruokatalous*. Suomalais-ugrilaisen Seuran Toimituksia 51. Helsinki: Société finno-ougrienne.
Johannessen, K. 1999. 'Åsetesrett', in S. Imsen and H Winge (eds), *Norsk Historisk leksikon*. Oslo: Cappelen Akademiske Forlag, p. 490.
Johnson, L.M. 2000. '"A Place That's Good," Gitksan Landscape Perception and Ethnoecology', *Human Ecology* 28 (2): 301–25.
Johnson, L.M. 2010. 'Visions of the Land: Kaska Ethnoecology, "Kinds of Place", and "Cultural Landscape"', in L.M. Johnson and E.S. Hunn (eds), *Landscape Ethnoecology: Concepts of Biotic and Physical Space*. Studies in Environmental Anthropology and Ethnobiology. Oxford and New York: Berghahn Books, pp. 203–21.
Johnson, L.M., and E.S. Hunn. 2010. *Landscape Ethnoecology: Concepts of Biotic and Physical Space*. Studies in Environmental Anthropology and Ethnobiology. Oxford: Berghahn Books.
Johnson, M. 1993. *Housing Culture: Traditional Architecture in an English Landscape*. London: UCL Press Limited.
Johnson R.B. and A.J. Onwuegbuzie. 2004. 'Mixed Methods Research: A Research Paradigm Whose Time Has Come', *Educational Researcher* 33 (7): 14–26.
Johnson, R.B., A.J. Onwuegbuzie, and L.A. Turner. 2007. 'Toward a Definition of Mixed Methods Research', *Journal of Mixed Methods Research* 1 (2): 112 –33.
Jåstad, H.L. 2011a. 'Northern Co-Residence across Generations in Northernmost Norway during the Last Part of the Nineteenth Century'. PhD Dissertation. University of Tromsø.
Jåstad, H.L. 2011b. 'Endring i samisk og norsk husholdsstruktur – Nord-Troms og Finnmark i perioden 1865–1900', *Historisk Tidsskrift* 90 (1): 33–61.
Jåstad, H.L. 2011c. 'The Effect of Ethnicity and Economy upon Intergenerational Co-Residence: Northern Norway during the Last Part of the Nineteenth Century', *Journal of Family History* 36 (3): 263–85.
Keane, W. 1997. *Signs of Recognition*. Berkeley: University of California Press.
Keilhau, B.M. 1831. *Reise i Øst- och Vest-Finn-marken:samt til Beeren-Eiland og Spitsbergen: i aarene 1827 og 1828*. Christiania: Cappelen.
Keith, D. 2004. 'Caribou, River and Ocean: Harvaqtuurmiut Landscape Organization and Orientation', *Études/Inuit/Studies* 28 (2): 39–56.
Kemp, W.B. 1984. 'Baffinland Eskimo', in D. Damas (ed.), *Arctic*, Handbook of North American Indians 5. Washington, DC: Smithsonian Institution, pp. 463–75.
Kent, S. 1984. *Analyzing Activity Areas : An Ethnoarchaeological Study of the Use of Space*. Albuquerque: University of New Mexico Press.
Kent, S. 1990. *Domestic Architecture and the Use of Space : An Interdisciplinary Cross-Cultural Study*. New Directions in Archaeology. Cambridge and New York: Cambridge University Press.
Kerttula, A. 2000. *Antler on the Sea: The Yup'ik and Chukchi of the Russian Far East*. Ithaca and London: Cornell University Press.

Kertzer, D.I. 1991. 'Household History and Sociological Theory', *Annual Review of Sociology* 17: 155–79.

Kertzer, D.I. 1995. 'Toward a Historical Demography of Aging' in D. Ketzer and P. Laslett (eds), *Aging in the Past: Demography, Society and Old Age*. Berkeley: University of California Press, pp. 363–83.

Kertzer. D.I. and D. Arel. 2002. 'Censuses, Identity Formation, and the Struggle for Political Power', in D.I. Kertzer and D. Arel (eds), *Census and Identity: The Politics of Race, Ethnicity, and Language in National Censuses*. Cambridge: Cambridge University Press, pp. 1–42.

Kertzer, D.I. and M. Barbagli (eds). 2002. *Family Life in the Long Nineteenth Century, 1789–1913*. New Haven and London: Yale University Press.

Kertzer D.I. and P. Laslett (eds). 1995. *Aging in the Past: Demography, Society and Old Age*. Berkeley: University of California Press.

Kharuzin, N. 1896. *Istoriia razvitiia zhilishcha u kochevykh i polukochevykh tiurkskikh i mongol'skikh narodnostei Rossii*. Moskva: AA. Levensop.

Khasanova, M.M. 2007. 'Reka i mirovozzreniia narodov Nizhnego Amura (k probleme kul'turogeneza)', in L.R. Pavlinskaia (ed.), *Reki i narody Sibiri*. Sankt-Peterburg: Nauka, pp. 182–215.

Klee, P. 1973. *Noteboooks, Volume 2: The Nature of Nature*, trans. H. Norden, ed. J. Spiller. London: Lund Humphries.

Klobystin, L.P. 2006. *Taymyr: the Archaeology of Northernmost Eurasia*. Washington, DC: Arctic Studies Center, National Museum of Natural History, Smithsonian Institution.

Korhola, A., K. Vasko, H.T. Toivonen, and H. Olander. 2002. 'Holocene Temperature Changes in Northern Fennoscandia Reconstructed from Chironomids Using Bayesian Modeling', *Quaternary Science Reviews* 21 (16): 1841–60.

Korhola, A., J. Weckström, L. Holmström, and P. Erästö. 2000. 'A Quantitative Holocene Climatic Record from Diatoms in Northern Fennoscandia', *Quaternary Research* 54 (2): 284–94.

Korpijaakko-Labba, K. 1994. *Om samernas rättsliga ställning i Sverige-Finland: en rättshistorisk utredning av markanvändningsförhållanden och rättigheter i Västerbottens lappmark före mitten av 1700-talet*. Helsingfors: Juristförbundets förlag.

Kropotkin, P.A. 1873. *Otchet ob Olekminsko-Vitimskoi ekspeditsii*. Sankt Peterburg: tip. Bezobrazova.

Kropotkin, P.A. 1904. 'The Orography of Asia', *The Geographical Journal* 23 (3): 331–61.

Krupnik, I. 1998. 'Understanding Reindeer Pastoralism in Modern Siberia: Ecological Continuity versus State Engineering', in J. Ginat and A.M. Khazanov (eds), *Changing Nomads in a Changing World*. Brighton: Sussex Academy Press, pp. 223–42.

Kultti, S. 2004. *Holocene Changes in Treelines and Climate from Ural Mountains to Finnish Lapland*. Typescript (available at http://ethesis.helsinki.fi/julkaisut/mat/geolo/vk/kultti/holocene.pdf).

Kultti, S., K. Mikkola, T. Virtanen, M. Timonen, and M. Eronen. 2006. 'Past Changes in the Scots Pine Forest Line and Climate in Finnish Lapland: A Study Based on Megafossils, Lake Sediments, and GIS-Based Vegetation and Climate Data', *The Holocene* 16 (3): 381–91.

Kuokkanen, R. 2009. 'Indigenous Women in Traditional Economies: The Case of Sámi Reindeer Herding', *Signs* 34 (3): 499–504.

Kuznetsova, V. 1957. 'Materialy po prazdnikam i obriadam amguêmskikh Chukchei', *Sibirskii etnograficheskii sbornik* 2: 263–326.

Kwon, H. 1993. 'Maps and Actions: Nomadic and Sedentary Space in a Siberian Reindeer Farm'. PhD Dissertation. Department of Social Anthropology: University of Cambridge.

Lambert, J.-L. (ed.). 2005–2006. *L'Orientation*, Special Issue of *Études mongoles et sibériennes, centrasiatiques et tibétaines,* 36–37 [Entire issue].

Laslett, P. 1972. 'Introduction', in P. Laslett and R. Wall (eds), *Household and Family in Past Time*. Cambridge: Cambridge University Press, pp. 1–90.

Laslett, P. 1977. 'Characteristics of the Western Family Considered over Time', *Journal of Family History* 2 (2): 89–116.

Laslett P. and R. Wall. 1972. *Household and Family in Past Time*. Cambridge: Cambridge University Press.

Latour, B. 2005. *Reassembling the Social: An Introduction to Actor-Network-Theory*. Oxford: Oxford University Press.

Lavrillier, A. 2000. 'La Taïga: le berceau des Évenks. Les représentations de la nature chez un peuple altaïque de Sibérie', *Boréales* 78–81: 25–44.

Lavrillier, A. 2003. 'De l'oubli à la reconstruction d'un rituel collectif: l'Ikenipke des Evenks. *Slovo* 28–29: 169–92.

Lavrillier, A. 2005–2006. 'S'orienter avec les rivières chez les Evenks du Sud-Est sibérien: un système d'orientation spatial, identitaire et rituel', *Études mongoles et sibériennes, centrasiatiques et tibétaines* 36-37: 95–138.

Lavrillier, A. 2008. 'Comment les Evenks de Sibérie méridionale ont modifié le rituel sur le gibier tué', *Annales de la Fondation Fyssen* 22: 112–21.

Lavrillier, A. 2011. 'The Creation and Persistence of Cultural Landscapes among the Siberian Evenk: Two Conceptions of 'Sacred' Space', in P. Jordan (ed.), *Landscape and Culture in Northern Eurasia*. Walnut Creek: Left Coast Press, pp. 215–323.

Lawrence, D.L. and S.M. Low. 1990. 'The Built Environment and Spatial Form', *Annual Review of Anthropology* 19: 453–505.

Leach, H.M. 2003. 'Human Domestication Reconsidered', *Current Anthropology* 44 (3): 349–68.

Lee, M., and G.A. Reinhardt. 2003. *Eskimo Architecture: Dwelling and Structure in the Early Historic Period*. Fairbanks: University of Alaska Press, University of Alaska Museum.

Leem, K. 1767 [1975]. *Beskrivelse over Finnmarkens lapper, deres tungemaal, levemaade og forrige avgudsdyrkelse*. København: Rosenkilde og Bagger.

Lehtola, V.-P. 2002. 'The Saami Siida and the Nordic States from the Middle Ages to the Beginning of the 1900s', in K. Karppi and J. Eriksson (eds), *Conflict and Cooperation in the North*. Umeå: Kulturgräns norr, pp. 183–202.

Lévi-Strauss, C. 1955. *Tristes tropiques*, trans. J. and D. Weightman. London: Jonathan Cape.

Levi-Strauss, C. 1979. *Structural Anthropology*. Harmondsworth: Penguin Books.

Lévi-Strauss, C. 1982 [1975]. *The Way of the Masks,* trans. S. Modelski. London: Jonathan Cape.

Lie, E. and H. Roll-Hansen. 2001. *Faktisk talt. Statistikkens historie i Norge*. Oslo: Universitetsforlaget.

Liedgren, L.G., I.M. Bergman, G. Hörnberg, O. Zachrisson, E. Hellberg, L. Östlund, and T.H. DeLuca. 2007. 'Radiocarbon Dating of Prehistoric Hearths in Alpine Northern Sweden: Problems and Possibilities', *Journal of Archaeological Science* 34 (8): 1276–88.

Liedgren, L. and I. Bergman. 2009. 'Aspects of the Construction of Prehistoric Stállo-Foundations and Stállo-Buildings', *Acta Borealia* 26 (1): 3–26.

Lightfoot, A. 2005. 'Skatten i Vesterled. Om sau, ull og tekstiler i det nordatlantiske kulturområde', *P2 Akademiet* XXXV: 153–64.

Linnaeus, C. (Carl von Linné) 1732 [1811]. *Lachesis Lapponica, or a Tour in Lapland, vols. I & II.* New York: Arno Press and the New York Times.

Loovers, J.P.L. 2010. '"You Have to Live It": Pedagogy and Literacy with Teetl'it Gwich'in'. PhD Dissertation. Department of Anthropology, University of Aberdeen.

Lowenstein, T. 1993. *Ancient Land, Sacred Whale – The Inuit Hunt and its Rituals.* Bloomsbury: London.

Lundmark, L. 2002. *Lappen är Ombytlig, Ostadig och Obekväm. Svenska Statens Samepolitik i Rasismens Tidevarv.* Bjurholm: Norrlands universitetsförlag.

Lurie, N.O. 1981. 'Museum Land Revisited', *Human Organization* 40 (2): 180–7.

Mack, J. 2007. 'The Land Viewed from the Sea', *Azania: Archaeological Research in Africa* 42 (1): 1–14.

Makarov, N.A. 1991. '"Eastern" Ornaments of the 11th–13th Centuries in the Sami Areas: Origin and Routes', *Acta Borealia* 8 (2): 57–80.

Marenenok. 1933. 'Mamont i zmei Chzhibdar', *Sibirskie Ogni* 1–10: 161–76.

Mary-Rousselière, G. 1984. 'Iglulik', in D. Damas (ed.), *Arctic*, Handbook of North American Indians 5. Washington, DC: Smithsonian Institution, pp. 431–46.

Mason, J.A. 1946. 'Notes on the Indians of the Great Slave Lake Area', *Yale University Publications in Anthropology* 34: 1–46.

Mauss, M. and H. Beuchat. 1979 [1906]. *Seasonal Variations of the Eskimo: A Study in Social Morphology.* London: Routledge and Kegan Paul Books.

Mebius, H. 1968. *Värro: studier i samernas förkristna offerriter.* Skrifter utgivna av Religionshistoriska institutionen i Uppsala 5. Stockholm: Almqvist and Wiksell.

Meschke, C. (ed.) 1979. *Kulturlandskap i älvdalar III.* Rapport 1979–2. Stockholm: Riksantikvarieämbetet och Statens historiska museer.

Morgan, L.H. 1877. *Ancient Society.* London: MacMillan and Company.

Morgan, L.H. 1881. *Houses and House-Life of the American Aborigines.* Contributions to North American Ethnology 4, Washington, DC: Government Printing Office.

Morphy, F. 2007. 'Uncontained Subjects: "Population" and "Household" in Remote Aboriginal Australia', *Journal of Population Research* 24 (2): 163–84.

Morton, C. 2007. 'Remembering the House: Memory and Materiality in Northern Botswana', *Journal of Material Culture* 12 (2), 157–79.

Mulk, I.-M. 1994. *Sirkas: ett samiskt fångstsamhälle i förändring Kr.f. – 1600 e.Kr.* Studia archaeologia Universitatis Umensis 6. Phd Dissertation. Umea: Umeå universitet.

Mullaney, T.S. 2011. *Coming to Terms with the Nation: Ethnic Classification in Modern China.* Berkeley: University of California Press.

Murray, A. 2002. 'Learning about the Land: Teetl'it Gwich'in Perspectives on Sustainable Resource Use'. MA Thesis. Department of Anthropology, University of Alberta.

Myreeva, A.N., A.M. Aizenshtadt, and I.I. Sheikin (eds). 1990. *Evenkiiskie geroicheskie skazaniia: Khrabryi Sodani-bogatyr, Vsesilnyi bogatyr Develchen v rasshitoi-razukrashennoi odezhde*. Moskva: Nauka.

Myrstad, R. 1996. 'Bjørngraver i Nord-Norge. Spor etter den samiske bjørnkulten', Dissertation (Hovedfagsoppgave). Department of Archaeology, University of Tromsø.

Nabokov, P. and R. Easton. 1989. *Native American Architecture*. New York: Oxford University Press.

Nadel-Klein, J. 2003. *Fishing for Heritage: Modernity and Loss along the Scottish Coast*. Oxford: Berg.

Nango, J. 2009. *The Saami Building Tradition: A Complex Picture. Northern Experiments: The Barents Urban Survey 2009*. Online Resource (available at www.northern experiments.net (accessed 20 July 2012]).

NAPP. 2012. North Atlantic Population Project, Minnesota Population Centre, University of Minnesota (available at www.nappdata.org/napp [accessed 20 July 2012]).

Nesheim, A. 1954. 'Den Sámiske grenevevingen og dens terminologi', in D. Strömbäck (ed.), *Scandinavica Et Finno-Ugrica: Studier tillägnade Björn Collinder, den 22 juli, 1954*. Stockholm: Almquist & Wiksell, pp. 321–41.

Nesheim, A. 1967. 'Eastern and Western Elements in Culture' in Instituttet for Sammenlignende Kulturforskning (ed.), *Lapps and Norsemen in Olden Times*. Serie A (26) Oslo: Institutt for sammenlignende kulturforskning, pp. 104–68.

Nickul, K. 1948. 'The Skolt Lapp Community Suenjelsijd during the Year 1938', *Acta Lapponica* 5 [entire issue].

Niemi, E. 1983. *Vadsøs historie*, bind 1. Vadsø: Vadsø kommune.

Nordin, Å. 2007. *Renskötseln är mitt liv: analys av den samiska renskötselns ekonomiska anpassning*. Umeå: Skrifter från Centrum för Samisk forskning.

Norge. Departementet for det Indre. 1872. *Tabeller vedkommende folkemængendes bevegelse i aaret 1869* C. No. 1. Christiania: Det steenske bogtrykkeri.

Norge. Statistisk Sentralbyrå. 1961. *Dødeligheten og dens årsaker i Norge 1856–1955*. Samfunnsøkonomiske studier 10. Oslo: Statistisk Sentralbyrå.

Nuvano, V.N. 2008. 'Etnoterritorial'naia gruppa "vaezhskie chukchi"', in L.S. Bogoslovskaia, V.S. Krivoshekov, and I.I. Krupnik (eds), *Tropoiu Bogoraza. Nauchnye i literaturnye materialy*. Moskva: Institut Naslediia, pp. 78–84.

Odgaard, U. and F. Kanal. 2003. 'Hearth and Home of the Palaeo-Eskimos', *Études/Inuit/Studies* 27 (1–2): 349–74.

Odner, K. 1983. *Finner og terfinner*. Oslo Occasional Papers in Social Anthropology. Oslo: University of Oslo.

Odner, K. 1992. *The Varanger Saami: Habitation and Economy AD 1200–1900*. Instituttet for sammenlignende kulturforskning, Serie B: Skrifter LXXXVI. Oslo: Novus.

Ojala, C.-G. 2009: *Sámi Prehistories: The Politics of Archaeology and Identity in Northernmost Europe*. Uppsala: Uppsala Universitet, Institutionen för Arkeologi och Antik Historia.

Okely, J. 1983. *The Traveller-Gypsies*. Cambridge: Cambridge University Press.

Olivier, L. 2001. 'Duration, Memory and the Nature of the Archaeological Record', in H. Karlsson (ed.), *It's About Time: The Concept of Time in Archaeology*. Göteborg: Bricoleur Press, pp. 61–70.

Olsen, B. 1984. 'Stabilitet og endring. Produksjon og samfunn i Varanger 800 f.kr-1700 e.kr.'. Magister Thesis. Department of Archaeology, University of Tromsø.

Olsen, B. 1986. 'Norwegian Archaeology and the People Without (Pre-)History, or: How to Create a Myth of a Uniform Past', *Archaeological Review from Cambridge* 5 (1): 25–42.

Olsen, B. 1993. 'Hus mellom steinalder og historisk tid', *Ottar* 1: 36–47.

Olsen, B. 1998. 'Saqqaq Housing and Settlement in Southern Disco Bay, West Greenland', *Acta Borealia* 2: 81–129.

Olsen, B. 2000. 'Nye tider, nye skikker. Om å leve sammen som samer og nordmenn for 1000 år siden', *Ottar* 229: 34–41.

Olsen, B. 2003. 'Belligerent Chieftains and Oppressed Hunters? Changing Conceptions of Inter-Ethnic Relationships in Northern Norway during the Iron Age and Early Medieval Period', in J.H. Barret (ed.), *Contacts, Continuity and Collapse: The Norse Colonization of the North Atlantic*. Studies in the Early Middle Ages. Brepols: Turnhout, pp. 9–31.

Olsen, B. 2007. 'Samenes fortid som arkeologisk forskningsfelt – virkningshistoriske utfordringer', in I. Lundström (ed.), *Historisk rätt? Kultur, politik och juridik i norr.* Stockholm: Riksantikvarieämbetet, pp. 192–207.

Olsen, B. 2010. *In Defense of Things: Archaeology and the Ontology of Objects.* Lanham, MD: Altamira Press.

Olwig, K. 2008a. 'Performing on Landscape versus Doing Landscape: Perambulatory Practice, Sight and the Sense of Belonging', in T. Ingold and J. Lee Vergunst (eds), *Ways of Walking: Ethnography and Practice on Foot.* Aldershot: Ashgate, pp. 81–91.

Olwig, K. 2008b. 'The Jutland Cipher: Unlocking the Meaning and Power of a Contested Landscape', in M. Jones and K.R. Olwig (eds), *Nordic Landscapes: Region and Belonging On the Northern Edge of Europe.* Minneapolis: University of Minnesota Press, pp. 12–49.

Osborne, R. 2007. 'Is Archaeology Equal to Equality', *World Archaeology* 39 (2): 143–50.

Osgood, C. 1970 [1936]. *Contributions to the Ethnography of the Kutchin.* New Haven: Human Relations Area Files Press.

Ostrom, E. 2003. 'Toward a Behaviour Theory Linking Trust, Reciprocity, and Reputation', in E. Ostrom and J. Walker (eds), *Trust and Reciprocity: Interdisciplinary Lessons from Experimental Research.* New York: Russell Sage Foundation, pp. 19–79.

Ovsiannikov, O.V. 1993. *The Arctic Russia in the Middle Ages: Recent Archaeological Discoveries and the Ancient Trade Route along the Arctic Coast.* Stencilserie, Tromsø: ISV, University of Tromsø.

Paavola, S. 2004. 'Abduction through Grammar, Critic, and Methodeutic', *Transactions of the Charles S. Peirce Society: A Quarterly Journal in American Philosophy* 40 (2): 245–70.

Paine, R. 1970. 'Lappish Decisions, Partnerships, Information Management, and Sanctions: A Nomadic Pastoral Adaptation', *Ethnology* 9 (1): 52–67.

Paine, R. 2009. *Camps of the Tundra: Politics through Reindeer among Saami Pastoralists.* Oslo: Novus Press.

Palmer, A. 2005. *Maps of Experience: The Anchoring of Land to Story in Shuswap Discourse.* Toronto: University of Toronto Press.

Palmore, J.A. and R.W. Gardner. 1994. *Measuring Mortality, Fertility, and Natural Increase: A Self-Teaching Guide to Elementary Measures*. Honolulu: East-West Centre.

Pehrson, R.N. 1957. *The Bilateral Network of Social Relations in Könkömä Lapp District*. Bloomington: Indiana University.

Permilovskaia, A.B. 2005. *Krest'ianskii dom v kul'ture Russkogo Severa (XIX- Nachalo XX veka)*. Arkhangel'sk: Pravda Severa.

Peterson, R. 1984. 'East Greenland before 1950' in D. Damas (ed.), *Arctic*, Handbook of North American Indians 5. Washington, DC: Smithsonian Institution, pp. 622–39.

Plattet, P. 2005. 'Le double jeu de la chance. Imitation et substitution dans les rituels chamaniques contemporains de deux populations rurales du Nord-Kamtchatka (Fédération de Russie, Extrême-Orient Sibérien): les chasseurs maritimes de Lesnaia et les éleveurs de rennes d'Atchaïvaiam', Ph.D Dissertation. University of Neuchâtel (Switzerland) and Ecole Pratique des Hautes Etudes (Paris, France).

Polomoshnov, I. 1991. *Poslanets solntsa, chukotskie rasskazy*. Anadyr': chukotskoe proizvodstvennoe poligrafob''edinenie.

Popkov, I.V. and D.Dz. Anderson. 2002. *Zdororov'e i zdravookhranenie*. Novosibirsk: Sibprint.

Popov, A.A. 1963. 'The "Kuoika," Guardian Spirits of Family and Clan among the Nganasan', *Arctic Anthropology* 1 (2): 122–30.

Posel, D.R. 2001. 'Who Are the Heads of Household, What Do They Do, and Is the Concept of Headship Useful? An Analysis of Headship in South Africa', *Development Southern Africa* 18 (5): 651–70.

Povoroznyuk, O., J.O. Habeck, and V. Vaté. 2010. 'Introduction: On the Definition, Theory, and Practice of Gender Shift in the North of Russia', *Anthropology of East Europe Review* 28 (2): 1–37 (available at http://scholarworks.iu.edu/journals/index.php/aeer/article/view/929).

Price, N. 2002. 'The Viking Way: Religion and War in Late Iron Age Scandinavia'. PhD Dissertation. Uppsala: Uppsala University.

Pyne, S. 1995. *World Fire: The Culture of Fire on Earth*. Seattle: University of Washington Press.

Qvigstad, J. 1893. *Nordische Lehnworter im Lappischen*. Christiania: In commission bei J. Dybwad.

Ragtytval', R.I. 1986. 'Meinypil'gynskaia kollektsiia semeinykh sviatyn', *Zapiski chukotskogo kraevedcheskogo muzeiia*, XIV: 170–91.

Rapoport, A. 1969. *House Form and Culture*. Foundations of Cultural Geography Series. Englewood Cliffs, NJ: Prentice-Hall.

Rapoport, A. 1982. *The Meaning of the Built Environment: A Nonverbal Communication Approach*. Tucson: The University of Arizona Press.

Rapoport, A. 1990. 'Systems of Activity and Systems of Settings', in Susan Kent (ed.), *Domestic Architecture and the Use of Space: An Interdisciplinary Cross-Cultural Study*. New Directions in Archaeology. Cambridge and New York: Cambridge University Press, pp. 9–20.

Rathke, J. 1907. *Afhandlinger om de norske fiskerier og Beretninger om reiser i aarene 1795–1802*. Bergen: J. Griegs bogtrykkeri.

Renbeteskommissionen af 1907. 1909. *Protokoll öfver de af kommissionen år 1908 i Tromsø amt hållna förhör: jämte register och det till grund för förhören liggande frågeformulär*. Stockholm: Norstedt.

Ridington, R. 1982. 'Technology, World View, and Adaptive Strategy in a Northern Hunting Society', *Canadian Review of Sociology and Anthropology* 19 (4): 469–81.

Ridington, R. 1983. 'From Artifice to Artifact: Stages in the Industrialization of a Northern Native Community', *Journal of Canadian Studies* 18 (3): 55–66.

Ridington, R. 1994. 'Tools in the Mind: Northern Athapaskan Ecology, Religion, and Technology', in T. Irimoto and T. Yamada (eds), *Circumpolar Religion and Ecology: An Anthropology of the North*. Tokyo: University of Tokyo Press, pp. 273–88.

Robbe, P. 1977. 'Orientation et repérage chez les Tileqilamiut côte est du Groenland', *Études/Inuit/Studies* 1 (2): 73–83.

Ruggles, S. 2003. 'Multigenerational Families in Nineteenth-Century America', *Continuity and Change* 18 (1): 139–65.

Ruggles, S. 2007. 'The Decline of Intergenerational Co-Residence in the United States, 1850 to 2000', *American Sociological Review* 72: 964–89.

Rundstrom, R.A. 1990. 'A Cultural Interpretation of Inuit Map Accuracy', *Geographical Review* 80 (2): 155–68.

Ruong, I. 1937. *Fjällapparna i Jukkasjärvi Socken*. Uppsala: Appelbergs boktryckeriaktiebolag.

Ruong, I. 1969. *Samerna*. Stockholm: Aldus/Bonnier.

Rushforth, S. 1984. *Bear Lake Athapaskan Kinship and Task Group Formation*. Canadian Ethnology Service Paper No. 96. Ottawa: National Museums of Canada.

Rushforth, S. and J.S. Chisholm. 1991. *Cultural Persistence: Continuity in Meaning and Moral Responsibility among the Bear Lake Athapaskans*. Tucson: University of Arizona Press.

Russell, F. 1894. 'Journal of a Trip from Edmonton, Alberta, North Via Lesser Slave Lake to Lake Athabasca, Saskatchewan, and along Mackenzie River to Fort Good Hope; and Also Between Great Slave and Great Bear Lakes and Coppermine River, Mackenzie April 26 – August 19, 1894'. Manuscript 1274, National Anthropological Archives, Smithsonian Institution.

Russell, F. 1898. *Explorations in the Far North*. Iowa City: University of Iowa.

Rybczynski, W. 1989. *The Most Beautiful House in the World*. New York: Penguin.

Ränk, G. 1949. 'Grundprinciper för disponeringen av utrymmet i de lapska kåtorna och gammerna', *Folk-liv. Acta ethnologica et folkloristica Europaea* 12–13: 87–111.

Sandstrom, A. 2000. 'Toponymic Groups and House Organization: The Nahauas of Northern Veracruz, Mexico', in R.A. Joyce and S.D. Gillespie (eds), *Beyond Kinship: Social and Material Reproduction in House Societies*. Philadelphia: University of Pennsylvania Press, pp. 53–72.

Sara, M.N. 2002. 'The Sami Siida Institution as a Social and an Ecological Regulation System', in P. Soppela et al. (eds), *Reindeer as a Keystone Species in the North: Biological, Cultural, and Socio-Economic Aspects*. Proceedings of the 1st CAES Phd Course, 1–15 September 2000, northern Finland, Finnmark, Norway, and Kola Peninsula, Russia. Rovaniemi: CAES, 23–27.

Schama, S. 1995. *Landscape and Memory*. London: HarperCollins.

Schanche, A. 2000. *Graver i ur og berg. Samisk gravskikk og religion fra forhistorisk til nyere tid*. Karasjokk: Davvi Girji OS.

Schanche, K. 1994. 'Gressbakkentuftene i Varanger. Boliger og sosial struktur omkring 2000 f. Kr.'. PhD Dissertation. Department of Archaeology, University of Tromsø.

Scott, C. 1996. 'Science for the West, Myth for the Rest? The Case of James Bay Cree Knowledge Construction', in L. Nader (ed.), *Naked Science*. New York: Routledge, pp. 69–86.

Scott, C. 2007. 'Bear Metaphor: Spirit, Ethnics and Ecology', in F.B. Laugrand and J.G. Oosten (eds), *Nature of Spirits in Aboriginal Cosmologies*. Québec: Les Presses de l'Université Laval, pp. 387–99.

Scott, J.C. 1998. *Seeing Like a State. How Certain Schemes to Improve the Human Condition Have Failed*. New Haven and London: Yale University Press.

Seccombe, W. 1992. *A Millennium of Family Change: Feudalism to Capitalism in Northwestern Europe*. London: Verso.

Segalen, M. 2002. 'Material Conditions of Family Life', in D. Kertzer and M. Barbagli (eds), *Family Life in the Long Nineteenth Century, 1789–1913*. New Haven and London: Yale University Press, pp. 3–39.

Semper, G. 1989 [1860]. 'Style in the Technical and Tectonic Arts or Practical Aesthetics', in H.F. Mallgrave and W. Herrman (trans.), *The Four Elements of Architecture and Other Writings*. Cambridge: Cambridge University Press.

Seppä, H. and H.J.B. Birks. 2002. 'Holocene Climate Reconstructions from the Fennoscandian Tree-Line Area Based on Pollen Data from Toskaljavri', *Quaternary Research* 57 (2): 191–99.

Serning, I. 1956. *Lapska offerplatsfynd från järnålder och medeltid i de svenska lappmarkerna*. Acta Lapponica 11. Stockholm: Hugo Gebers.

Seton, E.T. 1911. *The Arctic Prairies: A Canoe-Journey of 2,000 Miles in Search of Caribou, Being the Account of a Voyage to the Region North of Aylmer Lake*. New York: Charles Scribner and Sons.

Sheppard, W.L. 1998. 'Population Movements, Interaction, and Legendary Geography', *Arctic Anthropology* 35 (2): 147–65.

Shirokogoroff, S.M. 1926 [1928]. 'Northern Tungus Terms of Orientation', *Rosznik Orjentalistyczny* 4: 161–87 (Available at www.wpb.poznan.pl).

Shirokogoroff, S.M. 1929 *Social Organization of the Northern Tungus with Introductory Chapters Concerning Geographical Distribution and History of these Groups*. Shanghai: China.

Shirokogoroff, S.M. 1935. *Psychomental Complex of the Tungus*. London: Kegan Paul, Trench, Trubner and Co. Ltd.

Silver, C.B. (ed.). 1982. *Frederic Le Play on Family, Work, and Social Change*. Chicago: University of Chicago.

Simonsen, P. 1979. 'Juntavadde och Assebakte to utgravningar på Finnmarksvidda', *Acta Borealia* B 17: 3–55.

Sirina, A.M. 2006. *Katanga Evenkis in the 20th Century and the Ordering of their Life-World*. Edmonton: CCI Press.

Slobodin, R. 1962. *Band Organization of the Peel River Kutchin*. Ottawa: Department of Indian Affairs and Northern Development.

Slobodin, R. 1963. 'The Dawson Boys: Peel River Indians and the Klondike Gold Rush', *Polar Note* 5: 24–36.

Sogner, S. 1978. *Familie, husstand og befolkningsutvikling*, Heimen XVII. Trondheim: Landslaget for lokalhistorie.

Sogner, S. 1990. *Far sjøl i stua og familien hans: trekk fra norsk familiehistorie før og nå*. Oslo: Universitetsforlaget.

Sogner, S. 2009. 'The Norwegian Stem Family: Myth or Reality?', in A. Fauve-Chamoux and E. Ochiai (eds), *The Stem Family in Eurasian Perspective: Revisiting House Societies, 17th–20th centuries*. Population, Family, and Society 10. Bern: Peter Lang, pp. 151–73.

Sokolova, Z.P. 1998. *Zhilishche narodov Sibiri : Opyt tipologii*. Moskva: IPA "Tri L".

Solbakk, A. 2007. *Den elvesamiske kulturen*. Varanger: Varanger Samiske Museums Skrifter.

Solem, E. 1928. *Yngste sønns arverett hos lappene og andre folk*. Festskrift til rektor J. Qvigstad, Tromsø Museums Skrifter 2. Tromsø: Tromsø Museum.

Solli, A. 1995. 'Norge kring år 1800'. Masters Thesis. Department of Archaeology, History, Cultural Studies and Religion, University of Bergen.

Solli, A. 2003. 'Livsløp – familie – samfunn: Endring av familiestrukturar i Norge på 1800-talet'. PhD Dissertation. Department of Archaeology, History, Cultural Studies and Religion, University of Bergen.

Sommerseth, I. 2009. 'Villreinfangst og tamreindrift i indre Troms. Belyst ved samiske boplasser mellom 650 og 1923'. PhD Dissertation. Tromsø: Institutt for arkeologi og sosialantropologi. Universitetet i Tromsø.

Spencer, R.F. 1955. 'Map Making of the North Alaskan Eskimo', *Proceedings of the Minnesota Academy of Science* 23: 46–50.

Spink, J. and D.W. Moodie. 1972. *Eskimo Maps from the Canadian Eastern Arctic*, Cartographica, Monograph 5. Toronto: Department of Geography, York University.

Steadman, L.B. and C.T. Palmer. 2008. *The Supernatural and Natural Selection: The Evolution of Religion*. Boulder, CO: Paradigm Publishers.

Storli, I. 1991. '*Stallo'-boplassene. Et tolkningsforslag basert på undersøkelser i Lønsdalen, Saltfjellet*. Stensilserie B nr 31. Tromsø: University of Tromsø.

Storli, I. 1993. 'Sami Viking Age Pastoralism – or "The Fur Trade Paradigm" Reconsidered', *Norwegian Archaeological Review* 26 (1): 1–21.

Storli, I. 1994. '*Stallo'-boplassene: spor etter de første fjellsamer?* Oslo: Novus forlag.

Storli, I. 1996. 'On the Historiography of Sámi Reindeer Pastoralism', *Acta Borealia* 1: 81–115.

Strathern, M. 1999. *Property, Substance, and Effect: Anthropological Essays on Persons and Things*. London: Athlone Press.

Sundqvist, L. 1973. 'Kulturhistorisk inventering av byarna Kåtaselets och Hembergs omgivningar, Jörns sn, Västerbotten', unpublished research report. The Museum of Skellefteå.

Sushilin, N.V. 1929. 'K voprosu o novoi granitse mezhdu Priangarskim Kraem Kanskogo Okruga i raionom podkamennoi tunguski', *Sovetskaia Aziia* 3: 1114–125.

Suslov, I.M. 1936. 'Shamanstvo i borb'a s nim', *Sovetskii Sever* 1–5: 89–152.

Suslov, I.M. 1993. 'Contes chamaniques. Extraits de l'annexe du manuscrit de Suslov: Matériaux pour l'étude des représentations animistes et de la magie chamanique', *Études mongoles et sibériennes* 24: 101–21.

Suslov, I.M. and K.H. Menges. 1983. *Materialien zum schamanismus der Ewenki-Tungusen an der Mittleren und unteren Tunguska: Gessammelt und aufgezeichnet von I.M. Suslov 1926/1928*. Studies in Oriental Religions Vol. 8. Wiesebaden: Otto Harrassowitz.

Statistiska Centralbyrån 1900. Riksarkviet [The National Archives of Sweden]. Statistiska Centralbyrån (SCB) – samlingspost 1860/ Kansliet, verksledningen

1858 – 1971/Arkivexemplar av utgående handlingar/Avgångna skrivelser/ Koncept till avgångna skrivelser/Volym 93. Available online: http://www.napp data.org/napp/resources/enum_materials_pdf/enum_instruct_se1900a.pdf

Sverige. 1900. The Swedish National Archives, Umeå University, and the Minnesota Population Center. National Sample of the 1900 Census of Sweden, Version 1.0. Minneapolis: Minnesota Population Center [distributor], 2008 (available at www.nappdata.org).

Sverige. 1907. [BiSoS A 'Befolkningsstatistik 1900] Statistiska centralbyråns under-dåniga berättelse för år 1900. Tredje afdelningen: Folkmängden år 1900 efter kön, ålder, civilstånd, hushåll, födelseort, stamskillnad och yrken; lyten; frånvarande personer samt obefintliga. Stockholm: Kungl. Boktryckeriet P.A. Norstedt & Söner (available at http://www.scb.se/Pages/List____257387.aspx).

Sverige. 2005. Regeringskansliet. *The Sami – An Indigenous People in Sweden*. Stockholm: Ministry of Agriculture.

Tanner, A. 1979. *Bringing Home Animals: Religious Ideology and Mode of Production of the Mistassini Cree Hunters*. New York: St. Martin's Press.

Tanner, V. 1929. 'Antropogeografiska studier inom Petsamo-området. I. Skolt-lapparna', *Fennia* 49 (4) [entire issue].

Tegengren, H. 1952. *En utdöd lappkultur i Kemi lappmark: studier i NordFinlands koloni-sationshistoria*. Acta academiae aboensis. Humaniora XIX(4). Åbo: Åbo akademi.

Telle, K. 2007. 'Entangled Biographies: Rebuilding a Sasak House', *Ethnos* 72 (2): 195–218.

Thorvaldsen, G. 2009. 'Changes in Data Collection Procedures for Process-Generated Data and Methodological Implications. The Case of Ethnicity Variables in 19th Century Norwegian Censuses', *Historical Social Research* 34 (3): 168–90.

Thorvaldsen, G. 2011. 'Using NAPP Census Data to Construct the Historical Population Register for Norway', *Historical Methods* 44 (1): 37–47.

Tilley, C. 2004. *The Materiality of Stone: Explorations in Landscape Phenomenology*, Vol. 1. Oxford: Berg.

Tugolukov, V.A. 1978. 'Some Aspects of the Beliefs of the Tungus (Evenki and Evens)', in V. Diószegi and M. Hoppál (eds), *Shamanism in Siberia*. Budapest: Akadémiai Kiadó, pp. 419–28.

Turi, J. 1987 [1917 Facsimile]. *En bok om samernas liv: Muittalus samid birra*. Umeå: Två förläggare bokförlag.

Ukkonen, P. 2004. 'Early in the North – Utilization of Animal Resources in Northern Finland during Prehistory', *Iskos* 5: 103–30.

Urla, J. 1993. 'Cultural Politics in an Age of Statistics: Numbers, Nations, and the Making of Basque Identity', *American Ethnologist* 20 (4): 818–43.

Ushakov, I.F. 1972. *Kol'skaia Zemlia (Kola land)*. Murmansk: Murmanskoe knizhnoe izdatel'stvo.

UUL 1900–1910. Umeå University library. Parish records on microfiche. Norrbottens län. Jukkasjärvi parish. AIIa:1 1900–1910 A26263.

UUL 1896–1910. Umeå University library. Parish records on microfiche. Norrbottens län. Karesuando parish. AIIa:1 1896–1910 A23486.

Vasilevich, G.M. 1936. *Sbornik materialov po Evenkiiskomu (Tungusskomu) fol'kloru*. Leningrad: Izd-vo Instituta Narodov Severa.

Vasilevich, G.M. 1957. 'Drevnye okhotnich'i i olenevodcheskie obriady evenkov', *Sbornik Muzeia antropologii i etnografii* 17: 151–85.

Vasilevich, G.M. 1959. 'Rannye predstavleniia o mire u Evenkov', *Trudy Instituta Etnografiia* 51: 157–92.

Vasilevich, G.M. 1963. 'Early Concepts about the Universe among the Evenks (Materials)', in H.N. Michael (ed.), *Studies in Siberian Shamanism*. Arctic Institute of North America, Anthropology of the North. Translations from Russian Sources No. 4. Toronto: University of Toronto Press, pp. 46–83.

Vasilevich, G.M. 1971. 'Nekotorye terminy orientatsii v prostranstve v tunguso-man-zhurskikh i drugikh altaiskikkh iazykakh', in O.P. Sunik (ed.), *Problemy obshchnosti altaiskikh iazykov*. Leningrad: Nauka, pp. 223–39.

Vaté, V. 2003. 'A bonne épouse, bon éleveur: genre, "nature" et rituels chez les Tchouktches (Arctique sibérien) avant, pendant et après la période soviétique'. PhD Dissertation (anthropology) of the University of Paris 10 Nanterre.

Vaté, V. 2005. 'Kilvêi: The Chukchi Spring Festival in Urban and Rural Contexts', in E. Kasten (ed.), *Rebuilding Identities: Pathways to Reform in Post-Soviet Siberia*. Berlin: Dietrich Reimer Verlag, pp. 39–62.

Vaté, V. 2005–2006. 'La tête vers le lever de soleil': Orientation quotidienne et rituelle dans l'espace domestique des Tchouktches éleveurs de rennes (Arctique sibérien)', *Etudes mongoles, sibériennes, centrasiatiques et tibétaines* 36–37, 61–93.

Vaté, V. 2007. 'The Kêly and the Fire: An Attempt at Approaching Chukchi Representations of Spirits', in F. Laugrand and J. Oosten (eds), *La nature des esprits: Humains et non-humains dans les cosmologies autochtones*. Québec: Presses de l'Université Laval, pp. 219–237.

Vaté, V. 2011. 'Dwelling in the Landscape among the Reindeer Herding Chukchis', in P. Jordan (ed.), *Landscape and Culture in Northern Eurasia*. Walnut Creek, CA: Left Coast Books, pp. 135–60.

Vdovin, I.S. 1965. *Ocherki istorii i etnografii Chukchei*. Moskva-Leningrad: Nauka.

Vellinga, M. 2007. 'Review Essay: Anthropology and the Materiality of Architecture', *American Ethnologist* 34 (4): 756–66.

Vernant, J.P. 1969. 'Hestia-Hermes: The Religious Expression of Space and Movement among the Greeks', *Social Science Information* 8 (4): 131–68.

Vorren, Ø. 1966. 'Flyttsamenes husformer', *Ottar* 50 (4): 1–17.

Vorren, Ø. 1978. 'Bosetning og ressursutnytting i ressursutvalgets mandatom-råde under veidekulturen og dens differensiering', in O. Gjærevoll (ed.), *Finnmarksvidda natur-kultur*. Norges offentlige utredninger NOU 18A. Oslo: Universitetsforlaget.

Vretemark, M. 2009. 'Osteologisk analys av djurben från Kjerringsneset, Övre Pasvik I Sør-Caranger, Norge', unpublished research report. The Museum of Västergötland.

Vuntut Gwich'in First Nation and S. Smith. 2010. *People of the Lakes Stories of Our Van Tat Gwich'in Elders/Googwandak Nakhwach'ànjòo Van Tat Gwich'in*. Edmonton: University of Alberta Press.

Walkeapää, L. 2010. *Könkämävuoma samernas renflyttningar till Norge – om sommar-bosättningar i Troms fylke på 1900-talet*. Tromsö: Tromsö museum.

Wallerström, T. 1995. *Norrbotten, Sverige och medeltiden. Problem kring makt och bosättning i en europeisk periferi. Del 1*. Lund Studies in Medieval Archaeology 15:1. Stockholm: Almqvist and Wiksell International.

Waterman, T.T. 1927. 'The Architecture of the American Indians', *American Anthropologist* 29 (2): 210–30.

Waterson, R. 1991. *The Living House: An Anthropology of Architecture in South-East Asia*. Oxford: Oxford University Press.

Wegraeus, E. 1973. 'Pilspetsar under vikingatid', *Tor* 1972–73: 191–208.

Wheeler, D.E. 1914. 'The Dog-Rib Indian and his Home', *Bulletin of the Geographical Society of Philadelphia* 12 (2): 47–69.

Whitaker, I. 1955. *Social Relations in a Nomadic Lappish Community*. Oslo: Norsk folkemuseum.

Whitridge, P. 2004. 'Landscapes, Houses, Bodies, Things: "Place" and the Archaeology of Inuit Imaginaries', *Journal of Archaeological Method and Theory* 11 (2): 213–50.

Widerberg, K. 1980. *Kvinnor, klasser och lagar 1751–1980*. Stockholm: Liber Förlag.

Widlok, T. 2004. 'Sharing by Default? Outline of an Anthropology of Virtue', *Anthropological Theory* 4: 53–70.

Willerslev, R. 2009. 'The Optimal Sacrifice: A Study of Voluntary Death among the Siberian Chukchi', *American Ethnologist* 36 (4): 693–704.

Wilk, R. and W. Rathje. 1982. 'Household Archaeology', *American Behavioral Scientist* 25 (6): 617–39.

Wilson, E.T. 2006. 'Building an Arctic Community of Knowledge: The Promotion and Reception of Canadian Resource Management and Economic Development Models in the Russian North'. PhD Dissertation. University of Cambridge.

Wilson, P.J. 1988. *The Domestication of the Human Species*. New Haven: Yale University Press.

Wishart, R.P. 2004. 'Living "on the land": Teetl'it Gwich'in Perspectives on Continuities'. PhD Dissertation. Department of Anthropology, University of Alberta.

Woolf, T. and T.D. Andrews dirs. 2000. *Tlicho Ekwo Nihmbaa: The Dogrib Caribou Skin Lodge*. DVD Documentary. 29 min. Prince of Wales Northern Heritage Centre and the Tlicho Community Services Agency, Canada.

Wright, J.V. 1972. *The Aberdeen Site, Keewatin District, NWT*. Ottawa: National Museums of Canada.

Wright, J.V. 1976. *The Grant Lake Site, Keewatin District, NWT*. Ottawa: National Museums of Canada.

Yates, T. 1989. 'Habitus and Social Space: Some Suggestions about Meaning of the Saami (Lapp) Tent Ca. 1700–1900' in I. Hodder (ed.), *The Meaning of Things: Material Culture and Symbolic Expression*. London: Routledge, pp. 249–65.

Zachrisson, I. 1976. *Lapps and Scandinavians. Archaeological Finds from Northern Sweden*. Early Norrland 10. Stockholm: KVHAA.

Zachrisson, I. 1984. *De samiska metalldepåerna år 1000–1350*. Archaeology and environment 3. Umeå: Department of Archaeology, Umeå universitet.

Zachrisson, I. et al. 1997. *Möten i gränsland. Samer och germaner i mellanskandinavien*. Stockholm: Statens historiska museum.

Zetterberg, P., M. Eronen, and K.R. Briffa. 1994. 'Evidence on Climatic Variability and Prehistoric Human Activities between 165 B.C. and A.D. 1400 Derived from Subfossil Scots Pines (Pinus Sylvestris L.) Found in a Lake in Utsjoki Northernmost Finland', *Bulletin of the Geological Society of Finland* 66 (2): 107–24.

Ziker, J.P. 2002a. *Peoples of the Tundra: Northern Siberians in the Post-Communist Transition*. Prospect Heights, IL: Waveland Press.

Ziker, J.P. 2002b. 'Raw and Cooked in Arctic Siberia: Seasonality, Gender and Diet among the Dolgan and Nganasan Hunter Gatherers', *Nutritional Anthropology* 25 (2): 20–33.

Ziker, J.P. 2003. 'Assigned Territories, Family/Clan/Communal Holdings, and Common-Pool Resources in the Taimyr Autonomous Region, Northern Russia', *Human Ecology* 31 (3): 331–68.

Ziker, J.P. 2007. 'Subsistence and Food Sharing in Northern Siberia: Social and Nutritional Ecology of the Dolgan and the Nganasan', *Ecology of Food and Nutrition* 46 (5/6): 445–67.

Åhren, I. 1979. 'Tvångsförflyttning eller dislokation: Nordsamernas förflyttning till södra Lappland', *Norrbotten 1976–77*: 101–14.

Index

Adams, J. W. (and A. B. Kasakoff), 108
affordance, 2, 4, 9, 172, 267, 271
agency, 265, 268
Alaska, 76, 154
Alberti, L. B., 13–14
Aleut, 281n2
Alexander, C., 15
Allerton, C., 204–5
Alta-Kautokeino river, 77
Ampumaradan tausta site, 157, 166–67, 171, 182
ancestors: and Chukchi scenography, 184; and the Dolgan/Nganasan hearth, 260; and graves, 229; Gwich'in practices following, 67; and house ownership, 212; Inuit negotiations with, 232; Sámi settlement and dead, 85; of Samoeds, 251; and the San hearth, 257; and Scottish emigrants, 219; Tłı̨chǫ memories of, 268; Tłı̨chǫ offerings to, 44, 272
Anderson, B., 103
Apache, 223
archetypes, 251
architects: intuitions of urban, 278; Medieval land shapers, 14; Scandinavian and Sámi, 78; and shelter vs. buildings, 271; vernacular architecture without, 265; and views of architecture, 264
architecture, 1–6, 11; blended with kinship and landscape, 267; 'boxed', 280; and carpets in V. Flusser, 24; and cosmology 267–68; engagement

with, 205; Evenki shamanizing and, 238; and experience in M. Heidegger, 61; and fire, 272–73, 278; *goattieh*, *83*, 91, 96; Gwich'in circular, 56; Gwich'in log, 54, 278; Gwich'in pre-contact, 55; and an idealized past, 62; ideas and meanings of, 13–16, 204, 268, 270; incomer vs. local perceptions of, 203–4, 213, 214; mobile Dene, 30; *nasleg/ pogost*, 267; and partitions, 266; of patches, 42, 278; revitalised, 266; and sedentism, 278; skin vs. canvas, 57; social interaction within houses vs., 271; spanning *vs.* non-spanning, 264, 271; and textiles in G. Semper, 17–18; vernacular, 4, 264, 265–66, 278, 281n2; and writing in C. Lévi-Strauss, 27
Arctic Circle, 124
Arnesen, N. A., 147
Arnesen, O., 145, *146*
Arnøy (island), 145
Aronsson, L., 219
Arran, *78*, 90
Årvik, 147
Asker municipality, 131
Assebakte: graves, 154
atmosphere, 21, 26, 28
Aursjøen, Lesja (Norway), 155
autonomy, 45, 46, 273

baeljek (paired curved poles), 169
balok (skin-lined caravan), 274
Barents Sea, 124, 221n2